A Desert Country Near the Sea

BOOKS BY ANN ZWINGER

Beyond the Aspen Grove
*A Desert Country Near the Sea**
John Xántus: The Fort Tejon Letters (editor)*
Land Above the Trees (with Beatrice E. Willard)
*Run, River, Run**
*Wind in the Rock**

* Available from the University of Arizona Press

A
DESERT COUNTRY
NEAR THE SEA

A Natural History of
the Cape Region of
Baja California

ANN ZWINGER

Drawings by the Author
Photographs by Herman H. Zwinger

THE UNIVERSITY OF ARIZONA PRESS
Tucson

About the Author

Ann Zwinger holds degrees in art history from Wellesley College and Indiana University. She is the author of *Wind in the Rock*; *Run, River, Run*; *Beyond the Aspen Grove*, and numerous other books and articles, and she is the editor and annotator of *John Xántus: The Fort Tejon Letters* (University of Arizona Press, 1986). Ann Zwinger is the 1976 recipient of the John Burroughs Memorial Association Gold Medal, awarded for *Run, River, Run*. She makes her home in Colorado Springs.

THE UNIVERSITY OF ARIZONA PRESS
Manufactured in the U.S.A.
Published by arrangement with Harper & Row, Inc.

92 91 90 89 88 87

5 4 3 2 1

Library of Congress Cataloging-in-Publication Data

Zwinger, Ann.
    A desert country near the sea.

    Reprint. Originally published by: New York: Harper & Row, © 1983.
    Bibliography: p.
    Includes index.
    1. Natural history—Mexico—Baja California.
2. Desert ecology—Mexico—Baja California.   I. Title.
[QH107.Z84 1987]   508.72'23   86-24973
ISBN 0-8165-0988-3 (alk. paper)

British Library Cataloguing in Publication data are available.

For Herman.

And for three special daughters:
this amber time

CONTENTS

ACKNOWLEDGMENTS

This book benefits from the help, graciously given, of scholars in several fields; it could not have been written without it. I add the prescribed caveat with more than usual emphasis: in spite of their generous sharing of knowledge, if errors remain, they are mine.

Dr. Ira Wiggins, Professor Emeritus of Botany, Stanford University, read the whole manuscript and commented from his experience of fifty years in Baja California. I cherish his understanding and his delightful letters. He checked and corrected the Plant List, as did Annetta Carter, Research Associate, Herbarium, University of California at Berkeley, also an authority on Baja California plants. She brought nomenclature up to date as well as adding many Spanish names; her love of detail and accuracy saved me from unnecessary errors.

Dr. W. Michael Mathes of the Sutro Library in San Francisco, has published widely about the peninsula in both Spanish and English, and knows the Cape region well; he read sections on history and made comments and corrections, as well as suggestions in other areas that were of great use. He also checked the Chronology.

Dr. Richard P. Phillips, Coordinator of Environmental Studies, University of San Diego, was most helpful with the geology, not only reading manuscript but suggesting references that I had missed.

The following scholars are responsible for the plant and animal lists. Besides the Plant List mentioned above, my debt is to: Dr. Donald R. Patten, Los Angeles Museum of Natural History, for the Mammals List; Sanford R. Wilbur, Chief of the Division of Endangered Species, U.S. Fish and Wildlife Service, Portland, Oregon, for the Bird List; and Dr. John W. Wright, Los Angeles Museum of Natural History, for Reptiles and Amphibians. I am very grateful for their help.

Several writers with particular interest in Baja California read the manuscript *in toto*. Alex Kerstitch's work as an illustrator and biologist gave him insights I tremendously appreciated, and his comments were most helpful. Dr. George E. Lindsay, Director Emeritus of the California Academy of Sciences, read the manuscript in preparation, as did Paul Brooks, a superb writer of natural history who has written about Baja California. Dr. Richard Beidleman also read the manuscript in preparation.

Dr. Paul H. Arnaud, Jr., Curator, Department of Entomology, California Academy of Sciences, provided his account of the *Orca* Expedition to the Gulf of California and information about the Academy's insect collection. Dr. Alexandra Vargo, entomologist at Colorado College, advised on moth identification. Dr. Robert W. Kiger at the Hunt Institute for Botanical Documentation, Carnegie-Mellon University, and Dr. Rogers McVaugh, Department of Botany, The University of North Carolina, for information on the 1787–1803 Sesse-Mocino expedition to Mexico. Dr. H. Muramoto generously provided information on his research on varieties of wild cotton in Baja California being used in research on brown lung disease; Thomas H. Nash II, Department of Botany and Microbiology, Arizona State University, sent the study on Cape lichen.

The California Academy of Sciences Library is without parallel as a place to work, largely due to Mr. Ray Brian, Head Librarian, and Mrs. Ruth Oppa who could find any reference, any where, any time. I am also fortunate to live near the excellent Tutt Library of The Colorado College, headed by Dr. George Fagan. I thank all the reference librarians for marvelous help: Julie Eddy, Lee Hall, Yim Michali, Susan Myers, and Robin Satterwhite. I also thank Millicent D. Abell, University Librarian, University of California, San Diego, and Susan Starr, Head of Public Services. Susan Westgate of the Smithsonian Institution Archives was exceedingly helpful with the Xantus and Baird letters.

Mr. Glen Dawson of Dawson's Book Shop kept me posted on new material as it appeared, and graciously permitted extensive quoting, which was much appreciated.

Dr. David Nordstrom provided medical reports to which I would not otherwise have had access. Sidney Novis made available information about old maps of the area.

In Baja California I thank Miriam Parr for gracious friendship over the years, and sharing her knowledge of plant lore. Both she and Lee Stoner loaned me books that I otherwise would not even have known about, including some very hard-to-come-by copies of old books printed in Mexico.

In particular I thank our friends at Hotel Cabo San Lucas who in so many ways made this book possible: José Rivera Cassas, José Valle Alizondo, and David Yee Sanchez. Juan Arellános and Ruffo Arellános, and Misáel Vargas Perez provided information about the countryside, and Joaquin Palacias Aviles, information about deep sea fishing. For current information about *ejidos* I thank David Yee Sanchez, José Rivera Cassas, and Pablo Ortiz Reyes. And over many many years, *mis gracias a todos mis profesores pacientes de español:* Angel Rodríguez Jiménez, Jésus Castro Ojeda, José Castro Castillo, and Luis Manuel Navarro Garate, and Antonia Gastelum Alucano and Elisa Garcia Miranda. Hector Covi and Mario Covi helped with unfamiliar Spanish names and accents.

Profesor Nestor Agundez Martínez was a delightful host in Todos Santos and provided me with historical information on the area; Profesor Juan Pedrin, Mayor of San José del Cabo, was gracious and well informed about his city.

For a memorable trip into the backcountry, I thank Mary Shroyer and Gail Laughlin, and Franciso Reynoso of the Univercidad Autonoma de Baja California Sur at La Paz. That trip ended for me in the military hospital at La Paz, and Mary's help and comfort are the measure of friendship. My appreciation goes to a fine hospital and staff, Doctores José Islas Gonzalez and Hector Eduardo Flores Calleja, and the nurses who took marvelous care of me. And to Joe and Toni Duran, and Dr. and Mrs. David Hubbell, Herman's and my deepest thanks for help in time of need.

Bruce Simballa and Zita Szerlip, and our two forest service guides from Todos Santos, Julian and José, staffed an unforgettable trip to the high meadow of La Laguna. Martin Ramirez Marquez and Engelberto Agundez Seseina were excellent guides into the San Lázaro country, men who know the area well and how to travel in it, and my thanks to José Rivera for making the arrangements. I am indebted to all of them, for without their help I could never have gotten to where I wanted to go. I most particularly thank Maria Estero Ramírez Marquez for her gracious hospitality. Jim Jeffries, who now lives in Cabo San Lucas, was a knowledgeable and enthusiastic guide to the fossils of Baja California Sur.

This book was written on a Display Writer, for the care and feeding of which I thank Richard Kresge and Tom Coca, who faithfully administered to its crotchets.

I was privileged to have again as editor on this book Buz Wyeth of Harper & Row. My thanks also go to Florence Goldstein whose thoughtfulness is very much appreciated. I am grateful to those on the production staff especially who shepherded it through: William Monroe, Lydia Link, Terry Karten, and Coral Tysliava, and designer Charlotte Staub. My thanks to Margaret Cheney for copy editing a manuscript that would try the patience of Job, and to Timilou Rixon for an elegant job of going over the manuscript in detail with me. Fran Collin's professional guidance and friendship means more than I can say.

There are thanks of a more personal nature. For proofreading help of the most meticulous kind, my thanks to Kathryn Redman (who also helped with insect identification and index preparation), and David Kosley. Friends, who have read manuscript and offered frank and open comments, are Anne Cross, Ava Heinrichsdorff, Louise Marshall, Judy Noyes. I thank them for their honesty.

I wish I could thank all those with whom we have shared a meal and good conversation at the Cabo San Lucas over the years, but to begin a list like that is never to stop, and omitting someone by accident I find more distressing. I hope that those with whom we walked a sunny beach or shared a pleasant meal will know that those times are cherished in memory, *hasta un otra vez*. Herman's and my thanks also to Herb Moore and the forecasters of the National Weather Service in Colorado Springs, who provided us with many "severe clear" days for flights to Cabo San Lucas.

My loving appreciation goes to Mrs. Edwin Teale. Her reading of the manuscript aloud caught many stumbles in cadence and gave me an understanding of words; those were happy hours for me.

I thank Herman for his skill as a pilot and as a photographer. For the beautiful photographs that enhance the text, my gratitude for his patience and long hours spent in the darkroom to produce them.

Ann Haymond Zwinger

Constant Friendship
May 1983

*Now then! Those who have ears, listen! What is California? Nothing but innu-
merable stones and these you find in all four directions. It is a pile of stones
full of thorns—because this is the whole of California, that means beside
stones and thornbushes you find nothing else in California; or to quote the
scripture, a pathless, waterless thornful rock, sticking up between two
oceans.*

Jakob Baegert
Letter to his brother Father George Baegert
September 11, 1752

There is no more sharply defined faunal and floral area, that occurs to me now, excepting that of islands, than is embraced in the region above defined. Part of it lies within the Tropic of Cancer, and the balance along the Gulf shore and having mainly a Gulf drainage. The climate as influenced by its peculiar sea-bound tropical situation and rainy seasons is distinctively different from anything existing to the northward, but the climatic peculiarities will be noticed beyond. Mainly a mountainous section, some of the peaks being 6,000 feet high, it is separated for an hundred miles or more from the peninsula northward by a long expanse of low, level or rolling country. Such isolation combined with other causes makes it a region of peculiar scientific interest to both zoologists and botanists.

Walter E. Bryant
The Cape Region of Baja California
1891

INTRODUCTION:
THE CAPE

As on every flight, we depart the intricate jigsaw puzzle shoreline of mainland Mexico near Los Mochis and bear 193 degrees southwest over the Sea of Cortés.

The altimeter registers 8,500 feet. The sea is empty; not one ship drags a wake on the surface of the water, which, in this light, gleams nacreous as the inside of an oyster shell. A flock of low clouds lie beneath us, turgid sheep being herded northeastward, the inevitable stragglers leaving polka-dot shadows on the water.

Whitecaps blossom long enough to have a kind of permanency on the sea's surface, like stars in a constellation—aqueous Betelgeuses, marine Polarises, natant Aldebarans. Instead of looking upward to the stars I look down, the heavens reversed, or better still, all-surrounding, and the plane hangs suspended in the center of a dazzling lambent globe.

Overhead the empyrean ocean is feathered and foamed with soft white cloud-reefs and beaches—farther shores than I shall ever know. We drift under the most delicate mare's-tails, soft tubes of white fraying upward into delicate frizzled tentacles and think, where have I seen that before? and with the thought remember: kneeling at the edge of a granite-rimmed tidepool and watching tube worms unfurl tentacles into the still water.

No scribing horizon divides sea and sky. Blue simply blends into blue, and the barriers of my practical, pragmatic world disappear in a wonder of no gravity, no oriented ear, no tactile connection, a floating world glowing with light and color, dissolving the outlines of reality. Were it not for the drone of the engines and the question-mark-shaped reflection of my retinal cells in the Plexiglas window I could easily feel slipped out of these familiar bounds.

How many times, how many times, at this same particular time of day, have we followed this same sea path, pointing into this horizonless world of soft blurred blues, across this juniper-berry sea, into this gentle all-pervasive light? How many times, I wonder—with children, without children, with friends, just the two of us.

Why did we head here those many years ago? Simple, actually. We had reached fed-up time with the mania of Christmas and its pressures and wanted a family time unfraught with the usual saturnalia. I wanted a chance to enjoy my daughters as people before they all grew up and went away to their own horizons. I was tired of saying, "Pick up your room!" in my mother voice. I wanted to say, "Who wants to go down to the beach?"

Herman, then a pilot of nearly thirty years' experience, specified that wherever we went had to be within an easy day's flying time. So he drew a circle with a radius of that distance, and then drew radii from Colorado Springs going all the variations of south—Herman *hates* winter. The intersections occurred at Mazatlán and the tip end of the Baja California, Cabo San Lucas. Mazatlán was city, people, cars, noise, and we looked for empty beaches to wander, stars to track, sea shells to find, hillsides to explore. We picked the Cape. Unanimously.

Herman worked out weights and balances for the airplane, assigned each of us her poundage allotment. As we packed, we labeled each piece with its weight. We took off from Colorado on an icy morning, flying through a pale cold mean sky, above a familiar terrain gridded with tan section-line roads and quirked with arroyos, made unfamiliar by deep snow.

We landed in Arizona for gas, ate lunch on the ground, laughed at the first roadrunner we'd ever seen outside of cartoons, piled back into the airplane and droned southward. At La Paz we marveled at the softness of the air. As we took off, the tower wished us "Feliz Navidad!"

On the twenty-minute flight to the Cape, warm air filtered through the cabin vents. We wriggled out of sweaters and jackets. The ocean below glowed a lovely ultramarine. Surf ruffled white on deserted crescent beaches.

As he turned on final approach, Herman warned, "It's going to be a crosswind landing," and we all groaned. But with his usual skill, the stall-warning horn beeped precisely as the wheels touched ground. We parked, chocked the wheels with the nearest rocks, breathed in that incomparable pure air, and then looked around into a strange and starkly beautiful world, ocean and scrub desert, sky and sand, and each of us became, as Joseph Wood Krutch said in *The Forgotten Peninsula*, "a traveler who first saw the country more or less by accident . . . and was so struck by its wildness and its beauty that he returned again and again to poke his nose into some remote areas still seldom visited, and also to taste the pleasures of others less inaccessible."

And perhaps I knew at that moment, even though I had not published a book, that someday I would write about this place. But I did not know then how much it would become part of my life, that it would become another home. Or how many changes, how *many* changes would take place here, how many decisions would be made, how many corners turned, as if it were easier to see where to go in this clarity of air and time.

Herman discovered, learned, and became addicted to scuba diving here, going from ocean of air to ocean of water with equal ease, day after day slogging out of the waves like some creature from the lower depths, dripping camera equipment and tank, to report the beauty of another world to those of us who then only held down the sand on the beach or read or played interminable games of Scrabble—my mother, bless her, raised me on games.

Our daughters changed from children to young adults here. We shared Christmases here when it did nothing but rain, but everyone still voted to come back. We shared a Christmas when one daughter had had a brain scan for a tumor and would not know the results until our return (they were, mercifully, negative). One New Year's Eve the ocean bloomed with bioluminescence, surely an omen for a marvelous year. It wasn't. It was a terrible year. On another, something hit a glass I was holding and glass splinters spattered into my eye, surely a bad omen. It was a grand year.

There are no more family Christmases now because jobs intervene, but each daughter has kept this place in her heart in her own way, and maybe it means more now when they do get to come back: Jane taking off her shoes the minute she arrives and not putting them back on until ready to leave, surely a significant symbolic gesture; Sara, closing her eyes in delicious anticipation of a Mexican *cerveza*, taking a connoisseur's sip and smiling, "*That's* fresh-squeezed!"; Susan, entering with Herman that ocean world beneath the billowing silver ceiling; her drawings have been infused ever since with flickering fish shapes, schooling through deep-walled infinite skies that make inexplicable sense.

That first Christmas I didn't even hang my clothes on a hickory limb, let alone go near the water, didn't venture beyond the safety of the poolside—I, the inland freshwater child, still horrified in adulthood by that ruthless aggressive ocean. Then one year I put on a bathing suit, looked in the mirror, stopped deluding myself that I was not overweight and out of shape, went home, started running and exercising, and took command of my life. How many of the good things that have happened to me since have had their genesis here.

I remember one year near the beginning when José Vallé, who has since become our good friend, said to me one evening, "Señora, you seem *muy triste.*" I replied that I felt sad because we were going home tomorrow. "Oh, no, señora," he said solemnly, "here is now your home too." He was righter than he knew.

The airplane radio crackles softly and interrupts my reverie. Disembodied voices fall out of the ceiling speaker, giving directions from a place to which I am not going to a place I cannot see.

Now, nearly fifteen years and several dozen trips later, we make this trip, which has a sadness all its own for me. The last trip for this book. Behind my seat are all the signs: the once fresh U.S. Hydrographic maps now creased and dog-eared, full of scribbled observations. The once new sneakers now disreputable, salt-faded, full of convenient ocean-draining holes, shoestrings awkward-short from too many knottings. The once neat manuscript now bulging out of its battered binder. Another canvas bag filled with over annotated fieldbooks, pages softened from endless thumbings.

I've been rereading many of the books about the peninsula I first read years ago, and some of them are with me. (I think that, one spring, when I explored the stacks of the Library of Congress, I opened every book on Baja California that's been published, and closed most of them with a sigh, for they were concerned with the more accessible northern section of the peninsula, or four-wheeling, or off-road racing, or good fishing spots, not at all what interested me.)

The library that John Steinbeck and Ed Ricketts carried on shipboard with them in their 1940 Edward Abbey-like exploration that resulted in *Sea of Cortez* "contained all the separates then available on the Panamic and Gulf fauna," plus all the charts for the Gulf region they were covering. My book bag contains many of the same, now happily in paperback. Some of Steinbeck's references have been updated or replaced, and some were not yet published at the time of the first edition, such as Richard C. Brusca's *Common Intertidal Invertebrates of the Gulf of California,* a book enjoyable for both specialists and laymen; nor had Donald Thomson, Lloyd Findley, and Alex Kerstitch compiled the handsome *Reef Fishes of the Sea of Cortez,* with magnificent underwater photographs and drawings, largely by Kerstitch; nor had the monumental *Sea Shells of Tropical West America* by Myra Keen appeared. Joseph Wood Krutch had not taken the ten trips that illuminated his beautifully written account of *The Forgotten Peninsula,* nor had Pablo Martínez published *Historia de Baja California,* now available in English.

Since I've been interested in shore as well as sea I have a plethora of the field guides unloosed on the amateur naturalist in the last few years, on insects, plants, and birds, as well as the more specialized Peterson and Chalif's *A Field Guide to Mexican Birds,* Ernest Edwards's *A Field Guide to the Birds of Mexico,* and Blake's *Birds of Mexico.* There is no easily accessible or thorough compilation of peninsular insects, although there is considerable overlap with our Southwest; a 1926 copy of E. O. Essig's *Insects of Western North America* I found in a secondhand bookstore is of some help. William Howe's extravagantly illustrated *The Butterflies of North America* does include Mexican butterflies.

For plants, Jeanette Coyle and Norman Roberts's *A Field Guide to the Common and Interesting Plants of Baja California* is illustrated with color photographs and also gives plant names in Spanish, with some of the interesting lore surrounding them, for herbal remedies are still widely used on the peninsula. The definitive botanical reference is *Flora of Baja California* by Dr. Ira Wiggins, who, in the tradition of the botanists who explored the peninsula, made many trips here; his lucid introduction to the peninsula is superb. Each genus is illustrated, many of them handsomely so by Dr. Wiggins himself.

As I reread Steinbeck, Ricketts, and Krutch, I have the comfort of good company and a refreshed understanding of what this remote country gives to the stranger who is willing to take the time to ask questions, to observe, to learn. But Steinbeck and Ricketts were concerned primarily with the sea, Krutch primarily with the land. I cannot separate land and sea: to me they interfinger like the pattern in a moss agate, positive and negative shapes irrevocably interlocked. My knowledge of this peninsula depends upon that understanding: of the underwater canyons that are continuations of the land, of the shell fossils far inland that measure continuations of the sea in eons past.

Only the periphery would my predecessors find different—the paved loop from La Paz to San José del Cabo to Cabo San Lucas to Todos Santos, and back to La Paz, the hotels and condominiums along the coast between San José del Cabo and San Lucas. The interior remains much the same: fences woven of the ubiquitous *palo de arco,* courtesy, a grave simplicity. And so does the sea, curling in and out on its appointed tides.

Besides the "last-trip syndrome," today I have another reluctance to overcome. Herman intends to do some aerial photography, which means low altitudes, steep banks, and corkscrew climbs that plaster my stomach to my backbone. We will make landfall on the east coast above Punta Arena, and then cut westward to the Sierra de la Laguna and its high meadow, then follow down the Pacific Coast to the lighthouse at Cabo Falso, swing east and north around the bony spine of the peninsula that snubs out into the sea at San Lucas, take a look at the lagoon at San José del Cabo, cross the Sierra de la Trinidad tucked in the southeast corner of the peninsula, up to Cabo Pulmo and Pulmo Reef, and back past San Lázaro before landing. My stomach knots in anticipated misery.

When there are just the two of us, we have long since worked out a Jack Sprat agreement in flying: Herman sits front left in the pilot's seat; I sit second row right. My feet don't touch the floor in the front seat, and I have to hold maps for The Pilot. In the back I have another seat for workspace and am mercifully undisturbed to pursue my own nefarious activities like editing manuscripts and working double-crostics. But, when Herman photographs, I clutch the seat brace and the armrest and take my choice of staring up at a disorienting horizonless sky or straight down into an unwinding kaleidoscopic landscape that my inner eye and ear have never been able to agree upon.

Meanwhile, I orient myself on the hydrographic map, which is, thank heavens, printed properly. The trouble with the peninsula is that it runs cattywampus, a long gnarled finger pointing southeast. To make efficient use of vertical page space, most modern maps of Baja California cant it on the page at a 45-degree angle. Therefore the viewer never has a proper sense of how it lies. If there's a simplistic symbol of Baja California, perhaps that's it. Man's necessity to make things fit imposes a skewed reality on it, and the peninsula will *never* fit man's rational sensible demands. There is a slower reality and a richer pattern here, and Baja California runs northwest to southeast.

Another problem with Baja California is its name. One version says that Hernán Cortés and his company were struck by the dry, oppressive heat of the peninsula, and called it a "fiery furnace"—*calida fornax,* which through elision became *california.* Another, a Jesuit explanation, suggests derivation from the Spanish *cala,* which means "little bay," and the Latin *fornix,* which means "vault or arch," presumably after the arch at Cabo San Lucas.

The true explanation was discovered by Edward Everett Hale in 1862, buried in a novel first published in 1500, *Las Sergas de Esplandian* (*The Adventures of Esplandian*) by García Ordóñez de Montalvo, and exceedingly popular at the time of the conquest of Mexico. It is a true sailors' fantasy of an island inhabited by magnificent women called Amazons who wore solid gold armor, because gold was the only metal on the island where they lived. This island, "very near the terrestrial paradise," was called California after the Amazon queen, Calafia. Pablo Martínez, the modern historian of Baja California, speculates that the name was used in a derogatory sense by soldiers forced to serve on a peninsula where they found only misery, disease, and death. And no glorious women.

"California" first appears, as applied to the peninsula, in a diary kept by Francisco Preciado, who accompanied one of Cortés's men, Franciso de Ulloa, in 1539–1540. Long after Cortés's death, it was called Isla Carolinas after King Charles II, and so appeared on maps and charts as late as 1740. Drake in 1579 called the Pacific Coast of North America "New Albion," the only English-sounding name it ever had. After Jesuit settlements began in 1697, "California" became more and more current and was consistently used after the publication of a Jesuit history in the middle of the eighteenth century.

The peninsula was the original "California." The separation of "Baja" and "Alta" was not made until the end of the eighteenth century to differentiate the lower peninsula from the new Spanish settlements farther north at San Diego and Monterey. "Baja" of course means "lower" and applies to the lower part of the original California territory, the peninsula. Properly one should call it "Baja California" or "Lower California" or "Sud-California" or "the Baja peninsula." To call it simply "Baja" is no more correct than to call New York "New" or North Carolina "North." But the penchant for abbreviated names has created "Baja" as a noun, not an adjective, and a term considered insulting by some Baja Californians (which is not to say that many don't use it). Some of the best writers—Joseph Wood Krutch, for example—have consistently called it "Baja" and given further credence to truncated usage.

Ahead there are flourishes of clouds—except they aren't. They are mountains, of such a soft and faded blue that they mimic clouds. They are the backbone of the peninsula, a horizonful of mountains, as if the land were hinged on mountains. The ridge lines float above a sea out of which they rise magically, out of an unmeasured distance with no beginning and no end, no margins to this fanciful landscape, and it is easy to see how, once upon a time, Spanish mariners might have hoped this amorphous skyline belonged to an island around which lay easy passage westward to the spice and silk wealth of the Pacific, and portrayed it so on the maps, the printed image giving it veracity.

As we approach landfall, Isla Cerralvo far to my right shines clear and concise, an island set down with the finality of a chess piece at checkmate. Beyond, only the rimline of Isla Espíritu Santo is visible, thrown out in front of the horizon like an old doormat: please wipe feet before entering eternity.

Toward shore the colors warm, but I find it difficult to separate and identify them. I form a telescope with my fingers: thus isolated, the mountains are mauve, the ocean is ultramarine. The ridges partake of that coolness in the shadows, the ocean shares the warmness in the reflections of its waves. Faceted ocean, crinkled shadows, and across the peninsula, hung above the Pacific shoreline, a row of crimped white clouds. These small patterns animate the big masses of sea and land, subtle and soft, hard and crisp. The mountains, the sea, and the in-between: all of a part, all of a unity, but a strange unity, as if it were created in a cataclysm after everything else was finished, just as the German Jesuit Jakob Baegert wrote in 1772: "I have been wondering whether subterranean fires, an earthquake, or some other upheaval did not create this land and cause it in time to rise from the sea, after the creation of the rest of the world."

The sun burnishes a sheen on the water and the white surf line coils and kinks like a white string, bright between blue and tan, the vivid flexible line dividing two worlds. In one bay the water is so calm that the cliffs above the beach reflect perfectly in the sea. At a fishing camp the boats rest on the bay like little white water striders.

Ridges levitate above the beaches, edge after edge, until they cut into the sky, horizon at last, the crocodile-back profile suffused with color. An arroyo threads down the slope, fraying out as it reaches the ocean. Dry. Against the tree-dark mountains and scrub-furred ridges, the dry arroyos look raw and scraped, as if a large paw had gouged out the watercourse, splaying out into sandy streaks at the ocean's edge. The hard crystalline rock of the mountains squeezes the arroyos narrow; where they cross softer rock, they spread out into meandering and braided channels with their gritty absorbing silences. There are no glints of water, no streams, no rivulets, no ponds, no lakes, nothing to give back reflection; the whole landscape simply absorbs light.

The mountains, without the alluvial fans that ordinarily exist in dry country to form a transition between plain and slope, fairly crackle with vitality. They look as if made out of rumpled cardboard, and I feel that if I look away for even a second they will uncrumple themselves and explode into the air with horrendous thumpings and bumpings.

A dirt road wanders along the coast, connecting the few signs of life in an unpopulated landscape—the thatched roofs of a *rancho*. I remember them: neat little ranches with raked yards, with carefully woven walls and fences wreathed with bougainvillaea and the deep pink-flowered vines of San Mi guelito that bloom all year long; and sometimes unneat little ranches, full of empty tin cans and car remains—but somehow always with clean wash on the line. I look for the arroyo where we searched for fossils—huge thick oyster shells, thin delicately fluted scallop shells, sharks' teeth, whale verte brae—ten miles back from the ocean but part of the memory of the sea that lapped at old inland shores.

There are plans to pave this road someday. Joseph Wood Krutch quoted a "fanatical disbeliever in progress": "Baja is a splendid example of how much bad roads can do for a country. It must be almost as beautiful as it was when the white man first saw it in 1533—and of how many other regions can you say that?" These spidery back roads, sometimes rocky enough to jar every vertebra into a new configuration, sometimes deep with sand, are varied and fascinating—and *still* clean.

We bank sharply right, cross the Tropic of Cancer, and enter the mountains. Northward toward La Paz, a plain opens out, patterned with terraced farm plots undulating with the terrain's unevenness, flanked by short sharp ridges—no straight lines, everything curved and notched, cut up and fragmented. Bare rocks whiten some of the ridges as if the landscape were a plaster-of-Paris model from which the green paint has been worn off. As we look down on it, the scrub appears almost mossy, subtly greener and thicker along the creases in the land, giving an exaggerated sense of contour.

Ah, at six thousand feet the meadow of La Laguna! Once the meadow on top of the mountain held a lake until a storm broke its confines and drained the water away; now it is a lake of grasses. I can identify everywhere we walked, even pick out the little weather station, the glinting streams, one of which goes to the Sea of Cortés, the other to the Pacific. The trees surrounding the meadow encroach, chewing away at its periphery, and soon will swallow up this only open grassy space in the entire Cape mountains.

The mountains of the Cape lie to the west of center of the peninsula, sloping up from the Sea of Cortés, cutting down steeply to the Pacific, creating a landscape of endlessly repeated Vs: reversed Vs of mountains, true Vs of arroyos and valleys, and all variations between. No horizontals, no verticals, just diagonals, clamped by the perfect horizontals of the sea on either side. Herman makes a last circle. After five more *whisps* of the shutter, we climb to altitude and level out, and I relax.

The view now is all-encompassing and splendid. Below, the Sierra de la Laguna, and beyond it the Sierra de la Victoria. To the right, the Pacific, that endless ocean on which the galleons came. The land could look no more beautiful to them than to me this day. To the left, the Sea of Cortés. Rolling away ahead, the shimmer of ocean at Cabo San Lucas—land's end. Next stop: Antarctica.

Flowing beneath the plane lies what I have chosen to write about, not only because it is most familiar to me by choice and circumstance, but because it has a built-in fascination for those who ponder the questions of how the continents got to be where they are and where they are going and who lives here and why. Here lies the transition zone between the fauna of tropical western America and that of the North Temperate Zone, where there is a richness of juxtapositions that challenges the mind and provokes new understandings.

We cross Todos Santos, a pleasant town which lies protected from the Pacific behind a row of hills. Swaths of farmland with smooth, freshly plowed dark brown earth and neat green fields and their geometric boundaries contrast with the irregular scrub-covered terrain out of which they are cut. Smaller farms, with candlewick orchards, modestly green, tuck into the contours of the land. A road, paved, passes through a settlement, strings out of the farms. As we go south, along the Pacific, the farms become fewer, the roads dwindle.

The infinite Pacific—next stop west: Hawaii. Today it seems even more infinite, with just a smudge where the horizon ought to be, sea and sky one, world without end, amen. Wind trails pucker the surface, rasping out serpentines and banners. Crescent beaches stretch between bony headlands. We follow the shoreline, the breaking edge of the waves like white cartouches on an ancient map. From this altitude, they have a curious stillness, so unlike those heavy pounding rollers I know them to be.

Off the left wing tip shines the bald pate of Calaveras, its white granite dome gleaming in the sunlight. I found it more precipitous standing on that narrow ridge, buffeted by the wind, than flying over it, where one has at least the virtue of distance and none of the reality of vertical dropoffs. The land is fearfully beautiful in this light. I have a rush of feeling that I cannot explain, even to myself, compounded of love, ear pressure, and tilted horizons. If only I could reach out of the plane and gentle my hand over those rough contours, this inanimate unfeeling terrain, and by touching it, infuse it with the affection I feel. Maybe part of this landscape's appeal to me is the absence of the pretty, the nice, the sweet, the not-a-hair-out-of-place perfection. I prefer my apple trees gnarled, my paths rocky, and my landscapes rugged, surly, and forbidding. Never mind the superficials. Give me form, revealed in all its imperfections and confusions, all its variations and quixotic upheavals and fissures and errors of judgment. With the formal beauty of strength and endurance. Beginnings long since begun, understandings long since reached, vitalities still untapped.

As we approach Cabo Falso, the sand border widens and two lighthouses stud a wide apron of sand. The old lighthouse, so sensibly and unsensibly placed, was abandoned when blowing sand abraded its glass until the light shone blurred. The new one sits far back from the sea on top of the cliff.

Herman heads straight in for a close-in shot; I studiously write and don't watch the rapidity with which the altimeter unwinds, clear my ears again and again and again. He dips one wing, levels out, dips the other and turns and banks and climbs, and my stomach strains against the seat belt, then down toward cliffs and sand, so close I can count grass blades. I want to say, "Enough, enough!" but he has on his headset and can't hear me anyway.

Then up and eastward to land's end itself, and the landmark arch standing off Bahía San Lucas, one lurching turn and then another around the familiar spine. And sudden civilization. Packed into the last granite vertebrae of the peninsula are hotels, houses, streets, stores, all the imprint of man's pleasure at a reachable place in the sun. The bay where John Xantus collected his specimens of plants and animals then unknown to science, the beach where the English privateers careened their galleons, where once a tuna factory flourished, is now inhabited by large resort hotels and innumerable yachts. The deserted coasts of the Pacific and the Sea of Cortés give way to resorts and roads and tennis courts. The highway from La Paz binds them to the sea, as if all the new settlement were roped in, confining the visitor to the nice safe seashore.

Life on the other side of the rope exists on the terms of the peninsula: small *ranchos* tucked into a notch in the mountain slope or beside an arroyo or on a hilltop, blended in, sparse, spare, but a part of the landscape as the big hotels and the condominiums can never be. There life is predicated by rainfall, there women go out to gather herbs in the evening to help their husbands sleep well, a pickup truck stands by a woven *palo de arco* fence, and a quarter-mile horse race enlivens a summer afternoon.

The lagoon at San José del Cabo, where the Rio San José enters the sea, shines like a ducat dropped in the sand. We fly up the sandy river bed that runs up the eastern flank of the Sierra San Lázaro. The river comes down from the mountains to the north and furnishes irrigation water to the farms and ranches along its periphery and makes possible the vivid green garden plots startlingly visible from the air—bright green is a *very* uncharacteristic Baja California color. But there is no accompanying tinsel gleam of water from the air: the Rio San José runs underground, as Jakob Baegert wrote in a letter to his brother, "as if it feels sorry."

The peak of San Lázaro caps the Sierra, which rises to our left, a beckoning spire of bare rock. Being low altitude the Cape mountains are vegetated right to the summit except for San Lázaro and a lower peak behind it, which shine like bare bones. I have watched San Lázaro for years and yearn to climb it all the way to the very top, to perch up there on some small promontory, scratched and tired, scared and exhilarated. Someday I will.

The little villages of the valley shine like white pebbles tossed on the ground—Miraflores, then Santiago, very small in that big wild landscape, almost lost in the soft shadows of their valleys. Sometimes rock piles follow the ridge lines like the backbone of some huge animal. We turn out to the Sea of Cortés again, crossing the rough broken terrain that's as forbidding as any I know. We reach, turn, and follow the coastline southwestward.

The altimeter needle turns counter-clockwise. I watch for my own personal landmarks, the gray cliff that bites the ocean and holds my favorite tidepools, the perfect crescent beach, the old shipwreck, the far arroyo where Susan and I walked and found a waterfall, the beach where Jane and I play Scrabble and Sara made her first foray into snorkeling and where Herman and Susan dive.

I remember walking up from this beach one afternoon with a friend of many years, Kaethe Salomon. I stopped to look closely at a plant that fingered over the sand-pocketed granite cliff. Katie remarked, "It is enough for me to look at a flower and say it is beautiful. For you, you always have to know its name, why it is there, what it is all about." Her remark gave me pause. She was right of course. I just hadn't acknowledged this turn of mind. I *do* need to know who's eating whom and why and, if not, why not; and why does that cactus grow here and not there; and why is the sky blue and the sun warm, and why do the waves sometimes lap and sometimes boom, and why are the tidepool rocks slippery here and not there, and who is that tiny worm that drifts a red feather boa into the pool's current, and if far far out beyond my eyesight is there another horizon?

So I write about plants that have grown here for centuries, adapted by harsh realities to intriguing forms and shapes and the uses that an ingenious and aware population has made of them. About shells, those that totter over the rocks today, those that are extricated from rocks millions of years old. About the sound of the ocean, the sound of the mountains, the continuous sea, the seldom rain. Names given a century ago to creatures large and small, names not yet given to species not yet discovered. About small things that haunt the tidepools and bigger things that haunt the mind.

As we turn on final approach I find myself looking straight down into a sapphire-blue ocean with the ghosts of old ships and murdered captains and unnumbered creatures. As Herman levels out, I hear the wheep as the flaps go down, the high-pitched whine as the wheels lower, the deepening of sound as the propellers change into low pitch. Different as our sounds are— no wind luffing the sails, no creak of timbers, no slap of lines looping around a capstan—these sounds of navigation are still those of comfort, of things going the right way at the right time, of coming safely to land. The dirt strip rises before us and, as always, Herman sets some forty-five hundred pounds of metal, baggage, microscope, scuba gear, books, and bones down as gently as a leaf settling on the grass.

We thump along to the end of the runway, turn off onto the parallel taxiway, and bump back through our own dust plume. Herman pushes power to one engine, rotates the plane ninety degrees to park, pulls back the throttles, and waits for the engines to shudder to a stop, then pops open the front door.

Silence and soft warm air flood the cabin.

He turns from the front seat and says, as he has so many times, "Well, Annie, you're home."

1
THE SIERRA

The many ridges sloping down to the sea or to the San José Valley are all very precipitous and very narrow. Many are so narrow, indeed, that if one should slip he would be likely to fall down either side, as if from the sharp ridge of a roof. This sierra is imperfectly known. Few if any of the educated people of the country have ever visited the higher mountains or are at all interested in doing so. In Mexico there is no taste for athletic exercise, and no sierra or mountain clubs, no desire to enjoy the sublime scenery of the high mountains; all this is left to the poor cowboy, the arriero or mule-driver.

Gustav Eisen
Explorations in the Cape Region of Baja California in 1894, with References to Former Expeditions of the California Academy of Sciences
1895

Tronador *(Cardiospermum corindum)*

SAN LÁZARO

We've been getting to this crow's nest for fourteen hours, a space less than twenty feet long and a spare five wide. San Lázaro looms right above us. I think I had just assumed I was going to be climbing for the rest of my life, that this day began somewhere back in my childhood and that when I got here I would be an old woman. I'm so glad to be here I could turn somersaults. Except there's not room.

It all began with José Rivera asking two days ago, "You would like to climb San Lázaro day after tomorrow?" Good heavens, *yes!* I've only been trying to get there for two years!

José knows everyone and everything and everywhere around the Cape. He has the face and mien of an aristocrat in a Velásquez court painting: dark brown eyes, an expression of gentle amusement, a rising inflection in his speech that sometimes leaves sentences floating in the air. He walks catlike on the balls of his feet, his back ramrod straight, with a dignified precision of pace. He and Herman, two natural conservatives, communicate directly, seeing the world in much the same way. I suspect he regards me with considerable amusement for all the unfeminine things that, by a Mexican gentleman's definition, I do. But it is largely because of José Rivera that I can do

San Lázaro

them, for he knows whose sister has a cousin whose brother-in-law knows the area around San Lázaro or who likes to go oystering or where fossils are. And more than that, a boyish love of the countryside and what it holds.

Knowing someone who knows someone is often the only way to get into the Baja California mountains. Almost no accounts of climbing San Lázaro exist. The only one I found was written by Gustav Eisen in 1895, here under the auspices of the California Academy of Sciences; unfortunately all his personal papers for this trip, lodged at the Academy, were lost in the San Francisco earthquake of 1906. It is little comfort that his report could have been written yesterday. You can ask about these mountains, but you can get precious little information. It is not like going into wilderness areas in the United States. To say these mountains are remote is putting it mildly. And the remoteness is as much psychological as physical. The Cape mountains are not formidable mountains in the sense of technical climbs, but formidable because of lack of water and isolation. There are areas in the central part of the mountains which are possibly unreachable except on foot; neither horses nor mules can negotiate the boulder piles in streambeds and on ridges, nor penetrate the scrub, and generally no trails exist. But herein lies their beauty and their challenge. I have a goading curiosity to know what's growing up there that isn't growing down here, and what you can see from up there—what vistas, what understandings, what news of yesterday, what portents of tomorrow.

As dusk slides up San Lázaro's western flank, a row of palm trees in a furrow on the mountainside catches the last light, standing out bright against the dark green background. This graceful *la palmia* is endemic to the peninsula; its dead fronds fall away, leaving a clean strong trunk that may be over a hundred feet tall. A canyon wren carols one last time right beneath us, that liquid descending trill ending with a curling embellishment, and then is silent.

From this saddle I look westward into the interior mountains and their valleys, northeastward to the Sea of Cortés, east to the Rio San José Valley and south to more mountains that ground into being between a hundred million and sixty-five million years ago, that long slow heaving of massive scale and time that buckled up the whole Rocky Mountain chain when the peninsula was still part of the mainland. The Cape mountains, a confused mass of peaks that goes to within fifteen miles of land's end, are the rattles on the sinuous snake of the Rockies whose head lies in the Aleutians.

The mountains were formed by massive intrusions of granite welling up deep within the earth. These intrusions, called batholiths, pushed up the older igneous and sedimentary basement rocks that they entered, the age and history of which little is known. They jointed and shattered the older rock and metamorphosed it in varying degrees. Attached to western Mexico until twenty-five million years ago, the elevated basement rock was worked by erosion that carried its debris into the Pacific and exposed the granitic heart of the mountains—a granite webbed with intrusions of pegmatite, an exceedingly coarse-grained granite, or aplite, a granular crystalline igneous rock. When the granites cooled and solidified deep within the earth, they did so slowly enough that the minerals within them formed large grains, giving the rock its particular "salt and pepper" appearance now so marked in the Cape granites. Twenty-five million years ago the southern end of the Gulf began to open, and the peninsula began its move to the northwest.

Mainland Mexico and the peninsula are attached to different plates of the earth's crust, separated by the East Pacific Rise; the mainland is part of the American Plate, while the peninsula is bound to the Pacific Plate. The East Pacific Rise is an area of earth spreading where magma is constantly upwelling to the surface and pushing the plates apart. Some thirty million years ago, a large section of western Mexico tore free and became attached to the Pacific Plate; carried to the northwest, it became what is now the peninsular ranges, from Los Angeles, Alta California, south to central Baja California. As magma contined to well up into the rift, the volcanic mountains of central Baja California formed. The Rise worked its way north, widening the Gulf as it went. It reached the mouth of the present Gulf about four million years ago. The peninsula, as well as the portion of southern California linked to the Pacific Plate, moves northwestward between three and five centimeters a year. At the north end of the Gulf, the plate boundary is expressed in a series of faults, among them, the San Andreas.

In the Cape, the main sierras run almost true north and south for fifty miles, a single block in which transverse faults and erosion have combined to carve two separate complexes, the northern one called Sierra de la Laguna, and the southern, Sierra de la Victoria (although the latter name is often applied to the whole complex). Individual groups of peaks are often named after the commanding peak, as Sierra de San Lázaro. Since the opening of the southern end of the Gulf, the batholith in the San Lázaro area has been uplifted perhaps two thousand feet, and tilted southward, forming in the process the many fault zones that run both the length and width of the peninsula.

Because of the low altitude, most mountains are vegetated right to the top; nevertheless, they are ruggedly impressive. Low passages between east and west exist but are largely unused because the ruggedness of the terrain and the impassable thickets of thorny scrub discourage trails and travelers. The variations in elevation within the mountain system were caused by internal faulting, probably as the peninsula separated and moved northwestward away from the mainland. It is infinitely easier to follow the seacoast than to cut across country.

Now, as suddenly as if someone had pulled the light cord, it is dark. The heat of the day changes sharply to a cool evening. I spread my ground cloth before total blackness sets in. The lights of villages—Caduaño, Miraflores, Santiago—glitter in little clusters below. To the west and south, into the mountains, the valleys sink into deeper darkness. Not one pinpoint of light shines there. In the intense quiet I think back twenty-four hours to when Herman and José Rivera left me at Rancho San Miguelito. It seems an eon.

José, Herman, and I start out after lunch to find Ingleberto Agúndez—he's known as Néné (pronounced Neh–nay) who will be one of the two guides. He is working at the airport on the open-air waiting room, putting on palm thatch. He slithers down the ladder to greet us. He is slight and wiry, a boyish face beneath a three-day growth of beard streaked with gray, as is his dark curly hair. In the summer he trims palms, walking up the trunks and hacking off the old growth, which is an unsightly fire hazard.

The big palm boles that will support the waiting-room roof lie like huge matchsticks—they look odd, having pith but no rings. The Jesuit Miguel del Barco wrote that the trunks of *la palmia* are

> very strong and durable, and therefore people take advantage of them to make beams. But they do not shape them, rather they use them as they are, cutting them only according to the length that is needed. It would not be good to shape them, either, because on the one hand, they would lose much of their strength (which is in their exterior) and, in addition, they would end up too thin.

Miguel del Barco came to California in 1738 with one of the largest missionary groups sent out from Europe. He remained here thirty years, leaving when the Jesuits were expelled by order of the Spanish crown in 1768. Although his home mission was north of Loreto, he traveled widely and spent considerable time in the southern part of the peninsula. Like most Jesuits, he was well educated, and coupled this training with an observant eye and inquisitive mind.

San Lázaro

We go back to Néné's house to pick up his gear, which consists of a plastic shopping bag holding his food, gallon jugs for water, and a blanket. He harnesses his machete to his belt. He wears two shirts, with a *riata,* a long braided leather rope, wrapped several times around his waist.

As we drive north up the valley of the Río San José, the stone beak of San Lázaro to the west looks suddenly terrifying, like a knife stuck in the gentle ridges beneath. I have second thoughts. The plan is to stay at Rancho San Miguelito tonight (named for the ubiquitous deep pink-flowered vine), get up before dawn tomorrow morning, and climb to a camping spot on a high saddle beneath San Lázaro, where we will leave our gear, climb the peak, come down, camp, and be back to the ranch by noon the next day, since Herman and I must leave the day after. Not much leeway.

From Herman's face when he leaves me I know he is worried, concerned and perhaps angry at what seems to him my incompetent foolhardiness. No one here speaks English—or even Spanish as far as I'm concerned. To my ear they speak a soft singsong dialect with a rolling lisp, that I'm finding most difficult to understand. I suddenly empathize with the foreigner trying to learn English and being set down in a southern y'awl household.

After Herman and José are gone, I sit in the ramada at the ranch, a pleasant open living area typical of *ranchos.* Little María hurries up the piglets with "Ondule! Ondule!" as they scurry to be fed. The sun shifts behind the mountains and leaves a lavender haze over thatch roof, banana tree, and the huge boulders blocking the arroyo before me. Many big black carpenter bees called *moscoróns* drone through the air. Among the chickens two immense tom turkeys confront each other and display. At least two dozen baby pigs root and scatter. Only a couple of cows forage here, the rest being out on the hillsides. As the day cools the piglets congregate and flop on top of each other, noses all pointed in the same direction, as neatly laid as fur-trappers' pelts. One piglet scratches itself on a stone, a blissful look on its face. Another shoat stands on three legs and scratches its stomach with its fourth. The barnyard sounds quiet with only an occasional turkey gobble or piglet shriek. Had I but known, I would have enjoyed the quiet more: it is the most peaceful the barnyard will be until we leave.

A high fence surrounds the ranch buildings, all more or less connected by the roofing of the ramada. The floor is hard-packed dirt, clean-swept. The walls are woven of *palo de arco* withes. Trumpet bush, called in Spanish "arrow wood," for its straight shafts—is a shrub-to-small-tree that grows throughout the Cape, and flowers all year round. The flowers are large and bright yellow, giving way to long slender seed pods that dangle like green beans. The branches have remarkably even diameters. Their strength makes them ideal for this construction, and fences and walls all over the back country of Baja are made of them. They render windows unnecessary, for enough ventilation comes through the walls. Looking out from inside, the narrow interwoven triangles of the light patterns are intricate and pleasing.

In front of the kitchen several orange metal folding chairs and one wooden chair surround a table covered with fresh oilcloth. The kitchen, separate as it is on all ranches, is fire-lit in the darkness, larger than most, for this is a prosperous ranch. Counters line the sides, and on one sits a corn grinder, with a stone *metate* and *mano* beside it for grinding even finer meal. A big double fireplace in the middle has a pothook over one half and a grill for tortillas over the other. Corn boils in a pot. Water drops hiss as they fly into the coals.

Coralvine *(Antigonon leptopus)*

I stand at the doorway, fascinated, watching the eldest daughter (the rest of the children being in San José at school) make tortillas with a soft "tat tat tat." She picks up a piece of dough the size of a goose egg and, holding her palms vertically, pats it into a round shape. When it is the size of a salad plate she drops it on the skillet, dabs at its top with a crumpled paper towel to break the air bubbles and flatten it. When it's done she lays it on top of the stack already made, picks up another piece of dough, and resumes the rhythmic patting.

One of the things the Jesuit Jakob Baegert, who lived here from 1751 to 1768, found much to his liking was tortillas; he wrote his brother in 1752 that

> I did not speak of bread made of wheat or corn flour, but of little pancakes made of corn meal. The corn is lightly boiled, then ground by hand between two stones. The meal is formed into thin, flat, little cakes, made warm over a hot iron plate. These pancakes are eaten by all the people in all America, and are served like warm bread with meat and other foods. I found them a healthful food and very pleasing to the taste after having eaten them for several weeks.

La Señora lights a small kerosene lamp on the table, which she sets with spoons and milk glass bowls. In the center of the table she sets a pot of beans and an oblong plate of rice with a huge serving spoon. Next to these she places a little jar of what look like plump pale pink capers.

"Picante?" I ask cautiously. "Sí, Sí, *muy* picante!" they say, laughing. I ordinarily like peppers that would peel the paint off the side of a house but I doubt that this is the time to be brave, for these are *chiles pequeños* in vinegar, tiny but the most potent of all peppers. Capsaicin is the volatile compound that makes hot peppers hot, and the pepper pod placenta, where the seeds are attached, retains it in unreduced potency. *Capsicum annuum* originated in and grew wild in Central America and Mexico, and has been eaten for at least seven thousand years, and certainly cultivated nearly as long to spice up a fairly bland diet of maize, beans, and squash.

Hot to the table come fresh tortillas in which to roll up beans and rice. (Both beans and rice, and corn and rice, when eaten together, form complete protein.) The one thing I would miss in this diet is fresh milk and vegetables. None of the latter are grown here, although many remote ranches do have small gardens. And all fresh milk goes to make cheese. Without refrigeration perishables are difficult to preserve.

Whenever I have eaten at a ranch, La Señora serves and stands aside; she does not eat with the guests. I would like to ask her to sit with us but sense

Trumpet bush *(Tecoma stans)*

that it would be bad manners. Still, it bothers me, the *señora* from Colorado who always eats at her own table. After she clears away plates, she brings a cup of herb tea, heavily sweetened, that is absolutely delicious. I wonder if it is made from *damiana,* a small intensely aromatic plant with small bright yellow flowers common in the countryside.

I sleep in my sleeping bag on the ground at the foot of the clean-made bed in the sleeping room, a room about fifteen by fifteen feet with two half-partitions, one for the elder daughter, one for María, with two more big beds out in the middle. La Señora is clearly puzzled that I didn't sleep in the lovely clean bed; it was a matter of miscommunication, and besides I was dirty and I didn't want to make a lot of extra work for her. Inexplicable I may be, yet she regards me with a grave sweet smile and is courteous and kind.

Sleeping on the ground, my head up against the *palo de arco* wicker wall, seventy years fade away and I wonder if this was what it felt like if you were going to be executed the next morning in the Revolution? Confined in a tight space, watching the dim flickering light of freedom through those narrow interstices, listening to low voices plotting outside, the smell of dirt and death close by your head. The Revolution was very different on the peninsula, did not fire this land as it did the mainland. No Emiliano Zapata rode with his band of revolutionaries to give the land back to the farmers—there were no large holdings here to storm.

One rooster crows most of the night. Cape roosters have a maniacal crow, starting on a note of high hysteria and warbling into sheer panic. The first cries are as unnerving as those of a loon on an empty night, ending with one last lunatic ululation that jerks me wide awake again. And when the rooster didn't crow, the cowbells donged, or the eight dogs barked—if one leapt up at some imagined invasion, the rest rose in full bay. I've had quieter nights in New York City.

At four-thirty the radio comes on, the announcer shouting, "Cinco cinco *cinco!*"—wake-up programs must be the same everywhere, noisy and frenetic. La Señora's home-roasted coffee restores a partial sense of rationality. I watch Martín, Señora's husband and the other guide, cut a new leather thong with which to bind on his sandal, a kind of *huarache* with a rectangular piece of tire for its sole. We begin walking at first light, the datura flowers along the arroyo opening like great white owl eyes.

We follow a dusty path obviously laid out by drunk cows. Alongside, all the vegetation has the dry leaves of the season. Only one tree, that Martín calls *sambol,* shows pink and white sweetpea-like blossoms. I think blissfully that the walk is easy, upward but fairly open; a few bushes to avoid, a

Palo de arco wall

cholla or two to walk around, tree limbs to push aside. But enjoyable. Doves flute in the distance. Two of Martín's dogs accompany us, medium-sized both, very long-legged, with glossy black coats. One has a very haughty Egyptoid face and temperament; the other is younger and more amenable. They stay with us the whole thirty-two hours, without food or water.

Then we hit the open ridge and its spine of boulders. None of the rocks has a flat surface to step on. All the rocks are canted and sharp-angled. Many teeter treacherously. They range from basketball-sized boulders to truck-sized ones, with a long way down in between. Although most are granite, they display all shades of gray, some nearly black, some highly crystalline and cut with dikes that shoot through both granites and metamorphics like fine-grained angular snakes. Miguel del Barco wrote that these ridges are

> all covered with loose rocks, some placed on top of the others, of large and medium size, without allowing the soil which lies below them to produce either a small thicket or any other weed, as it does at other places where the great number of rocks is not piled up this way. These pieces of terrain, covered up with rocks upon rocks, are called *mal pais* with good reason, because they make an unpleasant sight, as one sees there nothing but dry stones whose surface, with the years, has become as if burned and some places it has the color of iron.

A few plants spring out between the rocks but there is no time to stop and look closely at those: a stalky spurge with long bare stems, white flowers almost half an inch across, centered with dark red, the ovary springing out of the side; showy pink composites—skeleton weeds familiar along the seacoast; desert lavender; orange mallows.

As I work along the slope I look for the one plant I would love to find above all others, a small endemic composite named *Faxonia pusilla,* not a glamorous flower, nor even very pretty; its charm lies in the fact that it has been collected only once, in 1893 by the botanist Townshend Stith Brandegee, and has never been found since. Not over three inches high, it raises flower heads less than a quarter inch tall held in involucral bracts with gland-tipped hairs. Since it blooms after the summer rains, we are probably months too early. But it never hurts to keep an eye out.

By now it is 85 degrees and heat radiates off the rocks. It's like walking in a reflector oven. The ascent is so steep that I spend most of my time looking at Martín's bare heels. Bare toes and bare heels. He leaps like an antelope. I, in my old Vibram-soled boots that protect my ankles, do not. When not looking at Martín's heels I am looking at his dog's heels because the Egyp-

Malacothrix *(Malacothrix xantii)*

tian dog feels it his prerogative to follow his master. If I try to shoo him away he simply ignores me. This is men's work, he seems to say, and dismisses me with a contemptuous stare. Martín has only to whistle at him once and he knows exactly what's expected of him, but he hears not one word I say.

Four muffled booms sound in quick succession. Martín explains that a new road is being built just north of here which will go from near Miraflores to Todos Santos. Through the mountains. Through *these* mountains? Over two hundred years ago Baegert observed that a missionary could travel between the two missions of Santiago and Todos Santos "in one day were it not for an almost insurmountable mountain range."

Looking eastward I spot a strip shaved out of the vegetation: the airport at San José del Cabo. A plane takes off—I see it only after I hear its drone. In this next to nowhere place, how ironic that the air age intrudes. A buzzard lofts over, and the plane's straight trajectory seems clumsy by comparison. Néné points to a *parajo azul,* a bright blue bird sitting on a limb close by—a lazuli bunting here for the winter.

Now there are intermittent periods off the boulders. Néné goes ahead with his machete, cutting stalks at a sharply lethal angle, eight to twelve inches off the ground, a perfect abatis. The ring of the blade echoes across the narrow valley beneath us. Blood red drops ooze out of the white core of lomboy, a sap of which Barco wrote that it "stains one's clothing with such tenacity that, no matter how the affected article is washed, the stain persists, and merely loses its bright color to assume a more subdued one." The clean turpentine smell of bursera and other pleasant scents lie on the air, clean or spicy or reminiscent of some long-lost aroma that evokes unformed memories.

Often, when I reach out for a branch with which to hoist myself, it's already been cut and pulls away with my weight. Vines weave interminable traps—resilient tronador loops all over plants and rocks. It has but two short curled tendrils on each flowering stem but they manage to anchor the vine into a deadly foot-catching mesh. I'd have caught my foot more than once were it not for its big and highly visible seed pods.

Martín stops to wait for me beneath a fig tree with a beautiful creamy white trunk and roots flattened and writhing through the rocks, anchoring the tree in a place no other trees grow. Barco said the roots "maintain the same color as that of the tree and they appear on the cliffs bearing some resemblance to water that has become frozen as it poured over rocks of the arroyo at the site." It bears a few tiny figs, on the tasteless side, about the size of large grapes, stuffed with brown seeds. The Indians reportedly would go miles to get them when they were ripe; Brandegee observed that when "the small figs are ripe the tree is full of animal life; numerous insects are buzzing around, attracted by the sweet exudations of the fruit, and hummingbirds are continually flying through the branches."

Fruit development is tuned to tiny fig wasps. Female fig flowers are filled with spines which exclude all insects except the eighth-inch female agaonid wasp. After she mates with a wingless male, she enters a flower in the short-styled female phase to lay her eggs. That flower then develops into "gall flower." As the wasp larvae grow, the flower becomes male and produces pollen. The larvae metamorphose into adults within the flower, and as they emerge, they brush against the anthers and are dusted with pollen which they carry out with them. When they enter another female flower, the pollen brushes off, thus fertilizing it. A fig tree can produce fruit only if its obligate wasp is there to fertilize it.

Four o'clock. We rest on the highest ridge of the peak just north of San Lázaro. As we came up over the rise, the bulk of San Lázaro rose out of the rock before me, rising as I rose, like some huge mysterious magical spaceship, as if I dreamed it.

Out of the somber greenness of its flanks rises a white stone peak, jointed like an old geological drawing, skimmed with brilliant apple-green and orange jewel lichens, the various hues of which lose their intensity with distance and simply rainbow the rock in delicate traceries. The configuration of San Lázaro's stone cap is the shape of the omphalos at Delphi, the parabolic carved rock that represented the navel of the world. Here it is on a monumental scale, tied with its ropes of crevices. Had the Greeks seen San Lázaro they might have thought twice about Delphi.

Clouds drift across the saddle between the two mountains and wreathe the top of San Lázaro, then swirl down the valley, and when I look up from writing, waft back up again. The wings of eight doves catch the light, gleam white, clouds distilled into birds. That the misery of getting here can produce such pure happiness will always remain a mystery to me. Some of it lies in the beauty of the mountain itself, some in the respite, and some in those unknown reaches of the human mind, which always searches and so seldom finds.

We still have a long way to go. Half an hour later we come to a sharp descent down fifteen feet of flat rock. I start to slide down when Néné's "NO!" stops me short. Above me Martín removes his braided leather *riata*

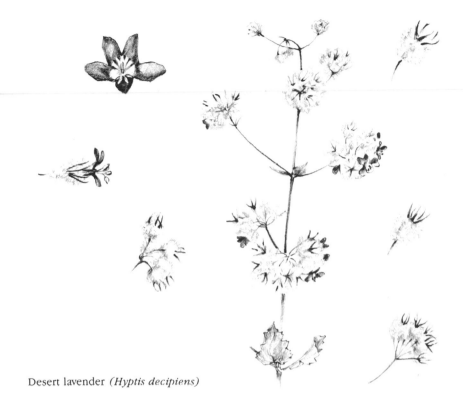

Desert lavender *(Hyptis decipiens)*

from around his waist, fashions a noose, braces himself against a tree and hands it down to me. I hang on with both hands and slide down the rock, scraping my belt buckle.

And then straight up again. I lose count of time and look up with surprise when we suddenly top out onto the saddle with San Lázaro looming immediately above. Two hours to San Lázaro from here, says Martín—do I want to go? Of *course* I want to go! That's what I came for! Then I hear Herman's voice in my ears and I glance at my watch. Two hours over means two hours back, and I think of traversing this terrain in the darkness. And that two hours over, I find, includes just going to the base. I couldn't do that   I'd have to go up to the top. I think all sorts of sensible thoughts, such as getting back when I promised Herman we would and and and.

Tronador *(Cardiospermum corindum)*

I remember the other knob of rock, bare as a gnawed bone, on the west side of the Sierra de la Victoria, named, appropriately enough, Calaveras— The Skulls. I remember what it was like on top, a vertiginous narrow rib of rock where I felt I could see the whole peninsula laid out like a map. It was fifteen hundred feet lower. What could I not see from San Lázaro? I look hard at San Lázaro, and write "INACCESSIBLE" in my notes. A snakelike word, full of sibilant warnings, ending with an explosive barricade. So be it.

For supper, Vienna sausage. I try to eat one of my tortillas and find I cannot. Food is the last thing I want. The puppy noses in the open can for the Vienna-sausage juice. When he's finished, I stomp on the can and put it back in my daypack. Martín and Néné nearly fall off the mountain laughing. Nor were they sobered by my account of how many people go into the wilderness in the United States, and if we didn't carry out, it would soon be paved with tin cans. Their depository was beneath a large rock, and from the number of cans there it had been in use a while.

We in the United States cloister our wilderness, philosophize about it, examine it, explore it, often fiercely defend its emptiness. Many see it as a museum containing the rich interwoven and untainted web of flora and fauna, a yardstick by which to measure the changes that man makes in his environment, or as a safety valve—for man. As Joseph Wood Krutch wrote about Baja California, one reason people came here is that "there is still a sizable minority who find the vanishing world, dominated by nature rather than by man, one of the things most worth seeing." Yet I also understand that wilderness is a luxury. It is for those who have time for it and don't have to fight it continually for living space. Néné and Martín know this country only because they hunt it.

Crickets, singing continuously at the ranch, fire in two- to three-second bursts up here. The sky blackens. The air chills to the low fifties. I snuggle into my sleeping bag. I think that Néné and Martín must have another place to sleep, and I shall have the singing quiet of a night beneath these glorious stars, a quiet which I desperately need after last night's cacophony and the day's duress. My bones want quiet. My muscles want quiet. My eyelashes and my fingernails want quiet. I find it hard to realize that exactly one week from tonight I will be in a New York hotel where I will crawl into a fresh bed and listen to the traffic sounds dim. No flickering fire, no fluttering evening wind, no stars so bright they're a hand's reach away.

It is not to be. When Néné dug a pit for the fire at the other end of the clearing, Martín dug a long trench right beside it, into which he snuggled, pulling dirt in over his feet. They build a fire big enough to roast an ox and keep it going all night. But, as the night really chills down, I suspect that they need the warmth, for neither of them has a jacket, and even tough calloused bare feet get cold. The disdainful dog sleeps at my right, as far away as he can sleep and not fall off the mountain; the puppy, who accepted my meager food offerings, snuggles close at my feet. Four watchdogs in all!

Of course I've heard all the stories of *zorrillo,* the rabid skunk. Walter Bryant, collecting birds here in 1890, said when he was in the mountains he heard so many stories of mad skunks "it was enough to make a nervous man keep his head covered at night," since it preferred to bite a man's face, and that it was "more feared by the inhabitants than drought, yellow fever, smallpox or cholera." The most sturdy guards against such skunks are ranch dogs. I give the puppy an extra pat.

Néné and Martín talk all night long. Néné never answers "sí" or "no" but "um-hum" or "hum-um" delivered in a melodious singsong. When one falls asleep the other wakes up and answers the question asked an hour ago. Once the fire almost goes out and I am so relieved—*now* there will be quiet! But Néné awakes almost immediately and quickly throws on more wood.

About four-thirty they begin making loud official noises, which I take to mean I should wake up, ridiculous because I haven't been asleep. I sit up. Néné is stirring a tin can full of coffee close by the flame; as it boils and foams he continually lifts a spoonful high and lets it fall back slowly so that it won't boil over. When he sees that I am awake, he takes it off the fire, lets it settle a minute, and then pours it into my mug and brings it over—*superb* coffee, thick and nourishing, loaded with caffeine which puts starch in my veins and lots of sugar which infuses me with momentary energy.

I compliment Néné. Martín says that's pretty good service; I reply, "El mejor en el mundo!"—the best in the world, better than a hotel. Martín says we will call this saddle "Hotel Anna." We laugh. "No llaves—no keys," I say, and Néné replies, "And no guests either—how do they get here?" A very exclusive hotel indeed, we agree, with an incomparable view. We sit talking around the fire for another two hours, waiting for first light. Martín points down the slope and says we will go quickly, "como las piedras" and makes a rolling gesture of rocks tumbling down the mountain. I laugh uneasily.

Part way down huge black carpenter bees hang and hover over empty space beside a ridge; we hear their heavy droning long before we see them. One holds an almost stationary station in the air until another comes and then zap zap *zap*—one of them leaves. Being territorial? They are not feeding, not mating, not doing anything but just hanging over an improbable mountainside and buzzing like crazy. Sometimes there are two or three at a time, and then like a magic trick but one remains, wings a blur, catching different light on its shiny abdomen as it adjusts to the vagrant updrafts. A carpenter bee looks for all the world like a bumble bee—big and bumbling and noisy. Its bare abdomen is the clearest visual difference, and the fact that the carpenter bees are usually all black, or at least not marked with the yellow banding sported by bumble bees. They feed on flowers, being big enough to bite right through a flower tube to get directly to the nectar.

They excavate tunnels, sometimes a foot long, in wood—hence their common name but do not feed on it. Partitions separate cells, with pollen and nectar placed in each, along with a single egg. When the larvae hatch, they have a handy food supply as well as shelter, for they also pupate there, emerging as adults. In spite of their huge size and bombast, they seldom sting.

José has asked me to bring him a flower from the mountain top. I keep looking on the way down. Big papery seed pods already replace ruellia flowers. Tiny purple flowers in fuzzy calyces haze desert lavender but fall quickly. Nor would San Diego sunflowers survive in my daypack in this heat. And then I see the answer, growing on a nearly vertical dirt slope, tucked around the base of a boulder. I bring José instead a curled fist of the clubmoss called resurrection plant. Now dry and tightly curled, when put in a cup of water it slowly unfurls into a brilliant green rosette, surely an appropriate symbol of friendship.

I tried to kid myself that going down was not going to be grim. Going down *is* grim. We come to a boulder pile that I think I cannot get across. I know that I am dehydrating, that I am descending toward heat exhaustion.

An early writer recorded that the "natives, it is said, never die—they dry up and float away." A high pressure zone centered over Lower California is responsible for a stable atmosphere most of the year and for the general aridity. Pleasant it may be, a great tourist attraction it may be, but when one is laboring in the sun, it negates one of the main sources of cooling for the human body—evaporative cooling through sweating.

Obviously body liquids lost by perspiration must be replaced. I have drunk so much water I feel as if I must slosh when I walk. Since the body can adjust to some loss of sodium salt for a period but cannot to loss of potassium salts, oranges, with their potassium (and sugar), have been a godsend. But I've eaten all mine. I focus tightly on keeping my good sense and getting myself down off this rockpile, knowing the worst is far from over.

When we finally reach the end of the ridge, Martín turns to me and says triumphantly, "El último!" The *end*. And somehow, knowing I don't have

San Diego sunflower *(Vigueria deltoidea* var. *deltoidea)*

any more to traverse, I trot along the next three hours with no more problem than toes ramming up against my boot toes as the descent continues to be very declivitous. Odd, I don't remember the going up as half as steep.

We haul into the dooryard just at one o'clock. *Mas vale tarde que nunca.* Herman receives me with a kiss and a cold beer, remarking on its excellence in restoring the body's electrolyte balance. I say nothing. Just guzzle.

La Señora stands aside, watching, smiling. In her blue dress, with her eldest daughter in brighter blue and little María in magenta, the three of them look like a bouquet of bright flowers, and we all take pictures of each other, everyone with everyone else. The banana tree leaves swish in the breeze, the *moscoróns* drone, the piglets fuss and squeal. I keep trying to cope with our mutual culture shock: I invaded their daily routine, came from a strange land, go back to a strange land, do things that no rancher's wife would do. Or would even *want* to do.

And so I say my *muchas gracias* to La Señora, ask "Con permiso," as we leave, then turn and say, as if it explains everything that cannot be explained between us, "San Lázaro es muy muy bonito."

When we fly home, San Lázaro studs the horizon of our leaving. San Lázaro: unclimbed. I am not as disappointed as I thought. Maybe what matters is that there are places you can't get to from here. Good. Perhaps we need inaccessibles, horizons beyond which we do not go. To which we are forbidden.

North of this sharp ridge the mountain top broadened and the trail led down
a long north slope thickly overgrown with a forest of pinyon pines and small
oaks into the basinlike mountain valley of La Laguna, where we camped at
the ruins of an old ranch in the extreme upper end. This open, nearly flat-
bottomed valley is about a mile long and from one-fourth to one-half as wide
with several small brooklets uniting near the upper end and flowing down
the middle. It is situated at an altitude of about 5,500 feet and surrounded
by steep mountain slopes covered with low oak and pinyon forest. Formerly
the bottom of the valley is said to have been occupied by a shallow lake, the
lower end of which was eroded during a season of heavy rains and the lake
drained. This occurred many years ago before [Lyman] Belding's visit here
in 1882, yet some of the people at La Paz and elsewhere in the cape district
still believe the lake exists.

Edward W. Nelson
Lower California and its Natural Resources
1921

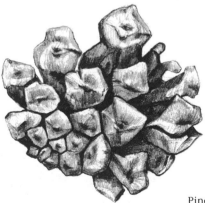

Pine cone *(Pinus cembrioides)*

LA LAGUNA

L a Laguna has been a magnet for naturalists ever since the first collector wandered into its unique high-altitude grassy meadow. Its fascinating flora and fauna reflect not only environmental conditions stunningly different from the remainder of the Cape, but provide keys to what sprouted and bloomed, scurried and hopped in previous epochs, and how they got here.

At four-thirty one December afternoon it's hem-and-haw time. With my daughter, Susan, and Zita Szerlip, one of two guides, I stand by the corral and watch the negotiations. Susan has on a pair of shorts and hiking boots, an overshirt tied around her waist and a baggy day pack on her back. Her hair is tied up, a lovely chestnut that matches her tawny eyes, and there's something Charles Dana Gibson about the face, possibly the hair up, possibly the dark brows. She has an enthusiasm for life that makes her a marvelous hiking companion.

The elder of the two ranchers is obviously in charge. He looks at the ground and draws arcs in the dirt with his big toe. A leather belt pleats his jeans to his thin waist; from it his machete sheath hangs loose. The problem is that two mules were to be provided for riding, plus five burros, to carry gear. But it is, after all, hunting season. The mules have gone with the hunt-

La Laguna

ers. Being sturdier, more reliable than horses, they were required elsewhere, *no es verdad?,* that "Is it not so?" that turns up at the end of so many explanations and indicates the logic of the espouser's viewpoint and the total untenability of yours. Only a fool wouldn't agree, "Sí, es verdad."

Our side is represented by Bruce Simballa, blond, bearded, and an experienced Baja California guide. He has a musical command of Spanish and interjects now and then. In the middle are the two Mexican Forest Service guides, José and Julian. Julian has been a forester for fifteen years, having first come as a guide for army firefighters putting out a fire here, liked it, and stayed on. Julian and his wife have thirteen children; when the oldest three were babies, they lived up on La Laguna, but when the children got older they moved to Todos Santos so that the children could have school. The rangers remain up at La Laguna for two-week shifts, alternating with two weeks off, which gives them time for other work. José and Julian are brothers who bear little facial resemblance, but they have been doing this for so many years now that they walk the same, dress the same, carry their rifles the same, and communicate without words.

The foot drawing ceases. The older rancher makes a pronouncement: we will spend the night at the trailhead, ready to climb in the morning. But *no* mules.

As we walk out, I watch the horizon, the way the hills flow into each other, that illusory Baja California skyline with vegetation that looks so soft and feathery but that is in truth so harsh. My foot raised for a step, I chance to look down, freeze in mid-air. Just where I was going to put my foot coils a small speckled rattlesnake. It doesn't move, lethargic perhaps from the coolness of the evening. Nonetheless, my heart still pounds. The rattlesnake gave me no warning. Normally a rattlesnake senses prey not by eyesight but by heat sensors located in loreal pits on either side of its head. They rattle when cornered or disturbed, to warn off non-prospective victims, retaining their precious venom to kill food animals. Grass patterns simply dissolve its shape as it lies curled; its dark diamonds outlined in white fade into the shadows, and the salt-and-pepper speckling of the rough scales matches the dirt. It is of no cheer whatsoever to know that these may be expected from sea level to high in the mountains, and frequent not only open brushland and rocky places, but piñon-juniper woodlands.

Jakob Baegert wrote in 1772 in *Observations in Lower California* that no missionary had ever died from the bite of one of these New World snakes,

> called *serpents à sonnet* by the French. The head is broad and ugly, the tail not pointed as that of other snakes, but blunt, and it consists of a number of

rings, which (as the Indians tell) indicate the age of the snake, one ring for each year. These rings are joined together like the tail of a crayfish. They are hollow and completely dry, and when these snakes hear or see anyone approaching, they produce a loud terrifying noise with the rings; it is terrifying because it announces the proximity of the snake and, consequently, the danger. Once at dawn, I heard that noise five times within half an hour's ride, and close to the place where I had slept in an open field the night before.

After my heart stops pounding, although I am not inclined to go back and check, I wonder, since the snake did not rattle, if it might have been a bullsnake, endemic to the area. It also has a black band under the tail and resembles the speckled rattlesnake. When on defense it flattens its head to make itself look like a pit viper, and at the same time vibrates its tail, a bit of mimicry that often works the wrong way: the resemblance is so close that it often gets killed by a rancher waiting to ask questions after.

Nearly stepping on a rattlesnake is just the beginning. At midnight I hear Susan rummaging for rocks to throw at a wandering cow, and then Bruce shouts at a pig that noses into the food boxes. Until four o'clock sounds of *"Ho!"* or "Get *out* of there, you bloody pig!" punctuate the night. All we need is Walter Bryant's *zorrillo:*

> One man of more than usual intelligence told me that while deer hunting in the Sierra de la Laguna he had lost a dog from hydrophobia, and one night while sleeping (with his head covered, of course), he had been awakened by the weight of some animal walking slowly along his body, and had waited until it was close to his head, when he suddenly threw it and blanket beyond his feet. Springing up he seized a stick from the fire in time to meet a skunk as it returned to attack him.

At four o'clock it begins to mist and drizzle. At dawn we sit bleary-eyed, eating dry cereal, too tired to build a fire, when José and Julian appear, jauntily leading four horses which, after all the reluctance of last evening, have been miraculously loaded, boxes and all. They walk at a vigorous clip up the trail, grabbing up mouthfuls of grass as they go. Given time, how simple it all is!

During the trek up, the weather changes every quarter hour—the sun shines or mists blanket the slope or rain obliterates the view—in short, at one time or another it does everything but snow. The temperature goes up and down like a yoyo. At first there are only views of facing hillsides, mirror images of those we ascend. With the rise in altitude, trees and shrubs become taller and denser. At a clearing, below us a sandy arroyo worms its way seaward. Further uplift and tilting have occurred within the last million years, rejuvenating streams that further cut the mountain flanks—the amount of uplift in the Cape has been estimated to vary between five hundred and two thousand feet. Since downcutting proceeded faster than valley widening, the valley walls are very steep, and some canyons may be four thousand feet deep. Intermittent storms wash sand and debris into them, creating the flat-bottomed arroyos that thread intricate patterns through the landscape far below us.

The trail rises more precipitously on the western flank of the Sierra de la Laguna than on its eastern flank, but on the east the trail is longer, access more difficult. The granites of these mountains weather quickly, crumbling from huge jointed blocks to individual mineral grains which are easily swept away. In addition, on the western side moisture coming in off the Pacific provides enough water so that most of the materials plucked off the mountainsides are carried down all the way to the sea.

Sometimes the path is respectable, a couple of feet wide, edged with wildflowers. Sometimes the path snakes across an open slope and it's just as well that mists fill in the abyss below. Since we are rising from a few hundred to nearly six thousand five hundred feet in less than eight miles, the ascent is steep, and it is made more so by having many descents along the way that have to be compensated for. Worst are those slots worn by pack animals, over waist-deep and scarcely wide enough to put one foot in front of the other. T. S. Brandegee wrote in 1890:

> The trails over the inhabited portion are pretty good, but those into the high mountains are decidedly bad; they are steep, rocky, often overgrown with vegetation that drenches the traveler with dew and rain drops. The summits are hidden during the rainy months by clouds, and about the peaks it almost always begins to rain and thunder at noon. Any one who collects plants in these high mountains during the rainy season must expect to be wet all day and kept awake all night by innumerable mosquitoes, but will be repaid by the sight of many strange and handsome plants, of which he may carry away specimens if his papers are not destroyed by the rain.

Until Annetta Carter's extensive explorations and Professor Wiggins's splendid and dedicated work, Brandegee probably did more to make the flora of the Baja peninsula known than any other botanist. He concentrated primarily on the flora of the Cape region, and although he sometimes accompanied California Academy of Sciences expeditions, most of his work was carried out at his own expense. He obviously loved the area, and I cannot help but envy him collecting in this Eden of unnamed plants.

During a hiatus in the rain the Pacific glows a pale milky blue, edged with a white shifting line that works slowly back and forth. Then mists curl across the high ridges, cutting off the view. Flights of white-winged doves whistle through the trees. A scrub jay grates. A rufous-sided towhee, brightly accoutered, darts across the trail. A small kestrel streams by, setting dozens of birds to twittering—they sound all around but are out of sight in the dense foliage.

The trees drip with old man's beard and Spanish moss, lichens that add to the misty outlines. Moss greens on rocks and ferns flourish in every crack. We walk through big oaks, pines, and madroño. This particular combination of plants is a remnant of the "Madro-Tertiary flora" which originated in northern Mexico, expanded northwestward, and by twenty-five million years ago reached the Pacific coast and began its spread south down the Baja peninsula. As the Pleistocene Epoch brought a warmer and drier climate, the woodland was largely replaced, at lower altitudes, by a desert and semi-desert flora. Oak-piñon woodland pockets exist today only in the mountains of the northernmost part of the peninsula and the Cape.

Although the hike turns out to be only six hours on the trail, when swathed in mists and bereft of visual reference, I lose my sense of time too. Finally the path levels out, then slopes downward. The bright open grass meadow of La Laguna shines through an opening in the trees, and its tawny color, on this dark afternoon, causes it to look lit with sunshine. My steps lighten and I feel a lifting of spirit, glad to be in this place where I have never been before except through someone else's words.

The trail strings to the shelter used by the foresters, who have a fire started, and it's more than welcome. The temperature has dropped to the low forties and a nasty little damp breeze snakes through the woven walls. There are two rooms in the shelter, built when La Laguna was a potato ranch. The left one is sleeping quarters, furnished with two bunks, spread with José's and Julian's sleeping bags. High shelves on the wall hold their stores, safe from the depredations of rodents and pigs. A small fire, built on the dirt floor, lights their faces from beneath, accenting their cheekbones and dark eyes, illuminating the undersides of their hat brims, like a sepia-print frame from an old Pancho Villa movie. The other room, their cooking quarters, has been graciously given over to us; the same size, about ten by fourteen feet, with a stone fireplace at the back wall, blackened from many fires. Anyone taller than five feet six stoops to come through the door in order to miss the central beam.

Outside, a spindly fence surrounds the neatly raked yard. The debris of decades, all the cans and bottles, have been thrown into piles outside the fence. There two dozen piglets, on dainty tiptoe feet, pick and root. Occasionally one dislodges a can, which clatters down the bank, sending them all squealing. The rangers maintain a small herd up here, selling off some, keeping others, having a ready supply of pork when needed.

Rain increases. The wind gusts. My pocket thermometer creeps down through the forties. I sit on one of the food boxes in the hut, writing down all I can remember about walking up. Outside, a dozen sparrows pick over the ground. In their midst a small junco feeds. As it turns, its bright yellow eye gleams—one of the birds I had hoped to see here: Baird's junco.

Ornithologist Lyman Belding discovered it February 2, 1883, here at La Laguna, which is the "type locality" from which the first specimen was found, identified, and described. It was named for Spencer F. Baird, then secretary of the Smithsonian Institute and himself an avid birder. William Brewster, the well-known Harvard ornithologist, reported on the next expedition to the Cape mountains in "Birds of the Cape Region of Lower California," based on the collection made by Anthony Frazar in the winter and spring of 1887. Brewster noted that these little juncos were very characteristic of the Cape bird fauna, and that they were so tame they often entered the shed where Frazar worked and hopped about his feet as he prepared his specimens.

These juncos are birds typical of the Madro-Tertiary flora that spread all over the Baja peninsula and most of Mexico when the climate was colder and wetter. The southward spread of this flora provided a dispersal route for other birds now found only in the Cape mountains, such as white-breasted nuthatches and acorn woodpeckers. They may well have been isolated here and forced to adapt, blocked from migrating outward by desert to the north and by surrounding sea. None are found at lower elevations and they are common only above three thousand feet; by now they may be adapted physiologically to the mountains. Originally considered a separate species, they are now classified as a geographic representation of the yellow-eyed junco, *Junco phaeonotus.*

The sky clears as we go to bed. In that breathless cold I never saw the stars so bright. Without competition from city lights, thousands of cones of starlight illumine the heavens. Each pinpoint is so crisp that the sky almost crackles. Cassiopeia glows in a sky through which Orion hunts, the nebula in his sword a glorious bright blur. I hold my breath, listening for celestial sounds, but only a total stillness pours down. A falling star streaks like a message across space, toward the big empty square of Pegasus, where the Babylonians thought the Garden of Paradise existed.

Last night's clearing sky removed the insulating blanket of clouds, and the night was bitterly cold. Susan was miserable with jellyfish stings. This morning our words hang like white cotton balls in the air. Frost crinkles on the tent. I contemplate not getting up.

In the shelter the thermometer holds to 36° F. and the fire gives precious little warmth. My ballpoint pen won't write. The ink is congealed. I have on all the clothes I can get on: a wool cap pulled down over my ears, a thermal underwear shirt, a wool shirt, a down vest, and an old down jacket, and over it all a windbreaker, very nearly what I slept in last night. A voice, rubbing its syllables over the fire, says *"This* is BAJA?"

By eleven-thirty the morning mists swarm away and the vista of La Laguna opens out, the long rolling meadow that Eisen estimated to be about a hundred acres. Mare's-tails streak the icy blue sky, attenuated by a brisk wind. A heavy squawking in an oak signals a clown-faced acorn woodpecker. It jabbers away, hopping from branch to branch, as if it too is trying to get warm.

In the middle of the meadow sits the small weather station, which the foresters monitor. The instruments are mounted on a raised cement platform, protected with a chain-link fence, padlock hanging open. These weather stations dot the peninsula, often in a school yard, sometimes in the middle of nowhere, where nevertheless they are read daily, and always locked—except here. Julian reads the maximum/minimum thermometer and announces that it was −2° C. last night, which translates to about 28.6° F., and only up to 12° C. yesterday, or 44° F. Left-handed, he holds the record pad perpendicularly as he fills in the spaces for the wind, checking off that it has been *ventoso y frío*—windy and cold. Now the wind is from the southwest, *medio nublado*. As he resets the thermometer he volunteers that he thinks we're odd to come up here at this time of year. Most visitors, nearly all students, come in the summer, when the meadow is in flower and cooler weather is a respite from the heat at sea level. I file that away: I'd like to come back then too.

Clumps of pitcher sage are interspersed among the grasses. Heaps of dirt lie at the entrances to old gopher holes. Coyote scat decorates the path edge. Band-winged grasshoppers clatter up everywhere, and smaller lubber grasshoppers spray out from our feet, so close in color to the path that they seem like animated gravel. They are short sturdy grasshoppers, with short wings and antennae, and a pronotum—the plate that covers the thorax—extended and roughly granulated, the body an inch at the outside, what Barco called *chapulines* that "fly little and jump a lot" as opposed to the larger ones that ravaged the countryside.

A tree island in the midst of the meadow turns out to be a dead tree fenced with prickly pear and cascaded with wild grape vines, that looks like some fanciful Italian stage construction dreamed up by Piranesi, or perhaps a drawing by Salvator Rosa, full of hidden meanings. Prickly pear cacti frequently indicate overgrazing because they come in quickly on disturbed ground. Disarticulating easily, the joints root where they fall. There is some talk of making La Laguna a national park, a different proposition from the National Park system as we know it, but if so grazing would be banned. According to Julian, there is pasturage elsewhere, but La Laguna is so convenient for the ranchers who live on the nearby slopes, the grass so ample, and the cattle so much easier to round up in the open, that it is well used.

Prickly pears also wreathe the periphery of the meadow. How very strange they must have looked to the first Europeans who saw them. The English privateer Edward Cooke, at the Cape in 1708, tried to relate them to what he knew from England:

> ... being a short Trunk, three or four Foot high, of a Willow green, shooting out into several Branches, bearing a Sort of Fruit, some longish, and others round at the End of the long, and a little flat on the Top, with several long sharp Prickles, and many downy Prickles, not unlike the Cow-Itch. It has no Leaves, the Inside of the round Fruit, is the best, and tastes like our green Gooseberries, making very good Sauce boil'd and sweeten'd with Sugar.

Many of these are loaded with fruit, a rich magenta inside, as full of seeds as they are juicy. Zita, who is addicted to them, cuts them open and scoops the meat out with a spoon. We eat ourselves sticky. Called *las tunas,* they are sold in Mexican markets and used for preserves and syrup; the pads are sold to be pickled or cooked fresh; Barco found they made "a tasty vegetable dish." Even the seeds can be used in soups or ground into flour.

Farther on in the meadow several towers of granite rise. A vivid, almost fluorescent, apple-green lichen scabs the rock along with a gray-green one common on granite, ruffling in circles. Orange jewel lichen limns many of the rock edges, a lichen which receives from animal urine the nitrogen it needs to grow. The rock is exceedingly abrasive, but as I scrape the surface with my fingers, fine grains sift into my open hand. They look exactly like salt and pepper: the white quartz is fine and sand size, while mica glistens in larger dark pieces like fresh-ground pepper. These are the granites that form the mountains, a complex of crystalline rock with a color and texture much the same throughout—coarse-grained, in color pale buff to gray.

In the rocks' protection grow a few of the piñon pines native to this area, graceful trees with supple branches that arch with the wind. In the midst of the meadow single pines grow well-shaped and rounded, well-needled limbs to within three feet of the ground. In the woods they are all scraggly and tall, laced with lichen, bearing many dead branches. After all the years of being accustomed to the lowland landscape of Baja California, these big trees astound the eye.

A tiny dry streambed meanders across the meadow, floored with granite gravel, a wavering string knotted with tiny pools cloaked with algae. Miner's lettuce, with its stem-encircling leaves, flourishes around the edge. Here, Julian says, there is always water. At La Laguna twin springs rise, this one which goes to the Sea of Cortés via Las Cuevas, the other which goes to the Pacific via Todos Santos. By the time they reach the lowlands both streams run underground, and farmers tap the subterranean flow through wells, their only means of irrigation.

From the edge of the meadow comes a lively chirping—a black phoebe flits from one grass stalk to the next, perching for a moment only, flicking its tail, always dancing just ahead of us, in and out of the shadows. The black phoebe is a fairly common resident below the 29th parallel, seldom far from water.

Two walkingsticks mate on a branch, improbable insects. As they move they look like nothing so much as twigs bowing in the wind. In the woods, ferns and mosses, hedge-nettle with rosy-red flowers, and small yellow marigolds with thin gland-scented leaves are totally unlike the vegetation of lower altitudes, where most leaves are haired, waxed, or reduced to spines. Shiny leaves, soft leaves, spiky leaves, all kinds of leaves, move against the stillness. Yet it strikes me as a nonsensical woods, one conjured up in the imagination of someone who's never been there, like that combination of expected and exotic in an Henri Rousseau painting: green carpeting of hair-cap moss, bedstraw twining in the shadows—natural. But then there's an incongruous *palmita,* sitting there like a yucca on a pole, that no realist would include.

Nolina beldingii, called *palmita* locally, was named by T. S. Brandegee for Lyman Belding, who first saw it at La Laguna while bird collecting; it is particularly plentiful among the oaks and pines of higher elevations. Brandegee, who climbed La Laguna in 1892, thanked Belding for telling him where to find it in this handsome manner. The fresh leaves, a yard long and an inch wide, splay outward and upward; the old leaves remain hanging on the trunk in a thick gray thatch sometimes many feet in diameter, a favorite nesting place of wasps as Brandegee found:

> Finding a tree growing on a steep hillside by the side of a cliff in what seemed a favorable situation for obtaining the fruit, I endeavored to reach it, but on touching the tree a crowd of wasps came pouring out of the great mass formed by the dead and adherent leaves of former seasons. Of course I did not wait to verify the truth of the reputation they bear among the Mexicans which, freely translated, is that they are "very brave little animals." Afterward I found that these wasps, so common in the peninsula and often attaching their nests to cliffs where they hang pendent from one end, make use of the Nolinas as well as the palms for a similar purpose, and it is difficult to find one not infested.

We pick up the little streambed again, following it until we reach the edge of the meadow, where the stream suddenly drops off into huge rocky stair steps. According to flood wrack caught fifteen feet up along the walls, flash floods are powerful enough to move tree trunks. Pools of water appear among the boulders, one wreathed with yellow monkey flowers, then a small trickling waterfall, and more pools, packed with evening primroses that grow in our Rocky mountains, and watercress!

A tiny Pacific treefrog, broad-headed with little round toe pads, sits in a shallow basin. I can't resist scooping it up to look at its coppery spotted back, white underside, the black line through its eye. It breeds in the pools here, spending two to three months of its life as a tadpole. A widely distributed frog, it occurs here from sea level to mountain top, adapted to exist in this variety of environments by adhering to no definite breeding season, keyed to the availability of water, which instigates breeding behavior. For such a little creature it has a big voice, which attracts others of its ilk so that large breeding populations assemble quickly. Both eggs and tadpoles develop rapidly, the latter able to feed on both plant and animal food, unlike most tadpoles, which feed only on the former.

We work down the giant stair steps until huge boulders block the canyon. In contrast to the abrasive crystalline granite in the meadow, here the rock is water-smoothed, almost silky. Today the water surface laps an inch below the pools' usual highwater line. Zita unpacks cheese and *bolillos,* the Mexican rolls shaped like shuttles. I gather fresh watercress and contribute smoked oysters and apples. Susan has brought oranges and the heady smell of the volatile oils in the peel scents the air.

I sit back against a sun-warmed rock and survey the series of pools, refulgent in their rock basins. Pale slabs of rock shelve downward, fluted and scoured. Bubbles froth off the little waterfalls that weave between pools, gurgling through sinuous streaming algae. Willow leaves plait across the ledge, golden brown on top, silvery beneath. A beautiful madroño angles over the stream, one large limb reaching almost all the way across. The red bark peels back in big scrolls, revealing a smooth pale beige wood on which water reflections quiver up and down. Animate and inanimate interwoven: granite gives this landscape character, the stream gives it light and color, the greenery gives it life.

On the surface of the pool at my feet water striders dart, the dents that their feet make on the surface reflecting on the sandy bottom in moving ovals. Small water beetles, their center legs stuck out like oars, ply just beneath. Through the clear water I watch a dragonfly nymph stalk the sand. Caddisfly cases, up to three inches long, roll on the bottom, made of minute grains perfectly fitted to form a quarter-inch-diameter tube. Inside, the larvae lie protected, anchored by hooks at the ends of the abdomens, feeding on the detritus that sifts downward.

As the air cools, we scramble up the steep slope flanking the stream to reach the meadow. At the shelter, we find chaos. When we left this morning, all the food boxes were stacked in the doorway as a barricade to keep the pigs out. All of them had their lids tied on tightly except the one at the bottom that contained all the meat and smoked fish. The pigs had pushed and shoved and dumped all the boxes over, nosed off the lid of the bottom box and gorged. About a dozen of them lie heaped together for warmth, like rag dolls, a charming scene of innocent porcine togetherness, which leaves me completely unmoved.

As we begin our walk down from La Laguna, I notice many more flowers than I did on the way up, no doubt the result of their not having been open that cold wet day, coupled with my lack of enthusiasm about anything except getting warm and dry. Crimson and yellow, cream and lavender, they grow in the rich sun-spattered soil. As if vying in color, a plodding caterpillar, dark gray bands separated by dark brown ones with red dots and yellow dots, glows almost iridescent, but heavy barbed spines at head and tail discourage me from picking it up.

We wind through dark forest crowded with wild rose bushes, wild geranium and strawberry, meadowrue and bedstraw, sorrel languishing across the ground with its shamrocklike leaves. Most herbs are long finished flowering and are in seed in this cold season of the year. *Mitracarpus* has odd little seed capsules that split open around the middle, the sepals persisting on the cap like little horns. *Heterosperma* seeds have barbed awns that catch in everything. It bears two kinds of seeds in its daisylike heads, those of the ray flowers being the miscreants. Julian points out *hierba de cancer*, a small plant good for rheumatism. He knows most of the plants by name and usually the uses to which they're put.

But an outsider wanting to learn plant names in Baja California is in for a nomenclatural nightmare: all the plants have, of course, scientific Latin names. They also have common names in Spanish, and since peninsular nomenclature is often different from that used on the mainland, many have two; there may be in addition an Indian name; and many have no common names in English. Anyone's botanical vocabulary quickly becomes rag-tag.

Suddenly a huge beetle flashes in front of my eyes and then hovers just a few feet away and turns into a hummingbird with a dark head and a sharp white stripe behind the eye. As he hovers, his pale grassy green throat shimmers above a lightly rusty breast. Poised with body almost vertical, advancing toward one flower, then another, wings an almost invisible blur so rapidly do they scull the air, tail constantly adjusting, fanning and twisting, it's one of the birds I'd almost given up seeing because of the weather: Xantus' hummingbird. Now called Black-fronted hummingbird, it is a peninsular endemic, especially plentiful in the Sierra de la Laguna.

John Xantus, for whom it was named, was the first to collect it. Xantus—misfit, charlatan, complainer, poseur, and no scientist—was sent here by Spencer F. Baird, then Secretary of the Smithsonian Institution. In the mid-nineteenth century in the United States, many of the collectors in western America were European immigrants; these talented amateurs were at the right place at the right time and, more often than not, collected for no more than the joy of discovery, and added greatly to the list of creatures that scrambled and flapped and dragged their carapaces across an unfamiliar terrain.

Fleeing the Hungarian War of Independence against Austria, Xantus arrived in the United States in 1851, in his words, "practically penniless";

unable to earn a living, he enlisted in the U.S. Army in 1855. At his first army station, Fort Riley in the Kansas Territory, he met salvation in the form of Dr. William A. Hammond, an army surgeon. Hammond was, in his spare time, an amateur ornithologist and a friend of Spencer Baird. Baird, who knew collecting opportunities when he saw them, exhorted those military men who went into unknown territory "to take advantage of their geographical situation by pursuing the naturalist's occupation."

Finding a willing student in Xantus, Hammond taught him something of ornithology, how to prepare specimens, and encouraged him to begin collecting on his own. But more important he put Xantus in touch with Baird. Hammond and Baird were instrumental in Xantus's next assignment, to Fort Tejon in California, by no small coincidence a place from which Baird wanted specimens. Characteristically, Xantus didn't get on with anybody and after a year, he was writing to Baird:

> I proposed to go out to the Gulf or [of] California, explore the peninsula as well, as the Sonora shore, & the gulf islands. I think there is hardly any spot on the N. American continent, which would reward more a collectors troubles, as the Vermillion Sea & environs. That Region forms something like a connecting link between the U.S. & Central American Zoology, & is almost unknown. You have some idea now dear Sir, what I could do under independent & favorable circumstances; and you may imagine what amount I could gather there, when properly supported.

Why did Xantus pick Baja California? His letters hold no clue. Whatever the reason, it sent the wily Baird into immediate action. He weaseled an appointment for Xantus as Tidal Observer for the U.S. Coast Survey at Cabo San Lucas, where he remained from April 1859 to August 1861. The specimens that poured out of Xantus's barrels and boxes Baird entrusted to leading scientists in appropriate fields for study. When Baird gave the type specimen of this hummingbird to George Newbold Lawrence, a leading ornithologist, Xantus sulked:

> If Mr Lawrence makes a speciality of the water birds; one of the songbirds, one of the hawks or owls, and at last will be nothing left to me.

In contrast is Lawrence's graceful description of 1862:

> Sent by Mr. John Xantus, whose investigations in the Ornithology of Western North America have been the means of adding many new birds to science. In compliment to him I have named it.

Lyman Belding noted that by April the hummingbirds had dispersed to lower altitudes, where he reported sighting one hundred at one time! Another ornithologist, Chester C. Lamb, who came to La Laguna in 1924, counted two hundred one morning on La Laguna before he gave up, and he wrote a charming description of how they bathed at a tiny waterfall, where they sat in the water and showered themselves by beating their wings, then would fly breast first against the streaming water and fall back into the pool below, while many more perched around preening and drying themselves.

When we are halfway down, clouds of tiny blue butterflies like scraps of sky flutter all around. When the sun goes behind a cloud, they whisk their wings shut and disappear into knife shadows and become old leaves. And when the sun comes out they whirl up again, landing on my pack, my shoulders, my head, rising in helices like blue leaves in a blue wind.

11

COUNTRYSIDE

The thorns in California are surprisingly numerous, and there are many of frightening aspect. It seems as if the curse of the Lord, laid upon the earth after the fall of Adam, fell especially hard on California and had its effect. It is doubtful whether in two thirds of the European continent there are as many prickles and thorns as there are in California alone

Jakob Baegert
Observations in Lower California
1772

The little boughs of each pole are full of thorns. This is a property of almost all the plants and trees of California, the exceptions to this being rare. Commonly, the difference is that some have more, others fewer, some have longer ones, others shorter, some have curved thorns, others have them straight.

Miguel del Barco
Natural History of California
1790(?)

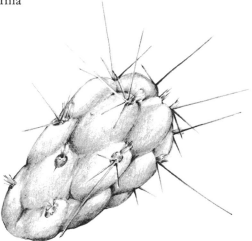

Cholla *(Opuntia cholla)*

THORNS

I f one were to draw a vegetative map of the Cape Region and color the mountains blue and the band of seashore yellow and all the in-between gray green, the last would cover more area by several times than the isolated islands of blue or wandering strips of yellow. One February afternoon Susan and I walk back from the ocean a mile or so just to explore that landscape that we see so much of from the air and so little of from the ground. We follow a small road that incessantly branches, becoming narrower and narrower. Susan is the explorer, yet patient with a mother who has so much to see and so little time to see it in, and we proceed at what Steinbeck considered "the proper pace for a naturalist" that allowed "time to think and to look and to consider"—walking.

Brickellia bushes, called *apan* in Mexico, line the roadside, sometimes almost vining over other bushes and low trees so that they reach high above my head. Slow-flying bees curl over the blossoms, clutching, consuming, so loaded with pollen they practically fall off the flowers. Neither the big lemon yellow hollyhocklike flowers of wild cotton, nor the brilliant yellow morning glories, nor the lavender blue wild nightshade, nor the wine red flowers of wild bean, nor the rich pink of San Miguelito attract so many insects.

Indeed, brickellia must be all things to all people. Once I complained to Miriam Parr, an impeccably groomed and elegant woman who has lived here for years, about some insect stings. "I have just the cure!" she said. I anticipated at the very least some new sophisticated ointment, but no—it turns out Miriam is interested in and knowledgable about native plants and their uses. She led me to a *Brickellia hastata* bush, picked a few leaves and ordered, "Rub them on." It *worked.*

Brickellia *(Brickellia hastata)*

A black pipevine swallowtail lofts high, a flashing iridescent black, missing one tail, witness to a bird's quick stab at the eye mark at the tail's end. The butterfly lives to fly another day, flight little impaired by the loss of an appendage which served its purpose well.

Gorgeous golden brown fritillaries flutter in the branches. One shuts its wings and shines the pearly spots on its underwing. The silvery gleam comes from microscopic striations in the scales that act like prisms when reflecting light. A small moth keeps its orange wings, banded with pale spots outlined in black, rolled across its back, and so looks more like a beetle than a moth.

There must be dozens of skippers, those often dark brown medium-sized butterflies, with distinctive hooked and clubbed antennae that make them easy to identify. They generally fly low enough to be easily seen. Their larvae are leaf rollers, living singly or communally in cigar-shaped leafhouses. Some species have tails (one such is heavily furred in iridescent deep teal blue on the inner edge of its tails), others are tailless, all of these have transparent "windows" in their wings through which the color of the flower upon which they alight shows.

Sulphurs land, snap their wings closed, and disappear, so much are their underwings patterned like dead leaves. Mexican sulphurs, yellow with a rough "dog's head" silhouette in the strong black border on the forewings, flutter everywhere. In spite of their apparent fragility and small size, they undertake extremely long migrations that include millions of individuals.

Dozens of queen butterflies drift about us, closely related to and colored like the monarch, and like monarchs their larvae feed on milkweed. Nearly all are male, recognizable by black scent patches on their hind wings. Each scent scale connects by an infinitesimal duct to a scent gland, and ends in a little brush which dispenses the scent. Males also are equipped with eversible brushes tucked in the end of their abdomens; when they evert the brushes and beat their wings together, scent from the scent scales transfers to the brushes, which they then dust against a female's antennae, evidently an offer she can't refuse.

But it's the two-winged flies that have me mesmerized. When I grow up, I confide to Susan, I'm going to study western Diptera. First there's a bulging-eyed assassin fly lying in wait on a brickellia leaf, long wings laid back over its abdomen. Their stiletto-like bodies give them a lethal aspect quite appropriate to their habits. The adults dart after insects much larger than they, delivering a lethal bite with a hypodermic-like stylet, clutching the victim in bristled legs and sucking it dry before dropping it.

Belonging to the same sub-order but with entirely innocent adult habits are the bee flies, the teddy bears of the Diptera world, darting between flowers and hovering over bare spots on the ground, where they drop their eggs. They hatch into frenetic larvae that search for the open solitary bee burrows; once found, they move inside, become sedentary, consume the pollen and honey the bee has stored for its offspring, and eventually feed on the bee's larvae, saving the vital organs until last so that the larva remains fresh and alive as long as possible. Then there are the big hover flies with translucent abdomens, that make them look larger than they are, and a snoutlike face to expedite flower feeding. And leaf miner flies and tachinid flies and a dozen others I am dying to know about.

And all so swift! In other insects the wings move up as one set of muscles in the thorax contracts and down as another pair contracts. But with two-winged flies, after the wings have passed the horizontal, there is a "click mechanism," which accelerates the speed of the last part of the cycle and makes possible a much faster wing beat.

Susan walks on ahead and when I cut cross-country to find her, I blunder into a spider web strung between two shrubs of wild cotton. Unlike domestic species of cotton, they drop their bracts, and do not produce cotton bolls. Brown lung disease, the bane of textile workers, comes from dust in the air,

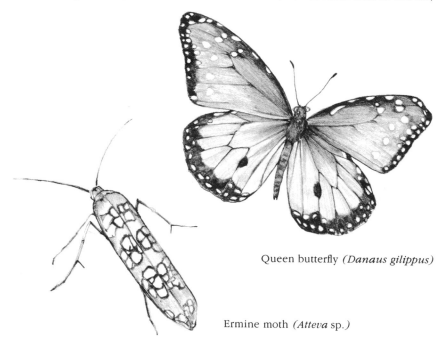

Queen butterfly *(Danaus gilippus)*

Ermine moth *(Atteva* sp.*)*

and two-thirds of the identifiable cotton dust comes from the bracts. Experiments are now being conducted at the University of Arizona on crossing wild varieties of cotton, endemic to Baja California and its adjacent islands, with domestic varieties to produce a plant whose cotton fibers develop in bract-free boll.

Hung in the middle of the web is a tiny spider with a hard shiny shell scalloped with six points, and a name bigger than she is: Crablike Spiny Orb Weaver, *Gasteracanthus cancriformis,* of a genus more common in the Tropics than in the United States. She hangs head downward, Arachne, on her thread of silk, condemned to spin eternally by the jealous rage of Pallas Athena.

Unlike the active wolf spider, the female orb weaver, with the exception of spinning a fresh web anew each evening to early morning, leads a sedentary life. Silk is produced from spinnerets at the tip of the abdomen, minute spigotlike structures surrounding the silk gland openings. Different glands produce different fibers, which, when extruded, twine together to form the silk—a liquid scleroprotein which hardens into a thread that may be as fine as 1/20,000 inch in diameter. The orb weaver produces a strong elastic thread for the web's framework and a sticky but weaker one in which insects catch.

The possible use of spider's silk has not gone overlooked for use in weaving cloth: in 1709 René Antoine Réaumur calculated that 663,522 female spiders were needed to produce a pound of silk, and in 1866, an American found that 415 female spiders were needed for one square yard of silk and concluded that spider silk was not likely to become competitive with that of silkworms!

I hold her in one hand and fish out my hand lens with the other. Her eight eyes are in two horizontal rows of four each, although she probably depends more on vibrations in the web than eyesight to locate prey. Such an intricate little creature for such a short life span: she will produce eggs late in the year, after which she will die. The young overwinter as eggs or spiderlings, disperse, and begin web weaving the following spring.

A large white snail shell crunches under my foot—so many speckle the ground here it's unavoidable. I pick another one up, thinking it empty as they usually are, and find it very much alive. Two dark eyestalks pop out and it extends a foot at least an inch and a half long. Gustav Eisen found in "certain evidently favored localities the ground is literally covered with the dead and white shells of land mollusks. . . . In places they glimmer on the ground as close and as prominent as white pebbles on a beach."

It's incredible that water-dependent gastropods are able to survive in this semi-desert. To do so, they underwent massive changes in their respiratory system. Gills atrophied. The mantle cavity became highly muscular and developed into a lung. To prevent water loss the edges of the mantle can be drawn together at the aperture, and a thin papery membrane is secreted across the opening. Since they are not totally successful in controlling evaporation, they are limited to humid micro-habitats and night feeding.

A bare rock outcrop on the ridgetop is one of the few places to sit free of spines, thorns, cow dung, and young cacti. There is a considerably higher knoll to our right, and a middle one between. I look at my watch. We really shouldn't. But, as I tell Susan ruefully, "shouldn't" is a word that deprives you of adventures, and another higher promontory so close by is just too much temptation when it's so hard to get here in the first place, but there's no way to explain this to a time-controlled husband to whom you've promised to be back at a certain time. Susan and I exchange a look of complete empathy and head for the next hill. Half an hour later we are on the highest ridge.

Beneath us dozens of big-trunked and small-branched elephant trees stalk the hillside, none over eight or nine feet high. *Palo blanco,* its white-barked trunks gleaming out from the dark scrub surrounding it, is the only treelike tree in sight, and it scarcely reaches thirty feet. I had assumed, as Barco did, that the *blanco* referred to the pale trunks, but Padre Norberto Ducrue, who served here twenty-eight years with the Jesuits, says not so:

> A species of tall trees is found in the mountains, the leaves of which have a pleasant green color, which in the local idiom is called *palo blanco* or white trunked tree. This is not because its bark is white but because in the month of May all the leaves and small branches exude a white, transparent, and sweet gum which is regarded by the Indians as a delicacy for some other effect which is not understood.

A legume, its feathery pale green leaves are composed of many small leaflets. The white flowers appear before the leaves; dangling pods, two to three inches long, enclose the seeds and turn a lovely bronze red as they ripen. Twisted when new, when cattle prefer them, they straighten as they mature. Barco records that missionaries used the bark for tanning, which was still an important industry at the beginning of this century. The trunks are used today for corner and fence posts.

The bark of elephant trees was also used for the same purpose when many tons were exported. The bark peels off in big translucent sheets. The wood beneath is pungently fragrant; an aromatic resin called "copal" flows

Assassin/robber flies *(Asilidae)*

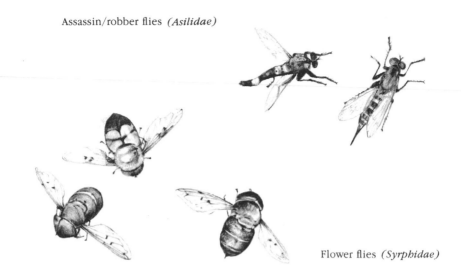

Flower flies *(Syrphidae)*

freely from a wound, and may have been used by missionaries in the celebration of Mass. The trunks and larger branches writhe in marvelous contorted shapes, fat in relation to the tiny branches bunched at the branch ends. Abundant cortex explains the thickness of the trunk, forming up to 70 percent of its diameter.

The drupes have the color and sheen of tiny Santa Rosa plums. Tri-partite, they pop open easily, leaving three little curved boats rocking on my notebook. Inside, a brilliant red orange exocarp covers the seeds, which are neatly three-angled, dark brown and shiny. The stems holding the drupes are alizarin, and when the outer coat of the seed falls off an exquisite color juxtaposition appears: orange red and plum red against wine red twigs.

Smudges of dark red smolder in the throats of big yellow morning-glory flowers; the vines twine over any low support or flow over the ground. The myriad buds twist tightly in their sepals, and pods in all stages of development hang from the curving stems. Called *yuca* by the Mexicans, it is always in bloom when we are here, which has been every month of the year but three. Barco found Indians eating the roots, which when roasted "have a good flavor but are stringy," and Edward Cooke, a privateer here in 1708 when anything edible must have tasted good, reported they tasted like yams. I hold one of the blossoms in my hand and look straight down inside: the anthers twist tight, having shed their pollen, and a single small flower beetle wanders within the mystery of this gold which lasts but a single day.

Lemonade berry grows all around, now only leafed with big round velvety leaves. Its seeds make a drink reminiscent of lemonade, long enjoyed
on the peninsula. Cooke, looking to augment a meager diet, must have become a gourmet of sorts:

> There is another Sort like a Curan, has a white Pulp, and eats tartish, having a
> large Stone within, which looks like a Bird's Eye, and has a Kernel, that may
> also be eaten. The Taste of it is pleasant enough, and I believe much es-
> teem'd by the Natives.

Its genus, *Rhus,* catches the eye of anyone allergic to poison ivy, but these
berries are not toxic, and when soaked in water or held in the mouth are very
refreshing and said to taste like piñon nuts.

A beautiful brilliant yellow-and-black bird common to the country, a
Scott's oriole, carols his song that reminds me of a western meadowlark.
Myth says the sight of this yellow bird cures jaundice—its genus name *Icterus*
means jaundice. It got its "Scott" after General Winfield Scott, a spit-and-
polish type whose sobriquet "Old Fuss and Feathers" scarcely seems to fit its
flash and color.

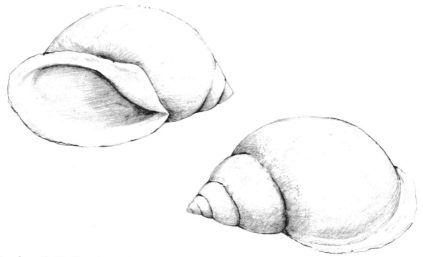

Land snail *(Bulimulus* sp.*)*

When we scrambled up this hill it took us only ten minutes and we had estimated thirty. Susan suggests that we misjudged the time because in our arid West, where we both live, faraway landforms look so clear and therefore close, but in reality are quite distant, and we are patterned into thinking this is so elsewhere. Here, if a hillside is in focus, it *is* close.

Elated at the tripling of the distance we think we can cover, we estimate our distance to the airstrip, cross country, to be fifteen or twenty minutes. We decide to walk to a landmark cluster of three utility poles, and then follow the right-of-way, assuming that it will be an easy short walk since in our part of the country a right-of-way once cut retains its clarity for years, and surely in this likewise dry climate, there will be more or less a clear path remaining.

In five minutes I know we've made a grievous mistake but it's too late. The terrain is sharp up and sharp down, covered with treacherous loose gravel. The right-of-way that we thought would be so easy to follow is in truth overgrown with all the vicious plants that spring up spitefully on newly cleared ground. The worst thing about the poor footing is that there's nothing to grab on to. It isn't that there are no plants for purchase—there are more than enough and that's the problem because everything has thorns. First there's a species of ocotillo called *palo adán* in Spanish, then a thicket of cholla, beyond which is a fishhook cactus among the worst of all, sour *pitahaya—pitahaya agria*. Two kinds of *pitahaya* grow here, producing fruit, one of which is sweet, the other sour, both high enough in vitamin C to have cured early sailors of scurvy. Organ-pipe cactus, *Lemaireocereus thurberi*, is *pitahaya dulce*. *Machaerocereus gummosus* is *pitahaya agria*, the misery that we are trying to avoid.

Jakob Baegert's account of *pitahaya agria* proceeds with typical German thoroughness:

> I became curious once and took it upon myself to count the thorns on a piece of plant cut from the center of a branch. It was a span as long and as thick as a fist. I counted no less than one thousand six hundred and eighty. . . . The thorns are arranged in little clusters, ten in a group, resembling the face of a compass and pointing in all directions in symmetrical arrangement. These little clusters sit on the ridges which divide the furrows running the whole length and completely around the branch, just as on the cardón. It is easy to see that, according to my calculation, a single one of these shrubs carries more than a million thorns.

Pitahaya agria redeems its over-endowed thorniness by bearing fruits as large as oranges, red in color, "so fresh and juicy," says Barco, "it is food and

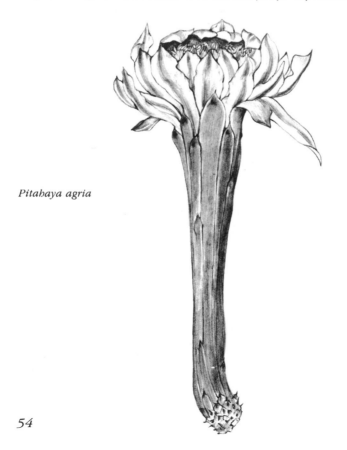

Pitahaya agria

drink at the same time, therefore those who eat a lot of it need little to drink." Walter Bryant described the fruit as "firmer than that of a watermelon, which it resembles, but the flavor is like nothing else known to me, having a slightly acid taste." This time of year only a few flowers are open; most are in bud, and fruit will not be available until the end of June. Stemless, they proceed out of an aureole as if glued on. One is just open, a six-inch-long tube flaring open to show white petals streaked with lavender, enclosing pure white anthers and stamens.

Unlike the fruition of most plants after a rainy winter, Barco noted that after the winter rains of 1739–40, "the entire country filled up with herbs in February and the following months and the trees renewed themselves, but the pitahayas did not bear fruit that year of 1740. It seems they complained of having had so much moisture." Indeed, the most abundant *pitahaya* years seem to be those preceded by drought.

The Pericu Indians timed their year by the fruiting of the *pitahayas,* a time of a surfeit of food that, to the missionaries' disapproval, led to the kinds of excesses that maintained the population. So meager were food supplies during the rest of the year that the Indians gorged (with no refrigeration it was either that or watch it go to waste), danced, and indulged in other traditional forms of jubilation.

The Indians also conducted what was called a "second harvest." In the fruit are so many black seeds that it's impossible to pick them out before eating, and they pass through the digestive system of man or beast without significant alteration. At *pitahaya* time the Pericu took to defecating on large open rocks, and when the feces dried, they broke them up, removed and toasted the seeds. Father Francisco María Píccolo was given a present of flour made of these seeds and, unaware, cooked with it, and was given a hard time by the other missionaries "for whenever any of them met with Padre Píccolo the story of the event provided an occasion for amusement and laughter."

When the Jesuits arrived in 1697, they found three principal Indian nations that lived as separate entities, each with its own language and customs, with no resemblance to the Aztecs or Mayas of the mainland. Those "from Cabo San Lucas to somewhat before the port of La Paz," according to Barco, were the Pericu. Baegert characterized them as "stupid, dull, stubborn, dirty, uncouth, ungrateful, lying, knavish, extremely lazy. . . ." They had no agriculture, no ceramics. Their spoken language was impoverished, with no words for "marry" or "honesty" in their vocabulary, which made it difficult for the Jesuits to teach such concepts.

There were perhaps five thousand Pericu by the time of the Jesuits' arrival. By necessity in this sparse place, nearly all their time was spent in finding and preparing food—men hunted, women gathered. Forced to live on whatever they could scavenge, and ate anything they could catch: rodents, snakes, small birds, ducks, worms, crickets, grasshoppers, caterpillars, spiders, their own lice. Sebastián Vizcaíno, a Spanish mariner and explorer who was on the peninsula between 1596 and 1603, wrote that the Indians "regaled me with lizards and dead snakes, food which must be held in high estimation among them, but was a manifest sign to us of the wretchedness and sterility of the country." Yet the Pericu were perhaps better off than the more northerly populations, since they were skilled at fishing and took other food from the sea.

The Pericu lived at the most primitive level. Barco commented that, even if they were not very clean, it was even worse if they washed

> because they wash themselves with hot water which has recently come forth from the natural fountain built into each one. This method of washing was common to men and women of all the nations of California, and some use it frequently, even every day.

The men went completely naked, sometimes painted their bodies, and wove pearls and white feathers into their hair in headdresses that even the missionaries noticed for their handsomeness. The women crushed palm fronds until the fibers were exposed. From these they fashioned a skirt, long in back, apronlike in the front, and to this they added a sort of cape, all tied on with small cords. They too adorned themselves with pearls and feathers and other ornaments. Both sexes wore sandals. Infants were carried in baskets, which were also used for seed gathering and drying. When the weather turned cold, the more or less nomadic Pericu made temporary huts out of branches, huts so small that "they have not room to lie at full length; so that they sleep in a sitting posture," wrote a Jesuit of these enclosures "half a yard high, one square, and without any covering but the heavens: dwellings indeed so scanty and mean, that an European tomb would here be reckoned a palace." This was the extent of Pericu architecture at a time when the Anasazi had already built and left Mesa Verde and Chaco Canyon, and the Aztecs had long since constructed magnificent temples.

The landscape we cross is as inimical now as it was then. The viciously spined whiplike branches of *palo adán,* full of brilliant red flowers, splay out from the crown. Adjacent plants interlace with its branches so that there simply is no way to get through. The Indians made a tea from it or ate the

Nightshade
(Solanum hindsianum)

stems raw. Despite their appearance, the ocotillos are not cacti but a separate family distinguished by the boojum tree, *Idria columnaris,* so delightfully described by Joseph Wood Krutch in *The Forgotten Peninsula.*

Because there's been no rain, the *palo adán* are leafless, since the small leaves spring out at the joining between thorn and stem only during moist spells and drop quickly when it is dry; this divests it of up to 90 percent of its surface area, effectively cutting evaporation and transpiration. The thin leaves can sprout and unfold in three days' time. When *palo adán* is in leaf,

Palo adán *(Fouquieria diguetii)*

it requires considerable moisture, and if enough is present, the leaves may persist for six months. If not, it may lose and put out leaves several times in one year. Two forms of leaves are produced. Those on old growth attach directly to the branch and fall without a trace. Those on new growth are stalked; when these leaves fall the pointed petiole remains and hardens to a thorn.

Susan and I take the worst of it because we're making a beeline, or as close as possible, and the worse it gets the more stubborn I get. We have long since gone our separate miserable paths, each determined that her way is the best.

All the botany books disclaim the common name for *Opuntia cholla*—"jumping cactus"—saying of course, be sensible, this segment of one year's growth doesn't jump, it only "dearticulates easily at the joint." Balderdash. It *jumps.* My hand doesn't even brush one, not even close enough to feel the spine penetrate, and as my hand swings forward with my stride, I am suddenly the unhappy possessor of a joint of cactus, the size of a small baking potato and as heavy, implanted on the back of my hand with, as William Gabb, traveling with Browne, remarked, "a pertinacity worthy of a better cause." I wish I had read Barco's description of how to free yourself:

> It is necessary then to take a small stick or some such object and tear off the little section of cholla because it cannot be touched with one's hands . . . though they go in easily, they come out with great difficulty, as if they were made of extremely fine scales which resist being pulled out.

I try to grasp it to pull it free, but it turns at a touch and locks in four more spines—barbed like a porcupine quill. I grit my teeth, take it by a sturdy spine, and yank. Each spine burns free separately. With amazement, considering the sharpness of the stings, I can see only one minute puncture. I feel as if I should be streaming blood like a santo.

We finally reach the airstrip, well over an hour later, sweaty, scratched, tired, and breathing hard—at sea level! I wonder if Susan's still speaking to me. I glance at her out of the corner of my eye.

She's grinning from ear to ear.

The next day Susan and I hike the upper reaches of a dry arroyo called El Tule—"tule" referring to reeds and bulrushes. I already know El Tule from its mouth, an apron of boulders which spread fifty feet out into the sea when

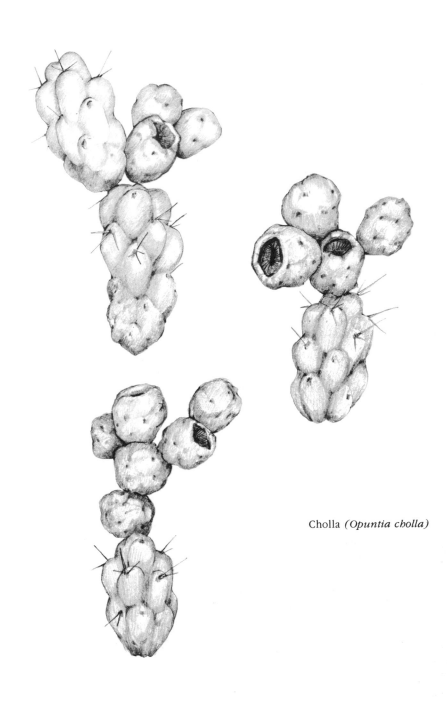

Cholla *(Opuntia cholla)*

the rampaging arroyo carried them down and dumped them in the ocean's lap. El Tule's fresh water runs underground and surfaces at the ocean's edge in dozens of little twinkling rivulets draining through the sand and escaping seaward. Someone has told us that if we go far enough back into the foothills we will find the arroyo running with water, and the idea of a bubbling stream in this land where there is no such thing piques my curiosity.

We set out, walking against the wind, against the sun. Nothing has changed since J. Ross Browne followed this valley in 1867, and found it "wild and unattractive, with dry, naked rocks and sand gleaming in the sun." Except perhaps the addition of cattle. Longhorn cows gallop off as we approach, but one calf, separated from its mother, follows us upcanyon half a mile—after all, we *do* have four legs.

Pleasant aromas waft from tall bushes of sage; people here pick a branch and inhale its freshness to clear the sinuses. Heliotrope patches the sand, leaves bluish-green, almost succulent, coils of tiny white flowers with green throats. Brittle bush, its leaves pale from a heavy coating of hairs, are spaced like checkers on a board. Their roots exude growth inhibitors that discourage other plants, a device fairly common in desert plant species, a kind of botanical territoriality. Nearly every bush has a pile of leaves under it, and these too may contain substances inimical to other plant growth.

Steep rock walls define the arroyo. If I read the angle of the walls to their subterranean joining, I calculate thousands of tons of sand must have been washed in to form this flat sandy bed, all plucked, grain by grain, off the surrounding granite mountainsides. The arroyo is bone dry today, and walking through bottomless sand is pure slogging. It's hard to believe that only a few months ago, when the arroyo flash flooded, water filled it from wall to wall. Barco recorded:

> The arroyos of California are commonly dry and they run only when it has rained abundantly for one or two days. In those instances their beds fill up and they run with a vigorous force like great rivers. This current lasts one or two days, or a little longer, according to the nature of the preceding rains, and within a few days they become as dry as they were before. Running water may remain in the arroyos for a longer spell if it happens that rains and large floods occur three or four times during the rainy season. This means in August and September, for although it sometimes rains in July also, storms then are usually short-lived.

The water is good for drinking, both above and underground, where it is tapped by wells for all water needs of the area.

A magnificent fig tree espaliers against the rock, bark white, trunk contorted, growing out of, into, and against the wall, woven and knotted into macramé patterns. On this blazing afternoon we pause in the cool shade beneath the solid overlapping layers of its leaves. Close by a cactus wren sings. An unusually large wren, it was described by Privateer Edward Cooke as "Shap'd like a Magpye, but not so big, his Top Feathers mix'd with white and black, being a charming Bird to look on." It builds tubular horizontal nests, sometimes a foot long, on the supporting arms of various cacti, not far from the ground. John Xantus found the first cactus wren at San Lucas. Like so many Cape species that had not yet been found elsewhere, it was thought to be an endemic; now it is the state bird of Arizona.

The arroyo narrows to a hundred feet. Susan and I agree to walk to a turn in the arroyo and no father. Enough sand plodding is enough. It is almost another mile before we round that corner, and as we do, the sand turns wet, and then becomes a larking sparkling little stream that swings into little meanders and shallows into sinuous braids. Yellow monkey flowers strain in the current; the white-and-yellow camomile or rock daisies Mexicans call *manzanillas* languish in the wet sand. We force our way through a head-high stand of reed grass that rustles sharply. Beyond the stream gutters out of a tumble of rocks that choke further passage. The rock shines white with black flecks, clean-washed and hollowed, walls rising to twenty-five feet on either side. The contrast of this Eden with the surrounding scrub desert gives it a fairytale quality. We splash in the frothing water, make sand dams, chase enameled damselflies, scramble around the rock, step on each other's shadows. For a little while we put aside all adult concerns and play.

When we grow up and go home, I find dozens of heliotrope seed pods stuck in my socks and jeans, minute spheres popping into separate small nutlets. On the outside of each nutlet are three ribs, each with tiny sturdy spines. The membrane on the inner face of most segments is torn open, the seeds gone. These are beautifully designed to be transported by an animal: not light windblown seeds, not round and rolling, not encased in an edible cover to be carried around unscathed in someone's digestive tract, but to catch on fur—in this case my socks. Many seeds must fall to the ground, wedge between two pieces of gravel, and remain, but some must get carried—coyote, fox, rabbit, ground squirrel, human—I rather like the idea of seeds galloping, trotting, hopping, and bounding across the desert.

Since the seeds provide identification clues, I sit on the floor as I so often do, Professor Wiggins's *Flora of Baja California* spread out on my knees, hand lens in one hand, seed case in the other, as happy, as my mother used to say, as if I had good sense. I cannot put into words why I so enjoy keying out plants. I only know that a new plant in one hand and a botany book in the other make for a serene time out of mind, obliviousness to hurricane and earthquake, tornado and tidal wave, appointments to be kept, chores to be done. Contemplating the tick of water through the stalk, the vein in the leaf, the pleat in the petal, the secrecy in the bud, the ultimate unfurling, I feel privy to all their little spinnings of immortality.

And now it's dinnertime and I'm not done looking at plants nor am I hungry. There are too many new things to savor. Little, fat, black flower beetles muck about in a forest of stamens; while I watch them through a hand lens, a bird squawks outside and I take up binoculars to spy a gila woodpecker on a palm bole, and then watch a pair of hummingbirds flit like little silvery fish in the late sunshine. Out there are untold numbers of algae waiting to be keyed out, holding untold numbers of minute creatures in their Lilliputian forests. Out there are new birds, new plants, new insects, new stars, new skies, new horizons, all crowding in to be discovered and identified, tugging at my sleeve like children and pleading, "Me next! Me next!"

And *I* have to dress for dinner!

For the first eight miles the country is rocky and barren, with a heavy growth of cactus and small trees, principally gum and mesquit. The trail winds almost continuously over desert patches of loose sediment, interspersed with boulders of granite. Deep arroyas [sic] are washed out by the rains, which at times sweep over the country, carrying away the soil.

Over the rugged points of rock that jut out into the sea we toiled for several hours.

J. Ross Browne
Explorations in Lower California
1868

Elephant tree *(Bursera odorata)*

4

HEADLANDS

The sirens of the Cape coast are not the legendary singers but the short steep hills along the coast that promise long views and fine vistas and understandings of landforms not available at sea level, and who knows what treasures just over the rim line? These are headlands that ballast the coast and shelve down into deep turquoise and blue depths. The intrepid J. Ross Browne wrote that he was unsettled by these rocky points "so rugged and precipitous that it required some nerve to sit coolly in the saddle. The sea dashed against the rocks hundreds of feet below with a fearful roar." Fitted out with saddle, blankets, revolvers, and sextant, Browne landed at Cabo San Lucas on January 5, 1867, to explore the peninsula.

Browne and his group came as representatives of the Lower California Company, which had received from the Mexican government land grants totaling 46,800 square miles. Between 1861 and 1865 the federal government of Mexico gave large land grants to foreigners in order to acquire capital. Grants were in the form of options which would become permanent providing that certain conditions were carried out within a specified time; the Lower California Company's time period was nearly up. Their land was advertised as

> on the eastern extremity of the Peninsula of Lower California, between La Paz and Cape St. Lucas; and the lands secured by the Company embrace an area of about 300 square miles, or over 125,000 acres of fertile and beautiful valley land!

Previous grantees had not fulfilled the terms of their contract and had lost their lands. Or had flagrantly advertised abundant and fertile tracts for farming, minerals for the digging, and precious stones for the finding. Some companies took the colonizers' money and then dumped them. Some found work, some made it back to the United States, some died.

The Lower California Company had the money (it was capitalized for $25 million), but no knowledge of the country, and Brown's reconnaissance trip was the first inland observation trip made to the peninsula. Not only was he to describe the country physically, but he was to ferret out the direction of the political winds; expansionists in the United States thought that the peninsula might profitably be joined to and become part of the United States, a philosophy Browne reflected:

> I regard the question of the acquisition of Lower California by the United States as one of great importance.
> This Peninsula commands the Gulf, the adjacent shores of Mexico, and the mouth of the Colorado. Its geographical position gives it a value, in a national point of view, to which its intrinsic resources can never entitle it. Combined with the acquisition of Sinaloa, Sonora, and Chihuahua, it would be not only of the greatest importance to commerce and navigation, but absolutely essential to our naval and military defenses. A strip of foreign territory could not be suffered to exist directly in front of our own possession.

Browne got his answer from Antonio Pedrín, the Governor at La Paz, who justifiably disapproved of the grants and of a foreign government within the confines of the territory. Browne attempted to smooth things over but his obvious loyalty to developers did not endear him to Mexican officials. His final report was negative:

> I should be very glad to be the humble instrument of promoting, even in a degree, the acquisition to the United States of Lower California. It would be, in many points of view, a valuable addition to our territory on the Pacific coast. Russian America and British Columbia on the north, and Lower California on the south, would complete a coast-line without parallel in the territorial possessions of the nations of the world. But with this grand object, and

Pitahaya agria

Wild cotton
(*Gossypium klotzschianum* var. *davidsonii*)

the magnificent future it reveals, fully impressed upon my mind, I should deem even such an acquisition costly at the expense of truth.

As he rode from San Lucas to San José del Cabo, the terrain that he saw about him must have been a powerful persuader. William Gabb, a geologist with the California Survey who accompanied Browne, made note of this stretch of shore "as a general thing dry, barren, and sandy, unpopulated, and destitute of all the necessaries of life, even wood and water."

Over the past years one of these dry hills has come to be a kind of backyard. The mile walk to and from is pleasant, and I enjoy following old paths rather than always seeking out new ones, because I learn more. This hill begins with a steep gravelly ascent, slippery going up, more so coming down, inhabited by too many acacias with thorny branches, scratchy euphorbias, whiplike *palo adán*, and prickly wild cucumber fruits half hidden under coarse leaves. The acacia, *palo chino* or "china wood," is full of small white flowers with a beguiling fragrance, a cross between lemonade and sweet-shrub. Every branch is full of freeloaders: a geometrid worm is colored the same wine red as the acacia buds, and so many pieces of stamen cling to it, it looks like a wilted flower cluster.

Fifty feet up, past the first scramble, a path a bare foot wide strings along above nothingness, tenable only because the rest of the slope is worse. The ground is so sparsely covered that there's scarcely one plant per square yard; the dryness, the south-facing sun-baked exposure, the well-drained gravel, and the lack of soil keep the plant population to a minimum, and those that are here web the ground so finely with roots that an intruder has a difficult time getting started. Although the surface is largely bare, there are crevices where small annuals cling and grow, among them, a tiny daisy and a delicate-stemmed houstonia with a cross of four pink petals—the bluets of New England turned pink.

One morning I walk here with Kent Roberts, Sara's husband, a young attorney specializing in admiralty law. A born naturalist, Kent started turtle watching as a child in North Carolina and went on from there. It's marvelous to have an extra pair of observant eyes, for Kent spots many things that I miss. First it is a five-eighths-inch hole in the bank at the side of the path, framed with cobwebbing. The opening faces east and the morning sun lights it full on. There is no visible occupant. I declare it empty. Kent chides, "You Midwesterners give up too easy," and begins pulling away the soil. After a flurry of digging, he unearths a large black female wolf spider.

Under my hand lens the distinctive arrangement of its eyes confirms the identification: four small front-row eyes in a nearly straight line, a much

Fishhook cactus

larger middle pair just above them; and lateral eyes in the upper row—with those in the middle the largest. Spider eyes are much keener than those of any other arachnids, with a cornea and a lens with a thick cuticle, vision further enhanced by their multiplicity and placement.

This female had excavated a tunnel at least twelve inches deep with a light collar of webbing around the opening. (Although wolf spiders do not construct webs, they do use silk in nesting and to tie their egg cases to their backs.) For desert insects, being able to dig is of inestimable value—often the only shelter available is beneath ground. Because they are diggers, the front legs of a wolf spider are heavy and strong, and the fourth pair of legs the longest, stretched out behind so that from above the spider looks somewhat rectangular. With highly sensitive tactile hairs, she picks up the slightest vibration— each fine bristle or movable hair has a knob at the attached end fitting into a socket with direct nerve connections to the brain.

Wolf spiders don't catch prey in webs, they lie in wait beside their burrows or are active hunters, pursuing and pouncing. A spider bites with formidable chelicerae, the prehensile claws that arm the proboscis of scorpions and spiders, the large basal segment of which connects to a venom gland; when the spiral muscle wrapping the gland contracts, the spasm forces venom into the bite, injecting enzymes into the wound that partially digest the victim's tissue by turning it into a kind of broth that the spider siphons. Their bites are not pleasant for humans either, and the remedies are as old as time. Pliny recommended cock's brain in vinegar, five ants taken in liquid, or a poultice of sheep manure and vinegar. Wolf spiders have also given their life for folk cures: applied in a compress of resin and wax to the temple they were thought to lower fevers.

Nothing was known about the spiders of Baja California before the first collection was made in 1924; that spiders have been long established here is evidenced by the large number of endemics—almost two-thirds of the known species are limited to the peninsula. As a group, they tend to be largely tropical in affinity, although the spider fauna is a very complex one, for spiders must have arrived with almost the first piece of bark floating on the sea or perhaps ballooning through the air on a vagrant wind.

As we pick across the path, a humming grows louder. Holes riddle a dirt bank two feet high. Several dozen digger bees pour in and out in a frenetic exchange of place, hovering, landing, looping. The bees look like small black bumble bees, unmarked except for a scattering of pale hairs, with pollen carried on their hind tibia and tarsal segments. They line their burrows with a protective waxy or varnishlike coating, and in them store a mixture of honey and pollen upon which their larvae feed. I wade right in for a look-see, having forgotten that indications are I am growing more and more allergic to bee stings and should be wary. But I am bewitched by that small bee, hovering in front of a small hole burrowed into a remote bank, for that bee carries with it a small chip of knowledge that adds something to human sentience. To watch that bee for a month could evoke a few phrases about beginnings and endings, yesterdays and tomorrows.

There are also wasps in numbers. Most common are the slow-flying polistes wasps which seem to float through the air, handsome with their exquisitely veined amber wings and golden brown bodies, abdominal sections variously marked with golden yellow patterns. Social wasps, they commonly build nests that hang by a stem from eaves and ceilings or protected outdoor places. The wasps masticate wood pulp and glue the walls together with their saliva, building two shells, marvels of engineering, with air spaces for ventilation and strong but light supports. The inner shell encompasses the hexagonal cells of the larvae; the outer one protects and insulates them. Polistes wasps have tufts of glandular hairs on the tip of the abdomen, and these they rub onto the nest stalk, coating it with an ant-repellent secretion.

And there are other wasps like those that Barco describes as "little, red, and very vicious." They form

> honeycombs, but without honey, and they locate them hanging from cliffs and steep rocks where there is some protection from the rain. They deposit their eggs in the little cells of the honeycombs. Worms are hatched from these later, and they become wasps in the end. These worms are a delicious treat for the Indians and that is why they sometimes wander about precipices with great risk to their lives, just to attempt to get some of these honeycombs.

Everything I spot seems to be venomous, including a flying warning signal: black and orange striped abdomen, orange-tipped antennae, and with orange and black brushes on the tibia of its flashy orange back legs. No Indian warrior ever strode forth to battle more handsomely arrayed. No small creature ever looked so lethal. But it's an innocent moth, garbed in warning clothing, taking advantage of the "avoidance image" in both color and form. Many insects that are relatively incapable of protecting themselves against diurnal predation often bear bright warning colors in imitation of non-palatable insects. For the predator which hunts by vision, the more distinctive the color pattern is, the easier it is to avoid. Monarch butterflies are the classic example of an insect that birds abhor. The larvae of the monarch butterfly feed on milkweed, and some of the plant's glycosides persist in the adult, causing vomiting in birds, and a healthy desire to avoid further contact. Of all the color schemes extant, orange and black (which the human species has chosen for Halloween) is the most characteristic, protecting such diversified insects as beetles, moths, ladybugs, and butterflies.

Farther up the hillside, Kent spots a young orange-throated whiptail before it patters under a protecting plant, but not before we see the black and yellow stripes and its three-and-a-half-inch blue tail, almost as long as it is. The young sport brighter blue tails than the adults, and their stripes are more vivid: the broad brown stripe down its back is edged with black and flanked by a conspicuous light stripe, in this one distinctly yellow, that runs from the nose into the tail. An inhabitant of desert areas, it feeds largely on termites.

Heliotrope *(Heliotropum curassavicum* var. *oculatum)*

The shrub under which the whiptail took refuge for a moment is an endemic spurge, which blooms with creamy yellow "flowers," in the distinctive configuration of euphorbias. Several small staminate flowers surround a single minute female flower, without petals or sepals; all are nestled in a ring of bracts. These have lobes bearing glands that are often colorful. The pistillate flower soon produces a tri-partite capsule which becomes prominent as it springs out one side on a curved pedicel. The best-known spurge is poinsettia with its large brilliant bracts; four less showy species grow wild at the Cape.

An endemic has developed distinctive characteristics in isolation to become a separate species, and to exist in only a single area. Because of the isolation and insular character of the Cape, one might expect many endemics, but in actuality, the number of endemic species for the peninsula is low (for the Cape it is slightly higher). Dr. Wiggins, in *Flora of Baja California,* suggests that paucity of endemics may be because the flora is so recent, the peninsula so recently separated from the mainland that there has not been enough time to develop indigenous species. Most of the endemics belong to genera and families generally common outside the peninsula, plants that have adapted to the heat and dryness of the environment. The flora of Lower California also contains many genera with only one or two species, another indication of a young flora. Dr. Wiggins suggests that this also indicates that it is easier for plants to adapt to higher or lower temperatures than it is to adapt to aridity.

Beside the spurge blooms an ill-smelling *Porophyllum* that has no common name that I know of. I reflect that if many of the insects are venom-

Cucumber *(Cucumis dipsaceus)*

Polistes wasp *(Polistes* sp.*)*

ous, many of the plants are odiferous—*damiana,* cinchweed, the brilliant orange-flowered dogweed, to name a few. Belonging to the daisy family, *Porophyllum* flowers are one of hundreds of variations on the theme of daisy flowers. Five bracts hold the flower heads, with a long slender purplish gland on the outside of each, which releases an unpleasant odor on touch. Similar glands stud the leaves. Likewise is dogweed, so called because some species are thought to smell like a wet dog; this one bears handsome orange daisy-like flowers and smells distasteful.

Cinchweed has a pungent, but not unpleasant, odor; it is a small bright yellow and orange marigold-like annual that threads across the ground, the leaves less than half an inch long, the flowers smaller than a dime. Their thickness and brightness stain the soil. Called *limoncillo,* glands also pattern both the bracts and leaves, which have a long hair on each tooth of the leaf. One of the several hundred desert ephemerals of the peninsula, cinchweed blooms after rain, germinating, growing, flowering, and setting seed at a rapid rate. By this adaptation it avoids drought pressures, and burgeons only when the season is favorable, largely unaffected by day length or temperature or soil, all factors of importance to perennials. Since there were recent rains their thickness stains the ground, far overshadowing other, less showy,

Commicarpus *(Commicarpus brandegeei)*

Houstonia (*Houstonia asperuloides* var. *asperuloides*)

Cinchweed (*Pectis multiseta*)

annuals such as *Houstonia* and *Solanum*—so many of the less conspicuous plants here have no common names, leaving one with a handful of Latin names like a bouquet of thistles. A small red fairy duster—such a small spare shrub to make such a display—is thought to be effective against high fever. A thin vine, almost leafless, with small white flowers, trails across it. The vine's intriguing seed pods are tiny capsules with rows of red dots around the lid. Its overwhelming name is *Commicarpus brandegei* and it has no common one whatsoever. A member of the Four-o'clock Family, it is named for T. S. Brandegee, who contributed so much to the botany of the peninsula; it is also a Baja California endemic.

We cut diagonally up the slope to reach a saddle linking two hilltops. The lighthouse at Cabeza Ballena—Whale's Head—lies below us. Violet-green swallows scythe the air slightly below us in graceful swooping flight; a black-throated sparrow chitters in a bush.

Nearby, on a rock pinnacle, a male iguana stretches out full length, facing out to sea. As we watch, a female lumbers onto another rock a dozen feet away; she is a soft buff, very much the color of the rock, on the side splotched with light gray. As fierce as they look, with the slight cresting of scales down the back—a baby dragon at least—they are almost entirely herbivorous.

The male iguana displays, rising up on his front legs, extending his neck, bobbing his head vigorously—in courtship, visual signals are important. No response. The male looks away. For minutes no one moves. The female sidles six inches, stops, sidles back. For a moment the male gives no evidence of noticing, then displays again. It is as if both are windup toy dragons with the mechanisms out of synchronization, so unrelated are their movements. The female ambles down, having remained fifteen minutes, and shambles away. The back view is that of an ambulatory well-weathered cow pat.

Later they are back on their respective knobs again, still basking but heads up, much more alert. Suddenly the male drops off the rock and scampers toward the female, who departs from her rock on the instant. It's a good roaring thirty-second chase, both of them equally swift. She ends up back on her knob, he on his, flanks heaving; they eye each other and stay put. The unexpected swiftness protects these iguanas from being caught for their meat, which is reputed to be excellent. When they dive into a burrow they inflate their bodies so that they are extremely difficult to extract. And they can deliver a nasty nip to a careless handler.

Diurnal lizards, these iguanas can be active an hour or so before they

Dogweed *(Dyssodia speciosa)*

emerge from their burrows, and then they may remain inactive near the entrance until their body temperature reaches between 100 and 104 degrees Fahrenheit. Once out and about, they maintain their internal temperature by behavior—choosing sun or shade, and even how they run. Through sand they shuffle, scattering the hot surface sand and contacting the cooler sand beneath their bodies. Climbing onto the rock pedestal may provide some cooling by exposure to breeze; they also may stand on tiptoe to keep from absorbing heat from the substrate.

I've seen this pair perform this chase-and-return sequence again and again, she always comfortably ahead, both returning to their individual starting points, from which they occasionally survey each other. Behind and below them, the crashing turquoise and white ocean provides the classic Hollywood accompaniment to a passionate scene, the director panning between him and her to display all those nuances of expression from awakening interest to mutual response to overwhelming desire. In like fashion I pan my binoculars from one to the other and find only drooped eyelids and what I judge to be, anthropomorphically, a phlegmatic passion at best.

Far below, the ocean laps limpid, green over the sand, purple-blue over the rocks. A very short swell runs, overlaid with crisp ripples, animated with prancing diamonds of sunlight. The swell began hundreds of miles away as waves kicked up by wind. But as the waves move away from the wind that instigated them, they change—become more symmetrical and rounded, close to a true sine curve, and go for miles across the ocean, retaining their size and shape.

Today, as lifeless as the slope looks, there is always movement somewhere. A white-tailed antelope squirrel bounds across the dirt, giving a good show of broken-field running from one bush to another. This shorter-eared and -tailed form of the antelope ground squirrel is more common in desert regions, and is one of the few rodents with daytime habits, made possible by a combination of physiological and behavioral adaptations for dealing with the stress of hyperthermia. They eat many foods that increase their water allotment (such as cactus stems), and depend upon salivation rather than panting for evaporation cooling. During the heat of the day they retreat underground, able to unload body heat by sprawling onto the cooler soil. On a very hot day they can remain active and above ground only a quarter hour and then must cool down before resuming active movement. They can also climb up into bushes, where they take advantage of a cooling breeze. Since antelope squirrels neither hibernate nor estivate, they face a difficult environment all year long.

As Kent and I turn back for lunch a small horned lizard jumps out from beside the path and scampers a few feet away, where it squats, flanks heaving, under a scraggly bush. These typical desert and semidesert inhabitants are the most numerous of the Cape lizards. This shaggy creature has little horns at the back of its head, which make it look very fierce, and pointed fringe scales on its flank, plus rows of enlarged pointed scales on each side of its throat. Its defenses are showy but relatively harmless: when attacked by a larger animal it inflates itself, making it difficult to swallow. It can bite in

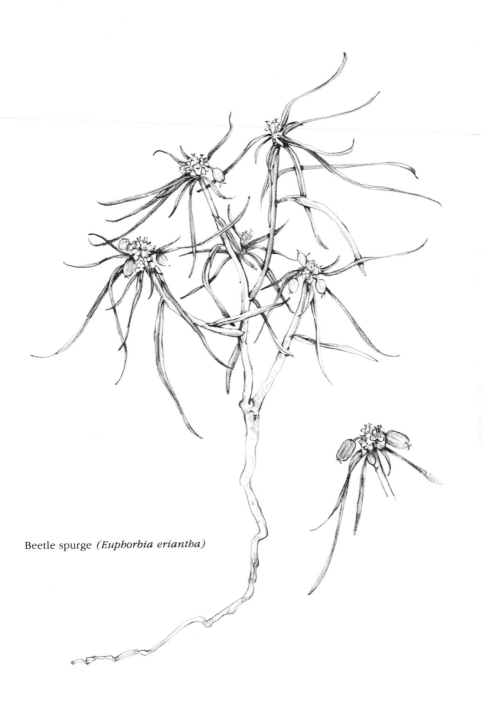

Beetle spurge *(Euphorbia eriantha)*

Fairy duster *(Calliandra californica)*

defense, and if this doesn't work, will "spray" blood from its eyes (actually the blood comes from a sinus at the base of its third eyelid); this so startles a predator that the horned lizard has time to escape.

Crouching and still, it is so close to the soil color, so patterned like the gravel, that I would never have seen it had it not run; its base color is laid with dark blotches which imitate the irregularity of the ground, and can be regulated by hormones to change color. Here is its ideal environment: open places for sunning, scattered plant cover, pockets of sandy soil in which it can bury itself, and a ready supply of ants and insects. Its hours of activity depend not upon temperature, but possibly some kind of internal clock.

They are active in the heat of the day, and adjust their body heat by where and how they stand, able to regulate their body temperatures within a surprisingly narrow range by their behavior.

Horned lizards protect their territories with great vigor, with a display of inhospitality that is more show than physical aggression. This territorial behavior seems to be inherent and not learned, and serves to assure a large enough feeding habitat for the individual. Such displays require considerable energy, and the exposed movements make the lizards more vulnerable to predation; that they continue to defend territories testifies to the necessity of doing so.

The vertebrates of arid regions are predominantly lizards. They occupy every possible niche—hard-packed soil, soft-packed sand, rocks—you name it, there's probably a resident lizard. The Cape lizard fauna is thought to be rather recent, ancestral populations having been periodically decimated because of climate swings, with at least four immigration waves from the north. With the barriers to migration presented by the Gulf and the Pacific, all species have had to come from the north, and those at the Cape have their closest relatives in Alta California.

The old cow path we tread bespeaks usage and civilization, and yet there is a wildness about this hill on the seaward side. One day, here alone, I looked down to the thousands of pinpoint reflections of the sun in the sea, as if the ocean were a grand camera obscura punctured with thousands of tiny apertures. Terrestrial wind has been defined as the movement of "electrically neutral gases," but the wind that sighed around the hillside that day was charged with the essence of wilderness. No one else had been here before. No one else would come after. Wilderness must be a state of mind.

*Doubtless it is easy for romanticism to exaggerate and overvalue these sim-
plicities but there is something very real about their attractions. However
low the "standard of living" may be, it is also a high one when measured in
terms of certain goods not commonly taken into account when the standard
of living is discussed. Though the inhabitants have relatively few time and
labor saving machines they seem, paradoxically, to have a wider margin of
leisure than many who live in more fully "developed" regions.*

Joseph Wood Krutch
The Forgotten Peninsula
1961

Morning-glory *(Merremia aurea)*

BACK COUNTRY

Having walked this inimical countryside, I find it difficult to see how anyone can make a living from the land, and when David Yee Sanchez asks if I'd like to visit some of his friends north of San José del Cabo, I am more than delighted to accept.

For it is on these isolated ranches that the traditional life of Baja California goes on, independent, largely self-sufficient, conducted by people whose way of life is not a lot different from that of a hundred years ago, who by understanding the earth are able to subsist from it. One simply lives here with what one was born to, a crease of mind, a turn of gesture, a world that belongs and fits, in which life is as sparse as the vegetation but in which people of substance live.

David Yee is a small sturdy man with a serious manner who prefaces most sentences with a courteous, "Well, ma'am, I would say . . ." and then gives me a lucid and patient explanation of whatever it is I have questioned. His Chinese father married his Mexican mother, whose last name was Sanchez; a Mexican man goes by his given and his father's name, as David Yee, but his full and proper name includes his mother's. David owns farmland north of San José, and although he no longer farms it himself, he maintains contact with his friends there and is very well informed about area ranching and

Iguana

farming, and to go into the country with someone like David is a privilege.

As we drive out of San José, he points out a big corral on the left side of the road to which rounded-up cattle are brought, usually beginning in January and continuing through February and March. Hands "wash" the animals in big bins to prevent insects from going out on them. Most cattle are raised for meat. Formerly they were shipped in and out by boat from old San José del Cabo; now they are mostly trucked out.

A white wooden cross marks a roadside shrine, decked with a wreath of red and white plastic flowers. On another, a brilliant blue bouquet leans against the base. These small commemorative shrines are erected where there has been an accident, a constant reminder to the traveler to take care.

A windmill stands by the road, one of few left on the Cape; now a rancher is more likely to have a gasoline engine to pump irrigation water. On the peninsula, for many years and many generations, farmers and ranchers have held their land in the homesteading sense. Since the government now requires residents to give proof of ownership and to register their land, it has made considerable monies available in government aid for this through CoReTT, the acronym for *Comisión para Regularización de la Tenencia de la Tierra,* the Government agency that does title searches, surveys, and provides registery papers.

We take the *ramal* to Santa Catarina, a *ramal* being a secondary unpaved road. A settlement of 1,000 to 1,500 people, Santa Catarina is a very old town, with a neat schoolyard and the small weather station one sees in nearly every settlement. Clean wash snapping on every clothes line makes the whole town look as if it were celebrating with multicolored banners. Although the houses are much the same—rectilinear cement-block construction, thatch roofs, and a ramada in front—they are set at different angles and among such a profusion of brilliantly flowering vines that the town has great charm. Gorgeous roosters pick and prance, opulently colored and tailed, reminding that cock fighting is still a keen sport in Baja California.

Next to one house are stacked neatly tied bundles of palm fronds, ready for thatching. What a satisfying roofing material: waterproof, easily replaceable, available for free, weathering to a pleasant color. What's more, a good thatch roof lasts up to thirty years. Even if strong winds peel off thatch, all the owner has to do is weave some fresh fronds into the empty spaces. And a well-thatched roof is also a handsome thing from beneath, a beautiful design made by the alternating splayed fans and split stalks.

The road through Santa Catarina is but a few blocks long, and soon we are back in the country again, following the shelf road, winding eastward.

Cattle range along the road. Since generally only waterholes are fenced, to keep cattle out, they wander anywhere they can find feed, although they generally stay within a day's walking distance of their home ranch, where water is available. Two dozen or so graze on the roadside shrubs. One carries a branch hung rakishly over a horn. Many joints of cholla cling to the flank of another. A third gazes stoically at us from behind a cactus; her calf kicks up its heels and flees as if the devil were after it.

Peninsula cattle are long-legged and rangy, with medium-long horns, high square rumps, and a hurried prancing gait that is almost horselike. The variety of colors is encyclopedic: Dalmatian-spotted black and white; black with brown; liver and white; cinnamon brown; tan and cream; speckled gray—one of every persuasion. According to David, at least fifteen acres per head are required, although twenty are better, and many ranchers in this area would prefer up to thirty-five. Over forty head in a herd is "not very wise because when we have a drought or a dry season, it's very hard to feed them."

Most cattle carry both ear and iron brands although there's scarcely any rustling. The only way to get a large load out is to come in with a truck, which is obvious and easily discerned. The intimation hangs in the air that local punishment usually supersedes judicial redress, making the latter unnecessary. Local ranchers are honest; if someone else's cattle appear at his watering place, the rancher drives them away—more cattle at *his* trough are not what he needs. Sometimes, says David, with the ruefulness of experience, you have to go and get your strayed animals from someone else's farm because they won't water them.

High on a tall cactus, looking like a part of it, broods a caracara, known in Mexico as *quileli* (rhymes with "ukulele"). The cries of the mythical Quilele foretold disaster; "caracara" is onomatopoetic, mimicking their high cackling cry. They often perch on top of a cardón early in the morning, wings outstretched, exposing their thinly feathered sides to the sun. These carrion-eating hawks are swift graceful fliers, alternating rapid wing strokes with long sailing glides.

When hunting, a caracara reportedly can chase and catch a jack rabbit through broken country, skimming with frequent twists and turns like a marsh hawk. Although caracaras eat carrion, they feed their young with fresh meat, a catholic diet of rabbits and skunks, rodents and reptiles, crabs and crayfish, opossums and turtles. According to David they smell dead animals before vultures do and prefer fresher food; they often fly along behind the plow and grab up lizards or mice or whatever else the plow turns up.

Thatch roof from inside

Lomboy (*Jatropha cinerea*)

They frequently nest in the branches of the large saguaro-like cardóns, using the same nest for several years as eagles do, by which time the nest attains a degree of pungent ripeness. Pairs produce only one brood per season, and the twenty-eight-day incubation period is shared by both parents. The young remain in juvenile plumage until the following winter or spring, when they molt to adult black and white.

We pass a farm where workers have harvested beans. The bushes are dry and brown, a foot or so high. Plants are dug by hand, as they have been for decades, spread on a cloth, then beaten to break out the beans. The edge of the field is planted in corn and squash, whose big orange flowers bedizen the sprawling plants, patrolled by flashing dragonflies and sulphur butter flies.

Fine sands and silts washed down in millennia past by the Rio San José form this good alluvial farmland. The San José, running well underground here, is the source of water for the valley. Recently, however, the water table has dropped, necessitating deeper wells. David owns several pieces of property in the area, among them one plot near the dry river bed. Once, David tells me, he could start digging at the dry river bed and trench out a five- to seven-foot-wide channel. By the time he got it dug to his land, water would be flowing in the ditch. No more. In 1966 he dug a thirty-foot well to reach water; in 1975 he was forced to dig a 60-foot well. When that well went dry, he abandoned the property for agricultural purposes. He laughs ruefully: "No sense for me to be a farmer here—I starve!"

The road parallels a straight irrigation ditch that waters a small orange orchard, water sparkling in narrow ditches through the clean ground beneath the trees. We pass another small farm growing lettuce, peppers, and corn. Tomatoes are grown here as well as onions and beans. Mangoes, plums, some citrus, and papaya have been grown here for years; avocados are just beginning to be cultivated. Farming, based on a growing season that lasts almost all year long, can be profitable.

Farther on we pass larger fields, the corn well over my head. A big pump drones. Water glimmers between the rows. Five men sit in the shade by a small cement pumphouse, eating lunch. David knows them all, stops to talk, asks about their yield, they wish each other *Feliz Año Nuevo* all around. He explains that this is the San Pedro Ejido (pronounced ay-hee′-dough), agrarian land held by the members of the *ejido,* that cannot be sold.

The concept of *ejido* or land held in common goes back to the end of the nineteenth century. It became of great importance during the Revolution of 1910–17/18 when Emiliano Zapata rode to secure land for the peasants who had none. It became a political reality in 1940 when Presidente Lázaro Cárdenas distributed forty-five million acres to *ejidos*.

To form an *ejido*, a group of farmers combine and petition the government for land that is currently not in use. Under certain conditions, the government grants them the land, helps with the purchase of equipment, bringing in irrigation, providing seeds, etc., through the government-supported *Banco Rural*. The debt is paid from crop proceeds. Some of the crops will be bought by a government food distribution corporation called CONASUPO which has first right of refusal and guarantees a fair price; the remainder of the produce can be sold on the open market. Some *ejidos* are more prosperous than others, often because of the skills and knowledge of their *comisario*, the man elected by majority vote for three- to six-year terms as head of the *ejido*. It is the only public office in Mexico in which the incumbent can succeed himself. Since the *ejido* is autonomous, he is often a man of considerable influence, and on some of the more remote *ejidos*, he may also serve as judge and justice in the absence of any civil authority.

We drive into the ranchyard of the Álvarez family where, in the hardpack dirt soil, a pomegranate blooms with beautiful orange red blossoms and small fruits in all stages of formation. Heretofore my image of pomegranates is woven into a brocade pattern on a Renaissance wall hanging as a symbol of fertility, which now seems sterile compared to the rich patterns of the growing plant. An orange tree bears "sour" oranges with thick lumpy skin. Several oleander bushes flower profusely, white, pink, and dark pink. Their plum tree first bears fruit, then leaves. Stalks of sugar cane rustle like palms when the wind blows. In their shade are native herbs. As in many back country ranches, this land is owned by the family, and privately farmed.

Señora Álvarez has a sweet placid face—broad forehead, broad cheekbones, wide mouth with a certain delicacy, and a lovely smile. Sparkly-eyed Alicia, who is a slender eight, wears bright red slacks and pullover, her dark hair pulled into two tight braids. Juan, only five, is much the shyer. Señor Álvarez, who has the high wide cheekbones of the Aztec, greets us with a huge grin and goes to get a picture of himself in full *vaquero* working dress. Practically the same as that the Spaniards brought to the peninsula, the leather garments provide protection for both horse and rider. Although worn less and less as the pickup replaces the horse, for off-road work there is no replacement. Originally they were made of deerskin but now are more likely cowhide.

None of the cattle are to be seen; in the dry season of winter, they come in only every three days, after which they must be chased out to forage. The big trough from which they drink is fenced off, the gasoline pump is silent. On the premises are chickens, pigs, and maybe two dozen sheep, amber to cream to golden fleeced; they too come to drink, then spend the rest of the day on their own, but remain closer to home. Señor Álvarez also raises corn for feed and hay for cattle. They begin milking in October or early November, and then turn the cows loose at the end of February to calve.

With the courtesy always observed at these ranches, we are offered dinner (which we refuse because of time) and a drink of water from the outside cistern beside the kitchen; it is surprisingly cool and refreshing without refrigeration. The thatch roof forms a band of shade around the kitchen.

Carlowrightia cordifolia

Shelves, made out of branches lashed together and varnished, hang from the roof and hold glasses and dishes; covered containers for food also hang out here, where they remain cooler. Everything is neat and well-arranged.

As we stand talking, two small cinnamon brown piglets become brave enough to investigate visitors, making Alicia laugh when I reach down to pat one and it gallops away in complete disorder. She wants to know about my girls—how old they are, what they do. She takes me by the hand and tells me the names of the plants she knows in Spanish, and I tell her the names I know for them in English. Oh my, how I wish I could spend the day with Alicia—it's been a long time since I've had an eager little girl holding my hand.

After we leave, we pass Álvarez's cornfield, a large field, totally planted to corn, a one-crop agriculture that is being practiced more and more. It looks woefully dry. The plants are stunted, their lower leaves brown. This year, David says, Álvarez does not have enough water for both cattle and crop irrigation. I ask what will happen if Señor Álvarez has a poor crop. "If bad corn, he will have to start selling whatever he can—a chicken, a pig, cattle—he makes most of his income from milking cows, but when the season is dry, feed poor, cows don't have much milk. La Señora also makes good cheese to sell, thirty- to thirty-five-pound squares at one time. But no milk, no cheese."

We stop off at another ranch, *Los Algodones, algodón* being Spanish for cotton—either cotton was once raised here, or it's named after the many wild cotton plants along the road. The ranch buildings and corrals spread out over a sandy arroyo bottom. Close by the house is a double *palo de arco* fence filled with stones and soil, two feet wide, built to divert flash floods, which a few years ago took out the house, the flowers, the fences—*todos.*

The ramada is shaded by huge trees, one of the several species indiscriminately called *palo verde.* This is shaped rather like an oak, but there the resemblance ends. The branches and leaves, which hang like tendrils, are all a mossy green. Belonging to the legume family, it has typically small leaflets arranged down a long pendent stalk; the leaflets fall early and the stem remains and carries on photosynthesis in the absence of the leaflets, in aspect looking somewhat like a weeping willow. The flowers, which we've just missed, are brilliant yellow in clusters at the ends of branches; now the long thin pods hang, swinging gently in the noontime breeze.

We enter the ramada through a bower of leaves and flowers—hibiscus, San Miguelito, and bougainvillaea—bright pinks and brilliant rose. Señora Amalia emerges from the kitchen, taking off her apron. Juanito, her husband, straw-hatted, rises to shake hands; we exchange "mucho gusto"—that gra-

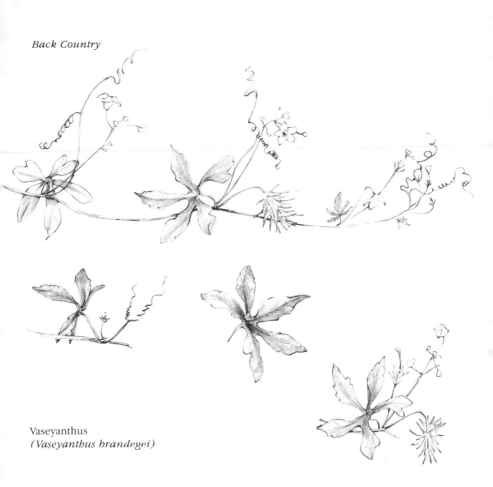

Vaseyanthus
(*Vaseyanthus brandegei*)

cious "much pleasure" of a Spanish greeting. Their son, Juan Ángel, has the wide grin of a man who loves life. La Señora's pleasure is birds. Two parrots swing in big cages from the roof, chortling about the vagaries of humans and the futility of it all. Hanging in a large cage behind the house is a handsome male pyrrhuloxia, that at first glance I take for a female cardinal. Pyrrhuloxia are fairly common in Baja California Sur, with a whistle somewhat like a cardinal's.

Dressed in black, La Señora has an easy bearing and a serene face, which reminds me of nineteenth-century novels that speak of women with "noble brows." She has just that. We speak of husbands, of daughters, of plants and their uses. She has mint growing in the flood fence; I finger a leaf and we share the aroma. A dragonfly bats over. Since it's not in my dictionary, I ask,

"Como se dice en español?" She smiles as she answers, "Caballerito del diablo." Wonderful!—"little horseman of the devil!" (Later I find they are also called *Libélulas.*)

Back of the kitchen the cheese press is in operation, weighted with part of an anvil and a boulder. The whey drips out and worms its way downhill, smelling pungently sour. *Queso fresco* is made from raw milk with homemade rennet prepared from a calf's fourth stomach. When it has clabbered, the curds are drained and then put into a press to get rid of any remaining moisture. It can be used as is, but more often is salted, then "ground" with a mano on a metate until it is pulverized, and repressed into cakes. It is light, slightly sour, and used in a variety of ways. Another cheese, *queso de apoyo,* is made locally from the small percentage of heavy cream; it is very rich, very good, and very scarce.

A couple of turkeys bustle into view; they are called both *pavo* and *guajolote* in Mexico. The usual chickens and magnificent roosters stalk around a pan full of grain, and then, to my amazement, a peacock flounces around the corner, dragging its exotic tail on the hard-packed dirt. Yes, says La Señora, we have two pair!

As we are driving out an incredible eye-catching strawberry red bird flashes out from a bush, brilliant against this grayed landscape. He perches on a post, darts out and back, sweeping low to the ground: a vermilion flycatcher, like a jewel spilling across the sand. I wonder if La Señora has seen this *cardenalito.* I suspect she has.

Our last stop is an agrarian plot, "owned" by David's son. Since his son is not old enough to work it, David does it for him by hiring a tenant farmer with whom he splits fifty-fifty. There is no one visible when we pull up. David honks the horn. From a far field a blue-shirted man in a straw hat comes running. He has not a single upper front tooth, but the merriest smile I've ever seen, one that pushes up the corners of his eyes into crinkled fans of infectious delight. When we leave David puzzles, "I don't know why they are so stubborn—there's not enough corn harvested for him to make a good living—but when I see him he is always happy—he has seven or eight children, he cannot make a living, but he is always so happy. I always envy him."

In spite of the amount of vegetation along the road, the landscape is essentially treeless, especially if one thinks of trees in terms of big oaks and spreading elms and sturdy maples. The lowland woods of Baja California Sur are stunted pygmy growths of limber, supple trees, often cluster-trunked, for the most part non-lumber trees. Wood is such a precious commodity on the peninsula that fenceposts are often cactus or ocotillo, or a living fence made

Cheese press

of *pitahaya agria* growing in a fierce barricade, or *lomboy* branches stuck in the ground to root, forming an impenetrable palisade. The best fence I ever saw was one made of cactus columns, each about ten inches in diameter and four feet high, set close together, forming an enclosure about eight feet by six, incarcerating a corpulent brown and white hog, kept from wandering by the most simple and painful of confines.

The ubiquitous *lomboy* lines the road, a limber-branched shrub-to-tree with smooth grayish brown bark. With the paucity of good graze and the abundance of *lomboy,* I ask if the cattle eat it. David laughs: "If cows only ate *lomboy,* we would all be the richest people in Mexico!" Actually cattle eat only the browned leaves of this euphorbia to avoid the sap, which is very bitter. It remains leafless until rains come, then leafs out quickly. The leaves are almost round, one to two inches across, sometimes just slightly three-lobed. Depending on rains, small pale pink tubular flowers bloom from August to November and often again in April. If no rains come, the leaves yellow and fall. The plump pods are easy to recognize, three-parted, nearly two inches across. The astringent bitter sap flows freely when a twig is broken, and is reported to prevent chapped lips and stop bleeding—indeed, common treatment for a child's skinned knee is to break off a twig and apply the sap. The isolation of these ranches demands a high sense of self-sufficiency, one of the facets of which is a thorough knowledge of medicinal herbs.

Driving home, I ponder the tenuousness of an existence on these remote ranches. Here nature seems at her most frugal, and a chain of bad years can deplete a family's resources. Nevertheless, life is good in many ways. Because I have always come with friends, I am greeted with a straight glance, a firm handclasp accompanied by that warm "Mucho gusto," an honest curiosity, and a graciousness that says, "You are a guest in my house, be welcome." I have always felt honored.

Ranching here requires hard brutal work, and the ability to endure years when crops are poor and cattle grow thin. But somehow, somewhere, there is always a helping hand. There are other options, should they wish—jobs in San José or La Paz perhaps. But many, especially the older people, according to David, choose to stay, and to maintain the strong fabric of life that suits them. I wonder: is it because they have no television, are not constantly assaulted by how much more others have, that they continue this life? Or would they still choose this, preferring the traditional celebrations, honesty among friends, self-sufficiency, and the reassurance of a life lived as they have always known it?

Farther north is a ranch called *Las Tunas,* after its abundance of prickly pear. It has become famous, not for the quality of its cheese or the graciousness of its hospitality, but for recent fascinating finds of land mammal fossils, savanna inhabitants whose closest relatives once lived in Texas—of the twelve mammalian species in the Las Tunas fauna, none are extant. Present only on the eastern side of the Cape in an area that once was covered by a meandering river, and possibly even connected to the mainland, the bones may indicate that southern Baja is of more recent origin than previously thought.

The first report on these terrestrial fossil vertebrates came out of discoveries made by Jim Jeffries in June, 1975. Jim Jeffries is a contented man, doing what he likes to do: scour the countryside for fossils. When he was a boy, his father built boats here. One day a workman brought in a shark's tooth. The incident haunted Jeffries until, after many years of searching, he finally found them where they lay. He took early retirement from the Beverly Hills Fire Department, built his house on the beach near San Lucas, and began to hunt for fossils in a serious way. A big hulk of a man, he strides across the landscape as if the very weight of his footsteps would bring them to light.

The fossil beds are in a non-marine layer of a primarily marine formation, the Salada Formation, which is probably of the Pliocene epoch. The fossils are restricted to a graben, a down-faulted block almost half a mile wide, flanked by older marine beds. Laid down between twelve and four million years ago, the Salada Formation underlies the area north and east of the mountains, and mostly is composed of sandstones, shales, and sandy limestones, with some loose gravels and sands.

Faults and warps jumble this whole area, making deciphering time relationships difficult. Folding and warping deformed the western margin of the Gulf and the eastern margin of the peninsula throughout the Pliocene. Very recent sediments overlie the fossil beds, uncomformably—that is, there is an erosional gap in the geological record of beds which ought to be here but are not. These recent sediments probably are remnants of old river or stream channels abandoned in the present episode of downcutting.

The fossil vertebrate fauna found here indicate a habitat with large slow-moving streams flowing across a subtropical savanna, very near the sea, much warmer and wetter than now, a habitat that would have remained well above freezing all year long, and been able to support animals no longer on the peninsula, such as crocodiles and large tortoises. The peninsula then was probably farther south, having migrated northwestward about 125 miles between the late Pliocene and the present.

Although the fossil fauna is not extensive, it is "significantly diverse"— this particular combination of animals only coexisted in a narrow time frame during the late Pliocene, providing an invaluable reference frame. The presence of *Crocodylus* implies perennial fresh water, as does that of a frog, *Rhynochotherium,* which required a year-round water supply. The presence of *Crocodylus* suggests that southern Baja California was still attached or very close to the Mexican mainland during or just prior to late Pliocene epoch six to four million years ago, which agrees with the "magnetic stripes" on the sea floor at the mouth of the Gulf and suggests that the northern peninsula split from the mainland some twenty million years before the southern end.

Many arroyos in this area cut through the more prevalent marine strata of the Salada Formation, baring the edges of hundreds of oyster and scallop shells, barnacle and sea-urchin fossils. One morning Herman and I went with a dove-hunting party to a ranch that would have required dropping bread crumbs to find one's way out, so remote was it. While the hunters spread out around a spring, we stood at the bottom of a dry arroyo like most of those on the Cape: flat-bottomed, steep-walled, characteristic of a stream developed on alluvial sediments, as Barco described them, with "very high banks on both sides, as if they were hillsides of the sierra itself." This entrenchment was caused partly by the lowering of sea level during the last glacial period when the sea may have been four hundred feet lower. Such lowering would have caused streams to flow faster down a greater declivity, carving out these deep channels. At the end of the Pleistocene era the general drying of climate also thinned the vegetation and reduced its ability to halt erosion. About the same time, weather patterns also changed; rain storms no longer came in gentle showers but in quick hard storms that at times reached hurricane force and caused the kind of fast heavy runoff that could carve these deep slots.

In the coolness of first light, looking for fossils, I stared instead, in some amazement, at the biggest swashbuckler of a grasshopper I'd ever seen, affixed to the wall just at eye level. Rendered lethargic by the coolness of the morning, it was just three inches from tip of antennae to spurred legs. The inward cant of its head marked it as a slant-faced grasshopper, often found in dampish places, rarely in damaging numbers. One of the most effective defenses from a predator is to be close to the color of the background or otherwise camouflaged, and to remain motionless, and since an insect of this size is most likely to be eaten by a large sharp-eyed bird, this immobile adherence to its background provides it considerable protection.

Then my eyes shifted focus and there, all around it, were shell edges laid every which way in the wall, a shambles of beach debris. Exposed by the flash floods that ream out these arroyos, they are protected by the compacted intermixed dirt and rock of arkose on top. When the waters of the Gulf crept into the lowlands and interfingered with the wrinkled terrain, shallow embayments formed and the Cape, at times, was probably isolated as an island. The shallow waters were warm, between 70 and 85 degrees Fahrenheit, nourishing a rich mollusk fauna. During the Pleistocene Epoch, between two million and twelve thousand years ago, sea level rose and fell with the rhythm of the Ice Ages, submergence, when marine shells were deposited, alternating with emergence.

That the climate was warmer then than it is now is indicated by the coral fossils imbedded here, species now found only farther south. In fact, at least half the species of shells found still exist today. Many are still living on the *east* coast of Panama, having migrated to the west during periods when there was sea passage between the Atlantic and Pacific.

Oysters grew where the water was six hundred feet or less, just as they do today. Some of them lie loose on the ground, monstrous shells almost too heavy to lift with one hand, riddled with the same kind of holes by the same borers that afflict present-day oysters. The same is true of the scallops, deposited in *Pecten* reefs that lay sixty to two hundred feet beneath the sea.

In another arroyo big heavy ark shells lie weathered out on the ground, and if I did not know better I could imagine myself on some beach along the Gulf, holding a sun-warmed and not too recently unoccupied shell in my hand. When I finally work a large fragment of a lovely scallop out and hold it

Fossil ark shell

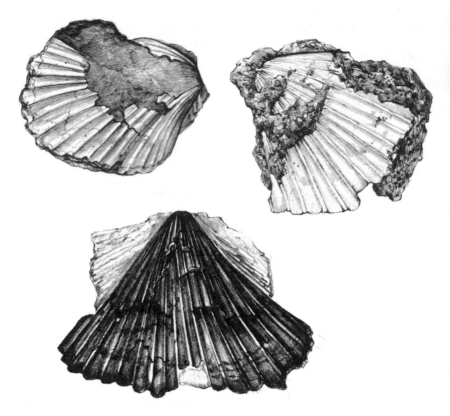

Fossil pectens

in my hand, the connection is too strong to miss: only a month ago, tired and depressed after a hospital stay in La Paz, I had scuffled along a flat beach and found gray scallop shells hidden in the sand like treasures. Nearly round, cupped just to fit in the palm, perfectly pleated, most of them retained their almost equal "ears" intact, the thin line muscle attachment still visible. The shape was satisfying and healing.

Thanks to Jeffries's guidance, Herman and I also look down on whale vertebrae, imbedded in the rock, each vertebra seven inches in diameter, lying linked in a loose white column. This is original bone, not replaced by other minerals; minerals have soaked into the pores, indurating it, and over the 5 to 15 million years it has lain here it has withstood erosion better than the parent rock. Dozens of small blue butterflies flit over it, a poetic contrast between permanence and the transient moment.

A few miles farther on, Jeffries points out a sharp, steep-sided valley where he has found many sharks' teeth, some of them huge, that armed the jaws of twenty-foot monsters. Sharks' teeth are like those of lizards, constantly replaced as worn ones fall out. In a quiet embayment, over the centuries, thousands must have sifted downward through the quiet water.

I work my way gingerly down the extremely steep slope, for it is coated with slippery shale, so dark in color it shimmers and reverberates with heat. By contrast, the streambed at the bottom is cool, pale gray rock fluted and potholed by water that one feels hasn't rushed here for eons, alternating with a sandy bottom but a few feet wide. On the other side, shiny in the sunlight, lies a small shark's tooth on the hot soil. Half the size of my thumbnail, the tooth is finely serrated on the protruding edges. Jeffries later identifies it as belonging to a still extant bull shark, *Carcharhinus leucas,* a belligerent shark and one of the few that goes up into fresh water. Some half of the genera of sharks that existed in those quiet seas are still swimming today.

Black butterflies lark up and down the hillsides, materializing out of the dark shale. From the bottom I look upward to the rim. That this dry oven of a slope, too hot to put a hand on, was once shallow sea bottom beggars the imagination. It is too hot and dry ever to have been anything other than what it is—hot and dry. In this confined slot I feel locked at the bottom of a well, immobilized by the weight of the heat, looking up through eons of sea, gazing through a silvery surface to a both strange and familiar sky.

Driving the miles between these far-flung ranches impresses me with their isolation. One of the festivities that alleviates this isolation is horse races, common over the countryside. One July afternoon, when José Rivera invites us to go to one at Santiago, we've accepted before he finishes asking because going someplace with José Rivera, as with David, is a treat. We drive up the San José River valley, a valley some forty miles long and two to three wide, making this valley far and again the best-watered area on the southern peninsula. The valley heads near Miraflores at about a thousand feet, an area which can receive twenty inches of rainfall a year, in contrast to San José, which may get twelve inches or less.

A bumper crop of *mala mujer*—"wicked woman"—a spiny prickly plant that stings like a nettle, flourishes along the roadside. It is one of those

plants that is practically impossible to ignore or to misidentify: the big pal-
mately divided leaves have near half-inch stinging hairs springing out of
white pustules. Male and female flowers are separate on the plant, the female ones being single and rather hidden, while the white clusters that are
showy are the male flowers with petal-like five-lobed calices.

In succession we cross the dry arroyos. These parallel streambeds follow
the drainage of the parallel valleys, with a dendritic pattern feeding into
each one at the head. Huge cobbles crowd the dry wash of Arroyo Caduaño,
also full of tree tobacco. Caduaño is one of the few native names retained on
the peninsula, most of them having been replaced with Spanish names; it is
said to have been a Pericu word meaning "arroyo verde."

The next wash is Las Víboras—"the vipers," hardly an enticement to walk
there. Its sandy bed is still corrugated from the last runoff. The water table
beneath these creeks rises quickly but sinks slowly, so the sand remains
damp sometimes for several months after a rain, allowing cultivation alongside their banks which is not possible elsewhere. Cattle tend to congregate
in the shade of the trees flanking a streambed, their manure adding concentrated nutrients, which flow downstream when it rains as a kind of natural
fertilizer. E. W. Nelson, who led a scientific expedition here in 1906, noticed
that

> Most of these streams flow permanently within their canyons, but during the
> dry season the smaller ones sink in the sand on reaching the border of the val-
> ley. At flood any one of them may increase to a roaring torrent down the steep
> canyon bottoms transporting great quantities of bowlders [*sic*], so that the
> broad stream beds, often 100 yards or more wide, are often covered with
> tumbled masses of water-worn rocks that in places render passage on horse-
> back impossible.

The *ramal* veers off to Santiago. The Jesuits established a mission here in
1723, which was abandoned in 1734 after the Indians rebelled and viciously
murdered the padre. No further crisis occurred until 1869, when the J. Ross
Browne expedition arrived just in time to miss a local revolution. The geologist for the expedition, William Gabb, reported that Pedro Magaña Navarette
and Antonio Pedrín were contending for the right to govern the peninsula.
Navarette held Santiago, not intending to give in to Pedrín who was expected from San José to replace him. When Pedrín arrived, Santiago became

> the scene of the decisive fight between the rival candidates for governorship
> in the last revolution, that took place before our visit. Navarette, the incum-

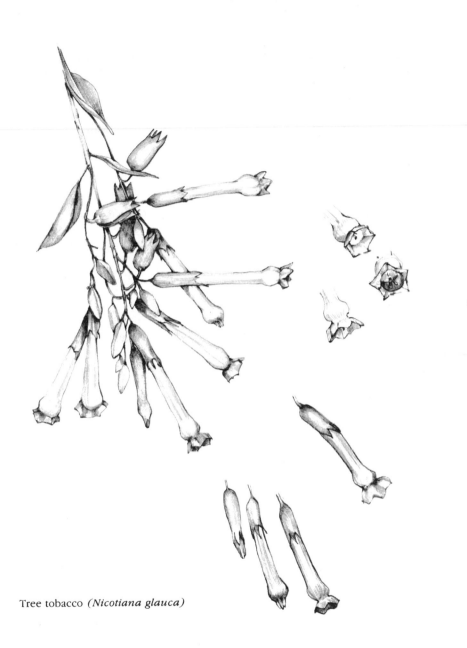

Tree tobacco *(Nicotiana glauca)*

bent, occupied with his forces the edge of the mesa on one side, and Pedrin, the aspirant, held the other side. They were at farthest not more than a third of a mile apart, and consequently there was some risk in exposing one's self outside the friendly cover of the houses and walls. The fight was kept up for two or three days—one man at a time peeping out from his shelter and, with fear and trembling, pulling the trigger of the flintlock with which he is armed. Each party being more anxious to protect itself than to injure the other, the battle might have continued a month, had it not been brought to a sudden conclusion by one of Pedrin's men crawling through the canes in the bottom, so near two men of the opposite party that he succeeded in killing both without being hurt himself. Navarette's party considered this as being a little more than they bargained for; they were perfectly willing to kill, but had no desire to be killed, so that as soon as the news of the death of their two comrades reached them, they became demoralized and fled in disorder, leaving Pedrin in possession of the field and of the government.

The road cuts between fields of sugar cane, lined by palms, then winds up the mesa side until we look down on all the fields. The Santiago valley lies verdant, exceptionally so from recent rains. It slopes gradually downward to the Sea of Cortés, topped with alluvial materials eroded from the nearby mountains that overlie the essentially marine-fossil-bearing deposits. In 1894, when Gustav Eisen was here, he found a permanent lake half a mile long and an eighth mile wide, which never dried up and whose waters supplied crop irrigation; it no longer exists. In 1960 the population was six hundred, and one of the main crops was sugar cane; once a sugar mill ran here, making panocha, a kind of brown-sugar candy.

At the gate to the airstrip, on which the race will be held, there are many policemen, every single one sharply dressed: crisp-pressed mustard-colored shirts, sharp-creased brown trousers with mustard stripes, ten-gallon hats. Many are armed enough to handle a major riot! A sign requires 150 pesos to enter. We are only charged 100 pesos. José asks why. The ticket taker replies, because there will be "solamente una raza"—not the usual two races.

Down the middle of the runway, covered with a thin layer of sand, two fences define the race course. The metal posts with tight-strung barbed wire are far more substantial than any farm fence. Policemen and ranchers stand at the fence; the women cluster in front of the cars and trucks that are parked twenty feet back. On one side beer and soft drinks are being sold; a band, composed of saxophone, guitar, and amplifier, caterwauls at full volume.

Only two horses run in each race. Keen rivalries exist between ranches, sometimes lasting for years, with many horses racing until they are thirteen, fourteen, fifteen years old. If a rancher thinks he has a good horse, he begins to train him and will perhaps begin racing him at three years. And if his neighbor thinks he has a better horse, there is a challenge. Generally a race is between very well-matched horses. Of course the race is much more than a race. It's a chance to see your neighbors, to brag a little, show off your fine horse, show dignity in defeat and honor in winning. For the women, it provides a chance to see each other and talk, and for everyone, a time of getting together that makes up for days of isolation.

Betting is spirited, albeit casual. As José describes it, someone just comes up to you, asks, "What horse you for?" A third party keeps the money for the two bettors, and José is the kind of man everybody trusts so often gets asked to hold bets. Nothing is written down, and no one ever reneges on a bet. "He does it only once," says José, "only once." The betting is so friendly that José claims that once he had to go look for the man who had won the bet he was holding, adding, "They trust you here." Then why so many deputies? "Oh," says José, grinning, "*every*body enjoys a horse race!"

The two horses prance back and forth, make practice starts, turn on a dime, the young riders showing off the horses. One rides with just a blanket, the other bareback. A strap about four inches wide is tied around the horse's girth and under this the rider slips his knees. One rider wears spurs. There are no stirrups, and only a rope halter.

There will be but one race this afternoon, and all attention centers on the two horses. One is a local favorite, *el caballo rojo*—"the red horse"—owned by a Santiago rancher. The other horse comes from a ranch about twenty miles away near Las Cuevas, a splotchy tan, gray, and white mare called La Loba because she is the color of a female wolf. Her small-boned rider wears dark red jeans and a white T-shirt and looks exactly like a teen-age Errol Flynn. He sports a thin mustache and a fierce scowl to make himself look older, well aware that he is the outlander here, the honor of the ranch resting on his shoulders.

The starting gate has no gate, simply uprights forming two portals. A horse race starts somewhat like a sailing race: everyone gets moderately into position and then the starter fires the gun. Here the jockeys bring the horses into the line together to "present" them, and the two gate judges yell "GO!" in unison. If they don't yell together, it is not a valid start. Today, the jockey of the red horse does not appear to hear the command and is late out of the gate. "Bad start," agree Herman and José, shaking their heads in the way of wise and judicious men. But the judges think it a fair start, and nobody argues with the judges. The three-hundred-meter course is run and the race over in seconds. At the finish line a judge on either side holds a rope strung between the last two fenceposts. The first judge to feel the rope pulled from his hand declares the horse on his side the winner. He calls out "La Loba!"

The young jockey is so proud he prances his horse. To come as a stranger here and to win is a triumph. He dismounts and holds himself very straight as he stands by his horse. The horse's owner, almost half again as tall as the jockey, comes over to congratulate him; he smiles only slightly, as befits his greater age and position. The jockey searches for his dignity and does not find it. In spite of himself, the fierce young face breaks into a radiant smile. He may never again be so proud as he is this moment.

Going home we detour through Caduaño, poor in comparison to Santiago. A decade ago students came here to suggest ways to help it economically, such as bee raising. In one field cows wander around hundreds of small wild plum trees, planted, José conjectures, as an agricultural experiment. Posters of Zapata and Che Guevera are nailed on a big tree.

Driving south, we parallel the east flank of the Sierra de la Victoria, ridge lines softened by the blue haze of a hot summer evening. Light rays shaft through the clouds, spotlighting the shining peak of San Lázaro. The road tops a rise and I look out eastward over the jumbled land, faulted and eroded, the quirking tan arroyos always disappearing in a tangle of landscape, those secretive arroyos that hold the messages of an ancient sea, and in the seeping darkness the land becomes those murky shallows that came and went.

On a hillside, dozens of plumeria bloom after the summer rains. Called by the residents frangipani or by a corruption of the old Aztec name, *cacalosúchil,* their leaves scarcely unfurl, but the branch tips are extravagantly flowered with huge white yellow-throated trumpets that mist their heavy fragrance into the air. The white flowers luminesce in the evening light, the spirits of ancient whitecaps, returning to claim their own.

III
TOWNS

I turned my mule for a last quiet look at San José del Arroyo. It was in those times a small village of under three hundred souls, and so near the ocean as our chubascos *permitted—for at times these winter storms lifted the sea and thrust it bodily over dry land. But to shelter our church God had placed a great mountain flank, jutting out into our valley and half-closing it; so that in the flat beyond stood both church and village, with a thousand-foot shoulder of hard rock between them and the sea storms.*

Through our valley murmured a little stream, which ended in a half-salt lagoon held back by sand-banks which only great flood or more resistless tornadoes could tear away. On one side, above all cultivated land, lay our zanja, *full always with clean water of a bathing temperature; ready, as the padres had taught us, to baptize the soil and bring forth proper harvests, God willing, in their season. Below, fertile acres covered with fruit trees and with that sweet cane from which* panocha *was made.*

Antonio de Fierro Blanco (Walter Nordhoff)
The Journey of the Flame
1933

Morning-glory *(Ipomaea pes-caprae)*

SAN JOSÉ

The population centers of Baja California Sur cluster on the seacoast—
La Paz, San José del Cabo, San Lucas, Todos Santos. Driving into San José del
Cabo, David Yee stops for gas. We wait in line. There is always a line since
there is only a single Pemex station, the label under which government-
controlled Petroles Mexicanos markets gas. There is another station in San
Lucas, and none between. So whenever one is in either, the first order of
business is to fill up.

Present-day San José is the third and what looks to be final settlement of
the second-largest town on the Cape, La Paz being the largest. In 1730, for
political as well as religious reasons, the Jesuit Padre Nicolás Tamaral and
another missionary established the original San José, the first mission on the
Cape. The Spanish galleons needed a protected harbor and way station before the home port of Acapulco, to ease the long difficult voyage. The fathers
built a church and a missionary's shelter right on the beach adjacent to what
is now the cemetery, at what is still called La Misión.

Because the area turned out to be unhealthy—the adjacent freshwater
lagoon breeds mosquitoes that call in for landing instructions, and the beach
is badly exposed to heavy storms—the settlement was moved around 1753

about five miles back from the sea to what is now called San José Viejo, where Tamaral built another church. The present and third San José grew up between the two on a site of 12,000 hectares given it by the federal government. San José was named after Don José de la Puente y Peña, Marques de Villapuente, who encouraged colonization on the southern peninsula by financing the mission; "del Cabo" was added to separate it from other San Josés.

Surrounding San José's 12,000 hectares was *ejido* land, of which 1,449 were "sold" to CoReTT, then passed to FoNaTur, another government agency—*Fondo Nacional de Fomento del Turismo*. The government-acquired hectares lie on the shoreside of town, and are being developed by FoNaTur. As a part of this development, a Mexican chain of hotels, part private, part federal, just opened a big hotel right on the beach, beside the lagoon of San José. Since the Baja California peninsula is essentially without mineable minerals (the silver mines at El Triunfo have long since been closed) and sufficient acreage for export farming, its greatest asset is a felicitous climate, and tourism is by far the largest industry on the Cape.

Poinsettias and jacaranda trees bloom profusely in the dooryards of San José. That combination of scarlet poinsettias, orange jacaranda, and magenta periwinkles and San Miguelito, with salmon bougainvillaea, create splendid vibrating juxtapositions of color. Joel Poinsett of South Carolina was the first envoy to Mexico from North America; he arrived in 1825 carrying the United States proposal to buy Texas, naturally most unpopular in Mexico. He took home with him not success but a colorful plant, *flor de nochebuena,* which he christened after himself.

Three-inch strips laid with pebbles are set between the squares of cement on the sidewalk. A quiet street marked Via de Mijares enters the plaza. It was not so peaceful scarcely a century and a half ago when Lieutenant José Antonio Mijares became a hero in the war between Mexico and the United States.

Secretary of State Daniel Webster, by some Machiavellian reasoning, proposed to lend Mexico $20 million so that she could then pay off her debts to England; for security the United States would get a first mortgage on Lower California as well as parts of northern Mexico. The proposition died a timely death. Webster resigned in 1843, and was replaced by John C. Calhoun, a former Vice-President, and an even more enthusiastic advocate of acquisition. The idea of uniting the two Californias was one that avaricious expansionist interests couldn't leave alone. Not only did the United States covet Alta but Baja California as well. Pressed by increasing migration to the West, and a certain uneasiness as to British intentions, some interests saw in the induction of California into the United States a solution to many problems.

When James Knox Polk came to office, he sent an emissary to Mexico with an offer of $40 million. When the Mexican government refused to receive the envoy, Polk used it as an excuse to declare war in 1846.

That July an American warship took command first of Monterey, then San Francisco and San Diego; all were declared to be United States territory. A strict blockade of the Mexican coast southward was established, and American ships sailed into La Paz. There the governor, Francisco Palacio Colonel Miranda, capitulated, fearing harm to the townspeople.

But the rest of a determined population, despite Palacio Miranda's position, decided to defend their native soil. When the U.S.S. *Portsmouth* appeared in San José harbor in March, 1847, the commander went ashore, raised the United States flag, and urged the residents to be peaceful; by July a contingent of volunteers had arrived at La Paz to secure the situation. Meanwhile, resistance was being organized in the peninsula, and when an American ship under false colors sailed into Mulegé, it was repulsed by the Mexican forces. Encouraged, the defenders split into two parties, one to unseat the Americans at La Paz, the other to go to San José.

In San José the American flag was torn down and all American civilians were expelled. The commander of still another American ship, attempting to calm the rebellion, left a contingent with one month's supplies holed up in San José. At the end of the month the officer in charge ignored demands from the aroused patriots to surrender. The siege, the relief of the siege, the resumption of the siege, went on for months. Lieutenant José Antonio Mijares heroically tried to storm the American position and was killed.

To end the conflict, the United States proposed keeping all of California, with a boundary smack down the middle of the Gulf of California. Mexico refused, making a counter proposal to cede Upper California north of the 37th parallel, and to retain Lower California:

> The cession of Lower California, of little importance to the Republic of North America, offers great embarrassment to Mexico, considering the position of that Peninsula, facing our coast of Sonora, which is separated from it by the narrow Gulf of Cortéz. It will suffice that Mexico would preserve Lower California, as it is necessary to have a part of Upper California, since otherwise the Peninsula would be without communication by land with the rest of the Republic.

On February 2, 1848, the war ended with the signing of the Treaty of Guadalupe Hidalgo. Article five ensured Mexican possession of Baja California and established an enduring border between the United States and Mexico.

But border problems did not end. In 1853–54 filibusters again attempted, without government support, to take Mexican territory in the name of the United States—*filibustero* is a Spanish word for a freebooter and plunderer. One Captain William Walker fitted out a brig, ostensibly to "explore" the peninsula, sailed with two hundred men, reaching Cabo San Lucas in October, then went on to La Paz and captured the city, where he proclaimed himself "William Walker, Colonel and President of Lower California." When he returned to the States, he was tried for abrogating neutrality laws and quickly acquitted, to the cheers of the California newspapers, indicating the sentiments of the times. He was killed on a like venture in Nicaragua.

Bad ideas die hard. Twenty years later, Captain John F. Janes, who described himself as "ex-sailor, ex-miner, ex-explorer, and ex-ward politician," set his sights on Baja California. He visited San José del Cabo in 1874, his stay convincing him that Baja California should belong to the United States, because it commanded "every line of trade." By 1884 he was haranguing:

> I hope to see the day when Southern California will become a state and Los Angeles the capital, and her government buildings the pride of her people, and Lower California will be to her what Los Angeles county is to California to-day. Lower California we must have; it belongs naturally to Alta-California. The United States must own the Peninsula as a protection against invasion, to reach from the Rio Grande to the Colorado River . . . Cape San Lucas, La Paz and Magdalena Bay, under the American government will secure us from invaders in case of war. The Peninsula in the hands of the Mexican government is worthless to them, and always will be. Her mountains and canyons are full of wealth, her valleys fertile, and only want American push and capital to show her natural resources. The government of this country must buy it, or we will have to take it for our own protection. Buy it if we can, if not we must take it.

All these ugly efforts came to naught, and their signal lack of success discouraged other parties from attempting the same.

David suggests that we stop at the Casa de la Cultura to see if there are any books that might be of use to me. Every town of any size enjoys a *casa de la cultura,* which may range from a treasure house of local lore and artifacts to a banal collection of modern "crafts," many of which are more plastic than indigenous.

In San José, a room approximately twenty by twenty feet has been set aside for the library and walled with bookshelves. The librarian talks eagerly of the town's history and its library. He shows me first Pablo Martínez's *A History of Lower California,* a source of great pride since Martínez came from San José. Books are filed according to category. I scan some of the titles, catching only those with big letters on the spines: A Spanish edition of *Los Miserables* in two volumes, *Santa Biblia, La Evolución de México,* many history books, *Entre la Cruz y la Flecha,* Bancroft's works on California and Mexican history, *A Tale of Two Cities, Fundamentos de Biología.* Before we leave we both sign the guest book.

As we walk through the town plaza, many workmen are involved in painting and refurbishing the City Hall. David tells me that they are readying for the celebration of San José's 250th anniversary, March 19–April 8, 1980, and I should really meet the mayor, who is the driving force behind it.

No sooner said than done, for the mayor is just climbing out of his light blue Jeep Wagoneer. David introduces me and mentions Harper & Row, and tells the mayor what I'm interested in; I notice that to each person he introduces me he tailors the description to fit the situation with a nicety of judgment and courtesy. The mayor immediately invites us to his office; on the walls are framed copies of *Acta de Independencia 1821 Pronunciada por su Junta Soberanía.* He stands very straight, balanced slightly forward, and speaks with the authority of a man used to being in command. His battle-jacketed navy blue suit goes well with his steel gray hair. In Baja California, mayors are elected for one term only; there are only four towns in Baja Sur with mayors, the *municipios* of La Paz, San José del Cabo, Comondú and Mulegé.

He launches, with great verve and enthusiastic gestures, into plans for the forthcoming celebration. He has collected old photographs of life in San José dating from around the turn of the century, had them blown up to twenty by thirty inches, mounted and labeled. They portray a far more formal San José than the one we see out the window today.

A picture of 1900 shows the El Mouno mill, where brown sugar was refined. (The old chimney still stands, close by the lighthouse.) In 1907 the first kerosene street lights are lit with proper ceremony; in 1912 the first steam pump brings water to San José, standing next to where the Casa de la Cultura stands now. A hurricane demolished the first Jesuit church in 1918, but its façade is preserved in a print. In 1927 the first road opens between San José and San Lucas, a very narrow single lane hanging precipitously on the hillside. The pilot, complete with goggles and white scarf, stands beside the first biplane to land here in 1929. The decade following 1920 saw the harbor visited by big ships with names like *Bolívar* and *Ángel* which carried cattle and tomatoes to the United States. In 1930 the first Ford dealer in San

José puts his hand proudly on the hood of his *Modelo "A"*—San José had one of the first dealerships in Baja California because it was one of the few places that could receive cars shipped by sea. (Now it has the highest number of cars per capita, save Mexico City, in all of Mexico.)

Several photographs show people arrayed on the plaza—men in black coats and ties and hats, ladies in becoming picture hats and starched ruffles. A charming group of schoolteachers sit primly posed, wearing long white dresses with leg-o'-mutton sleeves—schoolteachers then could only be unmarried women. In a 1923 picture flowers bedeck a car for carnival; its occupants face the camera with obvious pride and dignity. I remark upon this.

The mayor sighs heavily. He bemoans the lack of community pride and speaks of the value of the old ways—not that we should return to them, but that they had something to offer, that we have lost the spirit of doing things together. "Now it's all *dinero,*" he says.

He points out his wife in a 1930 parade picture. "Muy bonita," I say of her, to which he answers, *"Fue"*-was. Which I do *not* think is gentlemanly at all.

We leave the mayor's office and come out into the plaza behind the new City Hall, fronting the main church of San José, built in the 1940s. A mosaic in the lunette over the doorway commemorates the martyrdom of Father Tamaral in the rebellion of 1734, a few eloquent tiles portraying the whole bitter brutal history of Jesuit settlement and failure.

The Jesuits had been on the Mexican mainland since 1572, and they had had great success in proselytizing, but not until 125 years later did they come to the peninsula. They applied for, and in 1697 received, a license from Don Joseph de Sarmiento y Valladares to enter California that read:

> For the present I grant the license that the said padres Juan María de Salvatierra and Eusebio Franciso Quino of the Company of Jesus have asked for, covering permission to enter the provinces of California for conversion of the gentiles of those places to the society of our sacred Catholic faith; under the conditions that without the order of His Majesty they cannot engage in nor expend anything of the royal hacienda in this conquest, which is an express condition of this acceptance.

On February 6, 1697, Fathers Juan de Salvatierra and Eusebio Kino sailed for the peninsula to establish the first mission at Loreto, about a third of the way up the Gulf coast. From here Jesuits went out to explore the peninsula, and Father Kino, journeying northward from Sonora, established once and for all that the peninsula was just that, an unbroken strip of land attached to the main mass of the continent, not an island.

Late in the seventeenth century the Jesuits established the "Pious Fund" when it became obvious that they could not be self-supporting and would be forced to depend on donations. The Jesuits managed to survive through gifts from the faithful, such as Marqués and Marquesa de Villapuente, who left all their wealth "to be employed in the conversion of the indigenes of the Peninsula."

All told, the Jesuits founded eighteen mission settlements joined by a network of trails. They were an extraordinary group of men, well educated and trained, devoted and dedicated, and on this barren peninsula not subject to the excesses and temptations of life on the continent. The writings of the fathers who were here—Miguel del Barco, Jakob Baegert, Wenceslaus Linck, Norberto Ducrue, Luis de Sales (who was a Dominican)—are the accounts of perceptive observers of customs and language. They recorded their perceptions of an alien landscape, of political and judicial tribulations, as well as cures for snakebite, loss of innocence, and failure.

In this land, totally lacking in both skilled labor and abundant timber, they began building with branches, then adobe, and finally created impressive stone churches. They imported horses, which the Indians called "large deer." They developed mail routes between missions which became today's roads. They were the first farmers, who with herculean effort raised figs and olives and developed irrigation systems from the meager springs they found, sufficient only to water small fields. They introduced date palms in 1730, grapes in 1732. Now called *dátil* locally, date palms flourish wherever there is water. But they were never able to raise enough food for both themselves and their converts. As a consequence, only some of the Indians were permanent residents, supplying labor to the mission; the rest lived as wild as they always had, coming into the mission monthly and for big religious holidays for what one writer has described as "an intensive refresher course in Christianity."

When the crew of the Manila galleon, in extreme distress with but a few days' water left, stumbled upon the harbor at San José del Cabo in 1733, they found the mission established by Father Tamaral. Tamaral sent not only water but fresh meat and fruit, including *pitahaya,* which cured the cases of scurvy on board. When they reached the mainland, no one believed anyone in such good health could just have endured that voyage. The captain petitioned the viceroy to direct all returning ships to stop at San José for relief.

Father Tamaral had been modestly successful in his relations with the natives and many of them came to church. But the Pericu of the southern peninsula were much more reluctant than the tribes to the north to accept Christianity, resentful of the Church's interference in their patterns of living—they were polygamists and liked neither the curtailment of their freedom nor being publicly reprimanded for it. Their *guamas*—witch doctors—detested the new doctrines and smoldered at their loss of prerogative.

By 1733 four missions had been established in the Cape, with several thousand Indians, three priests, but only six soldiers for protection—one at La Paz, two in Santiago, three in Todos Santos. No garrison at all was stationed in San José del Cabo. The situation at that isolated mission was therefore more tenuous and precarious than any of the others. The first rebellion was fomented in Santiago, plotted by two Indians and the native governor. The padres were warned of the plot and negotiated a peace of sorts, only to have the plot erupt again in 1734.

When Father Carranco of Santiago was apprised of the conspiracy, he warned Tamaral at San José to abandon his mission. Tamaral refused, saying fears were born of cowardice. The rebels struck first at Santiago, finding Father Carranco at mass. They dragged him outside and shot him full of arrows. When he fell to the ground, they beat him with sticks and stones. Infuriated at his pious acceptance of his death, they derobed and defiled his body. They saw the lad who served him weeping, so they took him by the feet and swung him against the walls and rocks until they smashed his head open. They built a bonfire upon which they threw the bodies, feeding it with the holy objects of the church.

That was October 1. Father Tamaral was attacked and killed October 3. Indians forced their way into the mission, asking for unreasonable gifts, hoping to use Tamaral's refusal as an excuse to attack him. He tried to pacify them by offering them whatever they needed that was in the mission. But to no avail: the same Indians who had murdered Carranco hacked off Tamaral's head.

The next galleon that stopped for water at the end of its trip in 1734 found that the mission was closed, Tamaral murdered. The Indians captured and killed all the sick in the crew but nevertheless contracted the disease the ship carried and "developed putrid ulcers which appeared on the genital parts"—syphilis.

The other two missions on the Cape closed, and twenty-five years later the Jesuits were banished from the peninsula. Intrigue, complete with false letters and political machinations, persuaded Charles III of Spain to order them to abandon their missions. They were charged with accumulating great wealth on the peninsula (estimates ranged from $12 to $60 million!), of exploiting the natives by using them as slaves. Charles sent strict orders to the viceroy in Mexico that the priests were to take nothing but a few books and "If after embarkation there is found in any district a single Jesuit, even if sick or in pain, you will be condemned to death."

On February 3, 1768, the remaining Jesuits assembled for the last time at Loreto, where they had landed a century and a third before. The Franciscans reluctantly replaced them, but were equally unsuccessful. The expulsion of the Jesuits left the Indians with contempt for men of the cloth. The Franciscans had jurisdiction only over religious matters; temporal matters were handled by government troops reluctant to enforce discipline. The missions fell into ruin. At the end of five years the Franciscans left without a backward glance, holding mass to give thanks for their deliverance.

In 1772, Charles signed a concordat giving the whole peninsula to the Dominicans, who served from 1773 until 1790 with the same results. The local governor accused them of pilfering and stealing. Within a score of years syphilis spread by soldiers had decimated the Indians, and with the Indians gone, the missions lost their purpose. Years of deteriorating relations between church and local government culminated in 1833 in the Secularization Act; however it did not affect Dominican Missions of Baja California

Ground cherry *(Physalis glabra)*

Lagoon at San José del Cabo

which were considered the only vestiges of civilization. In 1857 strict separation between church and state was written into the Mexican constitution.

The lagoon at San José is still the only place along the whole southern coast where fresh water can be easily obtained, and it early earned the epithet of Aguada Segura—"secure watering place"—applied to any place where ships could count on replenishing their water supplies. In 1776, Captain George Shelvocke, an English privateer, described how to identify the bay:

> The watering place is on the *North* side, in a small river, which empties itself through the sand into the sea; this will be conspicuous from the ship, by the appearance of the green hollow canes which grow in it, which the Locusts do not touch. This water is excellent for sea service; in short, the Port in general is very convenient for such as may have occasion to lay in wait for the *Manila* ship, or lie for some time conceal'd after the coasts have been throughly [*sic*] alarm'd.

A berm of sand divides the lagoon from the sea. During the rainy season the berm used to break through on its own, but now, at least monthly, a channel is bulldozed through the sand to let the lagoon drain, both to keep down the mosquito population and to prevent the lagoon from backing up and flooding portions of San José.

In times past, before the underground river was so heavily tapped for agriculture, there was much greater flow into the ocean. Eisen wrote at the end of the last century:

> During the rainy season most of these tributaries are real torrents, sweeping everything before them, while in the winter time they may dwindle down to a mere seeping underflow, here and there rising to the surface. These combined underflows are sufficient to make quite a showing at the mouth of the river, where in the month of March I found at one time 500 cubic feet of water running to waste into the ocean. In very dry seasons this waste is, of course, less, while in the time of the rains the river swells enormously, and for days may be a mile wide and impassable for weeks.

Today the marker poles stand well out of water. Typical sand-dune flowers snake along the ground—the thick branches of wild morning glory, lavender flowers gone, replaced by spherical seed pods. Rough prickly beach grasses, ground cherry, and heliotrope with the ubiquitous spurges lie half-buried in the sand, along with the usual amaranths, nutritious plants in times past well utilized by the Indians. Privateer Edward Cooke wrote in 1712:

> A very small black Seed they grind upon Stones they have for that Purpose, and then eat it by Handfuls; my Men us'd to thicken their Broth with it, and said it serv'd as well as Flower. When ground, and boil'd in Water, it tastes somewhat like Coffee.

At the edge of the lagoon palm trees rise lush and tall and green, and seven-foot-high rushes march out into the water. Many ducks ply the lagoon, mostly female lesser scaups, against whose dark plumage the bills are startlingly light. These are ducks I've not seen before ever and I think of Walter Bryant's comment:

> San José del Cabo is a nearly perfect ornithological collecting locality, in fact it is the best place I have ever visited; first, the tropical situation makes it a desirable change to the collector accustomed to a cooler climate. Then the long stretch of sandy beach along the ocean must be suited to many shore birds, although during the weeks that I was there but few birds were found upon the shore, large and small ones alike preferring the brackish water of the lagoon or the sandy or grassy banks of the running stream just above. On the lagoon the ducks were arriving from the north, and cormorants were fattening upon the many small fishes.

A frigate bird skims the water, rises, circles, and skims again, as Bryant saw them feeding a hundred years ago,

> picking food from the water, they scarcely disturb the surface: descending airily, the object is taken in passing in such a manner that at the moment of seizure, the bird's head is bent under, then quickly throwing the head upwards, they rise again, silent and graceful.

They're more often seen high in the air, easily identified by silhouette of crooked wing, long forked tail (Mexicans call them *tijeras*—scissors), and unflapping wings, like some cutout bird rotating against a blue backdrop.

I stand on the lagoon side looking upward to a living frieze of gulls on the berm's rim: white throats, gray spotted breasts, pink legs, dark tails, white beaks with black tips—second-year herring gulls and some ring-billed and mature herring gulls. All face southeast, the direction from which the wind blows. They stand in all attitudes: one-legged, two-legged, head tucked under one wing. There is much sideways shaking of tails. Those at the outer edges are constantly moving, taking off and circling low, returning to a different place in the hierarchy—for all the stability of the frieze it is as restless as a honeycomb of bees.

The boom of the hidden surf pulses over the berm. I trudge up the sand and look over: the weight of the tumbling wave shakes the ground, falling like the wall of a demolished building. The water is yellowed with churned-up sand. The waves rush up and retreat with a hiss. The amount of beach sand here, enclosed by its flanking headlands, remains largely constant, the

Morning-glory *(Ipomaea pes-caprae)*

beach changing little other than steepening and narrowing when winter brings high surf, broadening under the gentle seas of summer. Essentially the sand is transferred to underwater bars during the winter and carried back to the berm during the summer, a continual exchange without much loss or gain in volume.

The large open bay, almost ten miles from end to end, is anchored by rocky headlands. I find it hard to imagine how small boats came in through this surf when San José was a major landing port. Benjamin Franklin Elliott, a preacher who wrote a little pamphlet called *Lower California—1917,* extolled the infinite green virtues of the peninsula, but even he was less than enthusiastic about landing at San José:

> It is situated on a cove at the end of the Peninsula on the east side. The sea is
> very heavy and landing is quite dangerous. It is done by means of small boats,
> mostly dugouts. These are rushed through the breakers on to the beach.

Palmer sand-bur *(Cenchrus palmeri)*

More precise was the description of the Dominican Luis de Sales in 1794:

> The bay of San José, open from the south around to the N.N.E., is very dangerous when in bad weather the wind blows from that quarter, the holding quality of the bottom being unsure and the anchorage so close to the shore that it would not be possible to get under sail with an on-shore wind. From this it follows that the bay ought to be used only from the end of November until May, the season of west and N.W. winds and good weather on all the gulf coast and also on that of Mexico. In fact it is during this season of the year that it is visited by the whalers and merchant ships which keep up commercial relations with Lower California.

During some months, the surf was too high and landings had to be made toward the west at La Palmilla, or even La Paz. The explorer Vizcaíno was detained here almost a month in the summer of 1602, forced back by high winds three times and then, as a final insult, becalmed.

In 1769 the first scientific expedition to Lower California was mounted and financed by the Spanish government in order to observe the passage of Venus across the sun. Although the English were eager to come to the Cape, relations between England and Spain were so poor that Charles III, who had just ejected the Jesuits from the peninsula, invited instead a Frenchman, Abbot Jean Chappe d'Auteroche, to be chief of the expedition. Chappe d'Auteroche was a Renaissance man—engineer, and geographer, watchmaker, alumnus of the French Academy of Painting and well-qualified for this task, having previously observed an eclipse in 1761 in Russia. Baja California was chosen as one of the widely separated stations from which to make time measurements, the coordination of which would give the sun's diameter more accurately than previously known. That one of the aims of Captain James Cook's first voyage was to set up an observation station in Tahiti underlines the importance attached to this eclipse.

Because of the unexpected slowness of the scientists' voyage across the Atlantic, provisions ran low and the Abbot wrote that

> we were obliged to stint ourselves to a pint a day, and even this was detestable water, having been put into vinegar casks. All these trifles would have been nothing, could we have flattered ourselves with some gleam of hope. We were in the 25th day of our passage, and only eighteen remained to the transit, and we were yet a great way from the place of our destination.

They landed on the east coast of Mexico and crossed to the west where they again embarked. When they cast anchor at San José del Cabo May 19, 1769, they blundered into one of the periodic epidemics that had ravaged the peninsula since the arrival of the Spaniards. But they were now weeks behind schedule. The Spanish wanted to go on to San Lucas in order to avoid exposure to the disease, and with good reason—several were to lose their lives here. But the abbot, afraid time was running out, insisted on remaining at San José del Cabo, less concerned about sickness than about losing precious time, feeling "confident his Catholic Majesty had rather lose a poor little pitiful vessel, than the fruits of so important an expedition as ours," and "would not stir from San Joseph, let the consequence be what it would." His adamantine set of mind jeopardized not only himself but other members of the expedition. At San José most of the expedition remained.

Chappe d'Auteroche's first concern was getting his instruments ashore safely. The first boats bucked through the surf and landed dry. Encouraged, the astronomer sent some of his boxed instruments on the second trip. The distressing report came back from shore:

> Mr. Pauly [his assistant] wrote me word from the water-side that they had been in great danger, the boat having been several times under water, but happily they came off with no other harm than their fright, and being very wet, as were all the chests. This last circumstance made me extremely cautious in removing my clock, which I had kept by me, and for which I dreaded the sea water. I therefore wrapped it up very close, and sat down upon it myself, to keep it dry in case the waves should chance to wash us.

Clock and astronomer landed without mishap. After weeks of worry about arriving too late, tension about getting his instruments safely to shore, certainly overfatigued and under stress, the abbot chose to sleep on the beach that night and to walk into the village the next morning. Sitting there on the sand, under the stars he knew so well, he put into words that infinite sense of well-being and serenity that comes so often in life as a prelude to disaster, as if whom the gods would destroy they first make serene. Looking over his shoulder as he writes, it breaks my heart because I know the cost of his choice and know the end of the story:

> Then it was, that casting my eyes upon my instruments that lay all round me, and not one of them damaged in the least, revolving in my mind the vast extent of land and sea that I had so happily compassed, and chiefly reflecting that I had still time enough before me, fully to prepare for my intended observation, I felt such a torrent of joy and satisfaction, it is impossible to express, so as to convey an adequate idea of my sensation.

The next day he set up his instruments in a large barn and on June 3rd he made his entry:

> The weather favoured me to my utmost wish. I had full time to make accurate and repeated observations for the setting of my clock. At last came the third of June, and I had an opportunity of making a most complete observation.

When his observations were published in 1778, they were the most accurate of all those made. On June 5th he took ill. On August 1, after much suffering, he was dead of typhus.

No stream runs from the adjoining high Sierras, but the water rises from the earth and is carried round about in irrigating ditches, so that a lowland two by three miles in area is watered, remains green and is a veritable oasis in the uninhabitable surrounding region. This tract is divided into small farms, separated from each other by dense hedges, six to fifteen feet high, composed of the native plants, and the paths or trails (there are no wheeled vehicles in the region) are bordered on both sides by these high walls of vegetable growth. . . . In the town nothing grows, and the whole surrounding region has a dry, sun-burned look, excepting during the rainy season; so that the view of the lower irrigated ground, with its orange and guava trees, its bananas and coca palms, and the large sugarcane fields is heightened in effect by contrast with the dry, dormant, rain-awaiting upland vegetation.

Townshend Stith Brandegee
The Hedgerows of Todos Santos
1890

Cardón *(Pachycereus pringlei)*

TODOS SANTOS

Herman and I set out for Todos Santos with our old friend José Vallé and his wife, Lupé, who is shy as a doe and as charming. Todos Santos lies on the Pacific Coast, smack on the Tropic of Cancer. On the east coast a large cement ball by the highway marks it; on the west, nothing other than the town itself. We have known José for as long as we have been coming to the Cape; he has been a teacher and traveled widely, and now is building his new house in San Lucas, where he heads the dining-room service of a large hotel.

North out of San Lucas, the dirt road is lined with trash. The well-traveled paved roads here at the tip sparkle with beer cans and bottles. It is my contention that the motoring Mexican reads only the first line of the highway sign:

DEPOSITO DE BASURA

and ignores the second:

A 500 METROS

Trash dumps flank the road for several miles. Five cows graze in one. In another, bedsprings gone crazy. Debilitated refrigerators. Dead cars. I recall with nostalgia Joseph Wood Krutch's comment of just twenty years ago:

No doubt there is a small element of truth in the explanation advanced by a cynical friend to account for the absence of visible rubbish: the inhabitants of Baja are too poor to have anything to throw away. Not everything they buy comes swathed like a mummy in three or four layers of cardboard, paper, cellophane, and plastic to be thrown on the street or to be blown there from overflowing trash cans. Most Mexicans cannot afford bales of Kleenex which will later decorate the shrubbery along the roadsides. And if they acquire something in a can they are very likely to save the container to carry water in it if it is large enough or to serve as a flower pot if it isn't.

We pass the turnoff to Rancho Hong Kong. Rancho *Hong Kong?* José explains that there are many Chinese shopkeepers in San Lucas, as well as a few Oriental ranchers. This rancher, who is about forty or so, recently married a very young girl. José was one of the guests at the wedding party. It is a custom throughout the peninsula that the groom order a beer truck to come to the festivities, so that guests can buy cold beer. Being from the mainland, José thought it more proper to provide beer for everyone and did not follow the local custom when he got married.

A roadside sign reads "TOPES."

"Que es 'topes'?" I ask, just as we find out with a jolt. "Topes" are speed bumps, and turn up in the middle of nowhere if there's a school nearby.

A vulture feeds by the roadside; we stop to see what it's pulling at—an old rubber tire! José calls them *zopiloti*. Barco watched them soaring so high that he expected them to be out of sight any minute:

> Their flight is very calm, beating their wings only rarely, or from time to time. When they are soaring like that, they form great circles in their flight in order to discover with their acute vision if there is on the ground some dead body on which they can feed.

Soaring high also puts them into cooler air and among favorable updrafts, which they can ride with a minimum expenditure of energy. In gold-mining days Indian and Mexican miners stoppered the primary quills, and used them for storing gold dust, wearing them strung about their necks.

Kestrels perch on the cardóns, a fine vantage point from which to lift off and stoop on prey. These brightly colored small hawks, bluish gray, chestnut, and black and buff, are found throughout Lower California in fairly open country with hunting space. The genus name, *Falco,* comes from the Latin word for sickle, describing the hooked shape of their talons; *sparverius* refers to both the small size of this falcon and its common food. They nest in old woodpeckers' holes in cardón, choosing those high off the ground. They pad pre-excavated nest holes with plant materials on which the female lays creamy white eggs speckled with cinnamon.

For some time there was thought to be a subspecies, *F. s. peninsularis*, the San Lucan sparrow hawk, collected by Anthony Frazar and described by William Brewster, who pronounced them smaller and lighter-colored enough to be a separate form confined to the Cape Region. Time has shown, however, that as in many other instances with the flora and fauna of the Cape these are merely color variations without sufficient difference to mark them as either subspecies or variety.

The road to Candelaria, which must be one of the few towns on the peninsula not named for a saint, shoots off to the right and is too much of a temptation to pass up—even José has never been there before. The old road to Candelaria was built by hand and is being replaced by a new road built by roadscraper, back hoe, and surveyor's tape.

In Candelaria there are no light poles. No telephone poles. In fact, Candelaria is enough off the beaten path so that one wonders why a town is here. The answer lies in the palms and bamboo thickets arrayed along the hillside near the center of town: Arroyo de la Candelaria, which runs most of the year to the sea. The valley is terribly steep and narrow and stone walls ballast at least twelve terraces. Voices carry from across the valley, remote but clear. A rooster crows. Dragonflies career by, crisp wings shining. The stream bed below is deeply shaded, with giant reed grass and palms, thick with greenery. I hear the quiet intricate sounds of water running, and finally I glimpse it far below, twinkling over the rocks. The sound of it, so seldom heard this far inland, falls on the ear like a melody. Standing here above the arroyo, listening to the distant goat bells chime in gentle progressions, I feel as if I were watching a movie with the sound turned down, running a few frames too slow. It's too beautiful a place to be true.

We ask a man directions to the cemetery. He does not speak, merely points—up there! Is he being symbolic or giving directions? The cemetery is indeed "up there," above the town on a little bald knoll that looks out to the Pacific, under the stars, above the world.

The *panteón* rests on bare sunbitten ground. Many of the graves are raised because the soil is too hard to dig in, a factor Father Baegert had to contend with: "For this reason, I had the four walls of my cemetery filled in almost to the top with soil, to lessen the work of the grave diggers and to spare the iron tools."

Even though it must have been difficult to hoist the cement slabs up here, they cover many graves. Although headstone dates tell that funeral rites were many years past, many of the tombstones look as fresh as if just laid. Many Candelarians lived to be ninety years old—Candelaria must be a healthy place to live. Plastic flowers embellish nearly all of them, in eternal golden yellow, immortal magenta and everlasting turquoise, trumpets of color, making the *panteón* somehow a joyous place, in contrast to the gray and tan dwellings of the living. Small but elaborate shrines seem to be part of every grave, containing the figure of a saint, a votive candle, and flowers. Flowers are placed on graves on All Souls Day—*Día de Los Muertos,* early in November, and on Father's and Mother's Day, and Christmas, all days of ceremony and remembrance.

On this bare hilltop a wonderful almost tangible peace surrounds me. Protected by higher hills, yet open to the sun, it is a place of comfort for those who remain to light candles and say prayers and ask for sustenance for the soul and forgiveness for sins. And I, suspended here between earth and sun, feel the strength that arises from the soil and the peace that descends from the sky: *Descanse en paz.*

In another half hour, back on the main road, we crest the divide and stop to look to the Pacific. A roadrunner hustles across the road, such a pompous self-important bird—who is, or course, neither, but it amuses the watchers to find him so. *Correrocamino* is a swift runner capable of speeding along at between twelve and twenty miles per hour, although obviously it cannot keep up that pace for any distance.

On the west side of the mountains that divide the Cape, there *are* differences. Hard to put your finger on, but differences. For one thing, there's no Río San José cleaving a valley and providing irrigation, so farms are almost nonexistant except around an oasis or where farmers can tap into underground drainage from the high mountains. There is no main stream into which small ones feed, only small ones that make their way straight to the Pacific. For another, the mountains themselves are closer to the sea, more precipitous, more of a presence. There are no resorts on this side of the peninsula above San Lucas, for the Pacific's fierceness discourages even the most opportunistic of developers. Only surfers frequent the long Pacific beaches, and relatively few of them.

On this side of the divide there are fewer *palo blanco* trees and many many more cardóns. There is a subtle change in color: the hillsides have an olive-green rather than a gray-green sheen in the midmorning light. There seems to me to be less variety and more of a few species: cardón, organ-pipe cactus, elephant trees with fat contorted trunks and tangles of small branches. Looking for all the world like a big bird's nest, ball moss clots many of the larger plants, an epiphyte related to the pineapple, a non-parasite that gets its moisture and nutrients from the air. On the Pacific side, where mists sweep inland, ball moss thrives, its plumed seeds well carried by the wind.

As we descend, cardóns become more and more numerous, and more and more are in flower. *Cardo* is Spanish for thistle, and Ulloa, sailing for Cortés in 1540, uses it in his account of the peninsula, which was also referred to at one time as "Isla de Cardón." On old plants, the green trunk has

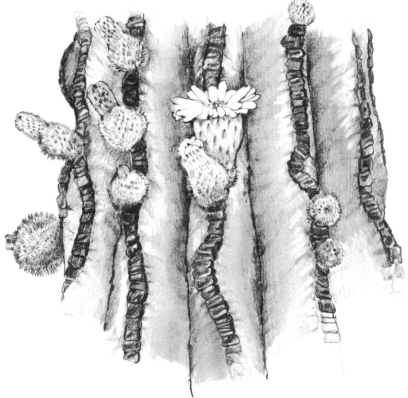

Cardón *(Pachycereus pringlei)*

133

faded to gray and the ribs have almost disappeared, so that they resemble nothing more than elephant legs—a forest of legs, without trunks, without tails, without ears—hence the *Pachy-* part of their genus name, *Pachycereus.* The blooms, each two or three inches across, are creamy white with a cool green cast and thick waxy petals. All pop out of the south side of the stalk in the most unlikely way, as if stuck on like doorknobs. The flowers are pollinated by bats, which, in the evening, arc from luminous flower to luminous flower. During the day, small beetles muck around in the pollen and no doubt transfer some to other flowers; every one I ever found seethed with tiny black flower beetles.

There are two species of cardón, most easily told apart by the difference of their fruit. *Pachycereus pringlei* (after its discoverer, the botanist Pringle) bears two-inch oval fruit with a brown furry covering containing a red pulp studded with black seeds—more seeds than flesh, actually. Barco describes the seeds as surrounded by a "viscous humor," so that there is little to eat, although he noted that the Indians toasted the seeds to keep them through the winter and they were much esteemed. The fruit of the other cardón, *Pachycereus pecten-arboriginum,* is covered with thick stout bristles, which were used, after drying, as combs by the Indians of the peninsula, therefore its specific name. It is slightly slenderer and smaller than *P. pringlei* and tends to be more southerly in its distribution.

If there is a plant family characteristic of Baja California it is the Cactus Family. With a high degree of adaptability, morphologically as well as physiologically, cacti have been able to grow successfully in this otherwise forbidding climate, and because of their adaptability there is a high degree of endemism; Dr. Wiggins estimates that some eighty species, making up 70.3 percent of the peninsula's cacti, are endemic.

Cacti from Baja California were first collected in 1839, by Richard Brinsley Hinds, the surgeon on the British survey ship H.M.S. *Sulphur,* who also served as botanist:

> We afterwards landed at Cape San Lucas, and not without profit. The *Cacteae* here, as elsewhere, were studiously sought after, and behind the raised beach is a fine array of trees, with all their singularity and interest. The afterpart of the vessel by this time presented a small forest of them, but though tended with much care, and with a due regard to their constitutions, they one by one pined and died during the subsequent voyage.

The collection was written up in 1844 by George Bentham, who labeled seventy-eight new species from Baja California alone.

Cardonales

Most of the cardóns along the road look as if every so often a string had been tied around the stem and drawn too tight. Since these are warm-climate plants, they are subject to frost damage. At the foot of mountain ridges, and on the Pacific side, momentary cold shocks may come from cold-air drainage as well as cold storms coming off the ocean, damaging tissue and momentarily halting growth.

When it rains, cacti are capable of storing large amounts of water in their pith and cortex. The very shallow root system extends horizontally within the top three inches of soil, able to absorb moisture over a large area. During a rain shower a cardón may absorb up to a ton of water, or 95 percent of its weight. Once the water is inside, the stem's thick waxy cuticle prevents it from evaporating. The stem's outer layer is packed with a thick layer of tissue, containing a large number of chloroplasts, enabling the stems to carry on photosynthesis.

Barco, that excellent observer, wrote that if a piece of cardón were mashed and wrung out, "liquor is obtained in great abundance. When this liquor is boiled and the foam is skimmed away, it becomes like a balsam, and it is surprisingly good to cure wounds and sores." However, Ducrue reported its use for toothache, and commented that "it does cause the teeth to fall out."

Without a deep anchoring tap root, cardóns are vulnerable to wind throw. Although the root system provides such efficient water uptake that few other plants grow within the perimeter of the roots' reach, they are seldom seen growing in solitary splendor. It has been suggested that the protection from upsetting winds achieved by growing closer together overrides the competition for water.

Providing support for all these trunks and stems, which average thirty feet in height, is a hardwood framework of vertical rods, which stiffen the ribs, a marvel of engineering, perforated with small holes placed vertically an inch or less apart, lightweight, yet extremely strong. With the lack of large trees for building material, the dead wood of the cardón is well utilized for a great many building functions—walls, rafters, and fence rails—as well as fish spears and bedsprings!

If the cardón is helpful to man, it is all things to smaller creatures and provides services to the who's who of peninsula birds. Early in the morning the resident vultures, dozens at a time, perch on the tips of the cardóns with their wings outstretched to warm; they look like northwest totem figures, brooding and symbolic. Just as we pass, a white-winged dove perched atop a cardón sinks its beak into a fruit. White-winged dove are very common in the country, and often hunted, usually flocking around water holes in the early morning or evening, the diagnostic white stripes on the wing conspicuous when they fly. Since these are plentiful birds of the desert and semi-desert, their physiology has been well studied. They can maintain a more or less normal body weight on a dry diet with their only source of fluid as seawater; their ability to do so may indicate some basic difference in electrolyte metabolism. Mourning doves, as well as white-winged doves, are able to rehydrate quickly, within five minutes after water becomes available. Many birds can retain their weight without drinking water if their food contains enough moisture—both house finches and Gambel's quail can survive on succulent vegetation. Insects provide considerable moisture to canyon and rock wrens. But birds, especially small birds, tend to lose great amounts of body weight during hot weather through evaporation; a finch can lose up to nearly 30 percent of its body weight. In drought seasons, the dryness of available food makes it difficult not only for adults to survive but to feed young; thus many desert birds' reproductive cycles are attuned to the rainy season.

The most industrious utilizers of the cardóns are the nesters. Gila woodpeckers and golden flickers excavate the trunks at the end of the nesting season; when egg-laying time again rolls around, a lining of dry hard scar tissue has formed. They use the nests but once. The abandoned nests are utilized by pygmy and elf owls, sparrow hawks, and flycatchers to name a few, and after the birds have finished, various rodents and lizards move in.

John Xantus found the cardón a gold mine for collecting the small pale screech owl named after him and once thought to be a Cape endemic. He found them calling noisily in the evening around the cardóns, where they nested in old woodpecker holes about fifteen to twenty feet from the ground, nests made visible by feathers snagged at the edge of the entrance. The birds are difficult to see at other times: their ear tufts break the normal bird outline, their facial patterns and body speckling all serve to blend them into their background. These owls are smaller than their relations to the north and east, illustrating Bergmann's Rule: the colder the climate in which the animal exists, the larger and darker will be the body because of the more efficient ratio of volume to body surface. In hot climates, lighter, more reflective color and smaller bodies prevail.

José must have been a tour guide in another life. He is full of information about politics and community life and gives us a sense of the Baja California he loves, which is impossible without such a friend who enthusiastically takes you into his world. In this desolate land, he says, there is an oasis on the way to Todos Santos, and we must stop to see it.

The perpetual desert scrub flanks the road. Then suddenly a verdure appears that astonishes the eye, with palm trees and green fields, and here we stop. Señora Refugio Garibay de León greets us. When she and her husband came here, she says, they prayed to the Virgin Mary for help and She showed them the water. To commemorate this she and her husband built a shrine, which faces the road, approached by a long paved walk flanked by bright pink benches. Fashioned like a little house, glassed across the front, the shrine is stuffed with flowers, both fresh and artificial. Señora says brides bring their bouquets here for good luck. And now at Christmas season it is further garnished with pink tinsel swags and blue bells knotted in here and there.

She has, she tells us, six children and thirty-five grandchildren, many of them with diplomas. As she speaks, she crosses the loose folds of her dress over her ribs, makes a basket out of her hands, leans back and pushes her hands upward, tilts her head back and smiles—a body language signifying complete satisfaction and pride.

"Look here," she says as she shows me her papaya trees. She asks if I know male and female are on different plants and laughs when I show her which is which: the male has small flowers on a raceme which vines outward from the stalk; the female has fewer flowers, larger, held closer to the stem. "Muy bueno, muy bueno," she says, to the plant more than to me.

It has taken us but a few hours to Todos Santos, even given our detours and time out for exploring, a considerable contrast to the 1890 account of botanist T. S. Brandegee:

> It was very difficult to reach this small out of the way place, situated on the shores of the Pacific Ocean, and the route I chose was by a trail one hundred and eighty miles long, which was followed on horseback. . . . Heavy rains had fallen in September, and the vegetation came rapidly forward and either matured its fruit or withered in the succeeding dry weather. At the beginning of my long ride there fell a steady rain of two or three days' duration, and for quite a while our horses waded through water and mud sometimes two feet deep, but the hot sun soon dried out the soil, and in a few days it assumed its usual barren appearance.

As we top the rise, Todos Santos spreads out in front of us. Here it is pleasantly breezy and cool, with wide streets lined with long-needled pines and blazing jacarandas, in many ways much as Edward Nelson saw it in 1906:

. . . a pretty place, consisting of 30 or 40 houses at an altitude of about 100 feet on a low bare ridge overlooking a narrow valley which is the lower end of a broad canyon leading from the west base of the Sierra de la Laguna. Below the road the valley was bright green with waving fields of sugar cane, and beyond, 2 or 3 miles away, lay the blue waters of the Pacific.

The Jesuit Padre Jaime Bravo first developed this area as a farming community around 1724 to supply produce for La Paz. Barco noted that "the entire exterior coast has been explored by land up to a latitude of 31 degrees and it has been found to be uniformly sterile and dry, with the exception of the place named Todos Santos in the South." A mission was founded here in 1733 by Padre Segismundo Taraval, who named it Santa Rosa. Completely razed by hostile Indians, it was rebuilt as Misión Todos Santos, sited on a high hill about a mile above where the town is now. Only remnants of the foundation remain. Missionary Jakob Baegert described the church as "vaulted, but with wood which was brought to the mission with the help of a great many teams of oxen over many miles from a very steep and high mountain range. It is large, richly and amply decorated."

The establishment of Todos Santos completed the circle of missions in the Cape, connecting La Paz, Santiago, and San José del Cabo. There were some two hundred Indians here when the mission was established, increased by the 1740s to over a thousand, dwindling to almost none after the epidemics of the mid-eighteenth century.

Todos Santos did not become a town until it received mainland immigrants. It was a center of revolutionary activity beginning in 1882, when Marqués de León organized against General Díaz, then *Presidente* of Mexico. Unsuccessful in securing La Paz, he retreated to Todos Santos and defeated those sent there after him. In need of funds, he traveled to San Francisco, where he successfully sought financial aid for his cause until word arrived of flagrant misbehavior on the part of his soldiers. He returned to Lower California, disbanded his troops and left the peninsula, still determined to overcome the bad government of Díaz. Fighting continued in desultory skirmishes, first at Santiago, then at San José del Cabo, then Todos Santos.

Nevertheless, by the end of the nineteenth century the peninsula enjoyed relative prosperity. Mission lands had been distributed and were being farmed. Schools were established. The pattern of life was much as it is today. The mainland revolution of 1910–11 had no counterpart on the peninsula, although there were isolated clashes. Even today the peninsula remains largely independent of the mainland. Todos Santos is now a town of over

2,500, and the fields around it are still fertile and productive, raising mangoes, as well as figs, oranges, bananas, and sugar cane.

The productivity of Todos Santos depends upon a reliable water supply
which comes from the mountains. An all-year stream enters the ocean about
two miles below Todos Santos, and there are three springs in the upper part
of the valley which supply irrigation water. Rainfall in the mountains sinks
through porous rock and fissures, and emerges below as springs, producing
a low but reliable flow. Now there are some small dams built back near the
mountains to prevent what happened some years ago. At the turn of the century either there was an attempt to tinker with the level of one of the springs
so that more land could be gravity-irrigated, or it happened naturally—
accounts vary—but somehow a shift in passage through subterranean fissures occurred and the spring disappeared, emerging again almost a mile
farther downhill, isolating the previously irrigated land above and taking it
out of production.

One of the big crops was sugar cane, and one of the important products
of Todos Santos was penuche or panocha, a kind of brown-sugar candy
boiled down from syrup as maple-sugar candy is. If ever there was an "industry" in Lower California, the making of panocha must have been it, for every
town had its own panocha factory. Sugar cane harvested in the spring was cut
into pieces and rolled to express the juice, which was boiled down until it
reached syrup stage, then poured into molds to harden. The candy was pack-
aged in little *palo de arco* baskets lined with sugar-cane leaves. The factory
was in operation until recently; today the walls stand empty, production
abandoned.

Professor Néstor Agúndez Martínez hosts our visit to Todos Santos's Casa
de la Cultura, which contains marvelous photographs as well as Indian artifacts. The local heroine of Todos Santos is Dianisia Villarino, known as "La
Coronela" for her participation in the revolution of 1911—her portrait shows
a formidable strong-jawed woman. On the walls hang a series of eight por-
traits, done in the precise and clear style we call primitive, smoothly and
carefully painted, features large and simple, the side of a nose modeled with
a strong and straightforward black stripe, the expressions stern.

Along with representative crafts from each state in Mexico, there is a glass
case with prehistoric artifacts found near Sierra de la Laguna. It is a hodge-
podge of Indian skulls, fishing arrows, and other artifacts discovered after a
storm washed out a dam. This area was one of the centers of the Pericu, who
hunted, fished, and gathered here. Unfortunately the artifacts are so jumbled
in the bottom of the glass case that I find it hard to make any sense of them,

except to perceive in their crudeness the most primitive solutions to survival.

We visit the grocery for some picnic supplies. It sells liquor as well as groceries and dry goods. Inside the meat counter are undefinable slabs of meat; unless enclosed in the case, nothing is protected from flies. A strong smell of fish emanates from the case although none are on display. Behind the counter, a shopping cart contains a flayed beef head still retaining the horns, curving upward and outward, in a surrealistic juxtaposition. There are apples and tangerines, shelves of marshmallow cookies and cakes in varying shades of lurid orange and shocking pink, and Christmas decorations. A loudspeaker blasts an obviously though modestly salacious song—the male voice rolls over the words, singing with gestures. The young woman behind the counter giggles self-consciously.

We stop by Apollinario's house. Apollinario, called Polie for short, snaps open a beer and gives us an expansive grin of pure sybaritic pleasure. Home only on weekends, he works "up north." His wife is a voluble lady, shaking hands, exchanging greetings, stirring something in a pot, shooing a chicken, bustling back to talk, her hands constantly describing this and that.

Oilcloth covers the big table, centered with jars of honey, mayonnaise, Tang, and Polie's beer supply. A treadle sewing machine stands on a table to one side. A big pot of soup simmers on the small gas stove, occasionally building up enough pressure to make the lid clank. Beside it a bowl overflows with chunked fresh cabbage and cut-up squash. A small chicken wanders through the forest of human and table legs. There are so many plants in various-sized cans standing all around that it has to pick its way carefully.

The jacaranda tree outside glows with orange flowers, and bougainvillaea —magenta, salmon, and crimson—cascades over the thatch roof, just as in any ranchyard. Two pickup trucks speed up the street, tires spitting gravel. The streets in San José are narrow and paved, in Todos Santos wide and dirt, inviting a little competition. Next door south the radio blares a mariachi band; next door north it blasts rock 'n' roll. That symbol of civilization, a bare electric light bulb, hangs by a wire in the center of the room.

The film rolls faster in town, ranch life without its measured cadence. It is more than the squealing of tires substituted for the squealing of pigs. It has something to do with pace and mechanical noises and cheek-by-jowl living, and a gas stove instead of a hearth, and a single light bulb to light up the canyons of the night.

IV

THE PACIFIC

The shore of the southern end of the peninsula from 15 miles south of Todos Santos to San Jose del Cabo is formed mainly by granite ridges varying from 100 to 500 feet high, which descend from the mountains a few miles inland and form a series of narrow rocky capes. Between the capes are small half-moon bays, commonly with white sand beaches about their heads.

Edward W. Nelson
Lower California and Its Natural Resources
1921

But who would believe it? The three days which I camped there in the middle of May were so cold from the strong winds blowing day and night from the west that I was forced to wrap myself up in my coat all day long and to draw the cap over both ears. This kind of wind blows in that area and on the entire western shore almost all year around.

Jakob Baegert
Letter to his brother
September 23, 1757

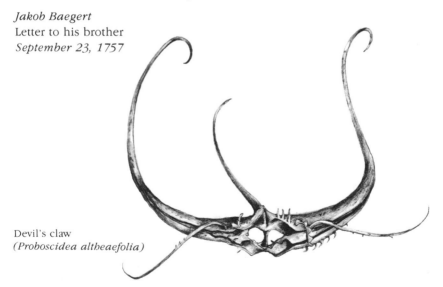

Devil's claw
(Proboscidea altheaefolia)

PACIFIC FRINGE

On a beach just south of Todos Santos, early one cool December morning, sleeping bag snugged close around my shoulders, I watch the Pacific pile in, rising in big slick dark gray waves before it spumes into a cold turquoise and white froth. I listen to the leading edge of foam slither up the beach and hiss down again, leaving the sand one shade darker, with a shining apron of moisture shimmering with sky until obliterated by the next wave. Southward, the water climbs the beach and rips across the sand. To the north, the concentrated force of the sea piles up against a headland and is flung cascading back into a confusion of peaked waves and high spray. No wonder Father Francisco Javier Clavijero described the Pacific Coast as one with "hardly a port where vessels can find shelter from the northwest winds which prevail there. Barks and other small craft cannot make the coast without risk of being lost on the rocks, in consequence of the heavy sea prevailing."

Through a notch in the mountain phalanx to the east the sky flames orange. Sun underlights the low clouds. Pink seeps over the whole quadrant, then all of a sudden dulls to a pale pearl dawn. The breeze freshens. The wind comes off the land, not the water, cool but not damp.

Last night I slept in stop motion, awakening once to see stars, and once not, when thin clouds blurred them to hurricane lights. All night long the surf cannonaded like distant Civil War artillery, a muffled percussive boom felt through the earth when a great wave broke all at once along its whole front. Short beach grasses rustled like tissue paper. All around my ground cloth this morning, lizard and bird and mouse tracks quilt the sand. Last night, as we came down to the beach, a fox streaked across the road above, tail streaming out behind, but there are no tracks to tell he came here.

Into this mountainous terrain of sand tracks, a velvet ant picks its way

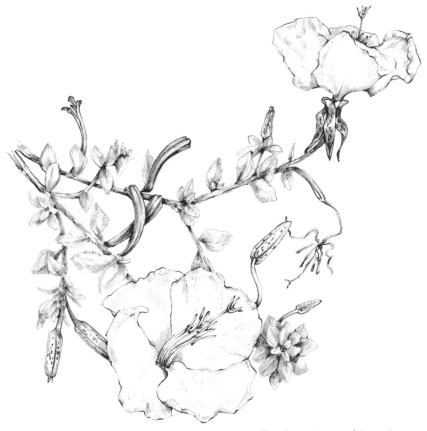

Evening primrose (*Oenothera drummondii* var. *thalassaphila*)

landward. The wingless females resemble ants, hence the innocent name that masks their true identity of wasp with a brutal wallop of a sting. These highly conspicuous insects are generally immune from attack by those who would normally prey upon them, such as birds or lizards, both of which depend upon their keen eyesight in hunting. Many velvet ants have venoms host-specific for their prey species—the wasps or bees into whose cocoon the female deposits her eggs.

At seven the little birds come, two pert sparrows chipping away. A gray scrub jay calls and putters across the beach, looking for food. The only jay in Lower California, it was first collected at Cabo San Lucas by John Xantus. Privateer Edward Cooke, here in 1709, described it as "a Bird of the Bigness of a Black-Bird, with a blue Head, Wings, and Tail, his Bill and Legs black, his back brown, mix'd with bluish Feathers, and his Belly of a light brown." It picks its way through patches of gray-green goosefoot and sprawling red-stemmed horse purslane that Barco says was used as a potherb. The succulent leaves and stems resemble the familiar domesticated portulaca, but it has no petals, just a five-lobed horned calyx.

The variety of rocks heaped up at the ocean's edge amazes me; for some reason I expected them to be homogeneous, instead they are extremely varied. Washed down from all the mountain slopes to the east by flash floods big enough to carry them, they glisten under the spray: pale gray granite shot with large flakes of glistening muscovite; gray granite salted with bits of quartz as big as peas; gray marbled with black and white; tan stained with iron; rocks sandwiched with layers of quartz—some remain rough and granular but most of them are sea-smoothed even though irregular in shape. The sea has a long way to go to work them to cobbles. They teeter in a long tumbled heap that must rumble and moan during high seas.

Ravens cruise the strand in search of scraps. A pelican wings by, just skimming a wave the split second before it breaks. And out of the north, beating a parallel banner a hundred feet off shore, come scores of Brandt's cormorants! Walter Bryant tells of seeing masses of them dive after fish:

> Many mornings I have been attracted by the noise of thousands fishing some distance off shore and have watched through a glass the dense, dark mass as they passed a given point. Those half a mile or more in the rear came flying forward in platoons and alighted at the head of the broad line, making the water turbulent with commotion while their numbers were being constantly augmented by the arrival of stragglers from the sides and rear. Mingled with the myriads of cormorants were often many California brown pelicans plunging for fish, while above all hovered Heermann's gulls, robbing at every

Pacific beach

opportunity. To all appearances, they were following a great school of fish, astounding numbers of which must be daily consumed by these voracious feeders.

Bryant also saw one robbed of a fish by a pelican, which deviled it until the cormorant dropped the fish; the pelican then snapped it up before it sank far below the surface. There were fresh eggs by mid-January, and he found them not too bad, "something of a gelatinous consistency, if I remember rightly, and although unsalted, I recollect that they were relished at the time. It makes a wonderful difference in one's opinion of such things whether they have dined well for a day or two preceding the experiment or not."

Cormorants and other sea birds feed here because cold currents upwell along the Pacific Coast. Deeper, cooler, nutrient-rich water (cold water generally contains more oxygen than warm) surges to the surface, replacing surface waters blown away from shore by the north and northwest prevailing winds, and bringing food to fish, bird, and mammal alike. Temperatures can be as low as 55 degrees where upwellings prevail. As a consequence, the Pacific Coast is an "overlap zone" when it comes to fauna. Because of the alternating warm and cold waters, animals from the north, more frequent in Alta California, mix with those from the tropical Panamic fauna, pockets of species from each zone in the local environments to which they are suited. This interchange goes on all the way north to the political boundary between Mexico and the United States; the more northerly forms drop out about Cedros Island; the more southerly forms disappear between the border and Magdalena Bay.

At noon one scorching summer day, Herman and I follow paths blown out in the sand between the wind timber on the upper beach. Low prickly-leaved beach grasses send out long rhizomes, rooting at the nodes, anchoring into the sand. Goldenweed and small spurges mat across the ground; the long leafless stems of milkweed make it look like the ribs of a spavined umbrella, set into the sand at a rakish angle. Ground cherry sprawls along the ground, its sharply angled stems bearing greenish-yellow flowers. Its inflated seedpods give it its generic name, *Physalis,* Greek for "bladder." The inflated pod (like a little Japanese lantern) encases a small cherrylike fruit, hence the common name.

The common Cape milkweed, in Spanish *yamete,* buzzes with huge black carpenter bees and spider wasps, and the stems seethe with milkweed

Milkweed *(Asclepias subulata)*

bugs. The complex corollas are pale dusty yellow with the elongated hoods soft rose, as shiny as if glazed. Instead of being loose, pollen is bound into pollinium sacs that resemble little bags; the sacs of adjacent anthers are joined by a yokelike structure, in which there are small clips. Insects coming for pollen are guided by the shape of the corolla to the clips, which become attached to their bristles so that they transport the attached pollinium sacs to other flowers. There, if the sac fits a matching pollination chamber, it breaks off and fertilizes them.

The genus (and family) name *Asclepias* commemorates the Greek god of medicine and healing. Some insects that feed on toxic plants are able to use the plant's poisons for their own defense, as the larvae of monarch butterflies use the digitalis-like cardiac glycosides that milkweed produces, which induce vomiting in birds. Possibly, plants like milkweed developed toxic compounds as a protection against being eaten; against this a herbivore must either not eat the plant, develop its own chemical counter-measures, or become immune to the plant's inimical chemicals.

Dozens of milkweed bugs, antennae waving, march up and down the stems. Small bugs, half an inch long, they are black with a red X on their backs and two white spots at the hind end of each wing; the young are pure red, and the wanderers, all stages between. Another species prowls the stalks: large milkweed bugs, orange and black striped.

The four-inch seed pods dangle, silvery green. One splits; inside, the seeds and their feathery tufts of hairs lie neatly imbricated. I split it a little more with my fingernail and several plumed seeds fall to the ground; on only one are the filaments dry enough to open and lift off into the wind.

Stalking the sand are two tarantula wasps that Baegert described as "almost thick as a thumb, . . . blackish with great, fiery-red wings, somewhat resembling the painted images of Satan." They are indeed striking creatures, with glossy iridescent navy blue bodies and cinnabar wings that they extend in full display as they walk. Strong fliers, they fly but seldom, spending more of their time walking about on stilted legs. On the peninsula they are known as *bitachi* and are justifiably feared for their sting, which, according to one entomologist, is the worst insect sting around.

The female wasp creeps up on a tarantula, easily as big as she if not more so, and delivers a series of stings that paralyze but do not kill. (Male *bitachi* have thirteen segments in their heavy black antennae, which are usually straight; females have twelve, and their antennae are usually curled.) She then drags the prey to her burrow, tucks it in, and lays an egg on top. When the egg hatches, the anesthetized spider serves as first food—were it dead it would be subject to drying or mold or bacterial decomposition, all of which would render it unfit for consumption.

Tarantulas are in themselves fascinating creatures, with an exceedingly bad press. They are long-lived, and it takes up to ten years for a female to become mature. Eggs are laid on a silken sheet that the mother manipulates into a protective bag. Barco found it "such a large spider that when it walks it appears as large or larger than a big hen's egg, but a round one." Called *araña de caballo* because they are believed to be dangerous to horses, in truth they are not. On the Cape there was a belief that a tarantula was an "unerring barometer" as a harbinger of rain within "four and twenty hours."

Just beyond the first screen of shrubs, my feet crunch through hundreds of translucent little husks, carapaces and claws of "lobster krill," crustacea a couple inches long, now translucent and fragile but when alive, bright red and a favored food of whales. They were observed by early travelers; the Dominican Louis de Sales wrote in the late 1760s that

> while the *Venus* was thus following the coast to enter the gulf of Cortés, the lookouts noticed red patches of great extent on the surface of the sea, which they took for patches of whale's blood. The presence of the whale-ships within sight might in some degree justify this guesswork supposition which, however, was soon contradicted by the reality for soon, as we advanced, we crossed over these patches and recognized that their red color was caused by a multitude of small vermilion colored crustaceans. These crustacea were like big shrimps but they had what shrimps lack, pincers like those of lobsters. We took some with a bag-net and preserved them in alcohol.

This coastline is visited by migrating whales and it is always an occasion of moment to see one broach and expel its breath. The warm air condenses as it hits the colder air at the sea's surface, making the spray visible from some distance. A toothed whale produces a single spout; a bone whale, which has double blowholes, produces twin spouts.

The Pericu believed that the great lord of the sky was Niparaja, who had several sons, and having created earth, did whatever he wished. One of his sons lived a long time on earth to help people, but he was abhorred and put to death, wearing a crown of thorns. Another, Tuparán, attacked his father but Niparaja was victorious; in punishment Niparaja took all the *pitahayas* away from him, and created whales to guard him.

The gray whale, which migrates once a year from Alaska to the lagoons of Lower California, is very nearly a relict, now surviving in a very restricted area. In prehistoric times it roamed the northern Atlantic and around Europe; a few may still exist in the northwestern Pacific. In the ocean they and other whales find favorable habitat, growing to 150 tons or more, a weight which would be impossible to support on land.

Whales have an incredible ability to dive deeply and surface quickly without the decompression problems that humans have. Ocean pressure increases by one atmosphere for every thirty-three feet of depth, one atmosphere being about fifteen pounds per square inch. Whales can dive half a mile and come right back up. (Generally speaking, below thirty feet, a scuba diver must take time to decompress while returning to the surface, although the length of the dive determines decompression rather than depth.) The usual duration of a whale's dive is ten minutes, although longer dives have been recorded; before and after diving, it exhales but once. Since respiration does not continue during the dive, there is no nitrogen buildup that causes the "bends" in humans; whales may also have blood capable of taking up excess nitrogen in the blood stream. Physiologically, the heartbeat drops from nearly eighty per minute down to ten. Circulation to main muscles, able to tolerate a lack of oxygen, can be cut off, conserving oxygen.

In the first half of the eighteenth century many whalers visited the bays of Baja California, taking sperm and other whales—one year fifty-two whaling ships were working Magdalena Bay. Not only whales were taken, but elephant seals, sea otters, and fur seals. By 1869, C. M. Scammon, after whom a lagoon on the west side of the peninsula was named, was writing:

> The sea-beaches of island and coast, once the herding-places of these amphibious animals, whose peltries were highly prized among the enlightened classes of both Europe and America, are now deserted; except at the most inaccessible points, there are but few found, and their wild and watchful habits plainly tell that the species is nearly annihilated.

One wonders what Mr. Scammon would think about people in rubber boats going out and patting whales.

As long as I watch, I see no spouts, only the spray from huge waves forming two hundred yards off shore, rearing up and breaking a quarter mile long in a great arching thud, throwing spray twenty feet, waves turbid with sand spun up from the constantly roiled bottom. With the curve of beach, the backside of the waves is visible, running, sloping upward, flying white splash from the other side. As these waves travel across deep water their passage is little impeded, and they come roaring into the beach around 15 to 20 miles per hour. But when they reach water with a depth of less than half their length or about 1.3 times their height, the waves steepen. Friction from the bottom holds back the base of the wave while the crest runs ahead, becoming unsupported. When the crest angle becomes less than 120 degrees, the oscillating water particles in the wave can no longer maintain their rhythm, and the wave charges and falls onto the beach, losing its energy in the plunge. Down the coastline the surf comes into slots and inlets and blows high, a series of fountains going off in sequence. The air rumbles with its constant noise. The wind streams spray off the waves' crests and fills the air with misty moanings and shakings.

The beach is unmarked by shells and pebbles. Trapped in a band on the beach, larger and coarser sand grains trail hundreds of little triangles downwind. Wind streams the sand about a foot off the ground. At water's edge it rasps the beach so fiercely that I go back and put on jeans to keep my shins from getting sanded down to bare bone. No wonder the beach is so clean: the wind keeps it so. I think my sunglasses are dirty but not so—it's a coating of the finest denominator of the ocean made airborne.

At water's edge the beach is flat, the sand fine, firm enough to drive on as intermittent car tracks show. I scarcely leave footprints. A line of white foam tats up the beach. Iridescent bubbles skid along the strand, shimmer and shatter. A fringe of sea spittle skitters toward the sea. Tiny holes fill with water, pop open, the inhabitants below getting sustenance—what a fever of feeding there must be beneath all this surface turmoil!

Head down, I trudge onward, looking up only to get a bearing on a rocky ridge down the way, and take a bearing as seldom as possible to avoid sand in my eyes, glimpse the secure edge of the beach, hedged with *mangle dulce* and *lomboy;* above them, a juniper blue thunderhead broods over the mountains.

A four-foot trough bears fresh ripple marks running at right angles to the incoming waves; the ripples are finger length from crest to crest, marking the drainage path of a stranded pool that recently emptied seaward. I keep looking for more life on the beach but the sea pulverizes everything. Out over the ocean, a single pelican circles low over a breaking wave, then tucks in its wings and drops in neatly just behind the breaker line.

All the rocky ridges that step out into the ocean gleam barren. But a small bay between two of them promises more. Here a few periwinkles and a limpet or two cling to the granite. Little pools inlaid in the granite ledge have sandy bottoms and clean sides. A thin coating of mauve coralline algae enamels the rocks precisely to where the water line now lies. One sill projects farther outward, formed of dark rock, Roman-striped with lines of paler intrusions, including a narrow white stripe of quartz. A small pool, a foot deep with a sandy bottom, contains four small fish, yellow and gray sergeant majors. Whenever a wave hits the pool it spins them topsy-turvy. Water twinkles in hundreds of tiny pockets in the rocks, runs in rivulets from one level to the next, sparkling, flashing, dancing. A crab skitters over the rock between pools, adding vibrating animal movement to flickering water movement.

Many of the rock edges are rounded, many of their flanks fluted. Sand fills every indentation. A few nerites graze the horizontal surface but they are scattered, not clustered as they are on calmer shores. I step farther out, watching carefully to see how far the waves are coming in. Every little crack is wedged with pebbles, pounded in by the surf. Larger pockets of sand are peppered with holes; barren the sand may be on top, there must be a rich sub-surface fauna.

Farther out on some of the rocks, where the waves are breaking, are patches of brilliant green. I want to get out to investigate but the waves break so hard and the undertow sucks at my feet so greedily that I hesitate, then chastise my cowardice.

I count intervals between the biggest waves. How long do I have to dash

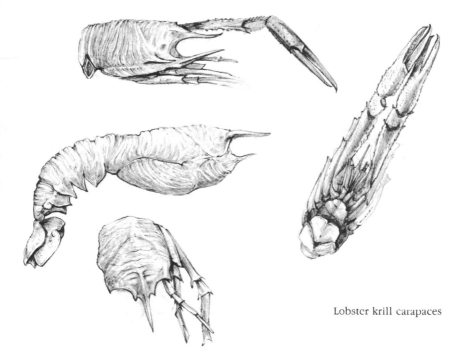

Lobster krill carapaces

Pacific beach

out, claw loose a tuft, and get back to safety? A series of four very low waves precede two higher ones, leading up to two or three monstrous ones that break high and smash over the rocks. According to Willard Bascom in his excellent book for beachcombers, *Waves and Beaches,* these periods are likely caused by the arrival of two sets of swells from two storms at the same time. When they coincide, they reinforce each other; when they are out of phase, they tend to cancel out. I count the cadence several times again, take a deep breath, and run—after all, it's only twenty or so feet.

I reach the algae, kneel beside it when I feel a change in pressure. There towers my recurring nightmare: the cruel cold curving gloss of a huge wave poised above me. The thin white ruffle line at its crest in ominous silence just begins to curl. I freeze with fear. With a sound like ripping silk the white line perforates. Spray blasts my face. Salt water stings my eyes. I cannot see. I lock my arms around whatever I can, digging my fingernails into the slippery granite. With an agonizing slowness and yet so quickly I don't have time to take a breath, the wave hits. The weight of the water falls on me like tons of rock. Water grabs my ankles and pulls, pulls my arms, twists, sucks, imbibes me. Darkness and cold. I am frozen with fear.

Brightness and warmth. Sunlight! I run awkwardly through a foaming nothingness of rock and wet saturated sand that holds my feet, wet clothes binding and dragging, then through damp sand, then through hot sand, and I crumple down into its comforting warmth and shake and gasp sea water and sea tears.

Yesterday or tomorrow. But no more today. No more today.

The beaches of the Pacific, compared with those on the Gulf side, are deserted, mainly because of the fierceness of the surf. Even Todos Santos is not on the sea but inland behind a protecting bluff, as is Pescadero. The most famous occupant of this fifty miles of strand is the lighthouse built in 1905 that stands at Cabo Falso—the "False Cape"—which was once thought to be the southernmost end of the Baja peninsula. Its status was destroyed by Spencer Murray, who in 1960 determined the point to be a "tumbled mass of broken rock" that "bisects the white sand beach which extends from the point of Cabo San Lucas to that at Cabo Falso." Actually there are two lighthouses, the old one which stands abandoned, and the new lighthouse high up on the cliffs built in 1962.

Herman, Jane and I take a likely looking *ramal* through view-blocking vegetation that leaves me wondering if we're on the right road. A woodpecker, a cardinal with a head the color of *palo adán* flowers, four top-knotted quail come within view, but Herman is not interested in birdwatching. He wants to lighthouse watch when the light is photographically perfect, and pushes on. We pull off and park at a likely spot in the road and find a path that leads down to the old light.

Herman and Jane hurry off; I dawdle along as is my preference. A branch rasps, unsettling as a rattlesnake's warning. *Lomboy* sprawls on the sand along the path, blooming with pink bells lined in red. The wind, laden with salt, nips back the branches, dries out the soil, and what remains is this bonsai border of lomboy. Other plants sprawl across the dune: golden-flowered *Kallstroemia,* yellow evening-primrose, and Spanish needle.

A big darkling beetle waddles across the sand. Heavily plated with rough black armor that protects it from evaporation, its main line of defense is its ability to squirt a blister-causing liquid, cantharidin. I stoop down to pick it up and it immediately elevates its rear end. I leave it alone.

Beach grass, like a compass, describer arcs in the sand dune. Its leaves are as sharp-tipped as thorns. Big sand dunes are unusual on the Cape. Generally, beaches are narrow, confined between rocky headlands, but here the wind has blown sand in over the cliffs and denied the original lighthouse survival, frosting its glass to uselessness. The late afternoon light softens the landscape, pours shadows into hollows, and draws a pale salmon gauze over sand, lighthouse, sea, rocks. The late breeze stripes the ocean like charvet.

By the time I reach the old lighthouse, rose suffuses the sky, glazes the

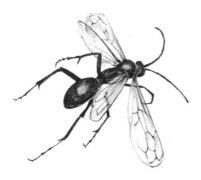

Tarantula wasp (Pompilidae)

walls. Where the stucco coating has fallen away, the wind has eroded the exposed bricks into fanciful shapes, like a Gaudi façade. Its handsome proportions show care in the building. Whoever lived here, even though isolated, was a man of importance. The lighthouse says so. The dignity and command remain.

Inside, six rooms, each with a spectacular view, flank a central hallway that leads seaward and ends in a tower with an iron spiral staircase. In the center was a wooden shaft, the bottom of which was mounted in a wheel, the top of which carried the light—unlike modern lights, the whole light turned. Shaft rotation depended upon a pulley-and-cable arrangement, working generally like an old clock. A weight hung on a cable which ran in an iron channel in the wall. The lighthouse keeper carried the weight upstairs at regular intervals, attached it to the chain, and as it descended, it turned the wheel at the bottom, which in turn rotated the shaft.

Outside, the sand falls away steeply to the top of precipitous cliffs and, two hundred feet below, big surf uncurls. Shards of glass, well over a quarter inch thick, lie half-buried in the sand, surface evenly frosted. I break off an edge with a rock and clear glass shows on the fracture—fragments of the original glass surrounding the light. Because the lighthouse was set too low, the new light was built on the cliff above in 1962.

We get back to the car as the sun flattens onto the horizon. As Herman loads camera gear, a distant diesel engine coughs. Herman's face lights up. "I'd know that sound anywhere—someone's cranking up the diesel to start the big light!" And before I know it we're zigzagging up to the new lighthouse at a speed suitable for Le Mans.

José Herrera Morales, one of the two lighthouse keepers, stands silhouetted in the lighted doorway. It turns out his father was the first lighthouse keeper, whose other claim to fame is that he was one of the few people in Baja California to die from a scorpion bite. He explains that this light is very important because it's the last light on the Cape. Rising 656 feet above the sea, it beams west, south, and southeast for 33 miles, flashing every six tenths of a second. An unmanned light, it needs to be lit in the evening and extinguished at dawn, a task which he shares with another keeper.

He invites us inside, where the works from the original lighthouse have been remounted, the turning stem now attached to an electric motor. Six cement steps, then five rungs on a metal ladder anchored in the wall, bring us to the platform below the light. The lantern turns evenly, silently, above us. On the brass stem a name plate is mounted. It takes me a couple of turns

Kallstroemia *(Kallstroemia peninsularis)*

before I can read it all the way through:

Bartier & Bernard
Rue de Curial 82
Paris

The light is surrounded by Fresnel lenses—Jane at one time in her life had Fresnel lenses on her glasses to correct an eye muscle problem. In 1822, Augustin Fresnel, a French physicist, designed a lens panel for lighthouse lights. In the center he placed a bull's-eye of glass, surrounding it with concentric prismatic rings, each with a different focal length depending on its placement, serving to concentrate the light many times over. Fresnel set these panels on a carriage that revolved around, in his day, an oil lamp, making possible a flashing light with a stationary light source.

Now, of course, radar and radio beacons are more accurate and reliable and, I suppose, more comforting than this pulsing light. But, being visual-minded, I feel the welcome of this beam across the endless darkness. Along this coast, there are almost no lights on the approach to Land's End. No quivering impersonal sound across the ether could possibly match the sight of that tiny, pulsing, votive candle of safety that marks a turning, a corner, a curving away, a here and a beyond.

The Entrance is about a League to the Eastward *of a round, sandy, bald Headland, which some take to be Cape St.* Lucas, *because it is the* Southermost *Land; but I believe that to be Cape St.* Lucas *which bears* E. *by* S. *from this bald Head, distant about three Leagues, and in the* Eastermost *Point. When you are in the Offing, the Land makes like an Island off the said Cape. When you come from the* Westward, *and are bound in here, the Marks are four high Rocks, the two* Westermost *sharp and tapering like a Sugar-loaf; the innermost of the two has an Arch, like that of a Bridge, thro' which the Sea has a Passage, leaving the outermost Rock about half a Cable's Length without you. Coming, as before, from the* Westward, *which generally must be, by Reason of the counter Current that runs in the Bay, steer in* N. W. *by* W. *which will carry you along the Rocks Side into the deepest Cod of the Bay, where you may anchor with your small Bower in ten Fathom, and moor on and off, the best Bower lying in 20 or 25, as you please, the Ground being a clear hard Sand, and Shoals gradually after you come in with the Bank. Here you ride land-lock'd from* E. *by* N. *to* S.E. *by* S.

Edward Cooke
A Voyage to the South Sea and Round the World
1712

Morning-glory *(Merremia aurea)*

9

LA VIGÍA

The Cape ends in a blunt spit of land that runs west to east. The lighthouse at Cabo Falso anchors its western corner. La Vigía—"the crow's nest"—anchors its eastern, a pinnacle of granite rising a steep 560 feet above the ocean. On a 20th of July at eight-fifteen, when it is already 88 degrees in the shade, I climb, scramble, and crawl to its crest. Toward the west, the Pacific sweeps far and away to infinity. To the north, long knife ridges lead up to the Sierra de la Victoria. Southward, if I ignore a few flyspeck islands, I can see all the way to Antarctica. Eastward, I see the lighthouse at Cabeza Ballena, and below, hidden from view, this granite ridge ends in the famous arch of Cabo San Lucas.

I sit wedged against a large boulder, locked against the empty space around me. The whole summit is a granite rock pile, jointed and riven, and in places scooped out in un-granite-like hollows, curved and tormented, once worked by the sea, now raised above it. Cracks between boulders look down to hell. I sight through one rift to a calm Pacific ruffling the sand below; the sound filters up in a faint but insistent rhythm. Clouds of sand finger out from the shore. The waves crowd close on each, churning up the sand and keeping it in suspension. Occasionally a larger cusp of waves roils up more and the sand stain plumes farther and farther out.

163

Close at hand two dragonflies patrol back and forth, paths separated by orbit. When the paths intersect they hover a moment, two inches from each other, *en face,* wings vibrating, then back off and separate to their own circuits again. One's patrol includes a big wooden cross, set facing the sunrise, hung with plastic flowers. Rags and oil on the ground lead me to infer that pyres have been built up here, which must have beamed for miles in every direction.

Rough and granular chunks of rock lie caught between the monster boulders that crown La Vigía. I pick up one and find a memory in the touch. I carted just such a rock all the way down from La Laguna—the same slow-cooled crystalline roughness, the same granular backbone at five thousand feet as at five hundred, the rock that holds the peninsula together, vertebra by vertebra, this dragon sleeping in the sun of millennia.

One of the boulders is scooped out like an old metal tractor seat. What a perfect place to sit and watch. Which is why I came. I wanted to see what the privateers' lookouts saw, tracking a glass slowly across the horizon, watching for gold and silks and spices. And now I know: their tomorrow.

Magellan, when he was killed, was, like Columbus, looking for the Spice Islands—the Molucca Islands, then claimed by the Portuguese. The islands he did find in 1521 were eventually named the Felipinas for the infant prince who became Philip II. Even then, the Philippines had been trading with China and the mainland for at least five centuries, perhaps longer. The potential for Spanish profits was not lost on the ambitious Charles V. In 1528, he decreed that a better route to the Philippines be found than that from Spain around South America. Under the direction of Cortés, who by then was established in New Spain, ships went out from Mexico to the East Indies. Five expeditions sailed but none were able to return to Mexico because they could find no winds favorable for eastern passage. In 1565, Miguel López de Legaspi established a permanent settlement in the Philippines; an eastward route was pioneered by López de Legaspi's chief pilot, Esteban Rodríguez, and an Augustinian friar, Father Andrés de Urdaneta. His solution was to sail northeast out of the Philippines, following the Japan Current northeastward almost to 40 degrees north latitude, until he picked up the northwesterlies off the California coast, then to parallel the coast southward. The establishment of the route made possible the yearly trips between Acapulco and Manila, sailed regularly by the Spanish galleons for two hundred and fifty years, making it the longest lasting trade line ever in existence.

The lightly loaded outbound ship usually left Mexico at the end of February or the beginning of March, carrying Mexican and Peruvian silver pesos, officials on their way to new posts, and supplies needed in the colonies, as well as soldiers and munitions. When the galleon arrived in the Philippines, it was unloaded, careened, and refitted for the longer voyage home.

Galleons were hulking wallowing vessels, three- to four-masted, the stern cut off straight, making a square-ended forecastle with a high poopdeck, so high out of the water that they would have bobbed like corks had it not been for their extra beam. Most of the early galleons were built in Nicaragua, but later ones were built in the Philippines, where Joló teak and other hardwoods were found serviceable—in particular lanang, a tough resilient wood that well withstood cannonballs. An authority, Woodes Rogers, an English privateer, who attacked one of these blundering ships, gave grudging admiration: "These large ships are built with excellent timber, that will not splinter, they have very thick sides, much stronger than we build in Europe."

To captain one of these treasure ships meant such profit that the captain need sail no more, and captaincies were sought-after political appointments. The galleons were often called the "China ships" because of their consignment of beautiful fabrics: brocades and damasks, filmy gauzes and elegant crepes, glistening taffetas and luscious velvets. One galleon carried more than fifty thousand pairs of stockings, and all the latest fashions finely sewn, plus napery and church ornaments, ladies' combs, ivory castanets, intricate

Spurge *(Euphorbia* sp.*)*

Old lighthouse at Cabo Falso

objects of jade, bronze thimbles, brass toothpicks, inlaid boxes. Bales of coveted spices stacked the decks.

The eastbound trip tried men's souls. Passengers paid 2,000 to 4,000 pesos to make the voyages but once at sea, often were short-changed as to food and water. Sometimes the only professionals on board were the pilots whose rutters, those impeccable records of observations of coastline and bay, were so valuable that they were often prize booty when a ship was captured.

For passengers and vessel the trip was debilitating. Water ran out early; after that they depended on dew or rain. Below, fumes from unwashed and seasick passengers, slop pails and bilge water, must have driven passengers to sleeping, shivering, on deck. One traveler wrote:

> The Ship swarms with little Vermine the Spaniards call Gorgojos, bred in the Biskit; so swift that they in a short time not only run over Cabbins, beds, and the very dishes the Men eat on, but insensibly fasten upon the Body. There are several other sorts of Vermin of sundry Colours, that suck the Blood. Abundance of Flies fall into the Dishes of Broth, in which there also swim Worms of several sorts.—I had a good share of these Misfortunes; for the Boatswain, with whom I had agreed for my Diet, as he had Fowls at his Table the first Days, so when we were out at Sea he made me fast after the *Armenian* manner, having Banish'd from his Table all Wine, Oyl and Vinegar; dressing his Fish with fair Water and Salt. Upon Flesh Days he gave me Tassajos Fritos, that is, Steaks of Beef, or Buffalo, dry'd in the Sun, or wind, which are so hard that it is impossible to Eat them, without they are first well beaten.

Gemelli Careri, a geographer, wrote, when they sighted land on December 14, 1698,

> Everybody began to take heart with the Hopes of being speedily delivered from so many Sufferings, and particularly from stinking Provisions which began to breed diseases.

Although others talked about doing it again, Careri felt that

> for my own part, these nor greater hopes shall not prevail with me to undertake that Voyage again, which is enough to destroy a Man, or make him unfit for anything as long as he lives.

As if the hardships of the voyage were not enough, the assumption that the Pacific was Spain's pond was rudely shattered when Sir Francis Drake

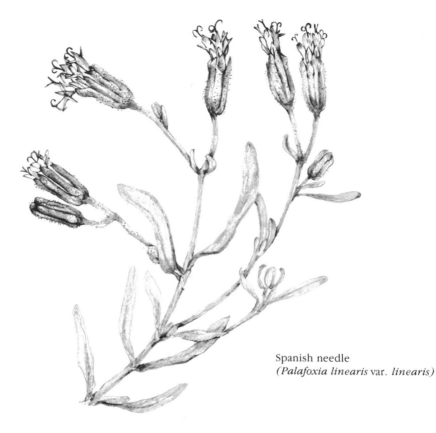

Spanish needle
(*Palafoxia linearis* var. *linearis*)

sailed into that ocean in 1579. By 1585 Spain's relations with Queen Eliza-
beth's England became openly abrasive, and the British crown itself encouraged attacks on Spanish ships. The bays along the coast between San Lucas
and San José provided excellent hiding places from which to harry Spanish
shipping, and the bobbing galleons were most vulnerable when they rounded the Lower California coast and turned east toward their home port of Acapulco.

Perhaps one of Thomas Cavendish's lookouts perched up here on La
Vigía. Cavendish was a young dandy of the Elizabethan court, influenced by
Drake's and Raleigh's tales of grandeur. When his debts piled up, he turned
to privateering; as such, he owned and manned his ship, but was "commis-

sioned" by the government or private concerns to harass the shipping of enemy countries, and owed a percentage of take to his sponsors. Cavendish left Plymouth at the end of July, 1586, with three ships, to capture a galleon and destroy Spain's port facilities in New Spain. Over a year later Master Francis Pretty wrote that on the

> 14 of October we fell with the cape of St. Lucar, which cape is very like the Needles at the Isle of Wight and within the said cape is a great bay called by the Spaniards Aguada Segura: into which bay falleth a faire fresh river, about which many Indians use to keepe: wee watered in the river and lay off and on from the saide cape of S. Lucar untill the fourth of November, and had the windes hanging still Westerly.

At San Lucas they waited. And waited. Almost ready to give up, the lookout spotted

> A sayle, A sayle, with which cheerefull word the master of the ship and divers others of the company went also up into the maine top, who perceiving the speech to be very true gave information unto our Generall of these happy newes, who was no lesse glad than the cause required: whereupon he gave in charge presently unto the whole company to put all things in readiness, which being performed we gave them chase some 3 or 4 houres, standing with our best advantage and working for the winde. In the afternoone we gat up unto them, giving them the broad side with our great ordinance and a volee of small shot, and presently layed the ship aboord, whereof the king of Spaine was owner, which was Admiral of the south sea, called the S. Anna, & thought to be 700 tunnes in burthen.

The decks of the *Santa Ana,* captained by Tomás de Alzola, were so crowded with merchandise that there was scarcely room for her three hundred passengers. After more than four months at sea, she approached Cabo San Lucas on the evening of November 14, 1587. Her lookouts saw two sails on the horizon that Alzola assumed were Spanish. As they drew closer "it was seen that it was the admiral's ship of an English corsair and thief named Don Tomas Candiens of Tembley, a young man of little age." Alzola gave out what arms could be found—"lances, javelings, rapiers & targets, & an innumerable sort of great stones" pulled out from the ballast. These stones provided what was probably the galleon's best defense as Master Pretty discovered, for the Spaniards threw them

> overboord upon our heads and into our ship so fast and being so many of them, that they put us off the shippe againe, with the losse of 2 of our men

which were slaine, & with the hurting of 4 or 5. . . . Our General encouraging his men afresh with the whole noyse of trumpets gave them the third encounter with our great ordinance and all our small shot to the great discomforting of our enemies raking them through in divers places, killing and spoiling many of their men. They being thus discomforted and spoiled, and their shippe being in hazard of sinking by reason of the great shot which were made, whereof some were under the water, within 5 or 6 houres fight set out a flagge of truce and parled for mercy.

After Alzola surrendered, Cavendish towed the galleon into the bay at San José and found he had a fortune in gold coin and pearls, to say nothing of silks and spices. With ultimate hubris, Cavendish presented Alzola with a signed receipt for the cargo. Cavendish had to leave behind five hundred tons of merchandise, which he fired along with the hull of the ship, and left passengers and captain ashore at San José,

> where they had a fayre river of fresh water, with great store of fresh fish, foule, and wood, and also many hares and conies upon the maine land. Our generall also gave them great store of victuals, of garvansas, peason, and some wine. Also they had all the sailes of their shippe to make them tents on shore, with license to take such store of plankes as should bee sufficient to make them a barke.

On November 29, 1587, Cavendish took the Spanish navigators and sailed for England. He arrived at Plymouth September 20, 1588, the same year in which the Spanish Armada was defeated. The survivors of the Santa Ana, with considerable ingenuity, salvaged the hull, sailed it for twelve days, arriving on mainland Mexico January 7, 1588.

The taking of the *Santa Ana* was a humiliating episode that ruined merchants in both Acapulco and Manila. After 1593, the tremendous expense of these galleons was borne by the government of Spain, and the crown regulated their size and number. They were not to be over three-hundred tons (this was never enforced—most were six to nine hundred tons), and two ships were allowed to cross yearly, with a third kept in reserve.

In 1602, Vizcaíno, to find a port to the north, discovered Monterey Bay and sailed as far north as San Francisco. Most of the California names as we know them today date to his voyage. For decades the bay at San Lucas was known as San Bernabé, for Vizcaíno sailed into it on that saint's day, June 11, 1602.

The galleons were relatively unmolested for over a hundred years until the War of Spanish Succession, when the English privateer Woodes Rogers set sail with two ships, the *Duke* and *Duchess* (captained by Edward Cooke), financed and equipped by Bristol merchants, who discerned that there were greater gains to be had from privateering than from regular trade. Also obvious was that Spain's ability to pursue the war depended upon the wealth brought her by the Manila galleons. The "Prize Act" provisions appended to an Act of Parliament in March 1708 provided incentives to trigger just such an expedition as Rogers's. Armed with a total of sixty-two cannon, Rogers set sail for New Spain that same year.

An able leader, skilled diplomat, and experienced sailor, he needed to be all of these, for his crew sounds like a Gilbert and Sullivan operetta. On the way, Rogers stopped at Juan Fernández Island off the coast of Chile, where he found and took on board a trained sailor named Alexander Selkirk, who had been put off there four years previously for quarreling with his captain.

That year two galleons were expected: *Nuestra Señora de Begoña* and *Nuestra Señora de la Encarnación y del Desengaño*. Rogers arrived at the end of November, 1709, and ordered his ships to sail stations so that they might see anything passing. Seeing fire on shore one evening, he discovered the presence of Indians near fresh water at San José del Cabo, where he estimated five hundred lived. He found them to be

> the poorest Wretches in Nature, and had no manner of Refreshment for us . . . a dull Musician rubbing two jagged Sticks a-cross each other, and humming to it, to divert and welcome their new Guests.

A month passed in patrols. Time and uncertainty hung heavy; Rogers was called upon to adjudicate countless disputes between crew members. One of Roger's crew members discovered that bread and sugar had been stolen and blamed it on the steward, who told Rogers that

> he lay next the Door, and the Key fastned to his Privy Parts, because he had it once stoln out of his Pocket, I suppose by the same Thief, who was so dextrous to get it now without disturbing him; but not being ingenious enough to fasten it to the same Place, he was discover'd.

The time in which the galleons were expected passed. Not seeing them, Rogers feared that they had eluded him and consulted with his officers about abandoning the search:

> By the foregoing Account it's plain what Flower and Bread-kind we have left, and the risque we must now run to get to the East-Indies, with so mean a

Stock. This I doubt not will be full Satisfaction to our Imployers, that we have prolonged our Cruize to the utmost Extent, in hopes to meet the Rich Manila Ship: But since Fortune has not favour'd us, we must think of other Methods to promote our Safety and Interest . . . 'tis my Opinion, that now our Time is so far spent, we ought to attempt nothing more in these Seas, lest our too long Stay might be the Loss of all, because the Worm has already entred our Sheathing. For these and other Reasons, I think it highly necessary, that from this Instant we make all manner of Dispatch to fit, and sail hence.

The *Duchess* went into San Lucas Bay December 31, 1709, the *Duke* stood outside the harbor, ready to leave the next day. At nine o'clock on New Year's Day morning, *Duke*'s lookout spotted a ship which turned out to be the *Encarnación*. Rogers attacked and boarded her, whereupon he learned that the larger, more valuable *Begoña* was behind her. But Rogers had been wounded in the attack on the *Encarnación* and was also shorthanded because many of his men had gotten scurvy during the long voyage and wait, and some had to be left to guard prisoners. When the *Begoña* was sighted a few days later, Rogers had to direct the battle from the harbor, getting signals from his lookout posted on a nearby hill—surely La Vigía. His ships were repulsed. The *Begoña*, though damaged, made Acapulco.

The thirty-year-old Alexander Selkirk was made first mate of the captured galleon, the first to be taken to England. On the 21st of January Rogers sailed for England, arriving a year and a half later, having profited (the reports vary) between 148,000 and 800,000 pounds sterling. Both Rogers and Cooke published accounts of the trip in 1712, and although popular, neither attained the fame of the book published by Rogers's friend, Daniel Defoe, about Selkirk, whom Defoe called *Robinson Crusoe*.

Safety from further harassment lay in securing the land north of the peninsula so that the galleons might have a safe port before rounding the Cape. For this reason Father Kino undertook his long trip in 1700, and by 1776 the ports of San Diego, Monterey, and San Francisco, connected by a chain of missions, were established. By 1804, with the Napoleonic invasions and the rebellion in New Spain, Spain had more pressing problems on her mind. In October, 1813, Ferdinand VII terminated the Manila trade and in 1815 the last galleon left Acapulco, bound for Spain.

When Woodes Rogers described the bay at Cabo San Lucas, he found the shallows good anchoring but "the rest of that Bay is very deep, and near the Rocks on the Larboard-side going in there's no Ground."

Sitting 500 feet above, I can see a deeper blue stripe snaking out into the ocean, the underwater canyon Rogers found too deep for anchorage. Although known at the end of the nineteenth century, these canyons were unmapped until a Scripps Institute expedition in 1940 took soundings and documented their existence.

Submarine canyons are concentrated at the southern end of the peninsula. Their V-shape cross-section resembles that of typical river canyons. They have dendritic drainage patterns (as terrestrial drainage systems do), and often wind downward counter to the general slope direction. Most of these submarine canyons are far too large to have been carved by underwater currents and look to be extensions of drainage systems already established on land. Dr. Francis Shepard, who first mapped the San Lucas Canyon, thinks that these underwater canyons were formed by running water with some contributing diastrophism, those large earth movements such as faulting which are so prevalent in this area.

Their concentration at the Cape, and their absence on the rest of the peninsula, is striking. Shepard feels that the lowering of sea level during the Pleistocene epoch would have provided at least part, if not all, of the impetus for such erosion. The tip of the peninsula shows evidence of elevation, and these submarine canyons are likely drowned land valleys. They are relatively young features of the seascape; the San Lucas Canyon cuts no further than through Pliocene sediments, which suggests that the cutting was done in the last two to five million years.

The San Lucas Canyon heads close to the granite spine of La Vigía, which descends beneath the sea to form one of its walls. The canyon descends steeply to a depth of some three hundred feet, then cants down even more sharply as it descends. In some places the steep walls rise over two thousand feet above its floor. This declivity provokes sandfalls. Sometimes the sand sifts slowly enough for fish to swim through it; other times there are swift massive falls and scuba divers have lost their lives here.

From the deep bottomless blue of the underwater canyon, the bay shallows toward a long sandy beach bounding the north side of the bay. The ultramarine water, cut with facets of darker blue by the surface breeze, phases to green, then fades to beige as it shallows out on the beach. Now open and sunny, it must have been a fearsome place for the seven Japanese sailors who were put ashore here in the dark of night over a hundred years ago. A Spanish ship had rescued them after they had been adrift at sea for over three months; once they were on board, the Spaniards treated them miserably—when water ran low and the Spaniards went on ration, the Japanese received nothing. They were taken ashore at San Lucas and abandoned. One of them remembered simply: "This place had a sandy beach, and more than five *chō* inland there were mountains, some of them quite tall."

Frightened, malnourished, unable to speak the language, in San Lucas they found kindness. Two days later they were transported to San José del Cabo to live and work, and stepped into a world that sounds like today's:

> The inside of the house had an earthen floor, and on it there were spread mattresses covered with cotton print, which served as beds. The cookhouse was built separately and had an oven made of clay. They cooked with iron pots and pans.

Some fifteen years later, in April 1859, John Xantus, then thirty-four years old, offloaded his nine tons of gear onto this beach. On top of the rise of sand as Xantus faced north was Mr. Ritchie's shack, Ritchie being an Englishman who had jumped ship as a teenager a few decades before and had settled into a semi-native existence. He had the only well; it provided the brackish water that Xantus had to walk miles to get. For decades he was the only European here; he supported himself by raising a little stock, fishing, farming, trading, smuggling, packing food to the silver mines then in operation, providing riding stock for whoever needed it and could pay for it.

Ostensibly there to set up and man the tidal gauge for the U.S. Coast Survey, in actuality, Xantus was there to collect for Spencer Baird at the Smithsonian. No wonder his first letter to Baird on April 13 was gloomy:

> The wind blows to hard all the time, and upsets every now & then my tent, as there is nothing but quick sand to fasten the pegs in. Besides it is too small, & so we [his helper, a Frenchman named Berlandier, whom he paid $30 a month] have to sleep on top of the boxes. . . . The whole shore is sand for about ¼ of a mile, & then commences a cactus desert about 6 miles deep, which is again girded on the Pacific side & north side by mountains of 5 & 6000' high. . . .

On the way down from La Vigía, looking for a cove where Xantus could have set his tidal gauge, I walk through hundreds of black and purple butterflies that I bat away to keep them from catching in my hair and fluttering in my eyes. No matter which cove he chose, he first had to build the housing and install the cumbersome foot-diameter pipe and its fittings. Then he had to wind the clockwork mechanism daily and change the chart paper monthly. At the end of the month he made a few days' worth of calculations, and sent them to San Francisco.

The records and calculations Xantus sent back were a shambles, and the Survey complained to Baird, who had the unpleasant duty of reprimanding his touchy collector. Xantus's carping holds the truth—he was existing under the most primitive, difficult circumstances, drinking marginal water, eating minimal food in miserable heat, day after day without letup:

> I am far from any shade whatever, & am constantly on the sandhill, under a vertical sun. My position is of course almost unsufferable, but I am firmly determined to hold out against all physical hindrances, until the service requires; as my honor has been assailed, a point for the vindication of which I am always ready to steak [*sic*] anything, and sacrifice anything.

Meanwhile, Xantus collected. And how he collected! With some taxonomic knowledge in mammalogy and ornithology, he did his most skilled collecting in these fields. Unlike most modern collectors who specialize, Xantus snared lizards and caught insects, snatched up crabs and starfish, gathered mollusks, netted fish. About the only things he didn't collect were algae and cacti, the latter posing a formidable problem not much relished even by modern botanists. He pressed innumerable plants, many of which honor his name, among them a shrub euphorbia with small creamy yellow blossoms that straggles up the cliffsides of San Lucas; a pink daisylike flower that grows on gravelly slopes above the sea; and a small lavender-flowered milkwort. One paper alone, published by Dr. Asa Gray on Xantus's specimens, contained 121 new species. New to science among the 290 species he collected were 57 mollusks, 48 crustacea, 66 fish, 25 insects, and 18 birds. And of these, nearly fifty were tagged *xantusi* or *xantusii* or *xantusiana* or *xantii*. That some of this nomenclature on further study has proved to be either obsolete or inaccurate in no way diminishes Xantus's contribution.

Xantus's second year at Cabo San Lucas brought him fewer new specimens, and exacerbated his problems. He had to make his own boxes for shipping; wood was, and still is, scarce and costly at the Cape. Boxes of specimens piled up on the beach awaiting chance calls from whalers; if too many accumulated, they had to be sent to La Paz or Mazatlán at his expense. His meager pay was always months late. Needed supplies appeared spasmodically, if at all. He was plagued by local vagabonds and out of touch with the rest of the world. All his despair sweats out in his words:

> I am quite sick indeed of this place, every day seems a long year, and every one with the same monotonous desolation around me, not affording the least pleasure, variety, or enjoyment of any kind. I have no reading matter whatever. . . . I am now of Gods grace nearly two years perched on this sandbeach, a

Land's End, La Vigía

laughing stock probably of the Pelicans & Turkey buzzards the only signs of life around me. To the E & SE the eternally smoky Gulf, to all other points of the compass the sandy desert, covered with white salina and ornamented with cactuses in every form, sticking out like candlesticks on a white cloth. . . . There is not a blade of grass in the country, & not a green leaf. Sand, salt, trunks of shrubs, Rocks & the like everywhere and covered everywhere with bleached bones of catle mules horses etc, died by thousands lately of starvation.

His letters mentioned Hungary more and more often. He made his last field book entry in December, 1860, months before he left. In August, 1861, he sold some of his government equipment, pocketed the proceeds, packed his shreds of clothing, nailed shut the last barrels of specimens, cleaned and oiled his guns, and disembarked from the beach on the same kind of heavy hot day as that on which he had arrived. He died thirty years later, never having achieved anything of as much worth as the collecting he did here. I envy him that wide-open landscape full of species for the naming, and all alone in that place where "the wind blows to hard all the time."

Beneath the rock mass of La Vigía and the arches of land's end, where each pinnacle has its resident sea lion, the sea has bellowed through a slot, and the wind has filled it with sand, creating a beach with one end on the Pacific, the other on the Bay. Walls rise at least one hundred and fifty feet high, as jointed as if wrapped in gray paper, tied and retied with string which cut into the surface, some Cristo invention come to life. And about halfway up the granite is fluted and full of holes. How many storms, how many centuries, how many times did the sea fly through here, slamming and wedging, its percussion loosening the grip of granite grain after grain, plucking them out, leaving the grinning solution holes? When the seas thunder that high, the sound must be awesome, and that immutable indivisible granite, rock of ages, symbol for eternity, gets eaten away like the most yielding sandstone. The power of the sea was never more clearly diagrammed to me: eighty feet up on those walls the sea has clawed portholes in the granite. The facing wall shoots up, equally scooped out, troughs that go upward in long sinuous Art Nouveau curves that curl themselves tighter at the end, a splendid façade, twisted and smoothed, cupped and curved, shattered and caressed.

The sea rules here and even the granite cannot withstand, where what one believes to be true and enduring is shot away with a pitiless torque of sea. It is all nothing to the ocean and tomorrow the water will roar through again and in millennia to come it will all be gone, and where I have sat, great fish who have survived it all will swim among these towers.

V
THE GULF
OF CALIFORNIA

It has a near resemblance to the Adriatick, a branch of the Mediterranean formed by the coast of Italy, and that of Dalmatia in Greece. The ancient discoverers called it Mar Barmejo, and Mar Roxo, the Red sea, from its resembling in form, and sometimes in colour and appearance, the gulf of Arabia, which runs from Suez, betwixt the coasts of Africa and Asia, and is celebrated for the Israelites passing it on foot. It has also been called Mar de Cortez, in compliance with the solicitude of the conqueror of the Mexican empire, in order to augment the glory of his enterprizes.

Miguel Venegas
A Natural and Civil History of California
1757

White-lined sphinx moth (*Hyles lineata*)

SEA OF CORTÉS

As the East Coast of Baja California curves northward into the Gulf of California, fishing camps take advantage of the excellent deep sea fishing. The Gulf is a narrow embayment that stretches nearly ten degrees in latitude and is seldom wider than a hundred miles. It was, and still often is, called the Sea of Cortés for its "discoverer," who first sailed and explored it in 1535.

In early times it was also called Mar Vermejo or Vermilion Sea because of its reddish cast. In the late winter and early spring minuscule plants often "bloom" in such numbers that they turn the water red and opaque; nearly all the early sailors of its waters note the "red tides." The autumn increase in dissolved phosphate and silica in the surface waters decreases as growing diatoms and other phytoplankton consume it in relatively rapid growth. Small patches of red water may appear by December. Over twenty species of dinoflagellates, so-called because of their two flagella, one wound round the body and the other trailing loose, cause the red tides. Dinoflagellates are on the border between plants and animals; they sometimes create their food through photosynthesis as plants do, and sometimes ingest it as animals do. In the latter state, some of them are toxic to fish, disrupting the nervous system, and a red tide is usually accompanied by considerable fish kill.

Gulf of California

At Punta Colorada fishing is especially good because an underwater canyon shoots out from shore here, roughly perpendicular to and eventually joining the main trough of the Gulf. The steep dropoff into deep water instigates the circulation and overturn of waters, bringing up cold water and ample food. In some places eighteen hundred fathoms deep, the deep water of the Gulf extends in close to land on the peninsula side while on the mainland shore there are wide shelves gentling into the sea. The lack of banks along the western shore tends to be typical of areas which have had diastrophic movement, such as the massive faulting common on the peninsula.

When we sit down to dinner family style, my first question is if anyone's explored the land back from the beach. I receive a chorus of "Oh no! We come here to *fish!*" The fishing-camp guests are predominantly men. And the talk is predominantly fish: a record-size 550-pound marlin caught today. Mexican ingenuity: how do you weigh a 550-pound marlin when you only have 220 kilo weights? You hack it into two pieces, weigh each piece separately, and add it up. Smaller marlin turned loose, five dorado, what kind of line weights, and are dorado going after red and white feather lures? "We gaffed a turtle—thought sure we'd have turtle soup for dinner!" "Want to go dove hunting tomorrow? Get a couple of dozen or so, use my .22 scatter gun." Where to go for "bill fish," where for "sails." Dorado congregate around any floating object—someone tells the story of a body found floating face down (apologetic looks at me, the only woman at the table) that the Mexicans left there because the dorado came in numbers and created such good fishing.

After dinner, Jeannie Briggs brings out a whole bucketful of beautiful shells her husband got from a shrimp trawler. We look at them with a mixture of awe and despair. All are alive. Some of the beautiful shells I've only seen in illustrations before. There are whole scallops of which I seldom find the smaller flat valves shaped like cats' paws, washed up on beaches, but often the larger bowl-shaped lower valves. Luminous moon shells. Lovely cockles. The shrimp man was complaining because there are so few fish this year, and added with a shrug, "In a few years—all gone."

When the shrimpers harvest, they trawl with a long V-shaped net attached to a rakelike dredge that rasps everything off the bottom, shrimp as well as all other marine plants and animals, which they call "trash." I cannot help but think of John Steinbeck's 1941 description of the twelve-boat fleet of Japanese shrimpers who were doing a very systematic job, not only of taking every shrimp from the bottom, but every other living thing as well. They cruised slowly along in echelon with overlapping dredges, literally scraping the bottom clean.

Steinbeck found tons of shrimp on the deck of one of the ships along with an appalling number of all kinds of fish, anemones, gorgonians—everything that lived on the bottom, all half-dead, to be thrown overboard. Steinbeck wrote:

> The Mexican official and the Japanese captain were both good men, but by their association in a project directed honestly or dishonestly by forces behind and above them, they were committing a true crime against nature and against the immediate welfare of Mexico and the eventual welfare of the whole human species.

Could it be that it has taken only forty years for his nightmare to begin coming true?

About five miles south of the fishing camp at Punta Colorada, the lighthouse at Punta Arena anchors a sandy point; a low lighthouse visible for only eleven miles, which does not matter for, unlike the other Cape lighthouses, this one is manned and equipped with radio antennae and radar beacons.

It sits on a cuspate foreland built up by strong southeast winds. Winter gales with high winds are not uncommon. Squall-like *chubascos,* which originate in the Caribbean off the coast of Central America and a few days later reach the Gulf, and occasional hurricanes rake the peninsula, often with devastating effect; both can do massive sand rearranging. The point develops on a shoal at an angle of the coastline and has two distinct sets of low sand ridges running essentially parallel to the northeast and southeast sides of the point, indicating most of the deposition of sand came from the south.

Herman and I start out early, fully intending to reach the lighthouse and be back before lunch. Little sandpipers totter back and forth just ahead of us. These cosmopolitan birds breed only in the Arctic, wintering to the south. They follow the foam line, making three or four quick consecutive stabs half-beak deep, the mandibles open by half an inch, at the end snapping shut on whatever tidbit turns up, searching for sand hoppers, isopods, worms. Their former generic name, *Ereunetes,* comes from the Greek word for searcher, or prober.

Out on a rock ledge an elegant gray willet, in morning attire of light gray

Boy with fish

plumage, stalks and pokes with its long, thin beak, then glides to another rock. When it spread its wings vivid patterns of dark brown and white flashed, but it tucked in its wings quickly and once again was only a soft dapper gray. A single black turnstone wanders among the rocks, short-legged and stout by comparison with its longer-legged companions, but also revealing vivid wing and back patterns when it flies.

The common shorebirds of the Lower California coast may have great bearing on the abundance, location, and shoreward evolutionary trends of invertebrate animals. Most of these birds are highly specialized, with long slender bills and long legs. Willets and godwits stick their long beaks deep into the sand for sand crabs or worms. Sanderlings, plovers, terns, and gulls are also adept at locating food buried in the sand. Turnstones do just that, finding food under rocks, or poking about in the beach wrack.

Seabirds have such evocative names: willet, sandpiper, dowitcher, tern, turnstone, godwit, petrel, loon, grebe, blue-footed booby, puffin, sanderling, tattler. Whereas land birds seem to me rather dull: robin or sparrow; or terribly literal: black-chinned gray warbler or yellow-bellied sapsucker. If I were a bird, I think I would like to be designated *Ereunetes desultorious*—the desultory wanderer.

Out in the Gulf, porpoises begin jumping, their black fins gleaming in ones and twos over a twenty-degree arc of ocean. Whatever fish it is that schools just beneath the surface, there are so many they change the water's sheen, faceting the surface, and sometimes jumping through as pale sparks of light.

Last night and this morning manta rays were jumping and the "whap whap" was audible over the beach noises. Joseph Wood Krutch remarked about their leaping that

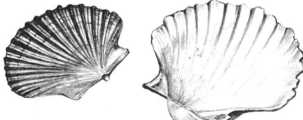

Pecten
(*Argopecten circularis*)

no one seems to know just why, perhaps out of sheer exuberance, perhaps, as the more prosaic suggest, to shake off parasites. These harmless though sinister-looking "devilfish" which swim through the water by flapping their bat wings, are ancient relatives of the sharks and they give birth to their young alive, dropping them one by one from the air in the course of a leap.

They are huge fish and made an indelible impression on Father Antonio Ascensión when he accompanied Sebastián Vizcaíno on his exploration around the Cape in 1602:

> The devil-fish are so large that one of them wrapped itself around the cable of the anchor-buoy with which the *Almiranta* was made fast, pulled it up and made off with it and the ship, so that it was necessary to kill it, but a large number of soldiers and sailors who were pulling it with strong ropes never succeeded in getting it out on land from the water. The mouth is like a half-moon, seven spans across from one side to the other, and from the head to the tail it measures seventeen spans.

Because of its size and shape, there were many legends about it:

> One fish which is like nothing else grows there; it appears to be a mossy blanket extending to several unequal points. . . . Its motion is scarcely perceptible, but when its prey is near it moves with great speed and enfolds and squeezes it. It is a very rare man who can save his life even though he is armed to strike out and defend himself.

I never do get to the lighthouse, having had too many things to see on the way, following my usual boustrophedon path looking for shells. On the way back I walk high up on the beach in the deep, loose sand to see what I didn't see while walking at the water's edge on the way. The biggest shells are far up on the beach, far above the storm line—lovely round deep scallops as big as my palm, along with cockles, olives, and ark shells.

Ahead of me a female turtle came ashore recently to lay her eggs. She gouged an unmistakable serpentine path through the sand, a trail about six feet wide formed by a series of scoops on either side of a central trough. She made no beeline out of the water but dragged up the berm in a wide curving trail maybe thirty feet long in an open arc that tightened into a close spiral, ending in three massive hollows marked with sand heaps on either side. From them a straight trough leads seaward. Nesting site found, work finished, she labored straight back to the safe sea—a thoroughly aquatic vegetarian, she comes ashore only to lay her eggs. In these big scooped-out fans in the sand I sense the ponderousness of the animal, the slowness of the pushing, the strain of dragging a gravid carcass.

Although not to compare with the eleven-foot turtles that paddled through the sea when salt water covered the North American continent from the Gulf to the Arctic 1,000 million years ago, present-day turtles still weigh up to four hundred pounds. I have no way of knowing of what species she was, although all the sea turtles of the eastern Pacific probably also occur on the west coast of the Gulf. The green turtle, named from the color of its fat, was reported as abundant in 1889, and these reach a length of five feet and two hundred pounds. Barco reports that when the Indians

> see a turtle near, they throw themselves into the water and attempt to turn the turtle over. Once this is done the turtle is theirs, because once in that condition it cannot get away. They put it into the canoe with caution, to avoid the turtle's strong bites as it defends itself.

The Spanish galleons "took on turtles" by the hundreds, for fresh meat and also for ballast—they would live in the hold for as long as eighteen months, and could then be butchered for meat and oil.

The carapaces of two dead crabs lie on the beach. One of them is bleached white, with an abdomen that curves up and under and snugs in a slot of the thorax; the other is fresher, and when I pick it up many little scavenger beetles dash for cover. These are brachyuran or "true" crabs, in which the reduced abdomen fits snugly in a shallow depression beneath. Most of the crabs living in the Gulf came northward from Central America, and of these the brachyuran crabs extend the farthest north.

The characteristics of the Gulf have made for a distinctive Gulf fauna. Generally the fauna is a northward extension of the Panamic province fauna with the northern boundary at Cabo San Lucas, although it may extend up to Magdalena Bay in warm pockets. With a very few exceptions, the Gulf littoral fauna is distinctly tropical in the southern Gulf, which differs considerably from the northern. The Pacific fauna probably immigrated to the Gulf either by past water connection across the peninsula (as across the lowland at La Paz when the Cape was an island), or by a southward displacement of present-day isotherms—warmer-water temperatures at Cabo San Lucas would have permitted immigration around the tip of the peninsula and up into the Gulf.

This same afternoon Herman and I walk northward from Punta Colorada, along the water's edge, our deep footprints in the saturated sand filling instantly with water. The sand is granitic and filled with black mica that adheres to my feet—at first I think it minute particles of oil, but on examination I'm relieved to find it mica.

Hundreds of quarter-inch holes pepper the sand. As a wave washes up they all spurt one-inch fountains and, as it recedes, they pop open. Hundreds of little sand-colored sea fleas spring off the beach like popcorn ahead of my footsteps. These tiny, leaping amphipods find their way back to their burrows by taking a reading of the moon, and possibly make adjustments nightly by orienting to the setting sun and rising moon. Not that they necessarily return to the hole they had dug—many sparring matches occur at the entrance of a burrow for possession thereof.

Five brown pelicans pass *in echelon*, followed by an egret, swift and purposeful, legs streaming out behind. A black tern fishes the breaking wave, in and out, patrolling, diving, swift and precise. Its pointed wings beat fast, its underside flashes brilliant white, black beak and forked tail sharp against the sea.

Farther down, the beach boulders are half-buried in the sand, with outcroppings extending twenty to thirty feet out into the water, rising in fanciful pinnacles above the sea, each one whitewashed and sporting its resident soup-tureen pelican. Such wonderful birds, ponderously dignified, taking off in an ungainly tangle of wings, toting beaks as big as fuller's shears, skimming with precision on the air cushion just above the surface of the water, then a controlled crash on a rock of choice, one elbow hooked in, then the other, a general shaking down and settling of frame, and again the immutable soup-tureen pose.

I've done some silly things in my life but I never thought I would be wading waist-deep into the ocean and waving and hollering to unseat six pelicans and four cormorants posted twenty feet away. The Photographer says go get them to fly so he can photograph them coming in to land. Photographers with motor drives are insatiable. The pelicans are unimpressed. Pelicans can look, when put upon, irritatingly superior. Supercilious. My extravagant operatic gestures impress neither them nor The Photographer. Finally one, with world-weary boredom, heaves itself into the air with such a slow wingbeat that it seems impossible that it can fly. It does not return. The rest remain unperturbed. I give up. Bait your own pelicans, Herman.

On the beach lies a pelican skull with massive eye sockets and a foot-

Slipper shells (*Crepidula striolata*)

long beak. A center ridge divides the beautifully sculpted top surface into three sections, the center ridge terminating in a hook at one end that just fits over my finger, broadening to the forehead at the other. Despite its size it hangs lightly from my hand.

The beach has completely changed in the last two months. Since then it has built out into a broad apron, where a group of willets now hold a convention. It is strewn with cockle and clam shells, some limpets, a few olives, and hundreds of slipper shells, which grow attached to offshore rocks. Cemented together in chains, at the bottom, are the oldest slipper shells—all female. At the top are the youngest—all male. And in the middle there are one or two in the process of remodeling. The chains attract free-floating larvae, which settle on the top and develop into males, although if one settles alone, it becomes a female, attracting a settling of male larvae. Older males remain male as long as attached to a female; if isolated, they develop into females. If a large number of males develop, then certain of these will become female.

Because these mollusks have become sessile, no longer crawling the sea bottom for food, some of the accouterments necessary for the meandering life have atrophied and others have been added. The radula, a kind of toothed ribbon used for scraping food, common to most gastropods, is reduced. Instead they extrude threadlike mucous secretions which entangle food brought by water currents. Sessile, they have lost the large muscular foot of most gastropods.

Among dozens of beached porcupinefish, six to eight inches long, lies one guinea fowl pufferfish. The skin, poisonous in life, has retracted around the mouth, revealing a bony structure beneath formed by fused jaw teeth that resemble nothing so much as a huge white beak. Porcupinefish are less poisonous than pufferfish, but when inflated their long, toxic spines become erect and make them formidable for their size.

Cockle shells are strewn all over, from fingernail to hand size, the fresher ones still rough, with short imbricated spines, in lovely pinks and roses and salmons marbled over ivory. The fossil record suggests that such bivalves probably arose from a common ancestor that lived in a single conical dome-like shell, something like a big limpet, with a mantle that hung down over its head and foot like a curtain. The foot lost its original creeping sole as the need to travel disappeared, and developed a wedge shape for burrowing efficiency. At the same time two shells developed out of one, hinged together dorsally. The gills enlarged and now serve both for food-collecting and respiration. Tubular prolongations on the mantle edges became siphons, which allowed the mollusk to burrow out of harm's way but still maintain contact with the open water that contained its food. All of these changes made it possible for them to abandon the hard and limited substrates to which their ancestors had been confined, and to take advantage of the much larger available area of soft-bottomed habitats. A cockle has not lost the capacity to move, however, and extends its foot and then forcefully contracts it, progressing in fits and starts.

As I walk back, a fisherman comes down to the beach with rod and tackle. He begins casting twenty-five feet out into the open ocean in beautiful slow arcs, patiently reeling in, walking slowly down the beach as he does so. It is

Pelicans and cormorant

as if the slow rhythmic casting has quieted the beat of the surf. I sit and watch. The dune shadow creeps across the beach and still I stay, content to watch the day rolling closed.

After dinner I gaze at a beautiful sphinx moth splayed on the pillar in front of the dining room. Behind me I hear the voice of one of the fishermen: "You like moths, little lady? This is no place to see 'em—they spray with pyrethrum down here to keep down the cockroach population. If you want *moths* you go up on the second story of the next building!" And there they are—composed on the wall like one of those composite pictures of all the colorful moths (or butterflies or beetles) in the frontispieces of books about moths (or butterflies or beetles), all the most gorgeous species on one page.

There are more than a dozen sphinx moths. Although varied in color and marking, all are easily recognizable: medium to large moths with heavy torpedo-shaped bodies. One, three inches long, is rose and gray with barred wings; a bigger one flares its gray flannel wings to reveal underwings the salmon pink of a small mammal's mouth agape. Deep yellow dots spotlight the length of another's abdomen, and it has a tongue at least as long as its body and comblike bristles on its legs. One is a striped morning sphinx, common throughout North America, a male with extravagantly feathered antennae full of sensors with which to pick up the scent of the females.

All are swift fliers that can reach thirty-four miles per hour, even faster with the help of a tailwind, in contrast to butterflies, which tilt frivolously through the air between six and nine mph. Some sphinx moths beat their wings so quickly that they blur, their fast flight and high maneuverability necessities for those that feed only in the brief half-light between day and night, just when bats come out to hunt. Since they fly in the cool of the day, they cannot use sunlight to heat up their flight muscles; instead they vibrate their wings so rapidly that approximately the same amount of heat increase is generated as if they were in the sun.

A large mousy-colored moth, disturbed, flares its wings, uncovering hindwings centered with eye patterns. The closer the circle is to a vertebrate's eye pattern the more effective this display is in discouraging bird predators. One sphinx moth, when it shows its eyespots, even shifts its wings to give the impression of eye movement. Since birds can learn to recognize and then to ignore eyespots, it is to the moth's advantage not to reveal them too often, and most moths keep them hidden, resorting to them as a second line of defense, the first being cryptic coloration and stillness.

Moth (*Agapema galbina*)

Moth (*Syssphinx* sp.)

Moth (*Noropsis hieroglyphica*)

The biggest moths of all are a handspan across, deep purple brown, with subtle lavender scallops and ringed eyes and exquisite variations of shading. I remember one year at the end of October when there must have been a mass hatch and dozens appeared, posed on every available vertical surface, as big as bats.

Several fat-bodied ermine moths bear delicately scaled white wings. This species is unpalatable to predators, but less so than one it closely resembles. The latter species hatches first and is so unpleasant to predators that they learn to avoid it; the second more palatable species hatches later, after predators have learned to avoid the original. My favorites are some I have never seen before, just an inch long, of pale gold figured with ebony, their intricate patterns resembling an Egyptian scarab. I'm not the first one to think so: their specific name is *hieroglyphica*.

Perched on the lintel above this array, a magnificent lime green mantis watches for lunch on the wing. The mantis stalks in slow deliberate motion, adjusting the position of its spine-studded forelegs each time it moves. Woe to the insect impaled there.

Long before I'm ready to stop moth-watching, Herman wants to take a flashlight and go walk the beach. As we walk down, yellow evening primroses have opened, perfuming the air, pale and luminous in the dusk, typical moth-pollinated flowers. The beach twinkles with little ghost crabs. The lantern light picks them up on damp sand, just above the swash line, where they stand on stilt-like legs, their eyestalks extended, giving them a look of great inquisitiveness. They crouch low so that the water smooths over them, then rise up on tiptoe before the next wave. Most of them stand their ground, and only skitter into the water when they feel threatened, the water sometimes tumbling them tail over teacup.

They spurt into the surf with deceptive quickness, and indeed are among the fastest of running crabs. When they run they move sideways, using only two or three pairs of their legs, kept from becoming entangled with each other by the width of their bodies. The forward legs flex and pull the body forward, the trailing legs extend and push. Because one set of muscles would tire if the crab kept its body always oriented in the same direction, it frequently spins its body 180 degrees without missing a beat, almost too quick for the eye to see.

One scampers up the beach instead of following the rest into the water and nestles into a hollow in the sand, ostrichlike. Herman scoops it up easily and hands it to me. Its carapace is pale tan, almost translucent, the shell suffused with pale flesh tones, speckled with soft gray, with a granular sand-like texture. It is pointed at the front corners, with a thin rim of white tracing its edges—a lovely little creature. Its eyes retract, its unequal chelae wave in threat (chelae are a crab's first pair of legs modified into heavy claws). Used for capturing and eating food, a claw is already open when the cheliped is extended, ready to snap shut on anything unfortunate enough to be within range. When the claw snaps shut, it is locked closed by a powerful muscle. These two actions—opening and closing—are innervated by a single axon, a fine economy characteristic of crustacean nervous systems.

Ghost crabs nest in burrows in the beach far up in dry sand, and above the windrow line are rimmed silver-dollar-sized holes. Several have busy bird tracks around them. On fresh ones, little crab claw marks punctuate the opening. The depth of the burrow depends upon how far damp sand is below the surface—they may burrow as deep as four feet to reach it. Once ensconced, they can produce a buzzing sound by rubbing their chelae together; this may serve as a warning that the hole is occupied, since there seems to be little compunction about occupying someone else's burrow. The crab unwittingly shares its burrow with many commensals, among them a mosquito that lives nowhere else. The mosquito remains in the upper reaches of the burrow during the day; equipped with elongate antennae, it gets early notice of the crab's return and vacates until the crab is back in

Ghost crab

196

Hermit crab

residence before re-entering. Often they swarm above the burrows during mating times.

I look up from the little fellow in my hand and scan the sky for its counterpart in the heavens. It is a breathtakingly clear and beautiful night, lit only by starlight. Cassiopeia and Aldebaran gleam, the Pleiades lie on the horizon. Polaris glitters to the north. To the south, Canopus glows low in the sky, like Polaris, one of the most ancient guide stars. The same stars that now guide spacecraft through the infinite guided the Spanish mariners through years of misadventure on this stubborn finite sea.

The color of the water changed, in the ocean it was blue, and now in the Gulf of California it is green-gray. I noted on the round world voyage, in the voyage to northern California, and now in southern California, that there where the color of the waters has the above coloring, which is mainly in gulfs, straits, bays, the water lights up strongly at night.

I. G. Voznesenskii
Aboard the Naslednik Aleksandr
1842

Puncture vine (*Tribulus cistoides*)

PULMO REEF

On a morning with a high overcast Juan Antonio picks us up on the beach at eight-thirty. His *panga* is fiberglass, with an outboard motor, a far cry from the slowly-crafted wooden ships of four hundred years ago that plied the Sea of Cortés. Nor does Juan Antonio resemble a conquistador: he wears a baseball cap and squint crinkles at the corners of his eyes. He does not smile much, but gets down to the business at hand of starting the motor. Rocks and shoals pack the shoreline, so we head straight out into open water on our way to Punta Pulmo, ten miles down the coast.

We bore toward a horizon which is all light, a sea emblazoned with sun diamonds. Heavily scrubbed slopes back the undulating beach line, all against a backdrop of blue mountains. Cerro Las Barracas rises 1,500 feet to the southwest, hazy blue behind a low sloping saddle of vegetated dune. Sometimes the ridges rise back from the beach and other times the headlands come down to the water, rocky faces split and riven, angular boulders hanging on the wall, angular boulders at the base, darker by being wet but just as sharp-angled as if they had fallen last night.

The bow of the *panga* smacks against a short chop. Most of the year water circulation in the Gulf of California is counterclockwise, entering at a depth

Gulf coastline, dry arroyos

of about 300 feet along the east, exiting along the west at about 150 feet below the surface. In the southern Gulf, onshore water temperatures may go down to around 62 degrees in winter, and up to 90 degrees in summer. Because of its warmer winter waters, the southern Gulf is considered a subtropical to tropical habitat.

Standing on the beach are two pelicans and six white egrets. The egrets always remind me of cartoon birds, fancy white feathers, long black legs, wearing yellow gloves on their outlandish feet. Elegant in flight, on the beach they look like perfect misanthropes, shoulders hunched against the world's injustices. Stalking across the tidepools, they lift each foot in exaggerated manner, stopping to peer into the water, then swiftly spearing a fish, tossing it up, catching it, and gulping it down. Since it's November, they have probably been here a month or so. Their specific name, *thula*, was the name given by ancient geographers to the northernmost place on the globe. Although their range does not reach that far north, they do migrate, and may nest and breed in Baja.

The motor misses. Juan Antonio runs it fast, then slow, listening to its sound so attentively I almost expect to see a stethoscope in his hands.

The engine quits. I see no oars, no oarlocks. "Tiene wrench?" Juan Antonio asks. "No tengo," says Herman, who can fix anything and so, I suppose, looks as if he would of course have a wrench with him. Juan Antonio looks at me. I shrug. "No tengo."

Juan Antonio pounds on a sparkplug. Ah, fixed—twin cylinders, one plug not hooked up. The motor starts with a jerk.

As we head out to sea, I sight back to the horizon line on shore, always uneven, as a child tears coarse construction paper to make mountains—some steep, some gradual, but always rough, always ragged, always softened by the light into haunting mysterious presences. Is this what the sailors who first saw this coastline saw—a gentle rim of mountains floating over light-filled valleys, a promising beauty that dissolved into brutal reality which, for many of them, became final reality? How many stood, spraddle-legged on the deck, steadied against the swell, glass to eye and tried to see the promised glint of gold? Or wondered at such a bleak and empty place?

When Hernán Cortés first sighted California's craggy horizon in 1525, there was hope that it was an island with easy passage west to the Spice Islands. Cortés went back to Spain in 1529 to raise funds and secure royal sanctions for further expeditions to the west of New Spain. The crown pressed him to discover a shorter way to get from New Spain to the spice supply which brought such high prices in Europe. In return for royal permis-

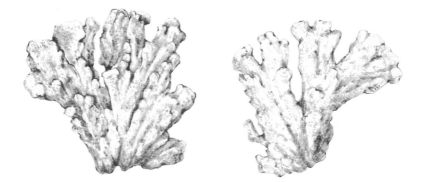

Coral (*Pocillopora elegans*)

sion the crown extracted a hard bargain: Cortés must finance the expeditions himself. Stories about a legendary island loaded with gold and rolling with pearls were lost on a hard-headed king.

In 1532, Cortés, back in Mexico, sent out two ships on an exploratory mission. The first was lost at sea. Sailors on the second mutinied, killing the captain. Command was assumed by the pilot, Ordoño Jiménez, who put off ship anyone who did not support him, sailed northward, and blundered into a large bay populated by what he thought to be friendly natives—Jiménez apparently was the first white man to set foot here. He named it La Paz— "peace"—because of the amiable Indians, a judgment fatally wrong. His men found pearls, bartering for them with the local Indians, and then extended their collecting to Indian women. Inflamed, the Indians murdered Jiménez and twenty of his crew; the rest escaped.

Three years later Cortés again outfitted an expedition. On May 1, 1535, he landed at La Paz with three ships and renamed it Santa Cruz because of the religious festival celebrated on the day. Supplies ran short and he was forced to sail back to mainland Mexico for replenishment. When he returned to La Paz he found that twenty-three of his men had died from starvation. He abandoned Santa Cruz to save the lives of the remainder, acknowledging that there was simply not enough food available to sustain colonists. Cortés's map of 1535, delineating that part of the peninsula below 26 degrees, was found in his papers but was never printed.

His last attempt took place in 1539. Cortés directed three ships to explore the Gulf, under the command of Francisco de Ulloa, the first mariner to record tides in the Gulf. Well knowing on which side his bread was buttered, Ulloa sailed the gulf to its upper end and named it Mar de Cortés. From this trip also dates the name of Vermilion Sea, for Ulloa and his men saw the phytoplankton blooms that colored the water. Then he sailed back down the east coast of the peninsula and around the corner to the southernmost end. He marked the distance from Santa Cruz to Cabo San Lucas, then doubled the Cape and neither he nor his ship were ever heard from again.

All in all, Cortés spent a fortune of 200,000 pesos on the Baja peninsula and had nothing but a few pearls to show for it. Cortés was out of favor with Charles V, who found Cortés's superior leadership ability a possible threat, and with the local viceroy, who had ambitions of his own. The King recalled Cortés to Spain and he never saw Mexico again.

The viceroy, delighted to be rid of Cortés, immediately funded his own expedition under the command of Juan Rodríguez Cabrillo, an expert Portuguese navigator who had been in Mexico since 1520. Cabrillo's orders were to explore the west coast of the peninsula, and since the peninsula was thought to be an island, to continue until he found a passage to the north. Cabrillo left the mainland June 27, 1542. Ten days later he reached Cabo San Lucas, and he entered in his *Relación*—his rutter— that it was "a clean coast, without any deviation; within, on the land, appear high and bare and rugged ridges." He sailed as far as the 44th parallel in northern California and returned to Mexico in April, 1543, not having found passage around the "island."

Fifty years later, the crown commanded Sebastián Vizcaíno to secure Lower California and make it safe for the Manila galleons, which passed there on their return trips. In 1596 Vizcaíno, who had been aboard the *Santa Ana* when it was captured in 1587, left Acapulco in three ships carrying soldiers and provisions. Looking for an appropriate place for a colony, he disembarked at Santa Cruz, remained two months, and then, like Cortés, was forced to return to Acapulco for supplies. He sailed out again in 1602, accompanied by Father Antonio de la Ascención, a priest who wrote a detailed diary of the voyage, which contained a mixture of valuable observations, interspersed with fancy, that only fueled some of the fanciful notions already in effect, such as, "I hold it to be very certain and proven that the whole kingdom of California, discovered on this voyage, is the largest island known or which has been discovered up to the present day." Vizcaíno had with him Cabrillo's rutter, which he found useless. Because of strong northwest winds Vizcaíno's second voyage took nine months instead of the usual one. The sailors contracted scurvy. Again the mission was abandoned. Like Cortés, Vizcaíno

Cabo Pulmo

went to Spain to ask for permission to further explore the peninsula, was denied, and never returned to New Spain.

The first printed map of California appeared in 1625 in *The North Part of America* and it shows Cabo San Lucas at the southernmost end of an island labeled "California." Maps continued to print it so. At about the same time, Henry Briggs, a lecturer in geometry and astronomy at Cambridge University, wrote the commentary that accompanied the map in *Treatise of the North-West Passage to the South Sea, through the Continent of Virginia, and by the Fretum Hudson:*

> . . . the Cape of California, which is now found to bee an Iland stretching it selfe from 22 degrees to 42 and lying almost directly North and South; as may appear in a map of that Iland which I have seen here in London, brought out of Holland; where the Sea upon the Northwest part may very probably come much neerer than some doe imagine.

In 1628 Francisco de Ortega received his royal sailing orders; he went out with a single small ship and returned from the peninsula with stories about gentle natives and lustrous pearls. Colonization again looked promising. Admiral Pedro Porter y Casanate was sent out in August, 1640, "continuing and bringing to fulfillment the exploration and financing of that country of pearls and peaceable Indians." His orders also included directions to find that much-desired "way of exit to the north." He was accompanied by a warship captained by Alonzo Gonzalez who found the port at Cabo San Lucas "capacious and deep" and Indians receiving "them with pleasure, throwing sand in the air and laying their bows and arrows on the ground." The expedition petered out, as did many others, through circumstances peripheral to the peninsula—ships not provided, sailors jumping ship, other ambitions, other times and tides. The admiral lost interest and went off to greener pastures in Peru.

Admiral Isidro de Atondo y Antillón made one of the final and most brutal attempts in 1683. He took seventy-four days to reach La Paz, arriving on the first of April, 1683. He invited the Indian leaders to dinner and shot ten of them on the spot. The understandable hostility of the Indians, plus a prolonged drought, served to end the expedition. He abandoned the peninsula at a cost nearly comparable to that of Cortés's.

Expeditions continued to go out every ten or twelve years or so. It was all very well to sit in Spain and issue orders, but orders and success remained disconcertingly disparate. Projects begun with great press foundered for lack of money and purpose; stories of a temperate, healthy climate and arable land and an ocean full of fabulous pearls faded against the harsh reality of little water, little food, and Indians who would or could not be friendly. This procession of treasure hunters and speculators accomplished nothing. Cortés strode over the horizon of Mexico in 1519 and it took but a few decades until Mexico's destiny was directed from Madrid. Not so on the peninsula. Well into the nineteenth century, history simply records a miserable monotony of failures on the peninsula, death by starvation, death by disease, death by murder, no gold, no riches—*nada.*

The one positive that came out of Atondo's expedition was Father Kino's report. When Father Kino sailed up the Sea of Cortés and saw unbroken land all the way north, and when he journeyed up the west coast of the mainland and crossed what was to become New Mexico to the Pacific Coast, he established once and for all that California was not an island, and undoubtedly influenced the respected French cartographer Guillaume DeLisle. DeLisle wrote, sometime around 1698, that since he didn't know whether the peninsula was an island or not, he would await further evidence. By 1702 the evidence was in, thanks to Kino's journey. News reached DeLisle who then drew it as it is, a peninsula. In 1705, Kino labeled this body of water the "Mer de la Californie" and so it has remained.

When Cabrillo left mainland Mexico that summer of 1542, on his way to explore the west coast of the peninsula and to find out what lay farther north, his first landfall on July 2 was probably Punta Pulmo. It is a clear landmark, the knob of Cabo Pulmo at water's edge connecting to an 830-foot hill that is the easternmost toe of the Sierra de la Victoria. The hydrographic map marks Punta Pulmo as dangerous as far as one mile from shore because of the coral reefs. From the air they splay out as dark fingers of deep purples, wine-dark stains in a turquoise sea.

Corals are well represented along the shore of the Cape, but most of them are solitary and generally not abundant. Because of the underwater rocky ridges to build on and the water temperature, the only prominent assemblage of reef-building corals in the Gulf exists in Bahía Pulmo. Steinbeck and Ricketts describe, in the *Sea of Cortez,* the field day of collecting they had when they set anchor here, a description as full of life as the corals they wrote about. The most recent study of the reef was done by Richard Brusca and Donald Thomson, the former a specialist in marine invertebrates, the latter in the study of reef fishes. Both are convinced that these are true

Cabo Pulmo

"constructional" reefs even though they are lacking in some of the characteristics of highly developed reefs, such as being based on rock outcroppings rather than formed completely of coral. These reefs are quite young,
less than twenty thousand years and possibly less than five thousand years
old, developed in Pleistocene times. Of the corals found in Pleistocene deposits on the peninsula, all are living in the Gulf today.

Corals begin as free-swimming larvae which attach themselves to a firm
substrate and begin a sedentary life. The colony grows from asexual propaga-
tion and the way in which budding or fission proceeds dictates the shape
and form of the colony, whether they are incrusting, dome-shaped, branch-
ing, or shrublike. Coral polyps secrete a rigid skeleton made of calcium
carbonate, within which all the polyps of colonial species interconnect. The
individual polyp strongly resembles a sea anemone in construction and in
the way in which it obtains food: long waving tentacles set up miniature
currents that swirl animal plankton within range of their stinging cells—
when the colony feeds, its thousands of beating tentacles haze the surface of
the coral with brown and retract on the instant at my touch. The principal
coral forming the Pulmo reefs is *Pocillopora elegans,* a branched coral which
grows in large solitary clumps; chunks of it make up much of the detritus on
Gulf beaches. The characteristic growth pattern of the deep polyp openings
gives it a distinctive sandpaperlike surface.

Reef corals are finely specialized in habitat. They are exceedingly sensitive to debris on their disks and tentacles, so can only live where the water is
clear and unpolluted. They cannot withstand sea temperatures below 70
degrees Fahrenheit, and so are limited to tropical seas. They cannot tolerate
even minor changes in salinity and so are never found living where fresh
water enters the sea.

It is thought that the reason these corals live no more than two hundred
feet beneath the water surface is because of the minute symbiotic plants

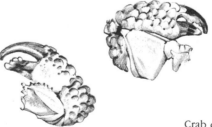

Crab claw (*Eriphia squamata*)

Thatch barnacle (*Tetraclita stalactifera*)

which live in their tissues and need light for photosynthesis. These are dino-flagellates in a vegetative stage, the same creatures that in an animal state cause red tides. They produce oxygen through photosynthesis, and utilize the waste products of the coral, particularly phosphorus, nitrogen, and carbon, the first two of which are in generally short supply in the sea. They form a self-contained recycling system, which, when once started, proceeds with little loss or gain from or into the environment.

I walk out from shore, walking on a ridge of rock so stuffed with pebbles and cobbles that it looks like a pudding full of dates and raisins. Occasionally, large dark smooth boulders are set in the matrix. Because the waves break sixty feet out, only a surge reaches here, ruffling the big shallow pools set on the landward side. The reef is irregular, uneven, full of potholes, with a coating of furry algae, and walking is tedious; even at low tide most if it remains covered by a few inches of water. Whenever possible, I avoid stepping on the corals. Under ideal conditions they grow a little under an inch a year, although reefs as a whole grow more slowly because of wear and tear.

A dark green tiny crab tucking itself into the reef's interstices blends into the olive-dark speckled shadows. Almost every niche holds one of these tiny crabs and, after I find one, I see a dozen more, often giving themselves away by slight movement which causes a change in light reflection. I finger one gently out of a rock crevice. Its carapace, smaller than a dime, is almost black; its legs are black with yellow markings, and its large chelae—almost half the size of the carapace—are lumpy with tubercules. Very territorial, it defends the borders of its estate with extravagant claw waving, quite ready to do battle with this behemoth holding it. On release, it scuttles to a bank of algae and backs under the overhanging fronds, fitting perfectly into the dark shadows, waiting for night to feed. Often small fish follow it about, snatching up leftovers from the crab's dinner of algae.

There are so few places to sit down and take notes in this water world that, when a rock protrudes, it's an invitation to stop and inventory. A crowded patch of thatch barnacles, called *el broma marina* by Mexicans, looks like many miniature Mount St. Helens as it now looks with the top blown off; inside, the animals are tightly closed, not to open until covered by water. In these, the usual six barnacle plates have been reduced to four and fused together to form a dark gray cone.

The boulder is studded with huge Dall's limpets, shells nearly two inches long, plastered to the side of the rock, each in its own special spot. The rule seems to be one limpet to a cobble, but boulders may have three or four, always with a good distance between. An empty shell lies rocking on the sandy bottom, outside finely and regularly grooved with white speckling on a dark ground, inside bluish white with a brown splotch in the center.

Each has its own "home space" to which it returns after grazing algae off the rocks; bare spots ringed in white on the rock mark an absentee owner. The shell conforms so precisely to a specific spot on the rock, curve to hollow, that the shell could not fit half so firmly anyplace else. Experiments have shown that limpets living on exposed rocks home more quickly than do those living on sheltered rocks, and that those which can return quickest are most likely to survive, for once snuggled into their own perfectly fitting niche they are difficult to detach. Heaviest predation is from starfish, which exude into the water a special protein that limpets sense, forewarning them to clamp down before the starfish arrives, thus avoiding being pulled off.

What looks like an old lime peel adheres to the same rock. At a touch it dimples, suctioning itself too tightly to be brushed off. Two tiny tentacles peep out and retract on the second. It is an opisthobranch, an odd mollusk that has adapted to the same habitats as Dall's limpets.

Hand-sized clumps of algae grow outward from the pools' sides, intensely iridescent, ranging from olive green to brilliant teal blue, one in particular set off by the brilliant orange feather tentacles of a worm mounted next to it on the wall. Out of water a sprig loses its color and becomes limp, a somewhat rubbery drab khaki color, each branch separating into two at the growing end of the thallus. It clings to the rock by means of a holdfast; holdfasts do not serve as roots which absorb nutrients, but simply as points of attachment.

Oyster white disks the size of a quarter, with inrolled edges, grow on both rock and sand. Concentric lines mark pulses of growth. This alga is a

Pulmo Reef

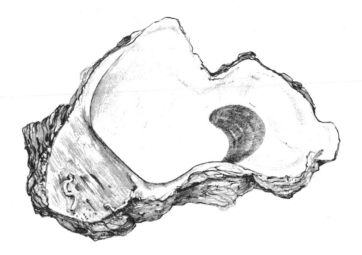

Oyster (*Ostrea columbiensis*)

short-lived annual (as are most of the algae in the Gulf) that begins growth in late fall. By the first of the year it begins to be tattered. There is little information on algal growth in summer, a field wide open for researchers, since, as one botanist points out with indisputable logic, all the expeditions mounted by sea tend to go in the winter when the sailing is good and the weather pleasant, not in the summer when the reverse is true.

The number of minute animals basking in the algae's protection must be astronomical, for every frond, every stipe, every thallus seethes with small creatures. Algae protect them by breaking the force of the surf and providing corners of dampness when the tide is out, and by hiding them from predators. I remember once looking at some fronds under the microscope. Sorting them out left small drops of water on the table in which were infinitesimal creatures pushing and pulsing against the rubbery dome of the water drop, responding to the warmth of the lamp.

Where the end of the reef drops off into deep water, a consortium of three herring gulls stands deciding the fate of the world. Herring gulls are large and common gulls, frequently with a wingspread over four feet. Two of these are adults, with clear white underparts and blue gray backs and mantles, black-tipped wings with white "buttons" at the wing tips, yellow bills each with a red spot near the tip of the lower mandible, and incongruous

211

lavender pink legs. The third gull is a young one, all restless picking and poking, in first-year plumage of dark brown, tan legs, black bill. Its first winter it will become an "immature," speckled brown and gray with a whitish head, dark eye and bill, and by then, pink legs.

"Herring" alludes to the fish that forms only part of its varied diet. Commonly they haunt fishing boats for garbage, but their tastes are catholic, from animal carrion to almost anything the sea has to offer; they are well known for dropping shellfish on the ground to break them open.

I walk as far out as I can safely see footing. Big heads of coral blossom beneath the surface. Although the water is beautifully clear, it is too deep to see detail, and the quivering reflections blur shapes and make outlines dance. I stand undecided whether to go on or go back. A heavy surge of returning tide reaches to my knees and pushes so firmly against my legs that it is all I can do to hold my footing. It makes my decision for me.

At many places along the Gulf coast, on the underwater granite ledges the sea has claimed for its own, lie oyster beds. Jésus, who used to live close by one of the best, says, "Every day in the summer, fresh oysters."

We've known Jésus since he was a boy; now he's married with a daughter. He has a big, sweet smile and a frequent laugh. From childhood he's known where the oysters are, and takes only those he can eat. He is also quite careful not to advertise their presence. He loops a net bag over an inner tube to hold the catch, takes crowbar in hand, and swims out, Herman following. I watch heads appear and disappear as they free dive.

Because oysters, once attached, are sedentary, oyster beds are built up year after year. The layering provides breathing space. They grow only in clear water where currents of water flow over them and where no sediment or mud curtails feeding. If not overharvested, oyster beds endure many years.

Large female oysters can shed as many as 500 million eggs in one breeding season, but a high mortality rate keeps the world from being encrusted with oysters. Egg and sperm are simply discharged directly into the water, where fertilization takes place haphazardly. The fertilized eggs hatch into minute larvae that swim free until metamorphosis prods them to settle on a firm substrate.

Jésus and Herman appear on the beach in half an hour with two dozen oysters, thick heavy shells as big as shoe soles, encrusted with all kinds of freeloaders, perforated by various borers. With a hammer Jésus gives the edge a couple of good whacks, then wedges the oyster open with his knife, and with the deeper shell cupped in his hand (since one oyster valve is cemented to the rock, mature oysters are usually misshapen and unequally valved), slips his knife underneath the adductor muscle and cuts it loose. (Oysters and scallops are similar in that both have a centrally placed muscle scar: the anterior adductor muscle has disappeared altogether and the posterior one has migrated toward the center of the shell.)

Jésus offers it to me. I hesitate a minute—it's *huge*. Jésus and Herman consume theirs in one gulp. Not me. I'm not an oyster aficionado, but biting into one is not as unpleasant as expected. It tastes little like the oysters with which I am familiar; it is very mild, rather sweet, tasting like oyster without being aggressive about it. The small disk of the muscle is like a tender scallop, firm and meaty.

I scrape off the fragments of muscle with my fingernail, scour the kidney-shaped adductor scar clean with sand. The attachment of the muscle to the inside of the shell interferes with the process of calcification and leaves a visible scar line. The inner surface of the shell gleams a pale nacreous bronze with glints of chartreuse, tints of rose, casts of ivory, sunlight and moonlight wavering across its enameled surface.

On the outside, the furry growth of seasons in the ocean encrusts it. I pick away at the covering to get to the shell itself and upset a tiny *café au lait* annelid worm that slithers quickly for shelter. The shell flakes off easily in fine crisp mica-like layers, years of growth snowing onto the sand.

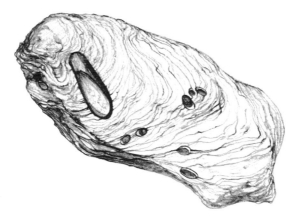

Oyster (*Ostrea columbiensis*)

A small date mussel has bored in slantwise, alive and well in its encasement, but doomed to remain there, for it has grown too large to exit. Its common name describes its size, color, and shape. It secretes an acid which enables it to bore in not only mollusk shells but calcareous rocks. Boring species normally have elongated slender shells, with the front margin of the valves armed with serrations which help in drilling. The toothed hinge and ligament that serve to hold the two valves together firmly are often absent on boring mussels, supplanted by a ball-and-socket arrangement so that the shells can withstand the torque of drilling.

The oysters that brought fortune hunters to La Paz were neither edible nor true oysters but bivalves somewhat resembling oysters. Although the shell is well designed to prevent foreign materials from entering, but in spite of that, a sand grain or a bit of debris occasionally gets between mantle and shell. The invading particle then becomes a nucleus around which concentric protective layers of shell form. If moved freely about during secretion, the pearl will be more or less spherical; if it lodges in one place or becomes imbedded in the shell, it becomes irregular and is called "baroque."

Once these shores supported a spasmodically profitable industry, and piles of shells on empty beaches witness to the large harvests that nearly decimated a species. Carbon dating documents that pearl fishing was going on up to seven thousand years ago. The Indians fancied pearls for hair ornaments, although they destroyed or marred most of them because the only way they knew to open the shells was to throw them on the fire. Not until the Spaniards brought knives and showed them how to open the shells was the beauty of the pearls preserved.

Father Antonio de la Ascensión, with Vizcaíno in 1596, wrote:

On the beach were found many heaps of mother-of-pearl shells in which pearls grow. There were many of these shells scattered through the sand, which, struck by the rays of the sun at midday, scintillated like stars, making it look like a starry heaven. From this the great richness in pearls in that sea can readily seen. It is certain that they are there and very fine ones at that.

While the beds were being exploited, pounds of pearls were shipped to Spain. By 1738, when pearl fishery was declining, the Spanish crown made an attempt to establish permanent beds, which was largely unsuccessful. Although Nelson, in *Lower California and its Natural Resources,* commented that the beds were flourishing in 1906, their end was in sight. They were heavily damaged during the Revolution in the early part of the twentieth century. Between 1936 and 1940 an unknown disease wiped them out.

The divers Barco observed and described went down just as Jésus did, with a minimum capital investment of a net and a stick, usually at midday.

> They dive each day about five hours, starting in the morning at ten or a little before, and leaving about three o'clock of the afternoon or thereabouts. During this time the sun, because it is at its highest, lights up the bottom of the sea better and, because that is where the pearl shells lie, the divers can see them clearly with everything else that there is on the bottom, without the necessity of any further industry other than opening their eyes.

The shells were put in the net and then thrown into the *canoa*. At the end of the day the divers dumped them all on the beach, where the shells were divided—one for the diver, one for the boss, one for the diver, one for the boss, and the *quinto*—the fifth—for the king. Then they were opened and searched for pearls. The broken shells were carted off and piled on the beach to decompose, then winnowed through again to see if any pearls had been missed.

Jésus hands me a second oyster. I subconsciously look for a pearl and wonder how many a Pericu had to open before one was found. I have a third oyster. It's not just the oyster, ocean-cool and wonderfully fresh, washed in sea water, that is so good, but all its surrounding world of fresh sea wind, hot sun, beautiful surf, and eating it out of my own hand. It could taste better only if I had dived for it myself.

The shore is an ancient world, for as long as there has been an earth and sea there has been this place of the meeting of land and water. Yet it is a world that keeps alive the sense of continuing creation and of the relentless drive of life. Each time that I enter it, I gain some new awareness of its beauty and its deeper meanings, sensing that intricate fabric of life by which one creature is linked with another, and each with its surroundings.

Rachel Carson
The Edge of the Sea
1955

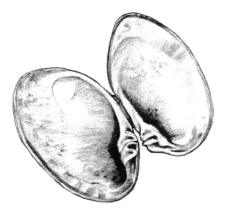

Venus clam (*Veneridae*)

CAPE BEACH

Today is my birthday and I sit on a beach watching the Sea of Cortés ruffle in, trying to think all the deep thoughts appropriate to birthdays and failing utterly. Instead I contemplate the physics of wiggling toes in loose sand. A hypnotic surf wrinkles in, stutters out.

The beach has steepened since last month. Like most beaches on the Gulf of California, this has a sharp slope up from the ocean, leveling off to the foot of cliffs a hundred feet back. The wavy reticulate line of last high tide garlands the beach with bits of urchin tests, barnacles and coral, scraps of wood, mole crab carapaces and crab claws, seeds and thorns. Interlocking scallops mark the lines of the last wave's reach. Higher, from the last storm, dark swags crisscross the beach, full of innumerable brown twigs, leaf bits, hard round seeds in many sizes, and all the fragments of other lives and other times, sorted, sifted, and dumped to dry in the sun. Two rather heavy shells move suspiciously through the dark lines—two hermit crabs laboriously toting their shells down the beach. While I am still several feet away they clamp into their shells and disappear.

Tucked in the midst of a knot of debris, a large hermit crab, ensconced in a golfball-sized shell, faces the sea, bedeviled by a scavenger fly. The crab's

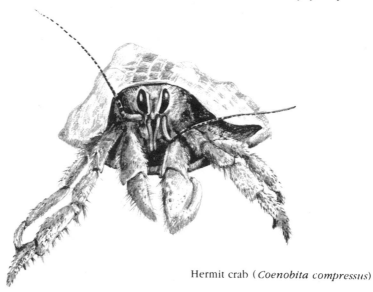

Hermit crab (*Coenobita compressus*)

stalked eyes protrude, its antennae flicker. The fly alights for less than a
second, then pops two inches away, explores, then back on the shell, then
on the ground facing the crab. When it alights too near, a claw flashes out
but always too late. The crab does not move, the fly bothers only this one.
None of the other hermit crabs probing the beach debris are so beleaguered.
The Mexican standoff continues for as long as I watch.

Because of the beach's declivity, the water piles up about twenty or thirty
yards out and comes pushing shoreward, standing up straight before it
crashes, a measured slatch of six or seven seconds. And as the water runs
back to join the sea it reams out tiny troughs in sinuous patterns of elongated
diamonds. Far out the sea glitters all the way to a firm horizon, a carved lapis
lazuli lid, above which the sky stretches thin and pale by comparison. The
sea picks up sunlight in pieces and tosses it back, a whole scintillating mingling of sea and sun and light all caught up together, dazzling and brilliant.
Even the sand glints light—sharp faces of feldspar, smooth chips of quartz,
flakes of mica. A dancing day, so full of flash and vivacity.

The grayish-pink sand is so coarse and irregular that I hardly notice it
when a piece jumps. But when it jumps again I look sharper and discover a
minute jumping spider springing hither, thither and yon with the alacrity of
a flea. It must be a female for its color is so nondescript; the males frequently
have bright decorations on their legs which they display during courtships.

Jumping spiders have exceptionally good eyesight and, combined with their ability to jump, are difficult to catch. I give up.

Some of the sand grains are nearly a quarter-inch in diameter—which must be the outer limit of "sand" and not far from "gravel." Coarse sand, very porous, yet fine enough to register the tiny scalloped ridges two or three sand grains high that the last wave scribed. And fine enough to contain, just above the swash line, dozens of small holes which house mole crabs. The egg-shaped contour of the shell is efficient for an animal that burrows in the moving sand at the edge of the surf. Most crabs can move in any direction, but mole crabs always proceed backward. Sometimes they move en masse up and down the beach for best feeding. If washed out, they reburrow, continually following the edge of the sea to remain in the wash. Sometimes in colonies of hundreds, grading from small to large, they face the surf, completely buried except for their stalked eyes and first pair of antennae, which can be fitted together to form a breathing tube. When the wave begins to recede, they uncoil a larger second pair of antennae and set them in a V to filter the food particles contained in the water. In the length of time that it takes the wave to ebb, the mole crab cleans its antennae of food several times.

In most of these species the males are minute and spend their lives attached to the female by suction cups on their legs. At first this was thought to be due to neoteny—that the males reached sexual maturity while they were still very small; now it may be that protandric hermaphroditism is involved—that is, males changing into females. Mating takes place in late spring to early summer, when several males cluster around a female; they deposit ribbons of sperm on her abdomen. As the eggs are laid they are fertilized, then carried by the female until they hatch.

Mole crabs or sand fleas
(*Emerita rathbunae*)

Today the remains of half a dozen mole crabs lie scattered above the waterline, but so delicate they shatter at a touch. The carapaces still bear the delicate apricot traceries that mark them in life, perfectly shaped for a tiny creature that burrows in the sand, but I discover that their particular curvature forms a large lift surface and if I put one on the palm of my hand, it floats away at the slightest breath, as light as thistle down.

I take a handful of sand and let it run slowly through my fingers, a personal hourglass, as if by doing so I can control the flow of time. Even though the bits and pieces are small, it's amazing how much can still be identified. Limpet rings, the dome long since worn away. A wisp of seaweed, bleached white. Whitened coral, pricked with tiny shadows, all that's left of the minutiae that built them. A Fabonacci spiral in a half-inch turrid shell sliced open vertically. Lavender sea urchin spines, sanded of their sharpness and intensity of color. A minute clam shell, halves still locked together like a tally. The remnant of a cowry aperture like a little toothed trap that gives them, even on the beach, the malevolent eye of a New Guinea mask. Barnacle cirri, lovely little curled combs half an inch long, casting a shadow more substantial than they are, wafting away at a breath. Minute dove shells, like grains of rice. An agate chama fragment, thick and rough as a bleached orange peel.

Gooseneck barnacles stud a scrap of wood, smooth shiny shells on leaden gray stalks lined up like a procession of bishops' mitres. An inch or less in length, they are a shiny pale lavender with the fine cross-hatchings of growth lines, rimmed with a thin vermilion line on the open edge. One is slightly open, with its little pleated cirri curled tightly in place. It amuses me to remember that they got their name because they were thought to produce geese, to "spawn as it were in March and April; the Geese are formed in May and June, and come to fulnesse of feathers in the moneth after." John Gerard, in whose *Herbal* these words appear, described how he found little birdlike creatures tucked inside. I give him his fancy of these little shells

wherein is contained a thing in forme like a lace of silke finely woven as it were together, of a whitish colour, one end whereof is fastned unto the inside of the shell, even as the fish of Oisters and Muskles are: the other end is made fast unto the belly of a rude masse or lumpe, which in time commeth to the shape and forme of a Bird; when it is perfectly formed the shell gapeth open, and the first thing that appeareth is the foresaid lace or string; next come the legs of the bird hanging out, and as it groweth greater it openeth the shell by degrees, til at length it is all come forth, and hangeth onely by the bill: in short space after it commeth to full maturitie, and falleth into the sea, where it gathereth feathers, and groweth to a fowle bigger than a Mal-

220

Limpets (*Diodora, Collisella,* and *Fissurella* sp.)

lard . . . which I have seene with mine eies, and handled with mine hands, I dare confidently avouch, and boldly put downe for verity.

Attached to floating objects, gooseneck barnacles are the only crustacea, other than parasites, to lead such a sedentary existence. The more primitive members of the barnacle family, they are the probable ancestors of the sessile barnacles now crowding on the shore-edge rocks.

Herman suits up to dive. He lumbers seaward, a medieval knight off to do battle with the underwater world. I carry down his cameras. He clanks off into the ocean. As he goes in, Susan, who's been snorkeling and free diving, materializes in front of me, laughing, holding the dripping shell of a lobster. As she swam out earlier, she kept seeing series of small bubbles, and followed them, thinking they belonged to Herman. Then all of a sudden, close to her head, down shot a dark form, which looped beneath her, then shot up again and broke through the surface. All she could see was a black creature with a long neck, two extended webbed feet, wings tucked in with shoulders jutting forward, picking something off a rock twelve feet or so down, moving horizontally with a frog kick or two. A cormorant! As it rose to the surface, it expelled air to adjust its body pressure, hence the stream of bubbles.

She holds in one hand the empty carapace of a big lobster with stalked eyes as round as tapioca, head and thorax still attached, and bearing four legs out of the original ten. She drops it on my towel. "Happy birthday, Mom," she says.

Inside, the shell is pearlescent, the conical hollows of the spines tinged with pale orange. Outside it is dark blue purple, studded with big thornlike spines that all point forward. These big spines are hollow, chrome yellow tipped, ringed with tan, orange, purple, ending in a thick translucent point. The small orange-tipped spines are the color of the carapace. At the broken edge, the three layers of its shell are visible by color: the outermost contains the pigment, the same kind of chitin-protein complex that covers insects; the

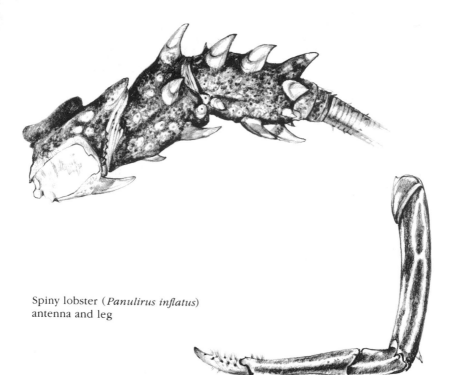

Spiny lobster (*Panulirus inflatus*)
antenna and leg

middle contains none; and the innermost, the thinnest, provides the nacreous sheen.

Miraculously, one of the long whiplike antennae has survived, that once sampled the water and gave warning of danger or scent of food. One of the smaller antennules is also still attached, in the basal segment of which are small cavities lined with sensory hairs. Inside the cavities, sand grains bound together by secretions roll about. Impulses from receptor cells of one cavity cause the animal to rotate to the opposite side, causing an opposite reaction on the other side, and the balancing of the two keeps the lobster level and upright. When it molts, the old grains of sand are lost and new grains have to be put back in; some crustacea do this by burying their heads in sand, and some crustacea actually insert sand with their claws.

The tough, slightly flexible membranes at the joints that allow movement are still intact, the membrane providing protection as well as mobility. I take it by a leg, manipulate it like a puppet: push here, pull there, in awkward jerks. I try to imagine it alive, backed into its crevice, legs making stiff arcs and circles of warning to predators, warning-bright spines protecting a prickly meal, tail and abdomen arched down, clamped into its safety, stalked eyes always at the ready. For some reason it clicks spasmodically as it dries, like a death beetle, making it strangely animate. Lying in the sun, splotched with salt, the carapace dulls. Already the tiny ants have found it, threading over and around and through this lagniappe on the beach.

I drowse, lying on my stomach, head on my hands, random small movements of the beach noted, processed, ignored. Individual damp sand grains dry, trickle down the side of a footprint, that kind of rhythmic filling-in that becomes part of the rhythm of a morning on the beach. Suddenly many sand grains fall at once and here comes a big nerite shell trucking across the sand. No self-respecting nerite travels on hot dry sand or at such a lurching tottering clip. Inside the shell is a tan hermit crab that, when I pick it up, immediately withdraws into its shell.

Its chelae, the left one being the larger of the two, block the opening of the shell as completely as the original operculum did. Slowly, slowly the claws unfold a centimeter or so, opening a slot just large enough for it to peer out. Then the legs emerge, glistening with amber hairs; the three legs on each side are held so closely together they look like little fans. Then two beady brown eyes on pink stalks extend. The antennae flicker, testing the air. It leans far enough out of the shell to get some torque, revealing, as it reaches for purchase, a pink tender back section with the last two tiny legs stretched out on either side, anchoring it to the shell's columella like grappling hooks. Its abdomen is modified to a right-handed spiral, to fit into what are mostly right-handed shells. Stretching almost out of the shell, it finally pops the shell over its back, its little chelae taking tiny nips out of my thumb. I put it back onto the sand. It must be frightfully hot inside that dark shell. It makes a beeline toward a spine of rock, going straight across every footprint, falling down the side, trundling across the bottom, backing up the other side. When it reaches the rock, it finds a tiny shadow and digs itself into the damp sand until it is completely out of sight.

Apparently omnivorous, the hermit crab scavenges by scent, following an odor downwind. Although terrestrial, it remains fairly close to the sea into which it must release its larvae. Housing is periodically a problem since a new shell of proper size has to be found as the old one is outgrown. In spite of that, hermit crabs seldom dispossess the original owner.

A cloudless sulphur butterfly, two-winged sunshine, flitters across the beach in erratic flight, alights in a depression in the sand at my feet. Its clear bright yellow color comes from the scales that cover its wings, achieved by an exquisitely timed program described by Jo Brewer in *Butterflies,* with beautiful photographs by Kjell Sandved. In the pupa, blood circulates through all parts of the butterfly's body, including the scales on the wings. Chemicals within the insect's body combine to form scale pigments, which are transported through the blood. But the scales do not firm, nor are they able to accept pigmentation, at the same time. Pigments must be injected into the bloodstream in a precise sequence, coordinated with the receptivity of individual scales. The wings assume the color they will bear in around three days.

A large angled-sulphur also hovers low over the damp sand at the water's edge, luteous with a single orange dot on the forewing. The sharp falcate outline of the forewings is unmistakable. The butterfly's wings are rather rigid, and when they fly they seem to bat through the sky rather than waft— in fact, one often looks like a scrap of paper caught by a vagrant breeze. The costal veins along the front of the forewings provide strength for flight. Even if its hind wings are damaged, a butterfly can still fly, albeit clumsily. But a shattered costal vein prevents it from taking off at all.

The air is full of flight. Above the ocean, thirteen pelicans glide, dipping down to fly just above the surface, scarcely moving a wing. The last one of the formation detaches itself and goes separately in a long curling sweep while the others remain tightly grouped, then swings around to rejoin them in the Tailend Charlie position. They undulate through the air like a silk banner in a slow wind.

The Creature from the Lower Depths appears. I go down to help him in, take his camera and flippers while he trudges out with the tank. After he

Hermit crab (*Coenobita compressus*)

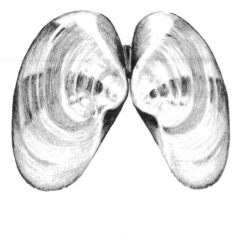

Venus clam (*Veneridae*)

divests himself of gear and peels off his suit, he hands me a five-inch murex, its tightly closed operculum looking like a dark brown mussel shell. The operculum is the thick hardened termination of the foot, the last part to retreat into the shell, thus providing protection to the tender foot. The shell's inner lip is china white, ending in a series of flaring ruffles edged with maroon, making a handsome shell that is much sought after by collectors. The scallops of the shell are practical as well as aesthetic, for they make the shell very difficult for a large predator to swallow or for another snail to drill into.

Bryozoa encrust sections of the shell, along with a tiny quarter-inch urchin and tiny barnacles. What I can't see I can feel with my fingers, so I search for my hand lens in the bottom of my beach bag and sit down in the sand to inventory the shell. Under the lens, the individual animals of the bryozoa are packed together like infinitesimal cliff swallow nests, little overlapping vases, at least fifty in a quarter-inch patch. From each little vase a minute animal stretches feeding tentacles into the water, winnowing out even more infinitesimal particles of food.

Cowry (*Cypraea annettae*)

When I've finished examining it, I walk out as far as I can on a rocky ledge and heave the murex back into the sea. Ambling back, I pause at a hollow in a rock ledge holding a small oval pool, a quarter of an inch deep with a sandy bottom. Low-tide spray does not reach it. The water warms. On it floats the empty shell of a tarantula, four inches across from tarsus to tarsus, light as a feather, plying from shore to shore like some Viking ship flamed and forgotten. A tan cylinder leg detaches and floats free, its bristles making dimples in the water as the wind pushes it around the pond. In the cracks of the rock above it cling four white and gray periwinkles and a dozen half-inch limpets—I see another every time I look. Innumerable tiny dark brown worm shells rim the edge, packed in tight curlicues like the stylized hair on a Persian relief.

Dark blue mussels, smaller than my little fingernail, tightly closed and glistening with salt crystals, are packed into a rock crevice. All are attached firmly at the narrow end by a series of fibers, rather as a balloon is tethered. A mussel puts down one thread, waits for it to harden on contact with sea water, then another a short distance away, and so on, until a conical bundle of fibers anchors it firmly. Since the shell is narrower at the attached end and wider at the other, many can wedge into a narrow space.

In housewifely fashion, neatening up Mother Nature, I run a fingernail through a sand-filled crack. To my surprise the sand grains are spongy, for they encrust the tubes of little half-inch cerianthids, small animals closely related to anemones. Being photonegative, they close under direct sun, which is damaging to their delicate tissues. On an overcast day they spread bluish white tentacles blending to pink. In closing they withdraw into their pebble-encrusted cases and simply disappear.

Highest up in the cracks are the periwinkles, neat little shells, pale gray crosshatched with darker gray lines, the color added in pulses of growth that give each its distinctive pattern. Many are only a couple of millimeters long, the largest not over a centimeter. Several dozen—make that several hundred—very tiny ones waddle across the rock, spires ticking back and forth like miniature metronomes as they also feed upon algae in the cracks. Periwinkles inhabit intertidal zones the world over, receiving no more wetting than comes from splashing waves. Their operculums close very quickly to minimize water loss, and can be held tight shut for long periods of time. It is thought that periwinkles may be the ancestors of today's land snails, and may be on their own tenuous trail to a fully land existence.

Considering the problems a shell presents to a gastropod—difficulties in breathing, reproduction, and getting rid of wastes, and hindering quick movement—the protection it provides evidently far outweighs its disadvantages. The ancestral spiral shell was formed in one plane like a cinnamon roll. It was neither very compact, since each coil lay completely outside the preceding one, nor easy to carry, because all the shell's weight hung on one side of the body. Evolution solved this problem by coiling the shell around a central axis, so that each coil was larger and lay beneath the preceding one. The spiral begins at the top, winding as it goes, producing a much stronger structure than a simple cone. The axis of the shell slants upward and somewhat back, and each one of these little periwinkles cants at the same angle as it proceeds across the rock.

Angled-sulphur (*Anteos clorinde*)

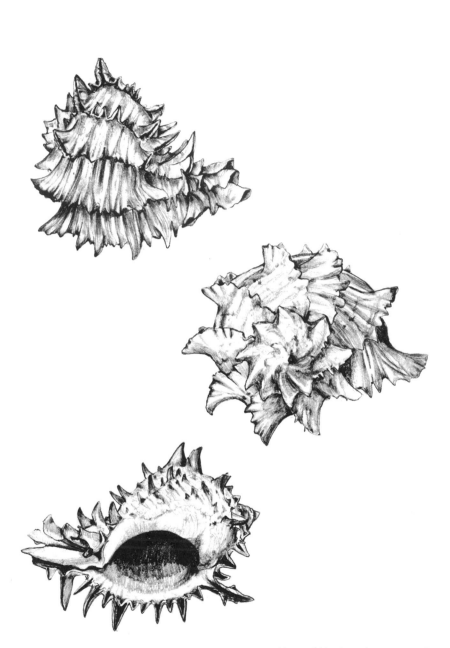

Murex (*Muricanthus princeps*)

Something else happened to gastropods which made it possible for them to fit comfortably within this spiral case. They underwent torsion—that is, the viscera rotated in a counter-clockwise direction, making it possible for the foot to be at the outer end, and the other organs to be arranged most efficiently for life in a shell. Holding a tiny snail in one hand and contemplating what evolution has accomplished, I feel it very dull to be so symmetrical.

A tiny limpet pivots on one end; they range from less than a quarter to nearly an inch, all with irregular dark brown and white stripes radiating from the worn knob of the umbel, a "true" limpet with a closed conical shell. The coiling of the shell, seen in most gastropods, has been completely lost. Hundreds cluster in all the cracks, all smaller than a dime, all the same species. I unseat one and flip it over. Contractions ripple across the exposed foot, it leans far out of its shell, and the minute it touches the edge of the rock it adheres and lifts itself over, right side up.

The sea runs up the rock beside them and sparkles down its granular flanks. But it is not the sunlight, I discover, that makes it sparkle—it is tiny amphipods, their flattened shape both identifying them and making it possible for them to cling to even minute irregularities in the rock. They have different legs shaped for different duties: the first five pairs are designed for feeding, and the last three are designed for creeping, since the animal spends most of its life on its side. Even the abdominal appendages are altered, the first three respiratory and the last three equipped for hopping. They are first-class scavengers, cleaning up whatever it is that needs to be cleaned up.

A shadow passes over; the osprey beats over low, lands on a finger of rock, tucks in its wings, and begins its vigil. Less than a hundred years ago ornithologists used words like "abundant," "plentiful," and "common" about ospreys here. Whether this is still so is not clear, but we always see at least one when we are here, perched for long periods of time on some promontory, usually in full sun, waiting, watching, and then launching into a swift stoop, hitting the water with a splash and, more often than not, rising with a fish in its talons, wings laboring with the effort of extra weight. When William Beebe sailed into port here he saw a nest on these rocks,

> great masses of sticks surmounting a pair of mighty granite columns, like some strange type of unrecorded architecture. Soon a bird appeared, carrying a large stick, detected first by its shadow rushing along the face of the cliff, leading the eye along the path of invisibility to the substance.

I take a wandering path up the beach, footprints as erratic as gulls' tracks, and yet this wandering is as sensible as anything I do, the pursuit of happiness from east to west, bending and stooping, examining and discarding, pausing, enjoying—not going anywhere in particular except down the beach, not getting anywhere on the dot of, a shuffling scuffling with the eternal optimism of *knowing* that just down the beach there's something marvelous, at the very least a frosted piece of beach glass for the sea jar I keep on my work table, at the very most, a new species never seen before. Today I find the whitened carapace of a swimming crab, beautifully whole, every spine intact. A shadow passes over: the osprey back on patrol.

Small hollows in the sand, where the surf swirled around a rock as the tide went out, are now filled with water. The most evanescent of habitats, warming in the sun, subject to surf on the return of the sea, never staying the same, coming and going with the vagaries of the waves, these pools are nevertheless occupied by a dozen small sea hares, which graze and lay their eggs here. The little sea hares are tan streaked with brown, given a ragged untidy aspect by their ruffled mantle. In sea hares, the shell is internal and completely covered by the mantle, and this lack of confining shell allows them to curl themselves along the sand in a graceful manner, tugging systematically at each sprig of algae, then moving on. Their eggs float on the surface like frayed snippets of tan yarn. Even though they are exposed, they are little preyed upon, for they exude a chemical substance that causes other animals to avoid them.

In the midst of these conservatively colored businessmen, there is one flower-child nudibranch, a shell-less snail in bright dark blue with yellow

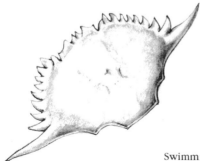

Swimming crab carapace
(*Callinectes* sp.)

and iridescent sky-blue stripes. It grazes along the side of a pool, very close to the surface of the water. On its back are two gray triangles like a bow tie, through which its heartbeats pulsate. Having no external shells for protection, they have developed other means. The papillae that stud their diaphanous bodies are tipped with small stinging cells that they acquire from the food they ingest. Due to these, most fish will not snap up a nudibranch, and if they do, they spit it out in a second.

I scoop it up in my hand, and it is as if I hold nothing but pure abstract color—no weight, no tactile sensation. It puckers itself up, elongates, moves on, nuzzling and snuffling along my hand in a mellifluous movement. I float it back into the pool, where it proceeds with unhurried measured grace, now down on the sand bottom, over a rock, stretching, coming within a couple of inches of a little sand-colored goby, which stays motionless only so long, then flicks off, the quickness of the fish's movement in direct contrast to the inexorable flow of the nudibranch. A breeze blurs the surface. In the tranquil safety beneath the surface the nudibranch undulates through the cycles of its life.

Tucked around some big round boulders are masses of overlapping, small eighth-inch tubes built of sand and cemented firmly together. Inside them, tiny dark forms come out, snap back. These imbricated tubes are inhabited by marine worms, which poke out their heads beneath the water, circulating the water about them by beating their cilia, bringing food to their mouths. To make the tubes they construct a collar of sand grains and mucus, slowly adding ring upon ring as in coiled pottery.

Farther on there's a grasshopper in the sand, rather unusual on the beach. Then a metallic beetle, then a dozen or more other species—including different grasshoppers and thorn-headed tree hoppers, all caught in footprint indentations. A strong wind blew this morning; was there a good gust that loosened these strange bedfellows, sent them sailing, and dropped them in this damp sand from which they could not escape? Most are still alive and move quickly once they dry out. Some are dead, already being explored by beach flies and infinitesimal beetles. I get a good look at things I have never seen except in books. Nice. Happy birthday, Ann.

I scuff a small brittle star out of the sand. It's the first time I've ever seen one both whole *and* quiet. A live brittle star is so slithery that examining it is out of the question. One often ends up with a couple of detached legs since they autotomize so easily. I take it back up to my beach towel and fish out my hand lens to enjoy it properly.

They differ from the familiar sea stars by having a differentiated central

Brittle star (*Ophiocoma alexandri*)

disk to which long flexible arms are attached, rather than being all of a piece as sea stars are. The mouth on the underside of the body is a little star, set in a tiny granulated disk, now gray instead of its pale green or brown in life. The arms are about two inches long, and taper from a quarter inch at the body to a sixteenth at the tip.

On top, the plates on the arms alternate between dark gray and pale gray—three dark, one light, three dark, three light, two dark, five light, light dominating toward the tip, dark toward the disk. The dark plates bear pale gray Chinese characters as if the creature were bearer of ancient legend. Toward the tip end, all the plates are light with a darker pattern. The light gray undersides of the arms bear smaller plates, with darker gray stripes running the length of the arm.

On either side of the arms are spines, a little longer than the plate they lie beside, groups of five toward the disk, down to three at the lower edge. In death, the spines are pale gray with a white spot at the base, tipped with salmon.

The brittle star retains its energetic writhing; now confined to two dimensions, each curve lies ready to uncoil, like those marvelously vital octopuses on Minoan vases that seem ready to bound right off the surface. With a hand lens, the more I look, the more the patterns come alive, perfect—no hand,

Cape Beach

how skilled or how careful, could replicate even this once what nature does a million times over without sneezing.

As I hold the little brittle star in my hand and take notes, it occurs to me that I can always come back to this time, these smells, these sounds, on this page. I remember the reason Edwin Way Teale gave for writing natural history:

> I suppose, if I answered truthfully, I would have to say that the first purpose was to preserve—as insects are sometimes preserved, with every wing-venation intact, in pieces of transparent amber—portions of our lives that seem especially precious to us.

Blowing spray tingles my face. Sun fires my bones. The ocean swirls in and tatters back. The wind buffets a white gull feather in the sand at my feet. The osprey hunts.

The exposed rocks [near Cabo San Lucas] had looked rich with life under the lowering tide, but they were more than that: they were ferocious with life. There was an exuberant fierceness in the littoral here, a vital competition for existence. Everything seemed speeded-up; starfish and urchins were more strongly attached than in other places, and many of the univalves were so tightly fixed that the shells broke before the animals would let go their hold. Perhaps the force of the great surf which beats on this shore has much to do with the tenacity of the animals here. It is noteworthy that the animals, rather than deserting such beaten shores for the safe cove and protected pools, simply increase their toughness and fight back at the sea with a kind of joyful survival.

John Steinbeck and E. F. Ricketts
Sea of Cortez
1941

Caesalpinia pannosa

TIDEPOOLS

On the way down to the beach I stop to watch a hummingbird, as still on her nest as if carved. She has tucked her nest into the crook of a dead *pitahaya agria* branch on a steep slope above the tidepools. The stalk, crooked like a bishop's crozier, leans back toward the slope, placing the nest only three feet off the ground. I sit on the slope watching her with the binoculars, and I think she's a Costa's hummingbird, not because of her markings (which, like those of most female hummingbirds, are undistinguished), but because of the distinctive nesting site.

When she flies, I hurry over and peek in. The nest is a cup an inch and a quarter in diameter at the top, an inch and a half deep to the rounded bottom. The eggs have already hatched into two black-bean birds with a sprigging of orange pinfeathers, heads smaller than a pea, infinitesimal beaks, almost too small to be birds. I stay but a second and retreat to my vantage point a distance away.

When she returns she stands at the far edge of the nest, facing me, lowers her bill into a waiting gullet and regurgitates food. She flies again, is gone four minutes, returns, and then settles back into the nest. Her whole body twitches slightly, as if the young beneath energetically resettle themselves. I watch a few minutes more and then continue down to my favorite little cul-de-sac beach, a mere pocket handkerchief of a beach tucked between the sphinxlike paws of granite cliffs.

On the way down to the beach, flowers bloom in every crack of the granite: *Hofmeisteria,* succulent leaves pale bluish green, with lavender flowers like marble-sized thistles; yellow-flowered *Tephrosia,* tiny cloverlike

Tephrosia cana

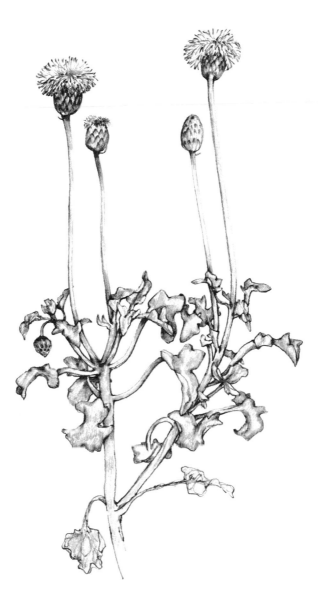

Hofmeisteria fasciculata var. *xantii*

leaves sticky with hairs, and *Caesalpinia*—none with common names although they belong to the two most prevalent plant families at the Cape, daisy and pea. Tiny cinchweeds and wild bean scramble in the gravel, along with some of the ubiquitous but nonshowy plants of the peninsula, and, as always, San Miguel vine.

The beach levels out into an apron of granite studded with tidepools that quiver and gleam in the sun. Here the headland gathers the waves as they angle into the bay and cossets the beach, although the debris in its back corners bears witness to the reach of the big storms that send a frenzied ocean dashing against the cliffs. The shoreline does not change much from year to year because there isn't that much sand to work on, and transport is blocked by the cliffs on either side. As long as I have known it, the little bay has remained a near constant. Its narrowness and its thin cover of sand attest to its youth.

From barnacle-encrusted rocks only sprayed by waves, to the outermost pools and ledges uncovered for only a short time, the bay is a study in zonation. The edge of the sea has been a zone of fascination world-wide for scientists and writers for generations, and the challenge to make order out of the sequence of inhabitants has attracted many marine biologists, who have proposed various classification systems. Most are based on the length of time the area is covered or uncovered, and this depends upon the amplitude of the tides. The highest tides come when the sun and moon are aligned and the gravitational pull of both causes "spring tides," on an average of every fortnight. Generally there are two high and two low tides per day, which bring food or exposure to sessile animals, depletion or renewal. Where the shore slopes gently, as here, a large area may be uncovered, although the tidal fluctuation here is only about three to five feet.

Four zones seem to be generally agreed upon, with individual variations according to the point of view of individual researchers. The high intertidal zone is wet only by the high tides, storm waves, and spray; the most plentiful mollusks in the zone are periwinkles. Otherwise, the fauna is largely terrestrial—many insects and spiders occur here. The mid-intertidal zone is alternately covered and exposed daily, and usually divided into upper and lower sections. The upper zone is uncovered more than covered; characteristic of this zone are barnacles, encrusting the rock, and nerites, rounded heavy-shelled snails; in all, this is the most densely inhabited zone. The lower mid-intertidal zone also has cycles of exposure, but coverage time exceeds exposure time. Best indicators of the next zone are green corals and colonial sea anemones, several crabs, and coralline algae: this fourth zone, the low inter-

Costa's hummingbird

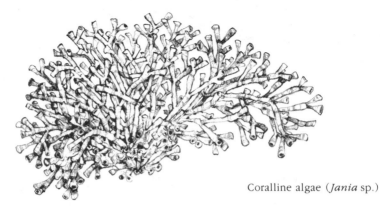

Coralline algae (*Jania* sp.)

tidal zone, extends from the mean of all the lower low waters down to the low water point on the beach.

Boulders rim the edge of this beach, a foot or two in diameter, rounded, all blackened with lichen, a noticeable color change from the tan granite of the cliffs from which they came. The dark color comes from encrusting lichen and algae that exist at this tidal level all over the world.

Lumps that look like black tar cluster around the boulders—my children long ago uncharmingly but appropriately christened them "sea turds." In reality they are sea cucumbers. Where there are puddles of water remaining, their luxuriant tentacles, like bronze seaweeds, sway in the water. I touch one and it retracts on the instant. When extended, these curled tentacles catch plankton on their sticky surfaces.

Sea cucumbers belong to the same order as the five-segmented starfish and urchins with radial symmetry. The cucumbers have reverted to their ancestral bilateral symmetry, and are cylindrical. Unlike their brethren, who have either heavy skins or shell-like tests, cucumbers are pliable and leathery, the skeleton reduced to multitudes of infinitesimal spicules embedded in the body wall. Like a skunk, the sea cucumber does battle from the rear. The tubules it ejects through the anus when under duress are actually part of the respiratory system as well the digestive system. Since they are sticky, they entrap any attacker.

Footsteps crunch in the sand behind me: Herman, burdened with camera, kneepads, and tripod, on his way to photograph tidepools. He has gloves stuffed in his pocket so I prevail upon him to turn over a boulder that I can't heft. The rock for all intents and purposes is polished bare on top, but the underside seethes with activity, a veritable nursery of young creatures that crawl, fall, plop, slither and wiggle across its now suddenly vertical surface: tiny sea cucumbers and baby brittle stars, marble-sized urchins and small sun stars. And worms. And hermit crabs by the dozen. The cucumbers, dirty white tinged with pink, with gravel and shell bits clinging to them, creep slowly down the rock face, each of them about thumb size. Another one is pale gray with blotchy mauve stripes; when I touch it, it spurts out a stream of milky water. Since none of them like all this fresh air, the movement is frenetic to return to a happier world below.

Herman, with gloves on, essays to pick up a nine-inch-long segmented fireworm, a segmented annelid worm. It is tannish-pink, almost flesh colored, with dots of deep red gills at the edge of every segment. He picks it off and brittle transparent spicules glisten in his glove; among all the wigglers and flippers here, the fireworm is the only one to cause considerable and lasting pain to the picker-upper.

Inching across the rock come three small sun stars, also a common species, although it seems to me we see fewer adults than we used to see. One of them, a soft gray-green mottled with rose dots, already has twenty legs, with a gap where two are missing. The young begin life with the regular complement of five arms but add additional ones rapidly as they mature. They move with measured slowness—most starfish can move about an inch a minute, following a leading arm which proceeds in the direction the starfish wishes to go, attaching and releasing its sucker feet as it proceeds.

The tube feet bear both suckers and tiny stalked clamps called pedicellariae. These fasten onto any available surface or crush smaller creatures intent on attaching themselves to the starfish. As a consequence starfish are always clean of the freeloaders commonly found on other shells. Starfish eat anything available, a catholic diet that encompasses the smaller animals of the whole intertidal community. When faced with tight shut mussel shells, they simply open them by force. They grip the shell so that the gape is positioned near the starfish's mouth, then apply a steady pull until the bivalve's adductor muscle gives way. The starfish needs only an infinitesimal opening in which to insert a lobe of its stomach and pour in digestive enzymes to soften the tissue of its victim. They are even capable of overwhelming urchins. Like the starfish, the urchin has protective pedicellariae which clamp onto the tube feet of the starfish. As the starfish pulls away it pulls off the urchin's pedicellariae until all are plucked off, leaving it free to feed with impunity.

Tidepools

A dozen baby brittle stars scull off the rock and drop into the water. Amazingly fast moving, these are off the rock even before I finish counting, propelling themselves in looping leaps. A single purple-red pencil urchin, test smaller than a marble, studded with heavy inch-long spines, clings to the rock. When grown, these sturdy urchins cling to rocks and reefs in mid- and low-tide zones, often hit by violent surf, and may live quite deep in the ocean, as much as five hundred feet. Since they are sedentary and their spines large and far apart, sponges or calcareous algae often take up residence on their tests.

Four chitons inch off the rock as speedily as possible, which, for a chiton, is not very fast at all. These are primitive mollusks that have remained confined to the hard substrate of their ancestors, and so are highly adapted for adhering. When threatened a chiton clamps down firmly by raising the inner margin of its foot, thus creating a vacuum which makes it extremely difficult to dislodge. The shell is formed of beautifully sculpted overlapping and interlocking plates, eight in all. The articulation of the plates enables a chiton to roll up into a ball like an armadillo, or to plaster itself to an irregular surface. Their flattened bodies have neither tentacles nor eyes; with the head under the shell, neither is needed.

Herman turns the rock right side up and jostles it gently to its original position. Before I can point out another one that I would like to see the underneath of, The Photographer has his tripod on his shoulder and is striding out toward the deeper tidepools with what seems to me unseemly haste.

Minute flies explore the rocks, bustling about between the barnacles. One is a long-headed fly, whose larvae live on algal encrustations, a little gray humped creature, scarcely a quarter of an inch long, with long hairlike legs and lovely little wings that can be read only with a hand lens. Another is a tiny beach fly with garnet eyes, and still another is a shorefly. As if to make sport of these insignificant poppers and fritterers, a pale chalky gray dragonfly makes figure eights between the pylons of granite pillars.

Charcoal gray nerites line up in the cracks of the granite. Most of the heavily ribbed shell is dark gray except for the flat white spire. According to Richard Brusca's *Common Intertidal Invertebrates of the Gulf of California*, a book that ought to be in every beachcomber's bag, it resorbs the walls of the inner swirls, an unusual strategy in sea snails but common in land snails. Several graze along the damp face of the rock. A snail moves by two waves of muscular contractions along the foot, one set on each side, contractions proceeding from front to back and out of phase with each other. As a wave passes any given point, the foot there is raised and set down again slightly in

Gulf fritillary *(Agraulis vanillae)*

advance of its previous position. One takes twelve seconds to cover its body length of an inch (only on a beach in Baja California would I calculate how long it would take it to travel a mile, should it wish to do so).

Most of the nerites are locked into a shaded vertical crack where some residual moisture remains, protected from inimical sun. I dislodge twelve of them and place them in a line. The reason for their common name, "baby's tooth," is obvious in the dentations along the inner lip. Only one, the small-est, closes its operculum and remains rocking, aperture up. The operculum has a flange that fits under the edge of the columella, insuring a secure closure when the snail retracts into its shell. Each of the others extends its foot, finds purchase on the rock and, in varying sequence, flips upright. I put them back in their crack where they adhere immediately.

I am amazed to see a cormorant in a tidepool twenty feet away. The cormorant dives four times in the shallow water, coming up four times with a fish. It dives with such vigor that its back arches out of the water, but the pool is so shallow that its tail sticks clear out. It raises its head, shiny fish clamped in its bill, a rapid wiggle, its neck thickens, the fish slides down its

244

gullet. Feeding finished, the cormorant cruises through a narrow slot not much wider than its body. It breasts a surge of water that pulses through the slot and lifts the bird so that its whole body is visible. Then the water withdraws and only the serpentine neck is visible. It turns, catches another surge, and skims back through the slot, sitting higher now, like a galleon under full sail. Fishing finished, it hops up on a rock; since a cormorant's feathers are not particularly waterproof, it needs to dry out after a fishing session. It sybaritically spreads its wings to the sun, snaps them in close, shrugging until every feather is in the right place. And then does it all over again.

As the tide goes out, the steps between the pools drain in scalloped ripples no wider than a hand. They look inanimate, these pools, so still, in muted rose, coral and olive, neutral tans and beiges. No bright colors at all. Tiny waterfalls between pools adjust the levels until there is no more adjusting to be done. The sound of the ocean diminishes and the landward sounds emerge, quiet poppings and clickings, tiny smackings as drying begins. A bubble on a pool's surface floats first in one direction, then the other.

A pistol shrimp snaps close at hand. These little shrimp, an inch or longer, remain in all the little damp crevices, and the sound of their little retorts accompany any walker. The pop! is made by the single enlarged cheliped with a trigger device that closes with a snap. With it a pistol shrimp stuns

Serpulid (*Serpulorbis margaritaceus*)

Nerites

prey that unwittingly pass by the door, snatches it in, dines, then scrupulously removes all remains. These shrimp are peculiar in that the front edge of the carapace has grown to completely enclose its eyes, but probably enough light penetrates for vision.

Serpulid worm cases patch the rocks so thickly that it's almost impossible to walk across the ledge without stepping on them. They range from tiny chocolate brown worm cases an eighth of an inch in diameter to those half an inch across, with the worms' heads retracted just to the plane of the opening. When about a millimeter long the young cement themselves to some substrate and begin their wandering tube growth. As water covers the shelf, they feed by extruding a mucus net to entrap plankton and detritus. When many worm shells grow close together, the individual nets extend into a communal sheet allowing them to act in unison so all feed at once.

Even though the tidepools have a superficial resemblance—irregular, not over four feet deep—they are all different. One will have many white worm shells, another colonial anemones, another a dotted line of purple urchins, for this is an urchin nursery, and there are hundreds, smaller than marbles, spines and all. Another with a paving of sponge, encrusting the rock. But the most animated has brittle star tentacles looping and unlooping, languid and beckoning, their bodies secreted, the disembodied arms like some part of a Gorgonian headpiece. Spicules line the tentacles, covered with mucus that traps floating food; when something interesting happens by, the tentacle coils around it and conveys it to its mouth. The life of the pool depends on a sense of touch: unfurling feeler, brisk antenna, feathered tentacle, groping arm.

A small nut cone shell steams slowly across the bottom, bubblegum pink foot extended. Cone shells provoke much interest because of the barbed tip on the proboscis, which shoots out with explosive force and injects venom into the victim. The venom's action is very rapid, and apparently acts like curare, interfering with the nerve-muscle junction. Some larger species are not toxic to humans, while several small species are highly so.

In this pool the little cones are the only original inhabitants in their shells. All the empty ones have been commandeered by the ubiquitous hermit crabs that give their occupancy away by the wobble of the shell they've occupied, nothing like the sinuous glide of the original inhabitant. And if their lurch and wobble didn't give them away, the two long vermilion antennae and two stalked eyes sampling the world certainly would. This little pool must be a veritable hermit crab nursery, for none are over half an inch in length, no antenna over three-quarters, no claw over a quarter inch. Out of

Caesalpinia pannosa

water, one is a handsome little creature, carapace and chelae black green, margined with scarlet, the little walking legs and antennae bright red orange.

A tar-covered rock rests on the bottom of a pool. I idly tap it with a stick. There is no answering "clack," no resistance. I look more carefully. It unfurls itself into a good-sized sea hare, dark velvety chocolate brown splotched with tan like tortoise shell. As it opens, it extends its siphon, opens out its "ears," then undulates across the pool, its mantle furling and unfurling over its back.

The tremendous number of eggs laid by marine animals compensates for heavy loss; an average-sized sea hare can produce 41,000 eggs a minute, and has been known to lay 478 million eggs over a period of 17 weeks. Only one out of each half billion needs to survive to adulthood for the species to be perpetuated. Since they are hermaphroditic they copulate somewhat as do earthworms, receiving sperm as well as discharging it—the MacGinities, in their delightful *Natural History of Marine Animals,* claim they've seen seven or eight in a complete circle, like elephants in a circus.

Over the years, this pool has provided continual entertainment for all of us, beginning with the day Jane found a foot-long jewel moray eel here. When the eel saw our shadow, it withdrew under a rock in a swift sinuous movement. I lowered my pencil into the water and the eel snapped at it quicker that I could see. At almost the same moment three puffs of ink blossomed in the pool and the tentacles of an octopus disappeared under the rock, a drama so quick and so silent that neither of us was sure we'd seen what we thought we saw.

Another time Kent picked up a rock in this pool to be greeted with a burst of ink. This time the octopus catapulted under a ledge. Kent, with a bravery I shall never know or understand, reached under the ledge for it. The octopus clamped on. Kent slowly retrieved his arm, grimacing at the unsettling suction. Against the sand the octopus had been sand-colored; on Kent's arm it flushed dark magenta. Many pigment-containing cells are scattered over its body surface. They are usually contracted, but under stress different sets of cells are activated and an octopus will run through its whole repertoire, phasing from one shade to another, stabilizing only if a particular combination seems successful.

It was a tiny octopus, with a head scarcely two inches, packed with the biggest brain and the best eyesight of any mollusk. The females lay their eggs in old bottles or tires or around rock edges, and are known for incubating the eggs with extreme care, keeping them clean so that no fungus can destroy the embryos. Once, when I picked up what I thought was an empty shell, a tiny octopus popped out, less than an inch long, a charming little creature that humped itself across my palm and dropped to safety in the water.

Once out into the light the octopus dropped from Kent's arm, opened like an umbrella, turned a splotchy pale green, contracted itself into a projectile, and shot away, leaving inky threads hanging in the water. The brown or black fluid that an octopus ejects contains highly concentrated melanin pigment; it seems not to serve so much as a smoke screen as to have some anesthetizing effects on certain fish, and can block a moray eel's sense of smell so that it doesn't even react to an octopus's presence.

Here, on another day, Sara found a four-inch pink pincushion of an urchin, of a most peculiar softness and completely covered with debris. The urchin's pincushion aspect comes from the shortness of its spines, and the odd-shaped pedicellariae between them which are usually held wide open, producing the flowerlike effect. Divested of its camouflage by meddling humans, it began immediately to restore its baggage. With its pedicellariae it picked up a pebble and, in just a few minutes, had passed it to its top. We left it garnishing itself with a piece of shell.

Tucked back in the corner of the pool that day was a little female Pacific spotted box fish, scarcely four inches long at most, a Disney-cute fish, blue gray with white spots, a stiff little box with tiny fins, like a blimp with its tiny propellers. In truth it is quite poisonous. In spite of its vegetarian diet and size, it has few predators since it secretes a poison from its skin glands lethal to gill-breathing animals. The males, wearing a gray-spotted saddle outlined in gold on the back and deep blue on the flanks, are so differently marked that once they were thought to be a different species. And here Herman found a ribbon worm, banded maroon and white, knotted in a heap. When he picked it up, it stretched out to two feet in length and then kinked up again like an old rubber band when dropped back into the pool.

Today I sit alone, contemplating the tidepool. A surge from far out brings in a trickle of water and the surface rises and falls an inch. As the angle of refraction changes, the illusion is that the bottom of the pool is being raised and lowered pneumatically, like a sophisticated operatic stage set. Bubbles float idly until the surface quivers with a light breeze. Beneath the water a bryozoa branch glistens with air bubbles, making it look like chenille. A blenny, speckled like a pebble, scoots along the bottom. A flatworm of undulating silken chiffon grace flows across the pool, alternately pouring itself over a pebble and swimming free. The voluted edges, rimmed with a thin

Bonaparte's gull

line of orange, curl in swimming; almost transparent, its internal systems form a nugget in the center of the little mottled oval.

During daylight hours, the water can be saturated with oxygen, releasing bubbles. Such tidepools have widely fluctuating conditions, requiring considerable adjustments from those who inhabit them. If the pool is shallow, the period between inundations may bring warming temperatures, increased evaporation and salinity, and wide fluctuations in acidity. During a rainstorm, there is also danger that salinity may be so reduced as to be fatal for some of the inhabitants.

As I watch the tufts of algae to see which way the current goes, one tuft ups and swims away. It turns out to be a knobby little crab with a narrow triangular carapace and very long knobby front walking legs, all olive green. When I drop it back, it sinks slowly to the gravel bottom, takes a moment to recover, then tumbles off again like an aimless scrap of plant, tips over backward, wafts from here to there, its behavior enhancing its appearance as a random plant frond.

Another crab is so covered with algae it looks furred. Out of water it makes way slowly, pauses at the edge of the pool, wipes water over its eyes with minute white claws, steps into the water, wipes its white-tipped claws over its eyes, then resumes its former pose of hanging on the wall. Two tiny speckled crabs crawl out of the pool, both smaller than a fingernail. They sit a second on an algae-covered ledge and feed, alternating claws. It is difficult not to be anthropomorphic, for their rhythmic intensity reminds me of nothing more than a child stuffing birthday cake in with both hands.

I remember how hesitant I used to be about visiting the tidepools that lie far out, for the tide has a way of coming back in with unexpected speed. But I would do so sometimes, especially if I had company who I assumed would save me from being swept off to Mazatlán.

One day Sara, Kent, and I edged far out on a headland, where the surf bores in. The rocks there are steeply canted and terribly slippery, jointed with deep cracks, piled on top of each other like a stack of old lizards. The tidepools are few and small, set in joints which hold water in long shining lines. On this exposed promontory, only a few tiny white periwinkles wedge in the rock cracks, and even fewer nerites. Even at low tide the sea froths and foams over the rocks, murky white, swashing back and pouring over again with the force of the rebound. It wets the seaweed-covered outermost rock with every wave, and thuds and works its way into every cranny, insistent, pervasive, insidious.

Sally Lightfoot crab

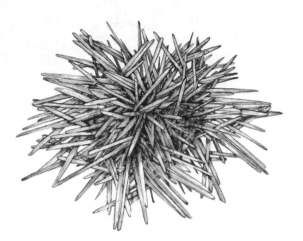

Urchin (*Echinometra vanbrunti*)

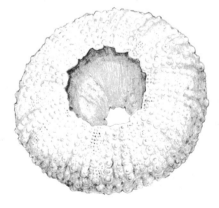

I remember that a long narrow quiver of water held a line of deep purple sea urchins with long needlelike spines. Each urchin had ground itself so firmly into the rock that it could not have left if it had wished to, and the line was punctuated with empty tennis-ball-sized holes. Some of the urchins were partly out of water and they looked disheveled, their spines falling every which way, full of pebbles and shell bits left by the last tide. An empty urchin test lay rocking underwater. It retained some of its spines, attached by a tough membrane surrounding a ball-and-socket joint that allowed 360-degree turning. The exquisite perforate patterns of the test diagrammed the placement of spine and pedicellariae. Under my hand lens a single spine looked like a jouster's lance.

Dark brick red anemones, a good inch across, also threaded the pennant-shaped pools. This anemone may be one of the most common in the Gulf, its dark color distinctive even from a distance. The column is neither adhesive nor buried, so the color, usually red or orange, occasionally brown, is highly visible. There may be as many as 150 tentacles crowded around the mouth, often patterned with yellow hashmarks. The anemones are carnivores, and when prey touches a tentacle, stinging cells paralyze it, and the other tentacles fold over it, basketlike. At high tide, a constant flow of water circulates over them; when uncovered, the anemones gather in their tentacles and close up shop, firmly anchored deep into the rock.

In a rock crevice I found clusters of thaids, dark gray with heavy evenly spaced knobs on spire and a salmon stain along the aperture; their "blood is the esteemed purple of the ancients," says Barco. Until aniline dyes were invented these close relatives of the murids provided the "royal purple" for regal garments. I pulled off one the size of a walnut and set it, opening up, on the rock. Before the operculum closed, dozens of minute orange mites sharing the shell scrambled for cover. The shell's operculum shut tightly and the opening filled with a white milky fluid that ran down into a rock crack, smelling faintly like rotten eggs. Some Central American Indians collected these shells, and when the snails exuded fluid, dabbed their thread in it, then replaced the shell to be used again, rather than crushing them as the Mediterraneans did murids.

In one of the wider channels between ledges, white pigeons floated on the water—except, obviously, they *couldn't* be pigeons. They were, in fact, Bonaparte's gulls, whose common name is "sea pigeon." Their plumage is simple and beautiful—pale gray, with a pure white tail and head (which in summer is black), and a dark gray smudge behind the eye. They lifted off and flew daintily over the water, tail fanned out and down, salmon pink legs dangling, picking debris off the surface. Bonaparte's gulls were first recorded here by Lyman Belding in the winter of 1881–82. Charles Lucien Bonaparte, after whom they were named, was the nephew of the Emperor and a respected ornithologist.

Mingling with the Bonapartes were three ring-billed gulls, all youngsters, and compared to the little sleek and elegant Bonapartes, they looked like big gawky teenagers got up in an adolescent's sense of high style: mottled feathers, dark bill tip without the ring typical of an adult, outlandish lavender legs, with huge paddle feet. These immatures will wear this plumage for three years before they molt to their handsome adult plumage. (Small gulls generally require two years, larger ones four, to reach adult plumage.) They feed on fish or scavenge along the coast. When nesting inland they take small rodents, catch flying grasshoppers, and pick up worms and insects. They commonly nest in colonies of thousands near fresh water. Both gulls have black wing-tips; melanin pigments which darken them have been shown to produce stronger feathers than non-pigmented ones, therefore of advantage on a part of the wing that gets extra wear. In addition, there are two slate gray gulls, the immatures of glaucous-winged gulls, recognized by their dark feathers and pink bills. Both are continually shoved out of the way by the young herring gulls.

Thousands of barnacles lined the rocks, all snugged shut. A white telltale circle of varying completeness, and sometimes a disk with fine growth lines spiraling out from the middle, remains after the barnacle is gone, re-

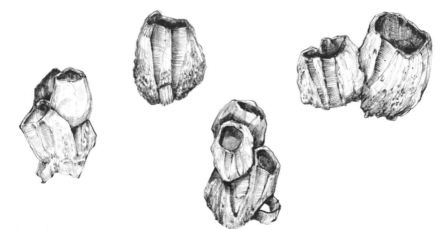

Barnacles (*Balanus* sp.)

Thaid shell (*Purpura pansa*)

vealing the pattern of shell growth. So many grew on the outer rocks that they gave the rock a pustulate profile. They are the only crustacea that use their appendages solely for feeding and not for moving about. Legs have become cirri, feathery appendages which comb the water to winnow the constant food supply swirling about them, opening and closing an average of 140 times a minute. Louis Agassiz, the well-known nineteenth century naturalist, described them as "nothing more than a little shrimp-like animal, standing on its head in a limestone house and kicking food into its mouth."

On another ledge the pools were larger and deeper. Brilliant emerald green coral nearly a foot across encrusted one wall. A branch coral with pencil thin branches gleamed dark magenta in a shaft of sunlight; where bubbles outlined a stalk it looked frosted. Yellow and black and red Cortez rainbow wrasse, like piscine Swiss guards, and ubiquitous in the Gulf reefs, looped around a head of coral upon which they were feeding. They are capable of stunning color changes. Spawning aggregations are usually of this rainbow color phase, but some females may revert to "secondary males," which are blue-purple with a bright yellow band, and these gather a harem of females, which they vigorously defend.

A blenny, visible only because of its high eye placement and eye markings, lurked in the shadow at the narrow end of the pool. Whenever another fish came near it darted out with a great rush and fluster, its tail beating the water and no mistaking the intent. Then it returned to its doorway and stood guard like a troll. Most species of blenny resemble each other so closely that

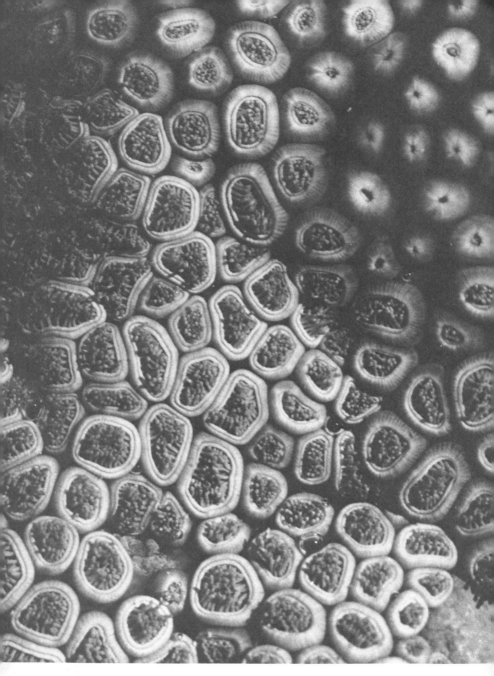

Colonial anemones

there could be a visual problem in identifying a prospective mate. To provide the right answers to the right questions, mating has become very ritualized with a series of visual and chemical clues, of action and reaction in proper sequence. Without them, there is no mating.

Scores of crabs scuttled all around us, beneath every overhang, all lined up, a phalanx of pincers and eyes, pincers and eyes, rustling like crumpled brown paper as they moved—Sally Lightfoot crabs. Sara counted two dozen in one crevice. Dozens more sidled across the rocks, but most of them clung to the edge of the rocks where the surf broke, retaining their footing even as big waves sloshed over them.

One Sally Lightfoot stood its ground in an old urchin hole, red chelae at the ready, pugnacious, bubbling at the mouth, viewing me with what I took to be unmistakable venom. Seldom are there any this far up on the rocks and alone; possibly this one was preparing to molt and seeking a shelter in which to split the old shell, and protected privacy in which to harden the new. Kent did the impossible and grabbed it, and thus gave the lie to one of the most oft-quoted passages from John Steinbeck's *Sea of Cortez:*

> They seem to be able to run in any of four directions; but more than this, perhaps because of their rapid reaction time, they appear to read the mind of their hunter. They escape the long-handled net, anticipating from what direction it is coming. If you walk slowly, they move slowly ahead of you in droves. If you hurry, they hurry. When you plunge at them, they seem to disappear in little puffs of blue smoke. . . . It is impossible to creep up on them. Man reacts peculiarly but consistently in his relationship with Sally Lightfoot. His tendency eventually is to scream curses, to hurl himself at them, and to come up foaming with rage and bruised all over his chest.

While he held her, I had my first chance to see up close the almost square shape and vertical front of the carapace; the triangular shape of the plastron beneath showed it to be a female. The smoky dark blue carapace was dotted with white, circled and splotched with pale blue, a lovely milky blue under the head. The blue comes from astaxanthin, a chemical which becomes denatured when heated and turns the shell bright orange-red. Bristly hairs studded her orange and red legs; although there are tactile and chemoreceptive hairs all over a crab's body, those on the antennae and legs, the first to make contact with stimuli, are the most sensitive. But she was not to be held for long: one claw made a triangle cut in Kent's thumb and he dropped her with appropriate comment. He said the claw itself felt dull, but when turned at the right angle and clamped with the force of the muscle, it cut sharply.

Large patches of colonial "anemones" paved the edges of many of the shallow pools set in the outer ledges. They were packed so closely that the usually round quarter-inch individuals were pushed into hexagonal shapes. Those below the waterline fed, short tentacles extended. Those above the waterline were closed, a pale softly iridescent gray green, fusing to a center ring of blue gray. The green comes from symbiotic single-celled algae within them. Individuals of the colony closely resemble "true" anemones, but the pedal disk is absent, and they are all interconnected, able to spread by budding, independent of sexual reproduction and the hazards of free-swimming larvae. I drew a finger across the feeding polyps which were velvety soft to touch. They closed immediately, and the message traveled outward until a wide stripe of animals had tucked in their tentacles.

That day Sara sat on a knob of rock, my textbook of invertebrate zoology on her knees, and read me the identification key. The night before, Sara, who played Scrabble every day at lunch hour, had snockered me 150 points and departed triumphant. As she flounced out she'd said, "After all these years!" How could she know it gave me vastly more satisfaction than it gave her? And somehow that added enjoyment to my saying yes, no, yes, yes as she read the key. What pleasure, that minute colony of humans, the only species to give and record names, sharing the accumulated knowledge of centuries, the sentience of sea and sun, water gurgling around our feet as the tide came back in, an irrevocable part of this time, this place, this affection.

And now, today, I remember that, as the surf sounds urgent behind me and small surges sweep in with more frequency and vigor. Still I sit, listening to the surf pound in on the outer ledges. Perhaps I linger because this pool is where we first explored a world that was new to us, and I keep seeing images of little girls discovering intriguing creatures that did peculiar things—it was a bad day for worm snails when Sara discovered that if you touched them, they withdrew convulsively and spit water. Jane always was first to find the sun stars that no one else saw. I remember Susan, snorkel mask on, lying on a ledge, face in the water, contemplating eternity.

A small trickle of water ruffles the surface, destroying its clarity. The sea returns, bringing food but also bringing turbulence. The surface flickers again and a narrow fall of water pours into one end, trickling and gurgling, pensive but purposeful sounds. Another surge reverberates off the narrow passage walls, echoing into intersecting arcs, that shimmer on the pool's sandy bottom. Somewhere, half the world away, the sea withdraws, baring rock and beach; here the sea sweeps in, covering barnacle rock and blenny pool, leaving them like the wavery shadowy shapes of memory.

Tidepools

Tidepools

As I climb up from the tidepool, the slope above lies in shadow, but a shaft of sun still lights the hummingbird nest. She is gone when I arrive, and when she returns, there are no more feeding forays. She sits facing the ocean sixty feet below. The pools on the rock shelf below reflect like steel mirrors, and the ocean filters in around the rocks between. She's nicely settled in, it is dusk, and I beam her my protective maternal thoughts and go up to dinner, having been reminded of how much I miss my daughters.

When I check the nest the next morning it hangs in tatters. Something got to it in the night. The black jellybean babies lie on the ground, wizened and dead. I pick up a piece of the nest—so soft, so gossamer, fashioned of bits of leaf, feathery sead-head filaments, fuzzy wild lavender calyces, lichen bits, all well-shredded before being woven together.

I know it's foolish and sentimental, but I hold that poor scrap of nest in my hand and tears blur my eyes. I wonder if she is still alive, still hovering somewhere, if she will nest next spring, will haunt the San Miguel vine, will lay pea sized eggs, if she will garland the air with her flight and remind me of the tenuousness of motherhood.

The first time I tried my large seine we captured about 3000 pounds in a few pulls, and my heart bursted nearly when I had to trow [sic] them away, so beautiful they were.

John Xantus
Letter to Spencer F. Baird
June 1 1859

With the nets which every ship carried, a great quantity of fish of many species and different forms, all very good, wholesome, and of good taste, was caught each day. That it may be known what the kinds of fish were, I give here the names of those I saw and had in my hands; sardines, chermas, *red-snapper, perch,* cornudos, *dog-fish, sharks, devil-fish, skate, salmon, tunny,* esmeregales, *oysters, ray-fish,* chuchos, *mackerel, roncodors, mutton-fish, bonitos,* puercos, *sole,* sirgueros, *newts, a great quantity of pearl oysters, and many whales.*

Antonio de la Ascensión
Account of the Voyage of Sebastián Vizcaíno
1602–1603

Pecten (*Argopecten circularis*)

14

BENEATH THE SEA

On October 25, 1764, Miguel del Barco, Jesuit missionary, wrote to his father procurator, saying, "My natural inclination leads me completely away from the sea." Yes. Freshwater child, raised on a river, summered on a lake in Michigan, I am firmly bonded to the fresh water heritage imprinted on me since birth. In addition, I inherited a predisposition toward seasickness. It is *my* further opinion that salt water tastes terrible and waves make swimming a lot of unnecessary effort.

I know exactly what the first fish that scooped itself out of the sea and up onto dry land and decided to stay thought as it slithered from the murky shallows on its tender finny feet and felt the whispery air. Enough of this vertiginous slosh. Enough of this flowing and ebbing. Enough of this salt water in my eyes. Give me a stable base from which to operate and a firm horizon on which to lock.

Therefore, not until a few years ago could I be talked into snorkeling. Herman smeared my face mask with something he called "whale spit" to keep my mask from fogging. Jonah didn't like it and neither did I. It made my eyes smart, and I had to wipe it out, and find something less irritating. Finally Susan, my water child, took me firmly by the hand, saying kindly but

Cortez chubs

firmly, "Come *on,* Mom!" in that tone of voice one assumes with a recalcitrant child and trapped me in her patience.

Because the water was not terribly warm, I borrowed Susan's wet suit. Susan is taller than I and her wet suit fit me like Dolly Parton's would fit Olive Oyl. I was so buoyant that I bobbed like a cork. Once in I had trouble keeping my flippers on; the foot extension necessary for flippers gave me foot cramps. A grain of sand lodged in one flipper. It stuck at a bony place, and as I worked it out with my fingers I let the snorkel tube dip below the surface. Even worse, beneath me was a whole moving world of vertiginous flickering light jiggling on wave-rippled sand, rocks wavering uncertainly, tufts of algae wafting about without apparent direction. The water went up and down, the patterns on the bottom swayed back and forth, and fish rotated at cross purposes to it all.

When I made my merciful retreat, the shore rose up and looked deceptively close, but when I put my feet down I was horrified not to touch bottom. The parallel troughs and ridges were a foot or so apart, scooped out by the roll of the waves as they come into shore, depending in dimension somewhat on the size of the sand grains. And just before shore was a steep step, formed from the backwash of the breakers that fed into the beach. As the waves go out, the sand is constantly sorted, with larger particles shifting downward until they reach a depth where they can no longer be picked up, forming a step with the angle of repose of the sand. When I finally dragged myself out, my stomach and head were so seriously uncoupled, my eye and ear so disoriented, I seriously considered taking Dramamine the next time I tried this, which I trusted would not be soon.

A summer passed, time in which to forget. Once again I set out, this time with my own wet suit. Visibility was excellent. Interlocking lozenges of light scampered up the rocks, fell off, coalesced, shredded, in a scintillating display of northern lights in an aqueous sky. A thin line turned, flashed into a fish; a foreshortened view slued into profile. Tail gleamed, flank pressed against water, head turned, gill flared, fish swam. Swift play of light, quick intensity of color, shine of scale and glow of iridescence, the curved flanks of silvery slivers, constantly turning and tumbling, rearranging like a pastel kaleidoscope.

The interface of water and air, a boundary I'd only seen from above, was a silken tent undulating in the underwater wind, gray blue with moving ovals, a scrim through which light billowed. A small fish shinnied up to the surface, popped the film, and slid back down again, all in silence. I was hooked.

Today, as I adjust my mask, I wonder at the discomforts of yesteryear. Beneath me, the sandy bottom moves. Dozens of fish, moving in braided unison, sweep over the bottom—young barracuda schooling with mullet, gray sleek fish curving through layers of water, pressing and turning, flowing, crowds and groups and streams. Milky-translucent needlefish, school near the surface, snagging tiny fish with their sharp-teethed jaws. Like ghosts, they fade in and out of focus.

Ahead of me a pelican floats, an improbable goose, thrown together of outlandish mismatching parts. I approach slowly, head down. Swirls of bubbles surround its webbed feet as it cruises slowly just ahead. When I look up, before me sails an eye dark as a berry, surrounded by brownish-gray and white feathers set in a bony head atop a long neck, hung with that capacious bill. It wallows just so far ahead, not fishing, just floating. A peaceable bird.

They are closer in than usual, brought in by large schools of "anchovies," and for the past week they have been diving so close to shore it looks as if they'll hit bottom. They beat over slowly, about twenty to twenty-five feet above the ocean, beaks tilted down at a forty-five degree angle, scanning. The moment of decision is obvious: the wings tuck partially back, the head points straight down and it plummets, its body making a half turn just as the beak hits the water, the bird having in that moment of descent made the necessary calculations of fish speed and direction, current, wind drift and direction, how deep it has to go, air density and water density and SPLASH! When the spray clears, there it floats serenely, bill horizontal, light shining through the stretched pink pouch, fish safely clamped inside. Below the surface it scooped in gallons of water as well as the fish and water sluices out of the sides of its bill. The bill points upward, and with a few shakes the fish slides down.

I plow through what looks like translucent pink Rice Krispies, in reality they are tiny jellyfish-like animals armed with stinging tentacles. The repeated stings range in intensity from a pinprick to a bee sting and galvanize me into kicking right through, for I remember Susan's reaction. She looked like an advanced case of chicken pox when we climbed La Laguna. Some people can be highly allergic, as Susan is, or just have a few moments of red welts, as Herman does. All that is known about the venom is that it is a protein, but the exact nature of the reaction is unknown.

The presence of these animals has undoubtedly caused the luminescence in the night ocean of late, sparkling as the waves pile up at shore, wreathing the land like some magical apparition. The cold light of bioluminescence is due to cells containing a substance called luciferin plus oxygen and water

Pelican swallowing fish

and activated by an enzyme. Such cells may be scattered over the animal's surface or localized in certain areas, and are jostled into luminescing by disturbance, such as being tumbled in the breaking water near the beach.

Once free of jellyfish, I hang suspended over a granite shelf, an extension of the granites of the land, slotted with sandy bottoms between noduled ledges. Today there are thin yellowtail surgeonfish, silvery with button-on yellow tails. Their common name comes from the razor-sharp spine set at the end of the body, just before the caudal fin. These can be flared away from the body and inflict a painful wound on any would-be predator as well as a human who handles them. Like most coral-reef fish, they are herbivores, brightly colored, and diurnal. Their sawtooth-margined spatulate teeth enable them to scrape algae from rocks, their primary food.

Many of the same species are common inhabitants of the coral reefs associated with western Pacific islands, and the reason that they are here is the like water temperature and habitat. Almost three-quarters of the resident species are common in the Panamic fauna. Some of these have come up the Mexican coast and undoubtedly crossed the mouth of the Gulf. The reef fish of the Gulf also share many genera and "species pairs" with the reef fish of the Bahamas, confirming both their shared ancestry and the recentness of their separation. Among them are quite a few species endemic to the Gulf.

Most of the species now restricted to the southern part of the peninsula are rocky shore forms, and since reefs are most prevalent from La Paz to Cabo San Lucas, this area is the richest in species in the Gulf. This distinctiveness may depend upon several factors, among them water temperature and substrate; the deep underwater canyons that reach outward from the Cape may have some influence, as well as the presence of coral reefs, rare elsewhere in the eastern Pacific.

Beneath me, two opulent parrotfish lurk among the dark rocks. One, an iridescent green, resembles some huge jewel floating in the sea. The other, a bicolor parrotfish, has a gray back end, and looks as if someone had held it by its tail and dipped its front half in violet ink. Their fused teeth resemble a parrot's beak, hence the name. A forehead bump often develops on some of the larger fish; ichthyologists once thought that this may have been used to nudge off pieces of coral, but no evidence has been found for this, for they are herbivores that scrape algae off rock. Many parrotfish sleep backed into rock crevices, but some secrete a mucus cocoon, the purpose of which, it is thought, may be to block off their scent so that predators cannot locate them while they are vulnerable.

I float over a shelf where sea fans spring out of the rocks, bathed in a

Yellowtail surgeonfish

Mexican goatfish

lovely opalescence. Colonies of polyps arranged in a flat lattice, facing into the prevailing current, make up these gorgonians. Mexican goatfish winnow the sand in the next canyon, bodies all canted upward. Twin barbels fold under the chin when swimming, but project forward for feeding when the fish is in a head-down position. Although primarily night feeders, they do search for food during the day, moving their sensitive barbels filled with chemo-sensory cells through the bottom sand, rooting out small crustaceans and mollusks.

A hundred white eyes flash and disappear as a school of scissortail damselfish turn in unison. Dark gray, their bodies fade into the background, but the dorsal white spot, just in front of the tail, is clear and bright. They remind me of nothing so much as birds of the sea, sliding and slipping, gliding and soaring, with the same flash turn of a flock of pigeons. Schooling has great advantage to small fish, sacrificing the few to protect the many. In a school, the individual fish has less chance of encountering a predator although the school as a whole is easier to see. One predator can only eat so many, seldom the number involved in the school; the larger the school the smaller the percentage that will be gobbled down. Some fish, if snapped at or up, release an alarm pheromone from special cells in its outer skin which activates the rest of the school. Generally the fright reaction causes them to scatter every which way, making them very difficult for a predator to track.

Sometimes a school of larger fish chases a school of smaller ones, and may drive them onto shore; Antonio de la Ascención in 1603 tells of a great quantity of sardines found thrown up on the beach, still fresh "and so good were they that on what was collected all those of the fleet supped that night and dined the following day." I remember a small inlet, where a school of jacks had cornered just such a school of fry; they whipped the water to a froth, fish flying clear out of the water in a frenzy of feeding and a frenzy of fleeing.

A king angelfish turns, a thin thread of brilliant fluorescent blue outlining the navy blue body and orange tail. I hang above it, enjoying the colors, watching it pluck food from the rock; it prefers sponges but also nips off algae and sessile invertebrates. Angelfish, along with butterfly fish, are some of the most brilliantly colored reef fishes. The young, although the same configuration, are burnt orange, outlined with the same fluorescent blue line. The king angel turns sideways for the perfect view, orange and deep blue with a white slash behind the front fin, and I know that, were it given to me to design a fish, I would hope I could do as well as a king angel.

I kick over toward an area where the reef is knobby with coral. There is

Jack

King angelfish

such a congregation of varied fish that I realize I've stumbled on a cleaning station. I remember when Alex Kerstitch, a superb illustrator and underwater photographer (he did the preponderant number of illustrations for *Reef Fishes of the Sea of Cortez*) took us out to Shepherd Rock to snorkel while he did a deep dive to check on some fish in the underwater canyon at San Lucas Bay. Shepherd's Rock is a well-populated cleaning station where many fish, sometimes thousands, congregate.

Cleaning is an essential activity for both cleaners and cleanees. Those wishing to be cleaned have a body language which indicates their peaceful intention to the cleaners, which are often butterfly fish, sergeant majors and wrasses, and juveniles of other species. Some fish even change color—the pale goatfish flushes dark and one guess is that its baggage of pale parasites shows up more clearly, making them easier to remove. Often fish signal the desire to be cleaned by posing with heads down and mouths open, something that can cause trouble in paradise. Groups of Cortéz rainbow wrasse, characteristic cleaners, are often infiltrated by a saber-tooth blenny, which closely resembles them. The blennies feed on skin mucus of other fishes, and when a fish comes in with its mouth open, the sabertooth darts at the victim and nips off a bit of mucus, usually with some skin attached.

A couple of dozen barberfish swim below, looking as if they wear raccoon masks. Half a dozen tend a gray mullet. As cleaning fish, they pick over the mullet, including the gill cavities and mouth; they likely eat whatever they find, although most cleaners, like the barberfish, also have other sources of food. Like most reef fish, barberfish are diurnal. At night they change color, the darkness on the back disappearing and the sides becoming blotched with pale spots. Butterfly fish patterning tends to be disruptive—a line passing through an eye, an eyespot at the base of the tail—all of which break up its outline and confuse its predators.

The sun shafts cleanly down twenty feet. Where granite walls drop off into slots of sand, a Moorish idol insinuates itself through the water, thin as a wafer, trailing a long thin dorsal fin, seeming to turn at more angles than a model going through a series of stylized poses. It is surely one of the loveliest of reef fishes. Scarcely seeming to do anything so plebeian as swim, it bends gently into a murky distance.

As I swim back along the cliffs I fancy the underwater landscape looks just like that of land with the color bled out: instead of clumps of bright-flowered cushion plants there are drab mounds of algae and coral. What is really different is the light: instead of the bright clarity and sharp shadows of land, there are amorphous shadows with a flickering fishnet of light that scintillates over every object, not a defining light but a quixotic arbitrary light as if the lighting director had abandoned the stage set, gone home, and left the lights to their own devices. And down there the wind is different too: on shore a tuft of grass bends and returns, bends and returns. Below, the underwater breeze of currents sweeps tufts of algae first in one direction, then another, swirling them in illogical patterns.

I persuade myself that it is good discipline to rely on my memory and not on pen and paper. In the water I count the things I want to remember on my fingers, then toes, then back on fingers again. I use every mnemonic device I can think of to recall what I saw: the seaweed fish that looked just that, hanging on the bottom and drifting back and forth with the current; how vividly the buttons on the tails of the surgeonfish tails shone; the disembodied white dots moving through space that focused into scissortailed damselfish; the upended goatfish resembling an odd fish-flowered garden; the "wounded" wrasse with a red splotch on its back.

When I climb out of the water, the world about me is unstable. It's fascinating when I'm swimming, but when I get on dry land the world sways. I write all that I can remember as soon as I get out, leaving dots of salt water on a wavering page.

When I look back out over the ocean I feel the illogic of it all. So much goes on out there underneath. The surface is a blank reflective mirror, a closed blue door, telling nothing of the teeming life just inches below, or hinting at all the information that my hand and head stumble over.

I stop writing to watch Sara. Now that I have become somewhat at ease with a mask and snorkel, I have a wonderful time watching Sara suit up. It's like watching myself a few years ago: the mask doesn't fit and it leaks; she can't get the beavertail of her wet suit fastened (a delicate situation at best); she can't get the flippers on without sand in them. Then she stands, waist deep in the water, fussing, putting the mask on and off, thinking, I'm sure, "Is it worth it?" but laughing all the while. A doting father hand delivers another mask, she sticks her face in the water, and it must work, for when I glance up again the sea where she stood is empty and she's gone in a flurry of foam.

The next day I watch Herman as he gets his gear together to go diving. He shakes his wet suit with great thoroughness. As I watch him I remember why. Once he left his wet suit over a wall to dry. He slipped on the suit to walk down to the beach, both one less thing to carry and to protect his bare

Moorish idols

back from the abrasion of the buoyancy-compensator straps. When he stuffed his arm into the jacket he let out a holler to wake the dead.

A scorpion had found the dark damp sleeve a pleasant place to rest and, when dispossessed by Herman's arm, it replied in the only way it knew how. I ran for help and was assured that peninsula scorpions are not fatal and that the cure for them is ammonia. It killed the pain but not the scare.

Baegert called them "pretty little animals" and thought it

> a lucky thing indeed, considering the great number of scorpions, that its bite is not fatal in California. It merely causes some swelling and is painful for several hours, as I have found out myself. The color of the California scorpions is yellow-green, and some are as long as a finger, not counting the tail.

Arching a curved stinger at the end of its abdomen forward over its back, it delivers a painful wallop fueled by two venom glands that open into the sting. The venom in poisonous species is neurotoxic and brings on convulsions and respiratory paralysis, and in extreme cases cardiac arrest. Mainland scorpion stings are often fatal, although they can be no worse than a bad bee sting.

This morning is, thank heavens, uneventful. I accompany him as he floats far around the end of a rocky promontory; there he dives and I cruise the surface, watching him in the murky blue below. Swimming near the cliffs I am surprised at how deep the surge of aerated water goes, as the wave hits the rock, a cloud of fine white bubbles ballooning outward. The strong rush of water blasts the seaweed, like strong wind, and it streams seaward; all the fish in the channel blow right along with it.

A Cortez angelfish checks out the funny blue fish with the tank on its back. It swims head on to within three feet of Herman's bubbles, circles around a rock, peeks over, returns, swims nose to nose again, repeats and repeats while Herman remains stationary, happily clicking away with his underwater camera. Less rectangular and brilliant than the king angel, it is a soft gray brown with amorphous yellow bars. The young are startlingly different from the adult, royal blue with curving brilliant yellow stripes, like cut-paper fish designed by Matisse.

Herman breaks open an urchin, and his faithful companion, a big old parrotfish, heaves into view. All of a sudden the fish spots a huge zebra moray eel and vice versa—they almost collide. The eel streaks for the nearest cavern. The parrotfish spurts into the distance. Total quiet lasts for about two seconds, and then the inhabitants, one by one, wrasses and damselfish and

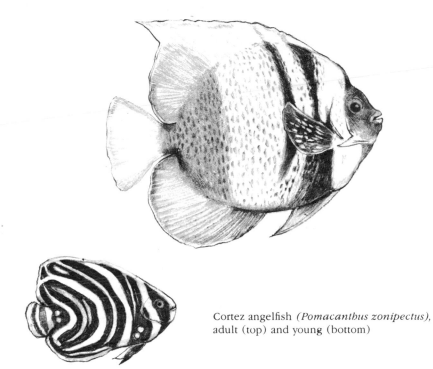

Cortez angelfish *(Pomacanthus zonipectus)*, adult (top) and young (bottom)

the small lurkers and pokers, reappear. I am unsettled by the soundlessness of the encounter--there ought to be a squeal or a scream, an indrawn breath, a rattle of warning. But there is nothing, just the crackling of water in my ears.

I am thankful not to be down there, although undoubtedly I shall be if Herman has his way; my first forays with tank and respirator have been less than successful, mainly because equipment tends to be too big, and I find it very unpleasant to have my buoyancy compensator and tank drift slowly over my head. But I suppose once one hears the sound of bubbles in one's ears, one must follow.

Herman disappears into the depths and I continue outward. Scores of baby sergeant majors school near the surface, neat little gray and yellow fish. I stumble onto a dozen Moorish idols—I've never seen more than one at a time before. Their milky white dorsal fins stream and flutter in the current. I hang above them, marveling. The water deepens. The water is warm, the day is pleasant, and I wander, much as I do on land, taking my time, fascinated by the varying landscape that unrolls beneath me. And I think of what I could see could I but see.

For out there in the deeper deeps the East Pacific Rise slowly pushes the peninsula away from the mainland. Afloat on this timeless water, I feel that if I could just go out far enough the rift itself would become visible, as indeed it did for the divers who went down a mile and a half and saw that identifiable boundary between continental plates, where the earth is being gradually expanded: a vast bulge of sea floor that developed perhaps fifty-five to sixty million years ago. At other places the earth turns in upon itself; here it tears apart, spreading about six centimeters a year, about the rate fingernails grow.

Along the ridge vents, where magma has risen to the surface and broken through, mineral-blackened water spews out. The water temperature at the vents is over 650 degrees Fahrenheit; it does not boil because the atmospheric pressure at that depth is 275 times that of sea level. Around the vents, which come and go, lives a biological community like none on land. It is entirely independent of green plants conducting photosynthesis at the base of the food chain. The base of the food chain there is chemosynthetic bacteria. The bacteria, which exit in astronomical numbers, metabolize the hydrogen sulfide pluming out of the vents into sulfur and various sulfates. Most of the organisms either live with the bacteria symbiotically or filter-feed on them.

Immediately around the vents the amount of food for the bacteria is perhaps five hundred times greater than in adjoining waters. Productivity is four times greater than that of surface water. The bacteria proliferate, growing in mats and clumps, in every interstice available. One of the divers found the scene

out of an old horror movie. Shimmering water rose between the basaltic pillows along the axis of the neovolcanic zone. Large white clams as much as 30 centimeters long nestled between the black pillows; white crabs scampered blindly across the volcanic terrain. Most dramatic of all were the clusters of giant tube worms, some of them as long as three meters. These weird creatures appeared to live in dense colonies surrounding the vents, in water ranging in temperature from two to 20 degrees C. The worms, known as vestimentiferan pogonophorans, waved eerily in the hydrothermal currents, their bright red plumes extending well beyond their white protective tubes. (The red color of both the tube-worm plumes and the clam tissues results from the presence of oxygenated hemoglobin in their blood.) Occasionally a crab would climb the stalk of a tube worm, presumably to attack its plume.

There are also whelks, barnacles, leeches, and a filter-feeding limpet, whose nearest relative is a Paleozoic fossil, plus a brachyuran crab new to science.

I float, arms outstretched, peering downward, searching for what the cormorant sees. Or what a pelican sees when it rolls downward in an unwinding helix. Or that wrasse, going about its appointed tasks with fidelity, at home beneath the silvered tent. And I reflect how simple it is for those who swim or pivot or rasp, supported and fed, adrift in an infinite womb, bathed in a life support medium full of needed nutrients, needing less to eat than their land-based counterparts, less plagued by temperature fluctuations and desiccation, no need to heat their blood, filled with body fluids with the same osmotic pressure as the sea, so needing less protective covering to separate them from an alien atmosphere, suspended easily in this friendly bath without having to battle the incessant pull of gravity.

I drift at ease, the salt water in my veins cooling to the temperature of the ocean, encased in an envelope that so recently left this safe world of filtered light and floating quiet, at one with what flickers and turns, flees and flutters, waits and watches below. The ties that bind dissolve and I float in a never-never land of flowing horizons, world without end, adrift between yesterday and tomorrow, contemplating a different way of chaining the world together.

I raise my head until the horizon in my mask encompasses half ocean, half sky. Each drop of water on the glass contains its own tilted quivering horizon. As I pivot like a free-swinging compass and turn northward toward the land, I see waves of mountains that sink and rise in far faster moment than they sank and rose in the cadence of eons, those times when the Cape was truly an island and where I have walked undulated with water waves instead of heat waves.

And then I take another bearing of space and time. In this interweaving of blues and multiple horizons is the meshing of time with the moment of motion and the sense of infinity. Adrift in this peaceful cradling ocean, it is difficult to believe that somewhere beyond a world is tearing itself apart.

NOTES

Introduction: The Cape

page

xvii Quote, Joseph Wood Krutch, *The Forgotten Peninsula* (New York: William Morrow, 1961), p. 6.

xviii Conditions still exist much as Gustav Eisen, "Explorations in the Cape Region of Baja California in 1894, with References to Former Expeditions of the California Academy of Sciences," *Proceedings of the California Academy of Sciences,* 2nd ser. 5 (1895), p. 737, found them in 1894:

The localities visited by the members of the various expeditions were only indifferently marked down on any previously existing map, and these mostly incorrectly located. The rivers and creeks were nowhere even hinted at and the mountain regions were everywhere found only indicated.

Maps published by the Defense Mapping Agency Hydrographic Center, Washington, D.C. 20390 (#21120, Bahía Magdalena to La Paz, printed in 1978) are an updated version of the first modern charting of the coast done by the U.S. Naval Coastal Survey Ship *Narragansett* in 1874. Current Mexican maps are available from Sección Distribución, Comisión de Estudios del Territorio Nacional, San Antonio, Abad 124 P. B. México, D.F., México.

Quote, John Steinbeck and Ed Ricketts, *Sea of Cortez: A Leisurely Journal of Travel and Research* (Mount Vernon, NY: Paul P. Appel, 1982), p. 12.

xxi For the naming of California see Edward Everett Hale, trans., *The Queen of California, The Origin of the Name of California with a Translation from the Sergas of Esplandian* (San Francisco: Colt Press, 1945); Bartolomé Ferrer, "Voyage of Cabrillo in 1542," *U.S. Geographical Surveys West of the 100th Meridian,* Vol. VII (Archaeology) (Washington, DC: U.S. Government Printing Office, 1879), p. 299 fn.; Miguel Venegas, *A Natural and Civil History of California* (Ann Arbor: University Microfilms, 1966), pp. 3–4; George Lindsay, "The Mission Period of Baja California," *Pacific Discovery* (July–August, 1965), pp. 2–3; and Pablo L. Martínez, *A History of Lower California,* trans. Ethel Duffy Turner (México: Editorial Baja California, 1960), pp. 89–91. Juan Rodríguez Cabrillo, "The Voyage of Juan Rodríquez Cabrillo," ed. Henry R. Wagner, *California Historical Society Quarterly* 7(1) (1928), p. 71 fn.: the 1562 map of Diego Gutiérrez was the first to use the name "California."

page

xxii   Quote, Jakob Baegert, *Observations in Lower California,* trans. and ed. Carl L. Baumann (Berkeley: University of California Press, 1952), p. 29. Baegert, who served on the peninsula 18 years, 1751–1768, published *Nachrichten von der amerikanischen halbinsel Californien* in Mannheim, 1772.

xxiii   Quote, Krutch, p. 14.

xxiv   Eisen, 1895 (p. 756), believed "the Cape Region of Baja California is one of the most interesting isolated points in the world as regards its fauna and flora."

    William Brewster, "Birds of the Cape Region of Lower California," *Bulletin of the Museum of Comparative Zoology, Harvard College* 41(1) (1902), the eminent Harvard ornithologist, who described one of the early bird collections from the Cape, quotes Townshend Stith Brandegee, the California botanist (pp. 3–4):

> I will answer that for the flora it seems best to include only the region south of a line between La Paz and Todos Santos. This line is nearly a straight line, and follows along the northern base of the Cape Mountains. The trail between La Paz and Todos Santos does not appear to ascend more than 150 feet above sea-level at any place, and there is a large extent of nearly level country to the north of it. The Cape Region will be, then, a mountainous country separated from the northern mountains by an extent of low land.

    Edward W. Nelson, "Lower California and Its Natural Resources," *National Academy of Sciences, Memoir* 16 (1921), p. 119, wrote in 1906 that the Cape "has been visited by numerous naturalists, and has contributed more material and had more published concerning it than any other section of the peninsula." Nelson led the first scientific expedition mounted by the U.S. National Museum in 1905–06.

    J. Wyatt Durham and Edwin C. Allison, "The Geologic History of Baja California and Its Marine Faunas," in "Symposium: The Biogeography of Baja California and Adjacent Seas. Part I. Geologic History," eds. J. Wyatt Durham and Edwin C. Allison, *Systematic Zoology* 9(2), p. 47, point out that the peninsula

> occupies a geographically and biogeographically critical site at the northern boundary of the eastern Pacific tropics. Nowhere else between the United States and Nicaragua is a Cenozoic record of the eastern Pacific recognized. Latitudes between the southern tip of Baja California and the transverse Ranges of southern California, the limits of the Peninsular Range province, embrace the transition between two great faunal divisions of the Eastern Pacific: the tropical west American and the north temperate west American.

    Paul H. Arnaud, 1970, "The Sefton Foundation ORCA Expedition to the Gulf of California, March–April, 1953," in *Occasional Papers of the California Academy of Sciences,* September 18, 1970, on a trip to collect arachnids, fish, insects (primarily Diptera) and mollusks, speaks of the peninsula (p. 1) as "an almost unique living biological laboratory which is infrequently duplicated in other parts of the world."

xxvi   Quote, Jakob Baegert, *The Letters of Jakob Baegert, 1749–1761,* trans. Elsbeth Schulz-Bischof, intro. and ed. Doyce B. Nunis, Jr. (Los Angeles: Dawson's Book Shop, 1982), p. 130.

Chapter 1. San Lázaro

5   Gustav Eisen, "Explorations in the Cape Region of Baja California," *American Geographical Society of New York Bulletin* 29(3) (1897), p. 277, found the interior peaks unknown and thought his party first to make any ascents; his only previous records were of "an

English sailor" and "an American newspaper man." The sailor must have been William Redmond Ryan, who in 1848–49 landed at San José del Cabo but did not climb any mountains. The newspaper man would have been J. Ross Browne (see Chapter 4), but nothing in his writing indicates he climbed San Lázaro.

John Xantus, at Cabo San Lucas 1859–61, wrote to Spencer Baird, Secretary of the Smithsonian Institution, January 25, 1860, a purely fanciful account of climbing "Santiago peak," the top of which was

> solid granit, thrown up in confused boulders, reminding one at the last day of Judgment, as we read in the good old book. The San Lazaro appears to be precisely similar, having in addition a crater as I am told. It is however not so high as the Santiago, as I could look over its top very well. At an altitude of about 6000 feet, there is a saddle between the two peaks, vis: [small sketch] and riding over to the west side, a fine country spread before the eye, a *mesa* or high table land of at least 25 [square] miles, with gigantic pines, oaks, & spruce, and without underbrush whatsoever.

His letters are in the Archives of the Smithsonian Institution, to which I am indebted for their use.

See Ira L. Wiggins, *Flora of Baja California* (Stanford: Stanford University Press, 1980) p. 846; and T. S. Brandegee, "Palms of Baja California," *Zoe* 5(10) (1904), p. 189.

5–7   Current papers on the geology of the Cape are W. R. Normak and J. P. Curray, "Geology and Structure of the Tip of Baja California, Mexico," *Geological Society of America Bulletin* 79 (1968), pp. 1589–90, 1597–98; J. Wyatt Durham and Edwin C. Allison, "The Geologic History of Baja California and Its Marine Fauna," in "Symposium: The Biogeography of Baja California and Adjacent Seas. Part I. Geologic History," eds. J. Wyatt Durham and Edwin C. Allison, *Systematic Zoology* 9(2) (1960), pp. 48–49; Edwin H. Hammond, "A Geomorphic Study of the Cape Region of Baja California," *University of California Publications in Geography* 10(2), (1945):45–114; Gordon Gastil, Richard P. Phillips, and Raphael Rodriguez-Torres, "The Reconstruction of Mesozoic California," *International Geological Congress, Proceedings* 1972:217–229; Gordon Gastil, Richard P. Phillips, and Edwin C. Allison, "Reconnaissance Geology of the State of Baja California," *The Geological Society of America Memoir* 140 (1975):1–170. The last two references focus on northern Baja California but contain information pertinent to the Cape. Although since replaced by recent work, N. H. Darton, "Geological Reconnaissance in Baja California," *Journal of Geology* 29 (1921), and Arnold Heim, "Notes on the Tertiary of Southern Lower California (Mexico)," *The Geological Magazine* 59 (12) (1922), are of interest. See also Armand J. Eardley, *Structural Geology of North America (Baja California and Sonora Systems)* (New York: Harper & Row, 1962). See also W. Hamilton, "Recogition of Space Photographs of Structural Elements of Baja California," *U.S.G.S. Professional Paper 718* (Washington, DC: U.S. Government Printing Office, 1971). For the East Pacific Rise, see also Ken MacDonald and Bruch P. Luyendyk, "The Crest of the East Pacific Rise," *Scientific American* 244(5) (1981):100–116.

7   Quote, Miguel del Barco, *Natural History of California,* intro. Miguel León-Portilla, trans. Froylan Tiscareno (Los Angeles: Dawson's Book Shop, 1980), pp. 107–8. León-Portilla gives an invigorating portrait of Barco, whose *Adiciones y Correcciones* provided firsthand accuracy and freshness for Miguel Venegas's *A Natural and Civil History of California.* Venegas had not been to the peninsula; he compiled his book, published in 1757, from letters and reports. Commission was given to Father Andrés Marcos Burriel to revise Venegas's manuscript; he compounded its errors, for he had not been to the peninsula either. Barco served in California with the Jesuits from 1738 to 1768 so wrote from experi-

page

ence. His charming and important work has been published in translation by Dawson's Book Shop, which is responsible for a series of beautifully designed books on Baja California, visual as well as scholarly gems; a list is available on request.

11 Jakob Baegert, *The Letters of Jakob Baegert, 1749–1761,* trans. Elsbeth Schultz-Bischof, intro. and ed. Doyce B. Nunis, Jr. (Los Angeles: Dawson's Book Shop, 1982), p. 121.

13 In Mexico datura is called *toloache,* which goes back to Aztec times. All parts of the plant contain alkaloids, among them atropine, a drug widely used today, as well as hyoscyamine and scopolamine; see Henry S. Wassen, "The Anthropological Outlook for Amerindian Medicinal Plants," in *Plants in the Development of Modern Medicine,* ed. Tony Swain (Cambridge: Harvard University Press, 1972), pp. 1–65. See also Charles B. Heiser, Jr., *Nightshades: The Paradoxical Plants* (San Francisco: W. H. Freeman, 1969), p. 142, who decries the elimination of plant species:

> Certain principles first delineated in *Datura* and other "worthless" plants have been of tremendous importance in the understanding of all plants, including those of great direct importance to man.

15 Quote, Barco, p. 296. Later intrusions, probably Cretaceous and early Tertiary, appear as dikes and veins. As a rule they appear to be finer grained than the coarser crystalline granites into which they moved; Hammond (pp. 64, 75) found that the dikes frequently outcrop as rocky spines along ridge crests.

Wiggins (p. 312) gives a complete description and illustration of *Faxonia.* T. S. Brandegee, "Additions to the Flora of the Cape Region of Baja California. II," *Zoe* 4 (1894), pp. 403–4, discovered and named it in honor of the botanical illustrator C. E. Faxon.

17 Quote, Jakob Baegert, *Observations in Lower California,* trans. and eds. M. M. Brandenburg and Carl L. Baumann (Berkeley: University of California Press, 1952), p. 115. Mary Shroyer, *personal communication* (January 7, 1983), writes that the ramal was

> beautifully done all the way up and across the pass. . . . Then, at the point of descent, everything went to pieces. Ford the streams, edge around mud and rock slides. We pushed the van in and out of an arroyo, knocking the bottom so badly we had to get a new muffler AND a new motor mount this week. We never could have made it *up* the down road!

Quotes, Barco, pp. 186–87, 126. F. J. Clavijero, *The History of California,* trans. and eds. Sara E. Lake and A. A. Gray (Stanford: Stanford University Press, 1937), p. 50 on *Jatropha vernicosa:*

> The bark is whitish. No use is made of this plant in California; but its stalks could be useful for making baskets and especially dye, because it contains a blood-colored liquid which dyes cloth so fast that, regardless of how often it is washed, the spot cannot be removed from it.

Clavijero published *Storia del California* in Venice in 1789; he had never been to the peninsula and depended heavily on accounts from others who had. He died before he had a chance to revise it.

17–
18 T. S. Brandegee, "The Distribution of the Flora of the Cape Region of Baja California," *Zoe* 3 (1891), p. 225:

> The Cape Region is quite thickly covered with large bushes and small trees with an abundance of climbing and twining plants using them for supports. These altogether sometimes become so dense that it is impossible to ride or walk between them, and to go through them is usually not to be thought of on account of the spines and thorns.

Quote, Barco, pp. 125 ff. See also Clavijero, p. 39:

The fruit is similar in shape and color to the early fig of the fig tree, but it is smaller, less juicy, and without the very sweet flavor of our figs. Notwithstanding this, the Californians esteem it so much that when they receive news about an *anaba* with ripe fruit they go quickly to look for it in order to provide themselves with it, although it may be twelve or fifteen miles distant from where they live.

Ducrue, in *The Natural and Human History of Baja California,* ed. Homer Aschmann (Los Angeles: Dawson's Book Shop, 1966), p. 51:

There are wild figs and grapes which bear fruit and which occur only in arroyos and deep ravines. The fig trees grow on and over the rocky cliffs in the fissures of which they establish their roots. If some rain showers have fallen the figs are passably tasty, but if there has been no rain the fruit is without juice and practically tasteless.

Edward W. Nelson, "Lower California and Its Natural Resources," *National Academy of Sciences, Memoir 16* (1921), p. 109, found fig trees from the foothills up to nearly 4,000 feet. Walter E. Bryant, "The Cape Region of Baja California," *Zoe* 2 (1891), p. 191, found woodpeckers, ravens, and both Costa's and Xantus' hummingbirds feeding on the figs.

21   According to the U.S. hydrographic map, the altitude of Calaveras is 3,695 feet, San Lázaro, 5,111 feet.

Quote, Krutch, p. 33. William Weber Johnson and the editors of Time-Life Books, *Baja California* (New York: Time, Inc., 1972), p. 23:

The reason Baja remains a wilderness seems to be none of these [inaccessibility, poverty of material rewards, etc.], but rather a sort of indomitable stubborness, a built-in resistance to the destructive impact of civilization, to the erosion caused by man's technology and acquisitiveness. Few of the world's wilderness areas have been so dreamed about, so dressed with fantasies, so desperately scratched over by men eager for wealth or power or renown. For more than four centuries man has been attempting to subdue the Baja peninsula, physically or spiritually, to exploit it or at least make it do his bidding. For all this human effort, most of the peninsula clings stubbornly to its primitive state. Much of it remains as it was a thousand, perhaps even a million, years ago.

22   Walter E. Bryant, "El Zorillo," *Zoe* 1 (1890), pp. 272–74, which Bryant misspells by omitting an "r"—the Spanish word is *zorrillo.* The type specimen came from Cabo San Lucas and it was designated by Dr. C. Hart Merriam *Spilogale lucasana,* which was replaced in 1952 by *S. gracilis lucasana,* the Western Spotted Skunk, according to E. Raymond Hall and Keith R. Kelson, *The Mammals of North America,* 2 vols. (New York: Ronald Press, 1959), pp. 930–32. *Spilogale* is a genus more common to the north; since the Gulf of California has blocked mammals from migrating from Mexico, the influx has been around the head of the Gulf with such species as black-tailed jackrabbits, antelope squirrels, and skunks; see also Robert T. Orr, "An Analysis of the Recent Land Mammals," in "Symposium: The Biogeography of Baja California and Its Adjacent Seas. Part III. Terrestrial and Fresh-water Biota," eds. J. Wyatt Durham and Edwin C. Allison, *Systematic Zoology* 9(2) (1960), p. 171.

The stories still abounded when John Xantus collected at the Cape; letter to Spencer Baird July 5, 1859; people at the Cape believed

that *this* skunk is highly poisonous, more so, than the Ratlesnake or Cobra coral. I at first ridiculed the stories, but Mr Ritchie assured me, that several of his horses & catle were bitten by the skunk, and some of them died, some turned mad & had to be shot.

page

Don Vicente Sesena a most respectable Ranchero near Cape San Lucas, told me the same story, adding that one of his sons was bitten by the skunk, & died in 2 hours. Don Antonio Pedrin formerly governor of Lower California & a highly educated gentleman told me many *facts* in this respect, corroborating the above stories; naming several men, women, etc who were bitten by the skunk, and died—got mad, deaf, lame, or crippled for life.—Now what you say to all this Sir; I at first laughed, then doubted, but I must confess I begin to believe—and whenever I turn up an old decayed tree, I hardly need say, that I look out sharply for black & white, much sharper as for ratling tails!

23   Asa Gray, "Enumeration of a Collection of Dried Plants Made by L. J. Xantus, at Cape San Lucas, etc., in Lower California, between August, 1859, and February, 1860, and Communicated to the Smithsonian Institution," *Proceedings of the American Academy of Arts and Sciences 5* (1861), p. 164, describes the woolly calyx of desert lavender as forming "a wide white *nimbus,* more than thrice the breadth of the enclosed flower, the hairs of which, moreover, are beautifully and dendritically branched."

Quote, J. Ross Browne, "Explorations in Lower California," *Harper's New Monthly Magazine* 37(1868), p. 584.

There are numerous papers on the effects of heat, among which are Douglas H. K. Lee, "Human Adaptations to Arid Environments," in *Desert Biology,* ed. G. W. Brown, (New York: Academic Press, 1968) pp. 512–56. I am indebted to Dr. David Nordstrom for George H. A. Clowes, Jr., and Thomas F. O'Donnell, "Heat Stroke," *New England Journal of Medicine,* 291(11) (1974), pp. 564–66. Once it was thought that loss of salt through body fluids had to be replaced by taking salt tablets; Jane Brody, *Jane Brody's Nutrition Book* (New York: Norton, 1981) emphasizes that *"the safest way to replace lost sweat is with plain water."*

25   I take some comfort from the fact that others have struggled with the same dichotomy. John Steinbeck wrote in *Sea of Cortez* (Mount Vernon, NY: Paul P. Appel, 1982), p. 100:

How can you say to a people who are preoccupied with getting enough food and enough children that you have come to pick up useless little animals so that perhaps your world picture will be enlarged?

Krutch, (p. 33) came to roughly the same conclusion:

What are we looking for? I have already suggested that fishing (which is the answer most would give) does not seem adequate. To most men the answer I give for myself—to see in their native habitat plants not to be seen anywhere else—will certainly seem even less so.

For the Mexican point of view, see Octavio Paz, "Reflections. Mexico and the United States," trans. Rachel Phillips, *The New Yorker,* September 17, 1979, pp. 136–153.

Chapter 2. La Laguna

27   Edward W. Nelson, "Lower California and Its Natural Resources," *National Academy of Sciences, Memoir 16* (1921), pp. 47, 142, 146; La Laguna "is a notable point from the fact that it is rich in species of plants, birds, and mammals peculiar to the cape district and is the type locality for many of them." Pp. 140–47 list the scientific expeditions to Baja California through 1911. La Laguna is also the type locality for several mammals which were given different specific names and are now recognized to be part of a larger complex, for example, the Big Brown Bat (*Eptesicus fuscus peninsulae*), the Desert Wood Rat (*Neotoma lepida notia*), and the Piñon Mouse (*Peromyscus truei lagunae*); see E. Raymond Hall and Keith R. Kelson, *The Mammals of North America,* 2 vols. (New York:

page

Ronald Press, 1959), pp. 184–86, 689–93, and 612–19. See also C. H. Townsend, "Voyage of the Albatross to the Gulf of California in 1911," *American Museum of Natural History Bulletin* 35 (1916), pp. 430–31; Gustav Eisen, "Explorations in the Cape Region of Baja California in 1894, with References to Former Expeditions of the California Academy of Sciences," *Proceedings of the California Academy of Sciences,* 2nd ser. 5 (1895), pp. 763–74; and Richard C. Banks, "Birds and Mammals of La Laguna, Baja California, " *Transactions of the San Diego Society of Natural History* 14(17) (1967):205–32.

29–
30   According to Jay M. Savage, "Evolution of a Peninsular Herpteofauna," in "Symposium: The Biogeography of Baja California and Adjacent Seas. Part III. Terrestrial and Freshwater Biotas," eds. J. Wyatt Durham and Edwin C. Allison, *Systematic Zoology* 9(2) (1960), p. 196, there is a high degree of endemism in the snakes of the peninsula. Of the rattlesnakes, the larger red diamond rattler is more common here than the small speckled rattlesnake, *Crotalus mitchelli.* John van Denbrugh and Joseph R. Slevin, "A List of Amphibians and Reptiles of the Peninsula of Lower California, with Notes on the Species in the Collection of the Academy," *Proceedings of the California Academy of Sciences,* 4th ser. 11(4) (1921), p. 72: Slevin did not find *Crotalus mitchelli* plentiful when he collected at the Cape in 1919. Savage divides the peninsula into four faunal areas: Californian, Colorado Desert, Peninsular Desert, and San Lucan. See also Wilbur W. Mayhew, "Biology of Desert Amphibians and Reptiles," in *Desert Biology,* ed. G. W. Brown (New York: Academic Press, 1968), pp. 195–356.

Quote, Jakob Baegert, *Observations in Lower California,* trans. and eds. M. M. Brandenburg and Carl L. Baumann (Berkeley: University of California Press, 1952) p. 41.

30   Quote, Walter E. Bryant, "El Zorillo," *Zoe* 1 (1890), p. 193.

31   Quote, T. S. Brandegee, "Notes Concerning the Collection of Plants Made by Xanthus at Cape San Lucas and Vicinity," *Zoe* 1 (1890), p. 270. Brandegee edited and wrote for *Zoe* at the turn of the century; his herbarium specimens were deposited at the California Academy of Sciences and lost in the earthquake and fire of 1906, as were Bryant's specimens (although the type specimens were saved); herbarium duplicates remain at the University of California at Berkeley. Many Cape plants were named after him, including species of *Acacia, Alvordia, Arracacia, Benthamantha, Brickellia, Calliandra, Chloris, Commicarpus, Echinocereus, Erythea, Euphorbia, Ficus, Leucaena, Populus, Quercus, Ribes, Vaseyanthus,* and a variety of *Houstonia.*

For further botanical collecting on the Cape, see Ira L. Wiggins, *Flora of Baja California* (Stanford: Stanford University Press, 1980), pp. 42–43.

Eisen's comment, pp. 277–78, is typical of every writer's remarks on the ruggedness of the trails:

The ascent and descent of the Sierra Laguna region is one of the most arduous in the sierra, especially when pack-mules must be brought along.

Chester C. Lamb, "Observations on the Xantus Hummingbird," *Condor* 27(3) (1925), p. 90:

These mountains are difficult of access, and it takes two days on mule back, over tortuous trails, to reach Laguna Valley, a small, uninhabited valley at an elevation of about 5500 feet.

Nelson, p. 47, "camped at the ruins of an old ranch at the extreme upper edge" and commented that the trail

would have been nearly or quite impossible to ascend it, owing to washouts along some of the steepest slopes, down which our animals were forced to slide in a half-sitting

page

position. In many places it was obstructed by trees and bushes which had grown in or across the trail.

See also Walter F. Bryant, "The Cape Region of Baja California," *Zoe* 2(1891), p. 198.

32 For a discussion of the origin of the Cape flora, see Daniel I. Axelrod, "The Stratigraphic Significance of a Southern Element in Later Tertiary Floras of Western America," *Washington Academy of Sciences Journal* 28 (1938), pp. 313–22, and *Studies in Late Tertiary Paleobotany* (Washington, DC: Carnegie Institution Publication 590, 1950); Ira L. Wiggins, "The Origin and Relationships of the Land Flora," in "Symposium: The Biogeography of Baja California and Adjacent Seas. Part III. Terrestrial and Fresh-water Biotas," eds. J. Wyatt Durham and Edwin C. Allison, *Systematic Zoology*, 9(2) (1960), pp. 148–65; Robert T. Orr, "An Analysis of the Recent Land Mammals," *ibid.,* pp. 171–79; Savage, pp. 200–201.

33 A. K. Fisher, "In Memoriam: Lyman Belding," *Auk* 37(1) (1920):33–45, eulogizes Belding for his contributions to ornithology. See also A. H. Miller, "Speciation in the Avian Genus *Junco,*" *University of California Publications in Zoology* 44(1941), pp. 173–434; Joseph Grinnell, "A Distributional Summation of the Ornithology of Lower California," *ibid.*, 32 (1928), pp. 170–71. In 1973 Baird's junco was determined by the American Ornithologists' Union to be a geographic representation of a single species, *Junco phaeonotus,* the yellow-eyed or Mexican junco. See also O. L. Austin, Jr., "Mexican (Yellow-eyed) Junco," in *Life Histories of North American Cardinals, Grosbeaks, Buntings, Towhees, Finches, Sparrows, and Allies,* comps. A. C. Bent *et al.,* ed. O. L. Austin, Jr., *U.S. National Museum Bulletin* 237 (Washington, DC; U.S. Government Printing Office, 1968), and R. C. Banks, "Baird's Junco," *ibid.*

William Brewster, "Birds of the Cape Region of Lower California," *Bulletin of the Museum of Comparative Zoology, Harvard College* 41(1) (1902), p. 11, judged La Laguna to be "one of the most interesting and productive, ornithologically, of any in the Cape region of which we have definite knowledge." Anthony Frazar, his collector, returned to La Laguna November 27–December 4 (p. 10) when it was cold, damp, and mist-shrouded and found few birds "most of the summer species having evidently descended to the lowlands or migrated to warmer latitudes, to pass the winter."

Another bird that remains strictly in the mountainous region of the Cape, not even ranging as far north as La Paz, is the endemic St. Lucas robin, *Turdus confinis,* similar to the North American robin but with underparts a very pale creamy buff, and common around the foothills of La Laguna; it is a subspecies in the 1983 AOU Checklist. It was first collected by John Xantus in 1860 although there is some question about its type locality, since Xantus said he found it in the town of Todos Santos and it hasn't been seen there since. Grinnell and Belding found some on the trail to La Laguna, but Frazar found them abundant (p. 218):

The song resembles that of the eastern Robin, but is weaker and less distinct, reminding one of the efforts of a young bird just learning to sing.

Miller thinks the avifauna originated, pre-Pleistocene, in the south or east, because had these typical cooler-climate birds come directly across the ocean, one would expect to have a greater number of species in common with the Mexican mainland than now exist. However, John Davis, "The Sierra Madrean Element of the Avifauna of the Cape District, Baja California," *Condor* 61 (1959), pp. 75–84, disagrees (p. 83):

It is concluded that the majority of the avian endemics in the Cape highlands show resemblance to Mexican populations because the vegetation of the Cape highlands has been relatively little altered since the initial invasion of the Cape district by the populations presumed ancestral to the modern endemics.

Davis places its origin in northeastern and eastern Mexico, where there are forms today with which they have the closest affinities, and suggests that of the 17 species and subspecies of birds endemic to the highlands of the Cape, 11 resemble species of the mainland and southwestern United States, and followed the Madro-Tertiary flora as it spread down the length of the peninsula, becoming isolated there: band-tailed pigeon, Xantus' screech owl, Xantus' hummingbird, acorn woodpecker, white-breasted nuthatch, Hutton and warbling vireos, rufous-sided and brown towhees, rufous-crowned sparrow, and this yellow-eyed junco. Since the Madro-Tertiary flora is thought to have originated in northern Mexico, the birds associated with it also derived from there.

See also Kenneth E. Stagner, "The Composition and Origin of the Avifauna," in "Symposium: The Biogeography of Baja California and Adjacent Seas. Part III. Terrestrial and Fresh-water Biotas," eds. J. Wyatt Durham and Edwin C. Allison, *Systematic Zoology* 9(2) (1960), pp. 181–82, who agrees, noting that the other birds characteristic of this flora are also found here; and Spencer F. Baird, "Notes on a Collection of Birds Made by Mr. John Xantus, at Cape St. Lucas, Lower California, and Now in the Museum of the Smithsonian Institution," *Proceedings of the Academy of Natural Sciences of Philadelphia* (1859).

The same relationship between birds of the Cape and mainland exists between two subspecies of piñon mouse, *Peromyscus truei lagunae* and *P. t. gentilis.* See D. F. Hoffmeister, "A Taxonomic and Evolutionary Study of the Piñon Mouse, *Peromyscus truei,"* *Illinois Biological Monograph* 21(4) (1951), pp. 1–104. The mouse is restricted to the Sierras de la Laguna and Victoria, and ranges between 4,000 and 6,000 feet; it is smaller, shorter, and lighter in color than other subspecies.

See also L. M. Huey, "The Kangaroo Rats (*Dipodomys*) of Baja California, Mexico," *Transactions of the San Diego Society of Natural History* 11 (1951), p. 226, who describes the Cape San Lucas kangaroo rat, *Dipodomys merriami melanurus,* as a race limited to the higher foothills around the Sierra Victoria from Cabo San Lucas to San José del Cabo, northward up the latter valley to Agua Caliente.

34 Gustav Eisen, "Explorations in the Cape Region of Baja California," *American Geographical Society of New York Bulletin* 293 (1897), p. 273:

The high mountains, which reach 8,000 feet, are always subjected to heavy frosts as late as March and April, and both at El Taste and Sierra Laguna ice is frequently formed on the surface of the water late in the spring. But from April to December no frosts occur even on the high peaks. Snow is never formed, no rain falling during the cold months.

In 1895 he wrote (pp. 752–53):

To-day the lagoon is dry, and forms an oblong somewhat irregular flat, on account of its dryness not worthy of the name of meadow. Through its center courses a tiny spring or two in the deeper channel which at the rainy season, or after heavy storms, undoubtedly has the appearance of a brook, but which at the dry season becomes almost entirely dry, most of the water which comes from the upper end sinking before it reaches the center of the flat. The flat contains probably about a hundred acres.

All the weather data is sent monthly to La Paz, and from there to Tacobaya, where the records are collated. There is no weather-forecasting service on the peninsula, although there is a network of weather-reporting stations at major airports throughout Mexico. Satellite weather reports are now available.

34– Hall and Kelson list a subspecies of the Southern pocket gopher (*Thomomys umbrinus*

page
35 *alticolus*) found at "7000" feet at La Laguna; see also Gordon L. Bender, ed., *Reference Handbook on the Deserts of North America* (Westport, CT: Greenwood Press, 1982), p. 301.

    Barco, pp. 78 ff., noted plagues of "locusts" at least eight times between 1722 and 1767 which

> When the locusts started to come down from the mountains [Sierra de la Laguna] in the year 1746, the Indians said that such insects were always in the sierra of the South in greater or lesser numbers. According to this, that mountain range is their proper territory.

35 George Lindsay, "Some Natural Values of Baja California," *Pacific Discovery*, 23(2) (1970), p. 9, feels that La Laguna should be a national park to protect a unique area, pointing out that once it was a rich habitat for deer, mountain lions, and bobcats, the latter two now largely hunted out; at the time of his writing there were only two national parks on the peninsula. See also William Weber Johnson and the editors of Time-Life, *Baja California* (New York: Time, Inc., 1971), p. 169, and Paul Brooks, "Baja California. Emergency and Opportunity," *Audubon* 74:2 (1972):4–23.

    Quotes, Edward Cooke in *English Privateers at Cabo San Lucas,* ed. Thomas F. Andrews, (Los Angeles: Dawson's Book Shop, 1979), pp. 57–58, and Barco, pp. 169–70.

36 Nelson, pp. 104–105: this first timber south of the San Pedro Mártir Mountains was where the missionaries went for wood for the missions. Wenceslaus Linck, *Reports & Letters, 1762–1778,* trans. and ed. Ernest J. Burrus (Los Angeles: Dawson's Book Shop, 1967), who served in the northern part of the peninsula with the Jesuits in 1762–68, p. 67:

> There is nothing to write about forests and trees in the peninsula, unless useless bushes and shriveled-up shrubs be considered as such. We would have spared no effort in our northernmost missions, even if it meant going thirty miles, to get a tree with which to help build a church; but nowhere was a tree to be found.

The black phoebe was first collected in Baja California by John Xantus.

See also D. C. Eaton, "A New Fern from Lower California," *Zoe* 1 (1890), p. 197, about *Asplenium bleparoides,* which he found at La Laguna.

36– Quote, T. S. Brandegee, "A New Nolina," *Zoe* 1 (1890), p. 306; also:
37

> The specific name is given in compliment to Mr. L. Belding, the well-known naturalist, who was the first to notice it in his ornithological expedition to the Sierra de la Laguna, several years ago, and who gave me directions as to the route by which I was enabled to find it.

37 P. L. Jameson, J. P. Mackey, and R. C. Richmond, "The Systematics of the Pacific Treefrog, *Hyla regilla,"* *Proceedings of the California Academy of Sciences,* 4th ser. 33 (1966):551–620, find the subspecies common at the Cape to be *H. r. curta.* It was first collected by John Xantus in 1859 (pp. 554–55) near Cabo San Lucas; there are also records from La Laguna.

38– Barco was sitting under a tree when a caterpillar like this one fell on him; when he
39 brushed it off (pp. 77–78) he "found out that the little hairs of the worm were hard and they not only pricked painfully at the slightest touch, but they left a smarting pain that lasted well into the night."

39 *Hierba de cancer* is a name applied to several species of *Acalypha,* a spurge. T. S. Brandegee, "Field notes on the plants of Baja California," *Zoe* 2 (1890), p. 151, noted:

> Nearly all the plants have local names, sometimes of Indian origin, often undoubtedly very old and many times evidently applied at a more recent date. The old women are

the best authorities in native nomenclature, probably on account of their habit of collecting and preparing the medicines for family use. In common with many people holding much higher rank they do not like to admit ignorance and whenever a plant is shown to them are sure to name it something, and although nearly all the plants really do possess distinct names, some of these names include several species and genera.

Dr. Ira Wiggins, to whom I am so indebted for generous help on this book, provided Spanish names from his copy of José Ramírez, *Sinonimia vulgar y científica de las Plantas Mexicanas* (Mexico: Oficina Tipográfica de la Secreturia de Fomenta, 1902), as did Annetta Carter from her field notes. Wiggins, *personal communication,* January 14, 1983, wrote:

> Another difficulty about finding common Spanish names for a larger percentage of the total flora is the tendency for a particular area to have names that are known only very locally, and also the tendency to apply the same name to a number of different technically named species! While in the field, I have received one local name from one person, a different one from another local resident—applied to the same plant.

39 I, for one, am sorry to see names in use like "Baird's junco" and "Xantus' hummingbird," which have a whole history in them, disappear from use. See Chester C. Lamb, "Observations on the Xantus Hummingbird," *Condor* 27(3) (1925), and W. E. Bryant, "A Catalogue of the birds of Lower California, Mexico," *Proceedings of the California Academy of Sciences* 2nd ser. 2 (1889), pp. 289–90.

40– Quotes, p. 40, *Letters,* Xantus to Baird, February 18, 1858 and August 10, 1860; and Henry
41 Miller Madden, *Xantus: Hungarian Naturalist in the Pioneer West* (Linz, Austria: Oberosterreichischer Landesverlag, 1949), p. 264, Lawrence quote.

There are two biographies of John Xantus: Madden's, and Leslie Konnyu, *John Xantus, Hungarian Geographer in America (1851–64)* (Koln: American Hungarian Publisher, 1965); he is also profiled by Edgar Erskine Hume, *Ornithologists of the United States Army Medical Corps* (Baltimore: Johns Hopkins Press, 1942), and his letters home published in *Letters from America,* trans. and eds. Theodore Schoenman and Helen Benedek Schoenman (Detroit: Wayne State University Press, 1975).

Madden (p. 51) notes that Baird, from his vantage point at the Smithsonian, had an overview of unexplored areas. See Philip Carpenter, "Supplementary Report on the Present State of Our Knowledge with Regard to the Mollusca of the West Coast of North America," *Smithsonian Miscellaneous Collections* 252 (1872), pp. 616–17:

> For obtaining data on geographical distribution, Cape St. Lucas was a peculiarly valuable station, being situated near the supposed meeting-point of the two faunas . . . ; and also, not being a place of trade, or even an inhabited district, likely to be free from human importations although we should be prepared to find dead exotics thrown on its shores both by northern and by tropical currents.

41 Clouds of butterflies seem to be fairly common in the Cape mountains; I have walked through them coming down from La Laguna, Calaveras, and La Vigía. Eisen, 1895, p. 761:

> I have seen so many butterflies filling the air in one of the high valleys of the Sierra El Taste that the air seemed thick with them, and this continued for several weeks. When at such a time a cloud over the sun caused a temporary shadow, this immense and innumerable host of butterflies suddenly vanished, having taken refuge on the under side of the leaves of trees, bushes and herbs. When in an hour the sun again shone out in all its warmth and brightness, the butterflies all at once left their hiding places and again filled the air.

page
Chapter 3. Thorns

45 Quote, John Steinbeck and Edward F. Ricketts, *Sea of Cortez* (Mount Vernon, NY: Paul P. Appel, 1982), p. 60. H. H. Behr, "Lepidoptera from San José del Cabo," *Zoe* 1 (1890), pp. 246–47, found many of coincided "almost entirely with specimens received from Mazatlan." The early life stages of most of these butterflies are not known; this would seem a wide-open area for research.

48– Hiroshi Muramoto, R. Sherman and C. Ledbetter, "A Progress Report on the Breeding of
49 Caducous Bract Cotton," in *Proceedings, Fifth Cotton Dust Research Conference,* New Orleans, and Hiroshi Muramoto, "Caducous Bracts in Cotton," reprint from *Proceedings of the 1978 Beltwide Cotton Production-Mechanization Conference and Special Sessions,* p. 96. I am indebted to Dr. Muramoto for these papers.

See W. J. Gertsch, *American Spiders* (New York: D. Van Nostrand, 1949), pp. 60–62.

49– Edward W. Nelson, "Lower California and Its Natural Resources," *National Academy of
50 Sciences, Memoir* 16 (1921), p. 113:

One of the features of the fauna of the cape region is the immense quantity of land shells found in some places. In certain evidently favored localities the ground is literally covered with the dead and white shells of land mollusks. We ride along for hours through canyons where the ground is thus strewn. Then as we turn into another canyon, we find no shells at all, not even after close search under rocks and trunks of trees.

See William Green Binney, "A Manual of American Land Shells," *Bulletin of the U.S. National Museum* No. 28 (Washington, DC: U.S. Government Printing Office, 1885).

50 Quote, Norberto Ducrue in *The Natural and Human History of Baja California,* ed. Homer Aschmann (Los Angeles: Dawson's Book Shop, 1966), p. 53. Ducrue, a Jesuit, was stationed on the peninsula for 28 years. Nelson, p. 45:

The village of Cape San Lucas contains about a dozen families who occupy a small group of adobe houses on a flat just back of the broad sandy beach and only a few hundred yards easterly from the base of the cape. It was formerly a much more populous and prosperous place. At the time of our visit the inhabitants were making a livelihood mainly by gathering tan bark from small trees on the sloping plain back of the town and shipping it to San Francisco.

51 Quote, Barco, pp. 231–32; Edward Cooke in *English Privateers at Cabo San Lucas,* ed. Thomas F. Andrews (Los Angeles: Dawson's Book Shop, 1979), pp. 42–43.

Walter E. Bryant, "A Catalogue of the Birds of Lower California, Mexico," *Proceedings of the California Academy of Sciences,* 2nd ser. 2 (1889), p. 295, was told by his guide that it was a meadowlark, and "the notes at a distance did resemble an imperfect song of a lark." He usually found them far from water.

54– Quotes, Jakob Baegert, *Observations in Lower California* (Berkeley: University of Califor-
55 nia Press, 1952), p. 33, and Miguel del Barco, *Natural History of Baja California* (Los Angeles: Dawson's Book Shop, 1980), p. 153; also p. 149:

The meat is juicy, white, delicate, and very tasty. It has no seed or kernels which impair, even in the slightest way, its enjoyment. This is because its seed, being as it is considerably smaller than that of mustard, is distributed over the fleshy part of the fruit, each little grain apart from the others. . . . Since the fruit is so fine and juicy the seed does not matter, nor is it even noticed when one eats it. These sweet pitahayas are the size of limes. . . . The skin of the pitahaya is meaty like that of a lime but without the bothersome juice of the latter, and much more rubbery, flexible, and easy to take off, and to such a degree that one peels the pitahaya without even thinking.

Lemaireocereus littoralis is a small species of *pitahaya dulce* that grows on the coast only between San Lucas and San José del Cabo; it bears delicious deep red fruits the size of grapes or smaller.
Quote, Barco, p. 151.
Quote, Walter E. Bryant, "The Cape Region of Baja California," *Zoe* 2 (1891), p. 193.

55–
56

Quotes, Ducrue, pp. 88–89, who describes the "second harvest" and tells the story of the discomfiture of Padre Francisco María Píccolo; Barco, p. 17; and Baegert in Pablo L. Martínez, *A History of Lower California* (México: Editorial Baja California, 1960), pp. 41–42. Jakob Baegert, *The Letters of Jakob Baegert, 1749–1761*, trans. Elsbeth Schulz-Bischof, intro. and ed. Doyce B. Nunis, Jr. (Los Angeles: Dawson's Book Shop, 1982), September 11, 1752, gives a long list of words that did not exist in the Pericu vocabulary, among them "pure, pious, moderate, kindly, virtue, envy, vice, mercy, decency, virgin, danger," and many more.
Miguel del Barco, *Ethnology and Linguistics of Baja California* (Los Angeles: Dawson's Book Shop, 1981), p. 17, speaks of "the *Pericú* nation, or following the Castillian form, *Pericúes*." English usage is Pericú for both singular and plural, with Pericus also acceptable. Their history is obscure, pp. 34–35:

They do not say when they came and, moreover, they are immersed in such a lamentable primitive condition, that it appears that no one among them has ever counted the years, or recorded the passing of time as was done by the Mexicans by means of the fifty-year cycles. . . . The cause that prompted them to leave their ancestral northern lands and come to populate those of California was, according to testimony of their ancestors, a great dispute that they had during a feast attended by many of various nations in competition with one another. The dispute led to an armed conflict and, after some fighting, the weaker ones, pursued by the more powerful ones, fled to the south and hid themselves in the mountains of the peninsula.

Quote, Vizcaíno in H. R. Wagner, "Pearl Fishing Enterprises in the Gulf of California," *Hispanic American Historical Review* 10(2) (1930), p. 206. Edward Cooke, pp. 38–39:

The Bay has Plenty of Albacores, Dolphin, Mullets, Breams, and other Sorts of Fish, which the Natives are very dexterous at striking, from their Floats, made of five Pieces of Wood, driving them with short Paddles, made like an Oar at each End, and carry with them their Wooden Instruments for striking of Fish, very often leaping off their Floats, and striking the Fish, when they are near the Bottom.

Quote, Barco, *Ethnology*, p. 75.
Quote, Miguel Venegas, *A Natural and Civil History of California* (Ann Arbor: University Microfilms, 1966), p. 77. Aschmann sums up the contribution that the missionaries made to a period that would otherwise be lost (pp. 9–10):

Although lacking the theoretical understandings of a modern ethnographer, and being subject to an especially heavy burden of professional prejudice, the typical missionary observer remained in intimate contact with a single alien society far longer than does the most field-work conscious modern anthropologist, often as much as twenty years.

See also William Weber Johnson and the editors of Time-Life, *Baja California* (New York: Time Inc., 1971), p. 33:

Although the Indians of mainland Mexico were in some cases sophisticated mathematicians and astronomers, those of Baja California could use only their two hands for counting. Higher calculations were not necessary; there just was not that much of anything. They were true wilderness dwellers, shaping their lives within the severe limitations of their particular wilderness, achieving a precarious and delicate balance between resources and needs. The struggle to maintain this balance permitted no luxury, no cultural flowering, no accumulation of wealth. And it did not tolerate interference. The arrival of the white man—and his diseases—interrupted the Baja Indians' marginal way of life in the mildest sort of way. At least it was mild compared with the violent conquest and subjugation of the better-developed Indian cultures of mainland Mexico. But while the mainland Indians survived to become a dominant factor in the life of modern Mexico, the Indians of Baja California perished—virtually obliterated by the time the white man got through with his unsuccessful efforts to make Baja California conform to an alien pattern.

59 Quotes, Gabb, p. 88, and Barco, *Natural History,* pp. 175–76.

61 Quote, J. Ross Browne, "Explorations in Lower California," *Harper's New Monthly Magazine* 37 (1868), p. 581.

Quote, Barco, *Natural History,* pp. 36–37; see also H. T. U. Smith, "Geological and Geomorphic Aspects of Deserts," in *Desert Biology,* pp. 70, 78.

62 Quote, Cooke, in Andrews, p. 47. Xantus collected the type specimen at Cabo San Lucas. See also Spencer F. Baird, Thomas M. Brewer, and Robert Ridgway, *The Land Birds of North America* (Boston: Little, Brown, 1874), pp. 133–34:

This is one of the most characteristic birds constituting the isolated fauna of Cape St. Lucas. Like nearly all the species peculiar to this remarkable locality, it is exceedingly abundant, breeding in immense numbers.

Bryant, 1891, p. 188:

The first bird that I heard on that morning was the ever-present St. Lucas cactus wren (Campylorhynchus affinis), a very characteristic species of Lower California; one of them was always about the garden in the rear of our house.

See also A. W. Anthony, "Notes on the Cactus Wren," *Zoe* 2, 1891, pp. 133–34, who described one building her nest.

Chapter 4. Headlands

65– Quotes, Spencer Murray, *Explorations in Lower California* (Studio City, CA: Vaquero
69 Books, 1966), pp. 11 and 36; Murray's introduction gives good background on the implications of the expedition and current political thinking. Browne traveled northeast to San José del Cabo, thence north to La Paz, across the peninsula to Todos Santos, thence northward to Magdalena Bay.

Browne's popular account, "Explorations of Lower California," appeared in three parts in *Harper's New Monthly Magazine* in October, November, and December, 1868, and was followed by his official report, *Resources of the Pacific Slope. A Statistical and Descriptive Summary of the Mines and Minerals, Climate, Topography, Agriculture, Commerce, Manufacturers, and Miscellaneous Production, of the States and Territories West of the Rocky Mountains* (New York: D. Appleton, 1869), containing articles by Charles Scammon and William M. Gabb, a geologist with the California Geological Survey and, on this trip, part-time botanist, and Alexander S. Taylor on the peninsula's history. Browne, *Harper's,* p. 578:

There is no doubt this point or terminus of the Peninsula would be a valuable acquisition to the United States. Situated on the highway from San Francisco to Panama, and to all the Pacific ports of Mexico, it is easy of access, affords good anchorage for vessels of the largest capacity, and possesses every advantage of position and climate that could be desired in a place of resort for supplies. A depot established here, with a dock for temporary repairs, and a light-house on the highest point of rocks, would be a great convenience to commerce. The country, it is true, can not be depended upon for any-thing more than fresh beef and indifferent water; but the advantages of the location for a depot, where coals and other necessary supplies for steamships could be kept, are not easily over-estimated.

Alexander S. Taylor, "Historical Summary of Lower California from its Discovery in 1532 to 1867," in Browne, p. 5: all the new transportation systems—steamer lines, railroads, etc.—

will very soon draw, voluntarily or not, the California peninsula within the periphery of events, big with the fate of the future states, commonwealths, nations, and empires of the great ocean which the Divine Father of All seems ordaining for the immediate future.

Pablo L. Martínez, *A History of Lower California* (México: Editorial Baja California, 1960), pp. 396, 405–7; this "black page" of the peninsula's history was closed in 1933 when 1,250,000 hectares (a hectare − 2.471 acres) were recovered from foreign coun-tries. See also Charles H. Townsend, "Lower California Versus the Acquisition of the Peninsula," *N.Y. Times,* January 26, 1919, who at this late date was not in favor of annexing the peninsula but favored access to the Gulf through a section of Sonora ceded to the U.S. Quotes, Browne, *Harper's* 38, p. 23.

69– See R. V. Chamberlin, "Expedition of the California Academy of Sciences to the Gulf of
71 California in 1921—The Spider Fauna of the Shores and Islands of the Gulf of California," *Proceedings of the California Academy of Sciences* 12 (1924), pp. 561–62.

According to Fred S. Truxal, "The Entomofauna with Special Reference to Its Origins and Affinities," in "Symposium: The Biogeography of Baja California and Adjacent Seas, Part III. Terrestrial and Fresh-water Biotas," eds. J. Wyatt Durham and Edwin C. Allison, *Systematic Zoology* 9(2) (1960), p. 169; several of the Baja California spiders have entered the southwestern United States, and several have peculiar distribution patterns—one is known at the Cape and elsewhere only in Saudi Arabia and India; another known from Upper and Lower California occurs elsewhere only in southern France and Spain.

Truxal, pp. 166–69, finds four rather well marked insect faunae on the peninsula, two of which are confined to the northern quarter of the peninsula, one to the central part, and the Cape Region fauna, which "is our richest and most ancient fauna." The present-day insect fauna has come primarily from dispersal centers in Mexico, Central America, and the west coast of South America, overland around the northern end of the Gulf, and down through the peninsula; there were also some early trans-Gulf dispersal routes when there was still a land connection. Because no insect fossils have been found, the routes of dispersal have to be postulated. The Cape fauna (p. 167)

has definite southern affinities and shows a close relationship with elements now found in the montane phases of southern Sonora and Sinaloa. It is probable that the Cape fauna is a remnant of a once more extensive biota that covered most of the peninsula but, because of ever increasing aridity, has retreated to its present state. As far as insects are concerned, the Cape Region fauna is our richest and best known in Baja California.

72 Quote, Miguel del Barco, *The Natural History of Baja California* (Los Angeles: Dawson's Book Shop, 1980), p. 98.

73 Jean M. Linsdale, "Amphibians and Reptiles from Lower California," *University of Califor-nia Publications in Zoology* 38 (1932), pp. 345–86, and Kenneth K. Asplund, "Ecology of Lizards in the Relictual Cape Flora, Baja California," *American Midland Naturalist* 77 (1967), pp. 473–74:

Some lizards are less specific in habitat selection in the Cape Region than they are in more xeric regions to the north. During the Miocene lizards may have had more generalized habitat selections in the widespread Madro-Tertiary geoflora. Lizards probably became locally restricted to habitats to which they were sufficiently preadapted during the segregation of components of the Madro-Tertiary geoflora into present-day associations. The generalized habitat occurrences of lizards in the Cape may be "nondifferentiated," paralleling the primitive nature of the community structure.

See also John van Denbrugh and Joseph R. Slevin, "A List of the Amphibians and Reptiles of the Peninsula of Lower California, with Notes on the Species in the Collection of the Academy," *Proceedings of the California Academy of Sciences* 4th ser. 11(4) (1921), p. 63, who found the orange-throated whiptail, *Cnemidophorus hyperythrus hyperythrus,* to be the most common lizard at the Cape.

74 For Dr. Wiggins's discussion of endemics, see *Flora of Baja California* (Stanford: Stanford University Press, 1980), pp. 26–36; plant families (p. 39) with the largest percent of endemic genera are, in descending order, Cactaceae, Polygonaceae, Asteraceae, Fabaceae, and Euphorbiaceae; see also Wiggins, "The Origin and Relationships of the Land Flora," in "Symposium: The Biogeography of Baja California and Adjacent Seas. Part III: Terrestrial and Fresh-water Biotas", eds. J. Wyatt Durham and Edwin C. Allison, *Systematic Zoology* 9(2) (1960), p. 164, in which he suggests

that the intrusion into the desert areas, by plants already well established in moisture adjacent regions, began comparatively recently, or that the genetic plasticity of many plants is less marked in regard to adapting them to low water supplies than for other vicissitudes of living.

Wiggins, p. 38, finds a relatively high number of plant families represented by a single genus (of 155 families, 42.6 percent are so), and thinks that this may be because the center of distribution of most of these families is at some distance from the peninsula.

75– Forrest Shreve and Ira L. Wiggins, *Vegetation and Flora of the Sonoran Desert* (Stanford:
78 Stanford University Press, 1964), pp. 127–33, estimate the total number of native ephemerals to be between 400 and 500 species.

78– Wilbur W. Mayhew, "Biology of Desert Amphibians and Reptiles," in *Desert Biology,*
79 p. 233, quotes one researcher who thinks that the head bobbing in courtship behavior possibly enhances depth perception. See also Linsdale, pp. 355–56; Calvin B. DeWitt, "Precision of Thermoregulation and Its Relation to Environmental Factors in the Desert Iguana, *Dipsosaurus dorsalis,*" *Physiological Zoology* 49 (1967):49–56; and Kenneth S. Norris, "The Ecology of the Desert Iguana, *Dipsosaurus dorsalis,*" *Ecology* 34 (1953):265–87.

J. van Denburgh, "Description of a New Lizard (*Dipsosaurus dorsalis lucasensis*) from Lower California," *Proceedings of the California Academy of Sciences* (4)10 (1920), pp. 33–34: this iguana was designated as a new subspecies in 1920 and further tagged *lucasensis* because the "rostral [is] usually separated from nasal by but one granular scale"; this was cutting it a little fine for establishing a new subspecies, a practice that characterized much of the early collecting on the Cape, both botanical and zoological. As the literature has been searched, distribution records expanded and refined, many of these subspecies, varieties, and even new species found in Baja California have turned out to exist elsewhere or to be units of a large variable complex.

80 George A. Bartholomew and William R. Dawson, in *Desert Biology,* p. 407:

The primary adaptations of rodents for a nocturnal and burrow-dwelling life have allowed them to occupy desert regions while still remaining in circumstances in which they need cope only with those limited aspects of the total physical environment for which they are suited physiologically. Paradoxically, an abundant rodent fauna lives in the desert by the simple device of avoiding desert conditions. Their primary adaptive pattern of nocturnality plus burrowing allows them to evade the dilemma of too much heat and insufficient water.

See also George A. Bartholomew and Jack W. Hudson, "Desert Ground Squirrels," *Scientific American* 205(5) (1972):107–16. For peninsular mammals see L. M. Huey, The Mammals of Baja California, Mexico," *Transactions of the San Diego Society of Natural History* 13 (1964):85–168.

80– Karl P. Schmidt, "The Amphibians and Reptiles of Lower California and the Neighboring
83   Islands," *Bulletin of the American Museum of Natural History* 46 (1922), pp. 614–15; pp. 620 ff., is interesting historically; in contrast, Savage cites a "Cape refugium" in the mountains and (p. 199) finds the

present herpetofaunal assemblage of Baja California consists primarily of northern migrants or western Mexican forms that have invaded the peninsula from the north after passing around the head of the Gulf of California.

Although modern species probably go only as far back as Pleistocene times, the essential characteristics of this fauna go back much farther. The uplift of the Rocky Mountain cordillera provided different altitudinal areas in which the differentiation of species could develop, and allowed entrance into the Cape of species normally adapted to cooler, moister climates. By early Pliocene the ancestors of the present-day genera were in place, an assemblage dominated by desert and plains types, with a few adjusted to the cooler climate of the oak and piñon woodlands. By late Pliocene the species most typical of the Cape today persisted in the thorn-scrub vegetation: horned toads, two tree frogs, a leaf-nosed lizard, a skink, and a spadefoot toad. The San Lucan division of the herpetofauna has more endemics than the other areas of the peninsula.

Chapter 5. Back Country

87   Edwin H. Hammond, "A Geomorphic Study of the Cape Region of Baja California," *University of California Publications in Geography* 10(2) (1954), p. 45:

Chiefly because of the aridity of its climate, the Cape Region does not support a dense population, although it is one of the less sparsely settled parts of the peninsula. Most of the land is used for grazing, and though forage for its herds of cattle and goats is scanty, the section usually produces enough meat for its own use and at other times exports small quantities of beef and hides to other parts of Mexico.

J. Ross Browne, "Explorations in Lower California," *Harper's New Monthly Magazine* 37 (1868), p. 578, on the side of the promoters, gave an unrealistic account:

The mesquit bean, fruit of the cactus, and green bushes keep them in good condition. Owing to the healthful nature of their food, and the advantage of an ample range, their flesh is tender and delicate. It is considered by sea-captains a great luxury to get a supply of beef from the Cape. The sailors, especially, are apt to bestow high praise upon it after a long voyage.

Edward W. Nelson, "Lower California and its Natural Resources," *National Academy of Sciences, Memoir* 16 (1921), on the peninsula in 1906, reported (p. 140) that raising cattle on a large scale was unprofitable because of drought years during which ranchers lost their cattle.

page

88– W. E. Bryant, "A Catalogue of the Birds of Lower California, Mexico," *Proceedings of the*
91   *California Academy of Sciences* 2(2) (1889), p. 282, remarks on the "extermination pol-
icy" then in effect in Mexico, a situation resembling the shooting of raptors in this country. He found caracara

> even more filthy in habits than the buzzards, resorting to an arroyo back of the village,
> where they scratched over excrement for food, getting their feet and bills smeared so
> that only those in good plumage were considered fit for specimens.

91   Ira L. Wiggins, *Flora of Baja California* (Stanford: Stanford University Press, 1980), pp.
17–18, says that in Valle de San Telmo in northern Baja California irrigation water was
pumped for agriculture and orchards:

> However, pumping apparently removed water faster than it was returned, the water
> level in the wells dropped to greater depths, and after a few years sizable areas were
> abandoned and the once-productive fields were reverting to the desert that had existed
> prior to the drilling.

Charles B. Hunt, *Geology of Soils. Their Evolution, Classification, and Uses* (San Francisco: W. H. Freeman, 1982), p. 314, points out that near the coast salt water may be drawn
up into wells, which then makes agriculture impossible.

Wenceslaus Linck, *Reports & Letters, 1762–1778* (Los Angeles: Dawson's Book Shop,
1967), p. 65:

> The peninsula can, in all truth, be termed the most wretched and most unproductive of
> all lands; for, although one or two of the missions did succeed in producing something,
> that fact is no indication of the general fertility of the entire region. The missions had to
> be established near some small stream or spring. Inasmuch as rain is so uncertain in the
> land, water was collected in reservoirs in order to be able to irrigate vegetable gardens
> or small plots of corn.

91– The concept of *ejido* goes back to the late nineteenth century, the right of every village to
92   common land, as opposed to the *hacienda* concept in which land could be owned only
by individuals of Spanish birth. To belong to an *ejido*, one makes application which must
be voted on by the current *ejido* membership (which is hereditary) that meets monthly to
discuss problems and matters of consequence; decision is by simple majority vote. *Ejidos*
on the peninsula follow the same general rules as those on the mainland but tend to be
somewhat different in practice because of different geographical circumstances: there are
no extensive areas of flat arable land (preventing wide use of large equipment) and a
much sparser population. Consequently one can find farming methods on the peninsula
that have been in use for decades if not longer, as well as sophisticated mechanized
equipment on the larger farms. The principle of forfeiting land for nonuse seems to be
much stronger on the peninsula.

CONASUPO (Compañía Nacional de Subsistencías Populares) was established by the
Mexican government in 1965 to supply "basic foods" to those of limited means. It has
expanded over the last decades to have a budget of over $2 billion, controlling corpora-
tions that produce cereals, milk, etc., and retailing these products (see *Lloyd's Economic
Report,* March, 1983).

98   Lomboy (*Jatropha cinerea*) belongs to the Euphorbia Family, one characteristic of which
is an acrid milky sap, which undoubtedly makes it unpleasant forage even to hungry
cattle. See Miguel del Barco, *The Natural History of Baja California* (Los Angeles: Dawson's Book Shop, 1980), pp. 186–87; also 35–36:

> And finally in a few corners and in the vicinity of arroyos and even on the hillsides after

page

a good rain, there is often some pasture for cattle. These would not be able to survive in such places on just the common grass because there is not enough of it. The cattle must avail themselves of the tops of branches and the new growth of trees and shrubs. They relish these as much or better than grass itself.

The identification and uses of medicinal herbs in Mexico is covered in a small paperback book by Dr. Jésus O. Cabrera, *Plantas Curativas de Mexico propiedades medicinales de las más conocidas plantas de Mexico, su aplicación correcta y eficaz,* for the loan of which I thank Miriam Parr.

99–
103

Research is being conducted jointly by the University of Mexico and Brigham Young University; see Wade E. Miller, "The Late Pliocene Las Tunas Local Fauna from Southernmost Baja California, Mexico," *Journal of Paleontology* 54(4) (1980), pp. 762–65. The area in which the fossils occur is now under federal control.

See also J. Wyatt Durham and Edwin C. Allison, "Symposium: The Biogeography of Baja California and Adjacent Seas. Part I: Geologic History. The Geologic History of Baja California and Its Marine Fauna," eds. J. Wyatt Durham and Edwin C. Allison, *Systematic Zoology* 9(2) (1960), pp. 65–66; W. R. Normak and J. P. Curray, "Geology and Structure of the Tip of Baja California, Mexico," *Geological Society of America Bulletin* 79 (1968), p. 1597; C. A. Anderson *et al.,* "The 1940 E. W. Scripps Cruise to the Gulf of California. Geology of Islands and Neighboring Land Areas," *Geological Society of America, Memoir 43* (1950), p. 48; and Gordon Gastil, Richard C. Phillips, and Rafael Rodriguez-Torres, "Section 3. Tectonics. The Reconstruction of Mesozoic California," *International Geological Congress, Proceedings* (1972):217–29.

Durham and Allison, p. 51; most of the fossils are "megafaunal"; J. Wyatt Durham, "E. W. Scripps Cruise to the Gulf of California, Part II. Megascopic Paleontology and Marine Stratigraphy," *Geological Society of America, Memoir 43* (1950), p. 7, thinks that the way the fossils have been collected probably has something to do with the apparent preponderance of gastropods; when fully collected (p. 16), Durham estimates the total number of species will be double or triple those currently known. See also William M. Gabb in *Resources of the Pacific Slope,* p. 114, for an historical note.

Indian middens confused the missionaries, who could not explain their presence so far from water; see Barco, *Natural History,* pp. 264–74, who refused to believe that the Indians could have carted that many shells that many miles, and knew that the Great Flood could not have deposited them for it lasted only "a single year." Therefore great uplifts were postulated to explain their presence on the hillsides. Richard P. Phillips, *personal communication:*

These are, indeed, the remains of Indian picnics. Live shell-fish were a way to carry fresh meat inland, and would keep alive and fresh for several days if you kept them cool.

See also M. L. Natland, "1940 E. W. Scripps Cruise to the Gulf of California. Part IV: Report on the Pleistocene and Pliocene Foraminifera," *Geological Society of America, Memoir 43.*

104

For Indian names on the peninsula see William C. Massey, "Tribes and Languages of Baja California," *Southwestern Journal of Anthropology* 5(3) (1949), and Miguel Léon-Portilla, "Indian Place Names of Baja California Sur. A Report Attributed to Esteban Rodríguez Lorenzo," *Southwest Museum Leaflets* 38 (1977). Captain Rodríguez Lorenzo was commandant of the presidio at La Paz and "faithful companion" to Salvatierra, one of the founding Jesuits. In 1974 a proposal was made at the Twelfth Annual Symposium of the Asociación Cultural de las Californias in La Paz that indigenous place names be officially

added to current place names in Baja California Sur.
104 Quote, Nelson, p. 82.
Describing the arroyos, Wiggins, *Flora,* p. 16:

> During storms that cause heavy run-off, huge boulders are carried out of the canyons and dumped near their mouths, and . . . the thunder of rushing waters and thumping of the transported boulders can be heard from a distance of several miles.

104– Quote, Gabb, pp. 83–84.
6 The mean annual rainfall at Santiago is about 10 inches; without irrigation, farming is impossible.

Chapter 6. San José

110 Walter Nordhoff, father of Charles Nordhoff, who co-authored *Mutiny on the Bounty,* wrote *The Journey of the Flame,* a vividly told, historically accurate account of a journey made at the beginning of the nineteenth century from San José del Cabo to Monterey.

111 One of the best sources of regional history is Pablo Martínez, *A History of Lower California,* trans. Ethel Duffy Turner (México: Editorial Baja California, 1960).
Miguel León-Portilla, "Indian Place Names of Baja California Sur. A Report Attributed to Esteban Rodríguez Lorenzo," *Southwest Museum Leaflets* 38 (1977), p. 10:

> Continuing north more than one league along the same arroyo, one arrives at another town, called San José Viejo, for it is here that the first mission was founded. But because the spring dried up and the water table became deeper, the town and mission were moved and this place was given the aforesaid name to distinguish it from San José.

112 George E. Lindsay, "Some Natural Values of Baja California," *Pacific Discovery,* 23(2) (1970), p. 1, who knows the peninsula well, perhaps puts it most soberly, especially in these times of financial stress:

> These changes are for the "good" of Baja California. Towns and cities are growing and the general economy has improved greatly. The advances and advantages, however, are not without cost. Much of that cost is the loss, already, of some of the peninsula's natural values. It is essential that these values be recognized, protected and cherished, if they are to survive. Their protection is an obligation of the present, an obligation to the future.

> William M. Gabb, in *Resources of the Pacific Slope,* ed. J. Ross Browne (New York: D. Appleton, 1869), pp. 82–83, guessed San José to be 1,500 inhabitants and found it a "little village of whitewashed adobe houses with flat-roofs." Now, a little over a century later, the population is close to 20,000.

112– For accounts of the war with Mexico, see Martínez, pp. 348–51; as well as Alexander S.
13 Taylor, "Historical Summary of Lower California from Its Discovery in 1532 to 1867," in *Resources of the Pacific Slope,* ed. J. Ross Browne, p. 55, and T. R. Fehrenbach, *Fire and Blood* (New York: Collier Books, 1973), p. 402. Mariano Otero was a young senator who, when the treaty was signed, saw in it "a death warrant for future generations"; he wrote a pamphlet that laid Mexico's failure to withstand a mere handful of invaders at the inability of the various interests—army, church, bureaucracy, *indios, mestizos, crillos*—to unite in common cause: "There is no national spirit because we are not a nation."

114 Robert T. Cochran, "Cold-eyed Soldier of Fortune Who Became a 'President,'" *Smithsonian* 12(3) (1981), pp. 117–26, characterizes Walker as a man who "had few principles, and they shifted without warning"; see also J. M. Reid, "The Ensenada," *National Magazine* 46, (1854), pp. 502–5.

Quote, John F. Janes in Anna Marie Hager, *The Filibusters of 1890* (Los Angeles: Dawson's Book Shop, 1968), p. 27. Janes looked with jaundiced eye on the happy native state and proposed to correct it (p. 24):

These days of simplicity, however, could not be expected to last forever. Heaven is not for man on earth. Nay, in the case of this earthly elysium, teeming as it is with gold and silver, and bordered by its gulf of pearls, the westward tread of man forbade it.

116–
20 Quote, pp. 116–17, Martínez, pp. 121 and 238. There are many excellent histories of the missions in California; among them are Peveril Meigs, *The Dominican Mission Frontier of Lower California* (Berkeley: University of California Press, 1935); Bryan James Clinch, *California and its Missions* (San Francisco: Whitaker & Ray, 1904); Francis J. Weber, *The Missions & Missionaries of Baja California* (Los Angeles: Dawson's Book Shop, 1968); Peter M. Dunne, *Black Robes in California* (Berkeley: University of California Press, 1952); Msgr. Francis J. Weber, trans. and annot., *The Peninsular California Missions 1808–1880* (Los Angeles: Dawson's Book Shop, 1979); and W. Michael Mathes, *The Mission(s) of Baja California: 1649–1849* (La Paz: Gobierno del Estado de Baja California Sur & Ayuntamiento de La Paz, 1977). The most telling are the accounts by the missionaries themselves—Barco, Linck, Ducrue, Baegert, de Sales—all of which have been published in translation.

Quote, p. 117, George E. Lindsay, "The Mission Period of Baja California," *Pacific Discovery* 18(4) (1965), p. 5.

Miguel del Barco, *The Natural History of Baja California* (Los Angeles: Dawson's Book Shop, 1980), p. 108:

When the missions of the South were founded there were many and frequent palm groves, because the Indians took absolutely no advantage of these large palms. With the occasion of the uprising of the year 1734, people from the province of Sinaloa came to that part of California in order to participate in its pacification. These people began to cut the hearts of the palms, which they called *palmito*, in order to eat them. The Indians learned to eat palmito from these or from others a short time before, because prior to that they did not know that it could be eaten. They liked it so much that in a short time they finished several beautiful palm groves.

Quote, p. 119, Martínez, p. 231. Pope Leo XIII appointed Francisco Melitón Vargas y Gutiérrez to make an inspection trip of the peninsula and to evaluate what he saw. His report, written in 1880, found great poverty, no cooperation between priests, and at San José (p. 75) the "parish church is very badly maintained and falling into ruins. The arches supporting the roof are propped up with supports." Because of poverty and small population, Vargas recommended that the peninsula should be part of the mainland Colima Diocese, and so affairs remained until 1921, when it was restored to its original status as a vicariate apostolic.

121 Quote, George Shelvocke in *English Privateers at Cabo San Lucas,* ed. Thomas F. Andrews (Los Angeles: Dawson's Book Shop, 1979), p. 89.

Quote, Gustav Eisen, "Explorations in the Cape Region of Baja California, Made under the Auspices of the California Academy of Sciences," *American Geographical Society of New York Bulletin* 29(3) (1907), p. 275. Nelson, p. 83:

The mouth of the San Jose is usually shut off from the sea by a heavy bar of sand built up by the waves. The water is thus held back to form a long narrow fresh-water lagoon immediately back of the beach. At flood time the water from the river backs up here until it spreads over most of the adjacent cultivated fields. At such times, if the water does not break a passage for itself through the bar at the mouth, the people dig a

page

channel across the beach and thus drain it into the sea.

Quote, Cooke, p. 42. Barco, pp. 195–96: since it was painful to rub amaranth between the hands while the seeds were still on the spike, the Indians simply bit off the tender young stalks raw.

Brandegee, "Notes Concerning the Collection of Plants Made by Xantus at Cape St. Lucas and Vicinity," *Zoe* 1 (1890), p. 272, and "Notes and New Species of Lower California Plants," *Zoe* 5(9) (1903), p. 166: the type locality of this ground cherry is Cabo San Lucas.

122 Quote, Walter F. Bryant, "The Cape Region of Baja California," *Zoe* 2 (1891), p. 191. Because of the surf in August, 1890, Bryant and his party had to land on a sandy beach two miles away at La Palmilla and walk into San José del Cabo, where they found excellent collecting.

William Brewster, "Birds of the Cape Region of Lower California," *Bulletin of the Museum of Comparative Zoology* 41(1) (1902), p. 12:

It is not surprising that so rare a combination of attractive conditions as that just mentioned,—especially in a country so generally arid and barren as Lower California— should have given San José del Cabo an exceptionally rich and varied bird fauna. The smaller insectivorous or seed-eating birds find congenial shelter and abundance of food in the luxuriant vegetation with which the village and its immediate neighborhood are varied; reed-loving species, such as Marsh Wrens, Yellow-throats, Rails, and Gallinules, inhabit the pools lower down the river; the shallow lagoon at its mouth affords a perfect paradise for waders and waterfowl of many different varieties, while Plover, Sandpipers, Gulls, Terns, Cormorants, Pelicans, and even such ultra-typical marine birds as Petrels and Shearwaters, frequent the neighboring sandy beaches or at least pass over or near them on their flights up and down the coast.

Quote, Walter E. Bryant, "A Catalogue of the Birds of Lower California, Mexico," *Proceedings of the California Academy of Sciences,* 2nd ser. 2 (1889), p. 261, who said that the Indians looked on them as "storm birds" and when a great number were about, they refused to go out in boats.

124 Quote, p. 104, Benjamin Franklin Elliott, 1917, *Lower California—1917* (undated), p. 25. Elliott, a preacher, had lived on the peninsula since 1894, and wrote this small paperback pamphlet extolling its beauties.

Willard Bascom, *Waves and Beaches* (Garden City, NY: Doubleday, 1964), pp. 22–23, 198–99: experimentally, the height of the berm above sea level is 1.3 × height of the deep water waves that formed it, and probably much the same relationship exists in nature.

William Redmond Ryan, *Personal Adventures in Upper and Lower California* (New York: Arno Press, 1973) is a collection of letters written in 1848–49 for the "amusement" of his family; Ryan signed up for an adventure and to (pp. v–vi) "experience an improvement in the general state of his health and spirits which had been greatly impaired by the sedentary and unwholesome nature of the pursuits in which he had been engaged." Pp. 184–85:

Our landing was effected with no further discomfort than was to be expected from our having to incur the chances of a ducking; as the boats were unable, on account of the shallowness of the water and the strong tide, to approach within a comfortable distance of *terra firma.* This, however, reckoned for nothing: nor did our tedious march to the town, though it was only three miles from the beach; nor our being several times nearly buried alive in the heaps of sand that filled the hollows of the road; nor our having to wade through a stream of some twenty feet wide that crossed it at the most inconvenient part, to say nothing of the broiling heat . . .

125 Quote, Luis de Sales in *The Human and Natural History of Baja California*, ed. Homer Aschmann, p. 109; Luis de Sales was a Dominican who served primarily on the northern part of the peninsula 1772–90.

Father Antonio de la Ascención, "Father Antonio de la Ascención's Account of the Voyage of Sebastian Vizcaíno," ed. Henry R. Wagner, *California Historical Quarterly* 7(4) (1928), p. 309, relates Vizcaíno's tribulations trying to get out of the bay, as

the wind was very strong, and the sea ran so high that it seemed as if it was going to bury the land and swallow up the ships. What the origin of this might be is well understood, and that it was the Devil, who caused it all in order to hinder the voyage and prevent the discovery from being made, so that he would not lose his lordship over the souls of the natives of that great kingdom.

125– There are several books on this scientific expedition, the most recent being *The 1769*
27 *Transit of Venus. The Baja California Observations of Jean-Baptiste Chappe d'Auteroche, Vicente de Doz, and Joaquín Velázquez Cárdenas de León*, ed. Doyce B. Nunis, Jr. (Los Angeles: Natural History Museum of Los Angeles, 1982). The journals have also been published in translation as *A Voyage to California*, introduction by Kenneth Holmes (Richmond, England: Richmond Publishing Co., 1973). Another account is Louis Marie Aubert Dupetit-Thouars, *Voyage of the Venus* (Los Angeles: Dawson's Book Shop, 1956); the original account was published in 1778.

J. Ross Browne, "Explorations in Lower California," *Harper's New Monthly Magazine* 37 (1868), p. 578, speaks of the problems of knowing the longitude of Cabo San Lucas:

Great difficulty seems to have been experienced by navigators in determining with accuracy the longitude of Cape St. Lucas. The early voyagers had no means of testing the accuracy of their reckoning; and those of later date have been subject to many difficulties in preserving the true time, owing to the great distance from the point of departure, and the various influences by which their chronometers have been affected. On the best chart now in use —that of Sir Edward Belcher— the longitude of the Cape is laid down about fourteen miles too far westward.

Quotes, Chappe d'Auteroche, *A Voyage to California*, pp. 56–57, 58, and 63–65. Chappe d'Auteroche's oblivious single-mindedness is well documented (Holmes, pp. 57–58):

From this time, it was my fixt resolution to land at the first place we could reach in California. I little cared whether it was inhabited or desart, so as I could but make my observation.

At last, by the help of some favourable gales and currents, we got sight of the land of California, which we judged to be near Cape S. Lucas, distant about eighteen leagues: we drew near the next day with a gentle wind. The 18th at night we were but five leagues from land. I was strenuous for landing at the nearest place, but as I was singular in my opinion the whole day was spent in altercations. The Spaniards wanted to go and land in the bay of San-Barnabe [San Lucas], which was fifteen leagues farther, consequently this would have prolonged our navigation perhaps for several days; for in order to get at this bay, we had to encounter the north and north-west winds, which blew almost constantly. These gentlemen objected to me that we ventured the loss of the ship in landing at Cape San Lucas.

Dupetit-Thouars, p. 59: "the same misfortune happened to all of them and one French

page
gentleman, a member of the Royal Academy of Paris, died."

According to Nunis, p. 82, Chappe d'Auteroche lies in an unmarked and unknown grave in San José del Cabo.

Chapter 7. Todos Santos

129 The town of Todos Santos is not to be confused with the islands to the north where Robert Louis Stevenson set *Treasure Island,* written while he lived in Ensenada during the 1880s.

129– Quote, Joseph Wood Krutch, *The Forgotten Peninsula* (New York: William Morrow,
30 1961), p. 259.

130 Quote, Miguel del Barco, *Natural History of Baja California* (Los Angeles: Dawson's Book Shop, 1980), p. 101; see also Edward W. Nelson, "A Land of Drought and Desert," *National Geographic Magazine* 22 (1911), p. 473. Although commonly soaring at midday, early in the morning these big black birds perch on cardón, wings outstretched, to warm; see Frank Heppner, "The Metabolic Significance of Differential Absorption of Radiant Energy by Black and White Birds," *Condor* 72 (1970):50–59. See also William Dawson and George A. Bartholomew, "Temperature Regulation and Water Economy of Desert Birds," in *Desert Biology,* ed. G. W. Brown, (New York: Academic Press, 1968), p. 364, who point out that soaring during midday heat allows them to reach cooler altitudes; updrafts provide an easy ascent with the expenditure of modest energy on the birds' part. Interestingly enough, William Brewster, "Birds of the Cape Region of Lower California," *Bulletin of the Museum of Comparative Zoology* 41(1) (1902), pp. 80–81, notes that John Xantus collected none, although at the time of Anthony Frazar's trip they were frequent (and still are) all year long. F. J. Clavijero, *The History of Lower California* (Stanford: Stanford University Press, 1937), p. 80: the Indians watched the buzzards land and checked the carrion; if not too badly decomposed, they ate it themselves.

131 Leland R. Lewis and Peter E. Ebeling, *Baja: Covering the Waters of Baja California from San Diego to Cabo San Lucas, to San Felipe, Including All the Offshore and Oceanic Islands* (Newport Beach, CA: SEA Publications, 1971), p. 153; although primarily for small boat navigation along the coast, this is a handsome book with a great deal of good information about the peninsula, including villages such as Candelaria. See also Walt Wheelock and Howard E. Gulick, *Baja California Guidebook* (Glendale, CA: The Arthur H. Clark Co., 1973), p. 149.

Quote, Jakob Baegert, *Observations in Lower California,* trans. intro., notes by M. M. Brandenburg and Carl L. Baumann (Berkeley: University of California Press, 1952), p. 25.

132 Walter F. Bryant, "The Cape Region of Baja California," *Zoe* 2 (1891), p. 192:

The road-runners were more common in the cape region than at any place upon the peninsula where I have been; probably the climate suits them and the country is certainly swarming with lizards, which constitute the principal article of their food. They were remarkably tame, too. . . . I have heard of people eating road-runners and declaring that the flesh was excellent; it might taste well to a hungry man.

One of several papers on roadrunner physiology is that of W. A. Calder, "The Diurnal Activity of the Roadrunner, *Geococcyx californianus,*" *Condor* 70 (1967):84–85.

132– To my knowledge, the only line transits to document changes in vegetation on the Cape
33 were done by T. H. Nash III, G. T. Nebeker, T. J. Moser, and T. Reeves, "Lichen Vegetational Gradients in Relation to the Pacific Coast of Baja California: The Maritime Influence," *Madroño* 26(4) (1979), pp. 149–63.

133– Henry R. Wagner, *The Cartography of the Northwest Coast of America to the Year 1800*

page
39   (Berkeley: University of California Press, 1937), pp. 9, 20 fn. See also T. S. Brandegee, "Cactaceae of the Cape Region of Baja California," *Zoe* 11 (1891):18–22. Norberto Ducrue in *The Natural and Human History of Baja California,* ed. Homer Aschmann (Los Angeles: Dawson's Book Shop, 1966), p. 49:

> . . . it grows straight up from the ground like a great green post, and sometimes, after the main trunk has grown, it puts out other post-like branches which are fairly long; some of these grow straight up, paralleling the trunk, and others are crooked. Its fruit is like the chestnut ball, but it encloses on the inside little more than a mass of round, black seeds; there is a very small amount of flesh which is reddish or white in color. The flavor of the seeds resembles that of poppy seeds.

Compare this with Miguel Venegas, *A Natural and Civil History of California,* 2 vols. (Ann Arbor: University Microfilms, 1966), pp. 42–43, who had never been to the peninsula; he wrote a good description of cardón but confused it with *pitahaya·*

> This tree is not known in Europe, and differs from all other trees in the world; its branches are fluted and rise vertically from the stem, so as to form a very beautiful top; they are without leaves, the fruit growing to the boughs. The fruit is like a horse chestnut, and full of prickles; but the pulp resembles that of a fig, only more soft and luscious. In some it is white, in some red, and in others yellow; but always of an exquisite taste: some again are wholly sweet; others of a grateful acid. And as the pitahaya is very juicy, it is chiefly found in a dry soil.

134   Quote, Richard Brinsley Hinds, in George Bentham, *The Botany of H. M. S. Sulphur under command of Capt. Sir Edward Belcher, During the Years 1836–42,* ed. Richard Brinsley Hinds, Esq., Surgeon (London: Smith, Elder, 1844), p. 5. This book, with magnificent illustrations, is the first published record of plants from the peninsula.
       A previous expedition sent out from Spain worked in Mexico 1787–1803, under the direction of Martin de Sessé y Lacasta and José Mariano Mociño. During 1791–92 a trip was made to the peninsula by a member of the expedition, José Longinos Martínez, and an assistant. He collected a few plants, some of which, according to Dr. Rogers McVaugh, *personal communication,* January 12, 1983, surely are from Baja California, but localities are not noted on the labels. See "Long-lost Sessé and Mociño Illustrations Acquired," *Bulletin of the Hunt Institute for Botanical Documentation,* 3:1 (Spring–Summer 1981). See also the introduction, *The Journal of José Longinos Martínez,* ed. Lesley Byrd Simpson (San Francisco: John Howell—Books, 1961), and Simpson, "The Story of José Longinos Martínez, California's First Naturalist," *Hispanic American Historical Review* 20(4) (1940):643–49.
       James A. McCleary, "The Biology of Desert Plants," in *Desert Biology,* ed. G. W. Brown (New York: Academic Press, 1968), pp. 163–64, 166–67, comments that the idea that spines reduce the leaf surface and therefore help prevent transpiration in cacti has been negated by recent studies indicating that because of the larger number of reduced leaves the surface area exposed is actually greater than in less xeromorphic plants. See also Volney M. Spalding, *Distribution and Movements of Desert Plants* (Washington, DC: Carnegie·Institution Publication 113, 1909).

136   Quotes, Barco, pp. 157 and 158. However, Ducrue reported, pp. 49–51:

> A piece of the cactus stem may be cut off and half-roasted, and if applied to the side where the flow of humors is disturbed or to an aching tooth it brings immediate relief or eliminates the illness completely; but it does cause the teeth to fall out.

Jeanette Coyle and Norman Roberts, *A Field Guide to the Common and Interesting Plants of Baja California* (La Jolla, CA: Natural History Publishing Company, 1980), p. 146, write

page

that cardón is still used that way, with thin slices of stem being cut and bound to an open wound: "It seems to act as a pain killer, disinfectant and healing agent."
Quotes, Barco, p. 158, and Ducrue, pp. 49–51.

136– According to John K. Terres, *The Audubon Society Encyclopedia of North American Birds*
37   (New York: Knopf, 1980), p. 732, the fruit of the giant cacti are an important source of moisture. Dawson and Bartholomew note that, as with mammals, birds' behavior helps them to avoid hyperthermia; they rest in the shade and remain inactive during the heat of the day. Very few birds take advantage of underground burrows for coolness. Of the nearly 300 bird species breeding here, less than 16 percent are actual desert dwellers; because of their mobility, many more temperate-environment species occupy the semidesert at various times, utilizing the wider range of habitat and food when available, and are not obligate desert dwellers. See also D. L. Serventy, "Biology of Desert Birds," in *Avian Biology,* eds. D. S. Farner, J. R. King, and K. C. Parkes, Vol. 1 (New York: Academic Press, 1971), and Walter Bryant, "The Cape Region of Baja California," *Zoe* 2 (1891).

137   Xantus' screech owl was named by Brewster after the man who first collected it. See also John Davis, "The Sierra Madrean Element of the Avifauna of the Cape District, Baja California," *Condor* 61 (1959), pp. 76–77; A. H. Miller and L. Miller, "Geographic Variation of the Screech Owls of the Deserts of Western North America," *Condor* 53 (1951), pp. 167–68, 175–76.

138   Quote, T. S. Brandegee, "The Hedgerows of Todos Santos," *Zoe* 1 (1890), pp. 179–80.

139   Quote, Edward W. Nelson, "Lower California and Its Natural Resources," *National Academy of Sciences, Memoir* 16 (1921), pp. 43–44.
Quote, Barco, pp. 34–35, and Baegert, p. 125.

140   Spencer Murray, *Explorations in Lower California* (Studio City, CA: Vaquero Books, 1966), pp. 41–42. The 1960 census gave Todos Santos 2,040 inhabitants.
Griffing Bancroft, *The Flight of the Least Petrel* (New York: Putnam, 1932), pp. 174–75, describes the candy-making process.

Chapter 8. Pacific Fringe

145   Quote, F. J. Clavijero, in J. Ross Browne, *Resources of the Pacific Slope* (New York: D. Appleton, 1869), p. 157.

146   Sherman A. Minton, Jr., "Venoms of Desert Animals," in *Desert Biology,* ed. G. W. Brown (New York: Academic Press, 1968), p. 496.
Quote, Edward Cooke, in *English Privateers at Cabo San Lucas,* ed. Thomas F. Andrews (Los Angeles: Dawson's Book Shop, 1979), p. 48. See also William Brewster, "Birds of the Cape Region of Lower California," *Bulletin of the Museum of Comparative Zoology* 41(1) (1902), pp. 123–25; and John Davis, "The Sierra Madrean Element of the Avifauna of the Cape District, Baja California," *Condor* 61 (1959), pp. 79–80.

147   Quote, Walter E. Bryant, in Brewster, p. 36. Edward W. Nelson, "Lower California and Its Natural Resources," *National Academy of Sciences, Memoir* 16 (1921), p. 471:

Whenever a cormorant, alarmed by our approach, flew away, the gulls swooped down on the exposed eggs and ate them at once; or, if we were too near, each gull transfixed an egg on its beak and flew away, draining the contents as it went. On two occasions I saw gulls light on nests and calmly pick up young cormorants weighing 5 or 6 ounces each and swallow them entire, the helpless victims being swallowed head foremost, their feet waving despairingly from the gull's widely spread beaks as they disappeared.

page

147– The temperature variations have been well documented and discussed in various papers;
48 see J. Wyatt Durham and Edwin C. Allison, "The Geologic History of Baja California and
Its Marine Faunas," in "Symposium: The Biogeography of Baja California and Adjacent
Seas. Part I: Geologic History," eds. J. Wyatt Durham and Edwin C. Allison, *Systematic
Zoology* 9(2) (1960), pp. 65 and 79; C. L. Hubbs, "The Marine Vertebrates of the Outer
Coast," in "Symposium: Part II. Marine Biotas," *Systematic Zoology* 9(2) (1960), p. 134
and "Changes in the Fish Fauna of Western North America Correlated with Changes in
Ocean Temperature," *Journal of Marine Research* (1948), pp. 461–62; E. Yale Dawson,
Marine Botany, An Introduction (New York: Holt, Rinehart and Winston, 1966), pp. 47–
49; G. E. MacGinitie and Nettie MacGinitie, *Natural History of Marine Animals* (New
York: McGraw-Hill, 1968), p. 3; Richard C. Brusca, *Common Intertidal Invertebrates of
the Gulf of California* (Tucson: University of Arizona Press, 1981), pp. 9–10.

149– See M. Edmunds, *Defence in Animals* (Essex, England: Longman Group, 1974), p. xv, and
51 Lena B. Brattsten, "Biochemical Defense Mechanisms in Herbivores against Plant Allelo-
chemicals," in *Herbivores, Their Interraction with Secondary Plant Metabolites*, eds.
Gerald A. Rosenthal and Daniel H. Janzen (New York: Academic Press, 1979), pp. 199
270.

151 Quote, Johann Jakob Baegert, *Observations in Lower California*, (Berkeley: University of
California Press, 1952), p. 43.
 Ross H. Arnett and Richard L. Jacques, *Simon and Schuster's Guide to Insects* (New
York: Simon & Schuster, 1981), p. 287: "This species probably has the most painful sting
of any insect." Sherman A. Minton, Jr., "Venoms of Desert Animals," in *Desert Biology*, ed.
G. W. Brown (New York: Academic Press, 1968), p. 497, comments that multiple stings by
large wasps and bees usually cause local pain and swelling; vomiting, diarrhea, and shock
may ensue. In sensitized individuals this may cause anaphylactic shock. While relatively
see also rare, more deaths occur from this than snakebites.
 Quote, Miguel del Barco, *Natural History of Baja California* (Los Angeles: Dawson's
Book Shop, 1980), pp. 59–60.
 Abbot Jean Chappe d'Auteroche, *A Voyage to California,* intro. Kenneth Holmes (Richmond, England: Richmond Publishing Company, 1973), p. 92, scientist that he was, nevertheless claimed that seeing a tarantula

 is an unerring barometer. This observation was communicated to me by a virtuoso, and
 I have never known it to fail. Whenever I have seen these spiders, the weather constantly changed to rain within four and twenty hours.

151– Quote, Louis de Sales, *Observations on California, 1772–1790* (Los Angeles: Dawson's
52 Book Shop, 1956), p. 107.

152 Quote, C. M. Scammon, "Report of Captain C. M. Scammon, of the U.S. Revenue Service,
on the West Coast of Lower California," in J. Ross Browne, *Resources of the Pacific Slope*
(New York: D. Appleton, 1869), p. 131. Pericu legend, Pablo L. Martínez, *A History of
Lower California,* trans. Ethel Duffy Turner (México: Editorial Baja California, 1960), pp.
57–58.
 Nelson, p. 111, in 1906, found the shores of the peninsula full of whales, elephant seals,
fur seals, and sea otters, although 50 years earlier, in the winters of 1846 and 1848, 52
whalers were counted in Magdalena Bay, leaving only when not enough animals were left
for the business to be profitable.
 Leland R. Lewis and Peter E. Ebeling, *Sea Guide Volume II: BAJA* (Newport Beach, CA:
SEA Publications, 1971), p. 361, illustrate whale silhouettes and blow patterns.

page

155 Willard Bascom, *Waves and Beaches* (Garden City, NY: Doubleday, 1964), pp. 36–38, 158–63: waves 1 yard high and 30 yards long land with a pressure of about 180 pounds per square inch.

157 Quote, Spencer Murray, *Explorations in Lower California* (Studio City, CA: Vaquero Books, 1966), p. 1.

Lewis and Ebeling, p. 153, place the light at Cabo Falso at latitude 22° 52′ north, longitude 109° 58′ west, conspicuous from the sea for the long "sand slide" on the coast. Edwin H. Hammond, "A Geomorphic Study of the Cape Region of Baja California," *University of California Publications in Geography* 10(2) (1954), p. 88: one of the most extensive accumulations of sand carried inland by wind on the Cape is at Cabo Falso. W. S. Cooper, "Coastal Dunes of California," *Geological Society of America Memoirs* 104 (1967): the escarpment on which the new lighthouse stands may be "an ancient subdued sea cliff." The lighthouse is 656 feet above the sea and half a mile above the old light, and is visible for 36 miles in clear weather. Other Cape lighthouses are set at Cabo Falso, Cabeza Ballena, San José del Cabo, Boca del Tule, Punta Arena, and La Paz.

The distinctive sand dune and sea-bluff plant communities are discussed in Ira L. Wiggins, *Flora of Baja California* (Stanford: Stanford University Press, 1980), pp. 24–25, 28.

Tenebrionid beetle species inhabit hot and dry regions and "exhibit a wonderful adjustment to their environment. The teguments are adapted to meet the demands against evaporation and to conserve the body fluids" by anatomical adjustments "practically sealing up the body against the drying effect of the desert," according to F. E. Blaisdell, "Expedition of the California Academy of Sciences in the Gulf of Califorina [sic] in 1921— The Tenebrionidae," *Proceedings of the California Academy of Sciences* 12 (1923), pp. 201–2. Walter E. Bryant, "El Zorillo," *Zoe* 1 (1890), p. 273, discussing rabid skunks, was told that "at times the skunks fed upon a certain species of black beetle (*Tenebrionidae?*), and forthwith went mad."

Gorton E. Linsley, "The Origin and Distribution of the Cerambycidae of North America with Special Reference to the Fauna of the Pacific Slope," *Proceedings of the Sixth Pacific Scientific Congress* 4 (1940), pp. 266–67 and 280–81, counts the neotropical beetle fauna as one of the richest in species; it spreads across Central America to the southern Mexican mainland and into the Cape region. In the Baja California insect fauna there are three groups: those species in common with California and farther north, mostly confined to the northern part of the peninsula; a fauna resembling that of Sonora, existing generally in the central half of the peninsula; and the Cape fauna. Of these the Cape fauna is the richest, and also thought to be the oldest, and contains most of the endemic species, both on a generic and specific level. Without doubt a larger fauna once inhabited the whole peninsula that was severely edited because of the increasing dryness during the Pleistocene era. The present Cape fauna appear to be remnants of those that migrated from Mexico around the head of the Sea of Cortés, or came by land when the peninsula was still attached to the mainland, and were able to adapt to the aridity.

See also John A. Grossbeck, "Lists of Insects Collected by the 'Albatross' Expedition in Lower California in 1911, with Description of a New Species of Wasp," *Bulletin of the American Museum of Natural History* 31 (1912), pp. 324–25, who lists some of the beetles of the Cape Region collected at that time.

Chapter 9. La Vigía

164– The definitive treatment of the Manila galleons is William L. Schurz, *The Manila Galleon*
68 (New York: E. P. Dutton, 1939). A *cédula real* of 1726, the official communication from

the King of Spain, prescribed dimensions: a keel nearly 120 feet long, beam of some 39 feet, depth from top of keel to first deck's lower surface, some 20 feet—about the size of a World War II PT boat. See also J. C. Beaglehole, *The Exploration of the Pacific* (London: A. C. Black, 1934).

Leland R. Lewis and Peter E. Ebeling, *Sea Guide Volume II: BAJA* (Newport Beach, CA: SEA Publications, 1971), p. 9: "Rutter" was derived from the French *routier,* a route book, which arose from meticulously kept ships' logs; they were guarded zealously and were often the most important booty because they provided experienced and detailed directions for difficult coasts and bays, where water could be found, etc. Urdaneta's *derrotero* was used for a hundred years as a guide between the Philippines and Acapulco. By 1734 there was a rutter for the Lower California coast, written by Admiral Joseph González Cabrero Bueno. See John Janes, "The Last Voyage of Thomas Cavendish as told by Master John Janes," in *Hakluyt's Voyages: Tales of Adventure and Exploration,* ed. Delbert A. Young (Toronto: Clarke, Irwin, 1973), p. 147.

Ersola, the Spaniard, was the greatest of the catch. As a pilot, he had made various voyages between Acapulco and the Ladrones [now Mariana Islands, east of the Philippines], therefore he could be prevailed upon to guide us to such isles as would provide us with fresh water, plantains, potatoes, and other necessities."

Quotes, p. 167, Schurz, pp. 196, 267–68, and 274. Careri sailed out in 1697 and returned the next year; his account was published in 1720.

168– Books treating of the privateers who used the Cape as a base from which to operate are
72 W. Michael Mathes, ed., *The Capture of the Santa Ana, Cabo San Lucas, November, 1587* (Los Angeles: Dawson's Book Shop, 1969); Peter Gerhard, 1960, *Pirates on the West Coast of New Spain 1575–1742* (Glendale, CA: Arthur H. Clark, 1960); Kenneth R. Andrews, *Elizabethan Privateering: English Privateering During the Spanish War, 1585–1603* (Cambridge: University Press, 1964); Thomas F. Andrews, ed., *English Privateers at Cabo San Lucas. The Descriptive Accounts of Puerto Seguro by Edward Cooke (1712) and Woodes Rogers (1712)* (Los Angeles: Dawson's Book Shop, 1979); and Young's edition of *Hakluyt.*

Quotes, p. 169, Master Francis Pretty in Mathes, pp. 24–29, and Alzola in Mathes, pp. 45–46, who said that the English "committed great harm and insolences until the twenty-ninth, when they had no more space to load."

Quote, pp. 169–70, Pretty in Mathes, pp. 26–27.

Thomas Cavendish, "A letter of M. Thomas Candish to the right honourable the Lord Hunsdon, Lord Chamberlaine, one of ther Majesties most honourable Privy Councell, touching the successe of his voyage about the world," in Young, pp. 445–46:

> I navigated alongst the coast of Chili, Peru, and Nueva Espanna, where I made great spoiles: I burnt and sunke 19 sailes of ships small and great. All the villages and townes that ever I landed at, I burnt and spoiled: and had I not been discovered upon the coast, I had taken great quantitie of treasure.

In truth, had Cavendish not found the *Santa Ana* the voyage would have been a financial disaster. As Cavendish's three ships left the Cape, one lagged behind and was never seen again, leaving stories of Spanish treasure to be found.

After Cavendish's successful raid, the viceroy, if there were rumors of marauders in the area, sent armed ships out to warn the galleons to stand well out to sea, and to escort them in. Nevertheless, the galleons remained sitting ducks; it was still more profitable to carry merchandise than cannon, and what armament there was was often stored in the hold, while the decks were piled high with goods.

page

Plans for exploring the California coast to find a safe harbor for the galleons came to nothing; Captain Francisco de Bolaños was sent out by the viceroy sometime around 1542 and probably named some of the places on the peninsula, among them San Lucas, although this is not certain; see Henry R. Wagner, ed., "Pearl Fishing Enterprises in the Gulf of California," *Hispanic American Historical Review* 10(2) (1930), pp. 86-87, and "Spanish Voyages to the Northwest Coast. The Voyage of Juan Rodríguez Cabrillo," *California Historical Quarterly* 7(1) (1928), p. 71.

Vizcaíno generally named places from the Carmelite calendar of saints, naming a site on the saint's day upon which it was discovered. See Bryan J. Clinch, *California and its Missions* (San Francisco: Whitaker & Ray, 1904), p. 23, and Antonio de la Ascensión, "Father Antonio de la Ascensión's Account of the Voyage of Sebastián Vizcaíno," ed. Henry R. Wagner, *California Historical Society Quarterly* 7(4) (1929), pp. 305-7: "As the fleet reached this bay on the day of San Bernabé, it was named 'San Bernabé.'"

171– Quotes, Rogers in Schurz, p. 322, and Woodes Rogers, *A Cruising Voyage Round the*
72 *World* (New York: Longmans, Green, 1928), pp. 208-12, and Rogers in Schurz, p. 326.

La Vigía is lower than two hills to the west at 620 and 845 feet repectively, but has the advantage of accessibility, being right on the bay, while the higher hills are over a difficult mile away.

Both Cooke and Rogers published their observations of the journey, of which Rogers's account proved the more popular. Roger's venture in turn inspired that of George Shelvocke. Shelvocke left England in February, 1719; on his trip a contentious first mate killed an albatross that supposedly haunted the ship, an incident which took poetic form in Coleridge's *Rime of the Ancient Mariner.*

172– Quote, Rogers in Andrews, pp. 63–64.
73 See Francis P. Shepard, "1940 *E. W. Scripps* Cruise to the Gulf of California, Part III: Submarine Topography of the Gulf of California," *Geological Society of America, Memoir* 43 (1950), pp. 19-27, and *Submarine Geology* (New York: Harper & Brothers, 1948). See also Ph. H. Kuenen, *Marine Geology* (New York: Wiley & Sons, 1950), pp. 485, 503-4, 525, and W. R. Normak and J. P. Curray, "Geology and Structure of the Tip of Baja California, Mexico," *Geological Society of America Bulletin* 79 (1968), pp. 1596-97. Other major canyons exist at Tinaja and Pescadero on the Pacific Coast, and at Los Frailes and Punta Arena on the Gulf Coast.

173– Quotes, Hatsuro, *Kaigai ibun, A Strange Tale from Overseas—Japanese Castaway,*
74 comps. Maekawa Bunzo and Sakai Junzo, trans. Richard Zumwinkle and Tadanobu Kawai (Los Angeles: Dawson's Book Shop, 1970), pp. 34 and 37.

174– In Spencer Murray, *Explorations in Lower California* (Studio City, CA: Vaquero Books,
77 1966), p. 2, is a grandiose sketch of Ritchie's house. For references on John Xantus, see notes for Chapter 2.

In his report to the Smithsonian Baird makes it sound as if he were doing the Coast Survey a favor:

> At this time the United States Coast Survey, desirous of establishing a tidal station at Cape St. Lucas, and of placing it in charge of a man of scientific training, was induced, through the efforts of this Institution, to offer the position to Mr. Xantus, who accepted it and proceeded to his post of duty early in 1859.

Baird, a member of the Coast Survey Board, weaseled the appointment for Xantus through his friendship with Professor Alexander D. Bache, superintendent of the U.S. Coast Survey. Bache had, just three years previously, made the first reliable measurements of ocean depth by comparing the recorded shock waves of an earthquake felt at sea with tidal

page

records; to get measurements from a such a remote place as the Cape must have intrigued him.

Quote, p. 174, Xantus to Baird, April 13, 1859. Willard Bascom, *Waves and Beaches* (Garden City, NY: Doubleday, 1964) has a diagram of the kind of gauge Xantus had to build and rig.

Quote, p. 175, Xantus to Baird, April 7, 1860; further:

> I am extremely sorry that Prof Bache thinks the fault is mine, and that I am neglecting the interests of the C.S. for the sake of other pursuits. I took very great pains to reap a credit although under most disagreeable and annoying circumstances, I expended not only my whole pay for the interest of the observations, but also a considerable amount of my private means, received since my arrival here. If I could not satisfy Prof Bache, my reasons I confidently hope will satisfy him, that the fault was not mine; I had a good will, zeal, & intention to do my best, this I say upon my honor; and if I had contributed largely to the Natural History, in exploring the flora & fauna of this little known section of the continent; I had certainly not done it on the expense of the interest of the C.S.

T. S.Brandegee, "Notes Concerning the Collection of Plants Made by Xantus at Cape St. Lucas and Vicinity," *Zoe* 1 (1890), wrote before any critical evaluation of Xantus's work had been made, and was puzzled by some of the lacunae (p. 270):

> Many plants grow about San Jose that Xantus did not collect, although they are very abundant and often very conspicuous; some because they are difficult to dry were perhaps intentionally neglected; such are the Portulacas, which abound, and are represented by five species. No mention is made of the cacti; a class of plants very difficult to prepare specimens from, but at that time the abundant ones were undescribed species.

In order of mention in text, *Euphorbia xantii, Malacothrix xantii, Hofmeisteria fasciculata* var. *xanti, Polygala xanti;* other plants named after Xantus are species of *Boerhaavia, Lyrocarpa, Heterosperma, Mimosa, Abutilon,* and *Sida.* See also Brandegee, pp. 272–73. Xantus's work *was* appreciated, and in print; witness the dedication of T. N. Gill, the ichthyologist who named two species after Xantus (Madden, p. 271):

> Mr. John Xantus to whom we are indebted for the noble collection of fishes and other animals of Lower California, and who has, more than any other single man, contributed to our knowledge of the natural history of the Western coast.

Quote, pp. 175–76, Xantus to Baird, February 27, 1861.

Chapter 10. Sea of Cortés

181–
83

The Gulf of California has been extensively studied; see G. I. Roden, "Oceanographic and Meteorological Aspects of the Gulf of California," *Pacific Science* 12 (1958), pp. 21–45; Roger Revelle, "1940 *E. W. Scripps* Cruise to the Gulf of California. Part V: Sedimentation and Oceanography: Survey of Field Observations," *Geological Society of America, Memoir* 43 (1950), pp. 1–6; G. I. Roden and G. W. Groves, "Recent Oceanographic Investigations in the Gulf of California," *Journal of Marine Research* 18 (1959), pp. 10–35; F. P. Shepard, "*E. W. Scripps* Cruise to the Gulf of California. Part III. Submarine Topography of the Gulf of California," *Geological Society of America, Memoir* 43 (1950), pp. 1–32; W. Hamilton, "Origin of the Gulf of California," *Geological Society of America Bulletin* 71 (1961):1307–18.

Boyd W. Walker, "The Distribution and Affinities of the Marine Fish Fauna of the Gulf of California," in "Symposium: The Biogeography of Baja California and Adjacent Seas. Part II. Marine Biotas," eds. J. Wyatt Durham and Edwin C. Allison, *Systematic Zoology*

page

9(2) (1960), p. 125, says it is the only evaporation basin in the Pacific and its large annual range of surface sea temperature (greatest in the north, less at Cabo San Lucas) is around 9° C.; these variations extend down to 600 feet. Depths frequently exceed 3,000 meters. See also Richard E. Brusca, *Common Intertidal Invertebrates of the Gulf of California* (Tucson: University of Arizona Press, 1981).

Revelle (p. 5) found "the waters over large areas were reddened and opaque, so great was the phytoplankton population."

Ara H. Marerosian, "Drugs from Plants of the Sea," in *Plants in the Development of Modern Medicine,* ed. Tony Swain (Cambridge: Harvard University Press, 1972) pp. 219–22, says there are at least 22 species involved in "red tide" poisoning.

Antonio de la Ascencíon, "Father Antonio de la Ascencíon's Account of the Voyage of Sebastián Vizcaíno," ed. Henry R. Wagner, *California Historical Society Quarterly* 7(4) (1928), p. 305, speaks of the sea which

some call "The Sea of Cortez," as he was the first who sailed on it when he went to the Californias in 1535, but others call it the "Mar Rojo," because the water has a reddish appearance.

184 Quotes, John Steinbeck and Edward F. Ricketts, *Sea of Cortez* (Mount Vernon, NY: Paul P. Appel, 1982), pp. 247 and 250.

186– Quote, Joseph Wood Krutch, *The Forgotten Peninsula* (New York: William Morrow, 1961)
87 pp. 206–207.

Donald A. Thomson, Lloyd T. Findley, and Alex N. Kerstitch, *Reef Fishes of the Sea of Cortez* (New York: John Wiley & Sons, 1979), p. 249, describe this manta as

a spectacular jumper, leaps high out of the water and lands flat on its belly with a thunderous "smack," which is audible from a great distance.

187 Quotes, Ascencíon in Wagner, p. 308, and Norberto Ducrue in *The Natural and Human History of Baja California,* ed. Homer Aschmann (Los Angeles: Dawson's Book Shop, 1966), p. 44.

187– Carl L. Hubbs, "The Marine Vertebrates of the Outer Coast," in "Symposium: The Bio-
88 geography of Baja California and Adjacent Seas. Part II. Marine Biotas," eds. J. Wyatt Durham and Edwin C. Allison, *Systematic Zoology* 9(2) (1960), pp. 142–43. C. H. Townsend, "Voyage of the Albatross to the Gulf of California in 1911," *Bulletin of the American Museum of Natural History* 35(1916), pp. 445–46, found hawksbill turtles *(Eretmoshelys squamata)* common at the southern end of the peninsula. See Jay M. Savage, "Evolution of a Peninsular Herpetofauna," in "Symposium: The Biogeography of Baja California and Adjacent Seas. Part II. Marine Biotas," eds. J. Wyatt Durham and Edwin C. Allison, *Systematic Zoology* 9(2) (1960), p. 195, and Archie Carr, "Great Reptiles, Great Enigmas," *Audubon* 74(2) (1972):24–35. Jack Rudloe, *Time of the Turtle* (New York: Penguin Books, 1980), pp. 232–33, describes the egg-laying firsthand.

Quote, Miguel del Barco, *Natural History of Baja California* (Los Angles: Dawson's Book Shop, 1980), pp. 248–49. John Xantus, in a letter to Spencer Baird, March 29, 1859, noted "innumerable turtles on the beach" of Guadalupe Island, off the west coast of the peninsula.

188 John S. Garth, "Distribution and Affinities of the Brachyuran Crustacea," in "Symposium: The Biogeography of Baja California and Adjacent Seas. Part II. Marine Biotas," eds. J. Wyatt Durham and Edwin C. Allison, *Systematic Zoology* 9(2) (1960), pp. 105, 117, and 119.

189– The type specimen for the brown pelican came from La Paz and was taken by Lyman
90 Belding in 1883; Joseph Grinnell, "A Distributional Summation of the Ornithology of

Lower California," *University of California Publications in Zoology* 32 (1928), pp. 71–72, found them "abundant."

William Weber Johnson and editors of Time-Life, *Baja California* (New York: Time, Inc., 1972), p. 129, note that as far as 300 miles below the Mexican border pelicans were producing thin-shelled eggs due to pesticide pollution. The numbers look to be fairly stable at the Cape, and it could be either that the effects are not making themselves shown yet, or more likely that there are no large spraying operations as there are on mainland Mexico, leaving this colony unaffected.

196–
97   For the crabhole mosquito, *Deinocerites mcdonaldi*, see John N. Belkin and Charles L. Hogue, "A Review of the Crabhole Mosquitoes of the Genus *Deinocerites* (Diptera: Culicidae)," *University of California Publications in Entomology* 14(6), 1959, pp. 411–20, 435–36.

Chapter 11. Pulmo Reef

198   Annetta M. Carter, "I. G. Voznesenskii, Early Naturalist in Baja California, Mexico," *Taxon* 28 (1,2/3) (1979):27–33. Voznesenskii was aboard a Russian ship that traveled around the Cape and upward into the Gulf looking for salt in the mid-nineteenth century. I am indebted to Miss Carter for a copy of her article.

The change in color noted by so many writers between the Gulf and the Pacific has some scientific founding; at Cabo San Lucas, the warm and salt-laden Gulf of California waters meet the cool low-saline Pacific waters and form a "front" marked by an abrupt change in the density of the water

201–
6   See Pablo L. Martínez, *A History of Lower California* (México: Editorial Baja California, 1960), pp. 72–73, 80–83, and George E. Lindsay, "The Mission Period of Baja California," *Pacific Discovery* 18(4) (1965), p. 2.

W. Michael Mathes, ed., *The Conquistador in California: 1535* (Los Angeles: Dawson's Book Shop, 1973) pp. 35–39. Gómara accompanied Cortés on his return trip when he found one ship aground and bailed it out "with the pump and with kettles"; he got the ship back in service but had to navigate it himself on the return trip to Santa Cruz because the "yard fell and killed the pilot Antón Cordero, who was asleep at the foot of the mast." See also Miguel Venegas, *A Natural and Civil History of California* (Ann Arbor, MI; University Microfilms, 1966), pp. ii–iii; Francisco Clavijero, *The History of Lower California* (Stanford: Stanford University Press, 1937), pp. viii–ix; and Henry R. Wagner, "Pearl Fishing Enterprises in the Gulf of California," *Hispanic American Historical Revue* 10(2) (1930), pp. 1–6.

Mathes, p. 53, quotes an account of one Diaz who reported that "once Ulloa was on land resting, a soldier of those he had taken in his command awaited him in a place where he stabbed and killed him." Ulloa clearly knew it was a peninsula, but the myth of an island persisted for 150 years more. Father Varegas gave an account of Cortés's journey, but Cortés left no detailed diary (Mathes, pp. 20–21), for

the discovery and possession of California was of such little consequence to the men who had conquered the great cities of central Mexico, Oaxaca, Yucatán, and Guatemala that the documentation surrounding them is rather perfunctory and devoid of description, particularly when compared with the excellent descriptions of central Mexico given by Cortés in his *Cartas de Relación* to Carlos V.

Quote, p. 203, Juan Rodríguez Cabrillo, "Voyage of Cabrillo in 1542," ed. Bartolomé Ferrel, *U.S. Geographical Surveys West of the 100th Meridian* (Washington, DC; U.S. Government Printing Office, 1879), p. 299.

Quote, p. 203, Henry R. Wagner, "Spanish Voyages to the Northwest Coast in the Six-

page

teenth Century," *California Historical Society Quarterly* 6(4) (1927), p. 26. Philip II issued his *cedula* to control discoveries in 1573, hence Vizcaíno had to go back to Spain to sue for permission to continue his exploration, according to Wagner (1930); Gonzálo de Franco accompanied Vizcaíno to Spain on this trip and reported to the King, p. 220:

> As a loyal vassal of your Majesty, I say that the conquest of this country is very important, because it has signs of great prosperity, the principal one being the many pearl oysters in which there can be much wealth once rich beds are discovered.

In December, 1665, a *cédula real* terminated all further expeditions for exploration.

Quote, p. 205, Emerson D. Fite and Archibald Freeman, ed., *A Book of Old Maps Delineating American History from the Earliest Days Down to the Close of the Revolutionary War* (New York: Arno Press, 1969), p. 130; a further note says that the idea that California was an island could be traced to maps taken by the Dutch from a Spanish ship soon after 1600:

> *California, sometymes supposed to be part of ye westerne continent, but scince by a Spanish Charte taken by ye Hollanders it is found to be a goodly Ilande; the length of the west shoare beeing about 500 leagues from Cape Mendocino to the South Cape there of called Cape St. Lucas; as appeareth both by that Spanish Chart and by the relation of Francis Gaule, wheras in the ordinarie Charts it is sett downe to be 1700 Leagues.*

Both Rogers and George Shelvocke showed some confusion as to whether Lower California was an island or a peninsula, but Thomas F. Andrews, *English Privateers at Cabo San Lucas* (Los Angeles: Dawson's Book Shop, 1979) says the idea persisted well into the eighteenth century. See also Admiral Don Isidro de Atondo y Antillon, *The Diary of the Kino-Atondo Peninsular Expedition,* intro. and trans. W. Michael Mathes (Los Angeles: Dawson's Book Shop, 1969).

206– Wagner (1937), p. 41: on June 3, 1542 they "cast anchor at the Punta de la California,"
9 which Wagner thinks was Punta Pulmo. See the U.S. Hydrographic Map *Bahía Magdalena to La Paz* #21120, and Leland R. Lewis and Peter E. Ebeling, *Sea Guide Volume II: BAJA* (Newport Beach, CA; SEA Publications, 1971), p. 196, for navigation warning. See also John Steinbeck and Edward F. Ricketts, *Sea of Cortez* (Mount Vernon, NY: Paul P. Appel, 1981), pp. 72–79; p. 309: "at Pulmo we have one of the few true reefs reported from the American Pacific." Besides *Porcillopora elegans,* two other corals are common here: *Porites california,* a brilliant green encrusting coral, and *Pavona gigantea,* a massive non-branching coral.

Richard C. Brusca and Donald A. Thomson, "The Pulmo Reefs of Baja California—True Coral Reef Formation in the Gulf of California," *Ciencias Marinas* 1(3) (1977), p. 40:

> Whether or not the Pulmo coral formations may be classified as true "coral reefs" may be a moot point; however, they clearly *function* as coral reefs judging by the species richness and coral associated fauna and flora.

P. H. Kuenen, *Marine Geology* (New York: Wiley & Sons, 1950), pp. 415–16, 420–21, says coral growth averages 2½ centimeters per year. Because of breakage, Robert Zottoli, *Introduction to Marine Environments* (St. Louis: C. V. Mosby, 1978), pp. 193–200, estimates 2–3 millimeters per year actual growth, and puts the salinity requirement of corals between 18 and 38 percent (pp. 186–88).

V. Fretter and A. Graham, *A Functional Anatomy of Invertebrates* (London: Academic Press, 1976), pp. 86–88, cite experiments using radioactively labeled carbon compounds to track the time of photosynthetically fixed carbon to travel into the animal tissue and found it surprisingly high. There are other corals which grow as deep as 2,000 feet, but none of these have symbiotic zooxanthellae.

Richard C. Brusca, *Common Intertidal Invertebrates of the Gulf of California* (Tucson: University of Arizona Press, 1981), p. 63:

> Ecological neglect is epitomized by the divers who strip the tropical subtidal regions of their populations of colorful animal life, especially taking corals and snails. . . . I do not mean in any way to condemn all SCUBA diving, but I do suggest that it might best be used for observational or scientific purposes, not for plundering nature. Corals are particularly fragile animals and are susceptible to quick death from such environmental factors as excessive rain (or fresh water runoff) and petroleum pollution.

See also pp. 61–62, 64, 400–401.

210 Experiments show that limpets in exposed situations home much more quickly than those in protected areas, and that probably selection favors those molded to a specific indentation, since they are more difficult to pry off; see M. Edmunds, *Defence in Animals* (Essex, England: Longman Group, 1974), p. 54. Hilary B. Moore, *Marine Ecology* (New York: John Wiley & Sons, 1958), pp. 61 and 364, found that limpets near shore are relatively taller than those seaward, suggesting that those in the wetter habitat do not need to lock onto the rock so tightly to avoid desiccation, and as a result the shell, "secreted by a more widely expanded mantle, had a flatter shape."

See Isabella A. Abbot and George J. Hollenberg, *Marine Algae of California* (Stanford: Stanford University Press, 1976), and E. Yale Dawson, "A Review of the Ecology, Distribution, and Affinities of the Benthic Flora" in "Symposium: The Biogeography of Baja California and Adjacent Seas. Part II. Marine Biotas," eds. J. Wyatt Durham and Edwin C. Allison, *Systematic Zoology* 9(2) (1960), pp. 94–96, 99.

214– Miguel del Barco, *Natural History of Baja California* (Los Angeles: Dawson's Book Shop, 15 1980), pp. 250–63 gives a thorough account of pearl fishing at the time of the Jesuit missionaries, as well as a listing of the various applicants for licenses and exploration. See also Martínez, pp. 220–21 and 433–34, and Michael Mathes, ed., *The Pearl Hunters of California 1668* (Los Angeles: Dawson's Book Shop, 1966), pp. 10–17.

Quote, p. 214, Ascensión, p. 307.

Quote, 215, Barco, p. 254. The royal *quinto,* or one-fifth of the worth to the crown, applied also to gold and precious metals, and presumably to anything else of value. See also Wagner, ed., "Pearl Fishing Enterprises in the Gulf of California," *Hispanic American Historical Review* 10(2) (1930), p. 198. As to whether the king ever got his *quinto,* Baegert, p. 45:

> The Lord only knows whether this one-fifth share of all the pearls fished out of the California ocean netted the Catholic King one hundred and fifty or two hundred pesos year after year, even if everything was done without cheating. I have only heard it said of two men, whom I also know, that they had something worth while after more than twenty years of pearl fishing. The others were just as poor after their pearl fishing as they had been before.

Chapter 12. Cape Beach

217 Willard Bascom, *Waves and Beaches* (Garden City, NY: Doubleday, 1964), pp. 200–206. I wish someone would write an illustrated field guide on the size, shape, location, and pattern of holes in the sand and their inhabitants.

218– W. J. Gertsch, *American Spiders* (New York: D. Van Nostrand, 1949), pp. 201–2: jumping

page

19 spiders do not have the enlarged hind legs that frogs and grasshoppers do; Gertsch thinks their extreme lightness makes the extra musculature unnecessary. Richard C. Brusca, *Common Intertidal Invertebrates of the Gulf of California* (Tucson: University of Arizona Press, 1980), p. 352: 3 species of *Pellenes* are found on Gulf beaches.

220– John Gerard, *Gerard's Herball. The Essence Thereof distilled by Marcus Woodward* (from
21 the edition of Th. Johnson, 1636) (London: Spring Books, 1964), pp. 283–85.

221 See C. L. Caster, "The Air Sac Systems of the Anhinga and Double-crested Cormorant," *Auk* 90(2) (1973):324–40.

221– For "rock lobsters" (as opposed to the large-clawed Atlantic lobsters), frequent on the
23 west coast of the peninsula and sought after since they are very meaty, see C. H. Townsend, "Voyage of the Albatross to the Gulf of California," *Bulletin of the American Museum of Natural History* 35 (1916), pp. 444–45; and Carl L. Hubbs, "The Marine Vertebrates of the Outer Coast," in "Symposium: The Biogeography of Baja California and Adjacent Seas: Part II. Marine Biotas," eds. J. Wyatt Durham and Edwin C. Allison, *Systematic Zoology* 9(2) (1960), p. 137.

223 See Steve A. Glassell, "The Templeton Crocker Expedition XI. Hermit Crabs from the Gulf of California and the West Coast of Lower California," *Zoologica* 22 (1937), pp. 242–43, and Robert D. Barnes, *Invertebrate Zoology* (Philadelphia: W. B. Saunders, 1974), pp. 443–44.

224 H. H. Behr, "Lepidoptera from San José del Cabo," *Zoe* 1 (1890), p. 246; evidently the indefatigable T. S. Brandegee collected more than plants:

> The species enumerated above were collected by Mr. T. S. Brandegee, in the southern extremity of Baja California, in August and September, 1890. His time being occupied almost exclusively by the collection and study of the plants of that most interesting region, the entomological collection consists chiefly, of course, of such as came into his possession by favoring chance.

225 See John D. Soule, "The Distribution and Affinities of the Littoral Marine Bryozoa (Ectoprocta)," in "Symposium: The Biogeography of Baja California and Adjacent Seas. Part II. Marine Biotas," eds. J. Wyatt Durham and Edwin C. Allison, "Systematic Zoology" 9(2), pp. 101–2: 50 percent of the Gulf bryozoa are tropical and strongly Panamic; 34 percent are warm temperate species and 16 percent from cool waters; this fauna extends northward from Cabo San Lucas to Magdalena Bay, where there is a transition to colder water species.

229 V. Fretter and A. Graham, *A Functional Anatomy of Invertebrates* (London: Academic Press, 1976), pp. 490–91:

> Torsion consists of a rotation of the visceral hump upon the head-foot so that what starts as its posterior surface, facing backwards over the hinder margin of the foot, is twisted forwards to become its anterior surface, facing forwards over the head. This has the effect of bringing the original left side to the right and the original right side to the left and of introducing a spiral turn into the narrow neck of tissue which connects the base of the visceral hump to the dorsal surface of the head-foot. This particular twist has nothing whatsoever to do with the spiral coiling of the gastropod shell, and is shown by all structures running from the one part of the body to the other in this region. From the relationship of the structures involved to one another, and from observation of its occurrence during development, it can be said that the direction of rotation of the visceral hump on the head is always counter-clockwise when the animal is viewed from above with the head anteriorly.

> Quote, Walter E. Bryant, "A Catalogue of the Birds of Lower California, Mexico,"

page

Proceedings of the California Academy of Sciences, 2nd ser. 2 (1889), p. 245.
Quote, Beebe, p. 191. William Brewster, "Birds of the Cape Region of Lower California," *Bulletin of the Museum of Comparative Zoology* 41(1) (1902), p. 92; Brewster finds it "apparently resident and about equally numerous at all seasons in the Cape Region." See also Joseph Grinnell, "A Distributional Summation of the Ornithology of Lower California," *University of California Publications in Zoology* 32 (1928), pp. 113–14. See also K. W. Kenyon, "Breeding Populations of the Osprey in lower California," *Condor* 49 (1947):152–58.

233 Edwin Way Teale, *The American Seasons* (New York: Dodd, Mead, 1976), p. xv.

Chapter 13. Tidepools

235– The name of Costa's hummingbird is a whole history in itself: Louis Marie Pantaleón
36 Costa, Marquis de Beau-Regard, was an amateur ornithologist (who collected hummingbirds) and archaeologist, a Sardinian historian and military leader, and present at many delicate nineteenth-century negotiations. See T. S. Palmer, "Costa's Hummingbird—Its Type Locality, Early History, and Name," *Condor* 20 (1918):114–16. William Brewster, "Birds of the Cape Region of Lower California," *Bulletin of the Museum of Comparative Zoology* 41(1) (1902), pp. 112–13, describes Costa's hummingbirds as thriving at low altitude in "barren, waterless tracts."

238 The Mexican government owns all beach land 100 meters up from high-tide mark, and all must be accessible to the public.
    After writing this chapter, I saw this beach five weeks after a hurricane. It, like other beaches near the tip of the Cape, lost a foot to a foot and a half of sand; here the granite base beneath was bared. Boulders rimming the beach were scoured clean, and the powerful surf had tossed some topsy turvy. On top there were only a few very small periwinkles and nerites, all nestled in cracks and crevices in the rock; underneath, except for three or four minute limpets, the rocks were empty. There were no brittle stars, no chitons, no flat worms, no sea cucumbers. Three months later, recolonization was well under way: chitons were back, brittle stars—though not yet in numbers—nudibranchs and anemones and others were present, and if not as numerous as before the storm, there still enough there to feel that they were well on their way back.
    Rachel Carson, *The Edge of the Sea* (Boston: Houghton Mifflin, 1955), p. 47:
    Though other elements of the intertidal world come and go, this darkening stain is omnipresent. The rockweeds, the barnacles, the snails, and the mussels appear and disappear in the intertidal zone according to the changing nature of their world, but the black inscriptions of the microplants are always there.

238– A primary treatment of zonation is that of T. A. Stephenson and Anne Stephenson, "The
40 Universal Features of Zonation Between Tide Marks on Rocky Coasts," *Journal of Ecology* 37(2) (1949), pp. 293, 297–98, 302–303; they identify (pp. 292–95) *Verrucaria maura* as the prevalent lichen. Robert Zottoli, *Introduction to Marine Environments* (St. Louis: C. V. Mosby, 1978), pp. 125–27; pp. 96–97, points out that the fungal partner of *Verrucaria* has very thick cell walls.
    The zonation scheme of Richard C. Brusca, *Common Intertidal Invertebrates of the Gulf of California* (Tucson: University of Arizona Press, 1981), pp. 26–28, is the most applicable; he differentiates 4 zones and lists the species most likely to be found in each in the Gulf of California.

241 John Xantus, letter to Spencer Baird, April 7, 1860:
    You will oblige me much, by calling the next bird—in my name—Kubinijii, in honor of

page

the Honorable August Kubinji, Director of the Hungarian National Museum. He is a very worthy gentleman, he saved the whole museum from the depredations of Genl Haynau, and he is since my childhood my true friend.

Instead, this sun star commemorates him; Xantus was clearly hoping for a position with the museum when he left Mexico. Steinbeck and Ricketts, p. 378, called it "the most common, obvious, and widely distributed shore starfish in the Gulf, often high in the intertidal."

243   Brusca, pp. 326–46, has a section on beach insects generally overlooked in most guides.

255   See Fred C. Ziesenhenne, "The Templeton Crocker Expedition. X. Echinoderms from the West Coast of Lower California, the Gulf of California and Clarion Island," *Zoologica* 22 (1937), p. 210.

Quote, Miguel del Barco, *The Natural History of Baja California* (Los Angeles: Dawson's Book Shop, 1980), pp. 274–75. Myra A. Keen with James H. McLean, *Sea Shells of Tropical West America* (Stanford: Stanford University Press, 1971), pp. 552–53.

Ducrue, in *The Natural and Human History of Baja California,* ed. Homer Aschmann (Los Angeles: Dawson's Book Shop, 1966), p. 45:

The fish or shellfish, so famed in antiquity, from which purple dye was obtained was found to occur on the Gulf Coast at the time of discovering by sea, and since then this shellfish has been seen and recognized in several places along the coast. In regard to its dye three things have been noticed: The first is an almost unbearable odor which is given off by the flesh when it is pressed and which stays in the stuff which has been dyed. Second, at first the dye is between green and yellow then it comes to be reddish in color then it changes to a beautiful violet. In addition it is not a fast color.

257–   If this blenny is *Labrisomus xanti,* then it was named after John Xantus by T. N. Gill in
58   1860. See also Donald A. Thomson, Lloyd T. Findley, and Alex N. Kerstitch, *Reef Fishes of the Sea of Cortez* (New York: John Wiley & Sons, 1979), p. 183; J. H. Todd, "The Chemical Language of Fishes," *Scientific American* 224(5) (1971), pp. 100–103; and Boyd W. Walker, "The Distribution and Affinities of the Marine Fish Fauna of the Gulf of California," in "Symposium: The Biogeography of Baja California and Adjacent Seas. Part II. Marine Biotas," eds. J. Wyatt Durham and Edwin C. Allison, *Systematic Zoology* 9(2) (1960), p. 128.

259   Steinbeck and Ricketts, p. 293, found the Panamic fauna quite well defined, with the southern limit well marked at 4°30′ and the northern limit generally at Cabo San Lucas, at 23°, but extending in favorable situations as far north as Magdalena Bay.

For Sally Lightfoot crabs, *Grapsus grapsus*—"crab crab," see Brusca, pp. 292–300; Jocelyn Crane, "The Templeton Crocker Expedition. III. Brachygnathous Crabs from the Gulf of California and the West Coast of Lower California," *Zoologica* 22 (1937), p. 77.

J. S. Garth, "Distribution and Affinities of the Brachyuran Crustacea," in "Symposium: The Biogeography of Baja California and Its Adjacent Seas. Part II. Marine Biotas," eds. J. Wyatt Durham and Edwin C. Allison, *Systematic Zoology* 9(2) (1960), pp. 106, 113–14, 118–20, finds that almost half of the crab species of the Pacific and the Gulf of California are Panamanian in affinity, 40 percent are indigenous, and 12 percent of northern origin.

Quote, Steinbeck and Ricketts, pp. 62–63.

260   If radioactively tagged carbon compounds are taken up by the colonial anemone *Zonathus,* 25–30 percent of the photosynthetically fixed carbon is back in the anemone within three hours, the carbon moving first into the algae and then back into the tissue of the animal; the rate at which this is done and the amount of carbon involved is "surprisingly

high," according to V. Fretter and A. Graham, *A Functional Anatomy of Invertebrates* (London: Academic Press, 1976), p. 88.

Leland R. Lewis and Peter E. Ebeling, *Sea Guide Volume II: BAJA* (Newport Beach, CA: SEA Publications, 1971), p. 186: mean high-water interval at the Cape is 8 hours, 8 minutes; the greatest range is 6.8 feet and the mean rise and fall is 2.8 feet, in contrast to the northern Gulf of California, where the tidal range is considerable. Tide charts can be ordered from the Superintendent of Documents, Washington, DC; The Department of Ecology and Evolutionary Biology at the University of Arizona puts out a Tide Calendar for the northern Gulf.

Chapter 14. Beneath the Sea

265   Quote, Miguel del Barco, *Natural History of Baja California* (Los Angeles: Dawson's Book Shop, 1980), p. 243 fn., letter to Father Procurator Ignacio Lizasoain, October 15, 1764.

A "long-snouted red crosshatch fish" was taken in 1952 off Bahía de San José del Cabo and proved to be the fourth recorded specimen of the genus *Oxycirrhites* and a then-undescribed species later named *O. seftoni*. Since the genus had previously been found only in the far western Pacific, this finding extended its range more than 8,000 miles, according to James E. Bohlke and John C. Briggs, "The Rare Cirrhitid Fish Genus *Oxycirrhites* in American Waters," *California Fish and Game* 392(3) (1953):375–80.

268   Walter E. Bryant, "A Catalogue of the Birds of Lower California, Mexico," *Proceedings of the California Academy of Sciences,* 2nd ser. 2 (1889), pp. 257–58, found them fishing in the company of large numbers of frigate birds that kept trying to rob them, and described one fishing (p. 258):

> With slow, laborious strokes and bill extended, he rises to a suitable height to enable him to see the fish beneath the rippled surface, then flying with measured beats as though he meant to go miles away, a fish is suddenly discovered near the surface, the wings partially collapse, and with a heavy plunge, a loud splash as he strikes, and the water flies upward. It is all over in a moment, the bird shakes his plumage, adjusts the wings, and sitting sedately upon the water with the bill drawn back close to the neck, the tip just below the surface, holding a wiggling fish for a few moments, then with an upward toss of the bill, the fish disappears in the pouch, there is a slight rustle of the plumage, a satisfactory shake of the tail and the fisher is ready for the next.

A. W. Anthony, "General Ornithological Notes. 1. Nesting Habits of the California Brown Pelican *(Pelicanus californicus),*" *Proceedings of the California Academy of Science* 2nd ser. 2 (1889), pp. 83–85, found 20–30 nests clustered together, clogged with accumulated filth of generations of pelicans. In one he found "hundreds of pounds of small fish . . . having been disgorged entirely undigested." See also D. W. Anderson, J. J. Hickey, R. W. Risebrough, D. F. Hughes, and R. E. Christensen, "Significance of Chlorinated Hydrocarbon Residues to Breeding Pelicans and Cormorants," *Canadian Field-Naturalist* 84 (1969):351–56; D. W. Anderson, J. R. Jehl, Jr., R. W. Risebrough, L. A. Woods, Jr., L. R. Deweese, and W. G. Edgecomb, "Brown Pelicans Improved Reproduction off the Southern California Coast," *Science* 190(1975): 805–8; and J. R. Jehl, Jr., "Studies of a Declining Population of Brown Pelicans in Northwestern Baja California," *Condor* 75 (1973): 69–79.

270   See Boyd W. Walker, "The Distribution and Affinities of the Marine Fish Fauna of the Gulf

page

of California," in "Symposium: The Biogeography of Baja California and Adjacent Seas. Part II. Marine Biotas," eds. J. Wyatt Durham and Edwin C. Allison, *Systematic Zoology* 9(2) (1960), pp. 126–33, who cites a high proportion—17 percent—of endemics; Panamic species make up 73 percent of the total species, and San Diegan, 10 percent.

273 Quote, Antonio de la Ascención, "Father Antonio de la Ascensión's Account of the Voyage of Sebastián Viscaíno," ed. Henry R. Wagner, *California Historical Society Quarterly* 7(4) (1928), p. 307.

278 Quote, Johann Jakob Baegert, *Observations in Lower California* (Berkeley: University of California Press, 1952), p. 42. See Stanley C. Williams, "Scorpion Fauna of Baja California, Mexico: Eleven New Species of Vejovis (Scorpinida; Vejovidae)," *Proceedings of the California Academy of Sciences* 37(8) (1970):275–331. *Vejovis vittatus* is one of the new species "found throughout the southern part of the peninsula from Comondu to Cabo San Lucas. It was one of the most frequently encountered of all the Vejovis species."

280–81 Quote, Ken C. Macdonald and Bruch P. Luyendyk, "The Crest of the East Pacific Rise," *Scientific American* 244(5) (1981), p. 104.

CHRONOLOGY

1492	Columbus "discovers" America.
1510	García Ordóñez de Montalvo publishes *Las Sergas de Esplandian* which becomes source for name of California.
1516	Charles I becomes King of Spain and Netherlands and is elected Emperor Charles V of the Holy Roman Empire in 1517.
1517–24	Cortés occupies Mexico.
1521	Magellan discovers the Phillippines and is killed there, his men imprisoned.
1528	Charles V orders Cortés to send out an expedition to search for Jofre de Loaysa, who was shipwrecked in the Phillippines in 1525, and to develop a trade route across Pacific; Spanish ships reach East Indies but are unable to return eastward across the Pacific to Mexico.
1530	First recorded landing of Europeans on Baja California; Fortun Jiménez leads a mutiny, sails into La Paz Bay, and is killed by Indians.
1535	Cortés sails to La Paz, names it Santa Cruz. New Spain is organized to be ruled by crown-appointed Spanish-born viceroys.
1537	Francisco de Ulloa sails up Pacific Coast to Cedros Island and is not heard from again.
1542–43	Juan Rodríguez Cabrillo explores the Pacific coast of North America as far north as southern Oregon; finds site of what will become San Diego.
1556	Charles V abdicates; Philip II begins Spain's "Golden Century."
1558	Elizabeth I becomes Queen of England.
1565	Lopez de Legaspi conquers the Philippines; Esteban Rodríguez and Father Andrés de Urdaneta pioneer homeward route for Manila galleons across northern Pacific taking advantage of the Japanese Current.
1566	Annual roundtrip voyage of Spanish galleons established between Acapulco and Manila, with the Cape Region of Baja California becoming an important landfall.
1572	Spain claims the Philippines and develops Manila into a key port, receiving goods from China and spices from the Moluccan Islands.
1573	Philip II issues *cédula* that all exploring expeditions must be licensed by the Spanish crown.
1578–80	Sir Francis Drake enters Pacific, raids American littoral, ending Spanish domination of Pacific; names North American coast "New Albion," and completes circumnavigation of the globe.

1587	Spain's relations with England, under Elizabeth I, deteriorate; Thomas Cavendish captures Manila galleon *Santa Ana* at Cabo San Lucas.
1588	Spanish Armada defeated.
1593	Crown assumes jurisdiction of galleons which are henceforth supported at royal expense.
1596	Sebastián Vizcaíno sails to La Paz hoping to explore the peninsula.
1602-03	Vizcaíno explores west coast of California and northward; discovers Monterey Bay.
1609	Fray Antonio de la Ascención, who accompanied Vizcaíno, recommends to king establishing a settlement at the Cape for convenience of returning galleons.
1665	All further private exploration in Baja California forbidden by royal decree of Charles II.
1668	Francisco de Lucenilla receives license to take expedition to Baja California; attempts to establish settlement near La Paz but fails; in 1683 his second application to explore denied.
1683-85	Admiral Isidro de Atondo y Antillón applies and receives permission to explore peninsula but abandons attempt after difficulties with Indians. Father Eusebio Francisco Kino founds Mission San Bruno.
1697	Father Jaun Salvatierra, with permission of the crown, arrives at Loreto to establish first permanent Jesuit mission.
1701	Kino goes north, from Sonora to mouth of Colorado River, ascertains that Baja California is a peninsula; dies in Sonora in 1711.
1701-13	War of Spanish Succession heavily financed by returns from Manila galleons.
1708-09	Woodes Rogers, English privateer, attacks and captures Spanish galleon *Encarnación* at Cape; publishes his account in 1718 as does his companion captain, Edward Cooke.
1719-21	George Shelvocke and John Clipperton, hoping to emulate Roger's success, raid along western Mexican coast and Lower California, about which Shelvocke publishes an account very much resembling Rogers's.
1720	Padre Juan Ugarte explores California coastline in *El Triunfo de la Santa Cruz*, first ship built in the Californias. Padre Jaimé Bravo establishes mission at La Paz.
1721	Mission founded at Santiago, to which Padre Lorenzo Carranco comes in 1726.
1724	Mission founded at Todos Santos.
1726	Royal *cédula* on galleon dimensions (keel 117 ft, beam 39 ft, 300-ton capacity) little observed.
1730	April 8, Father Nicolás Tamaral founds mission at San José del Cabo. Philip II issues a *cédula* allowing only two galleons per year to sail between Acapulco and Manila.
1732	First Manila galleon stops at Cape on homeward trip and receives food and water from Tamaral's mission; the Captain recommends that this be made an obligatory stop.
1734-37	Great Pericu uprising at the Cape. Fathers Carranco and Tamaral murdered in 1734 by Indians at Santiago and San José del Cabo respectively. First rutter published in Manila, covers coastline from San Diego to Cabo San Lucas.
1736	Galleon lands at Cape, passengers and crew murdered by Indians.
1739	Miguel Venegas publishes *Empresas apostólicas de los Padres Misioneros de la Compañía de Jesus, de la Provincia de la Nueva España, obradas en las Conquista de California*, compiled from missionaries' letters and reports, the first book about Baja California (Venegas never saw the peninsula).
1742-44	Epidemics of smallpox, measles, syphilis at Cape; remaining Pericu from Todos Santos and San José restricted to Santiago.
1748	La Paz abandoned as a mission.

1757	Andrés Marcos Burriel makes extensive revisions and publishes Venegas's *Historia o Noticia de la California* (Burriel never visited the peninsula).
1767	Charles III issues *cédula* expelling Jesuits from Spanish domains.
1768	Jesuits depart from peninsula in February; Gálvez, Viceroy of New Spain, sends expedition to Alta California to establish Spanish presence there.
1768–71	Franciscans serve as missionaries on peninsula, going northward to establish missions in Alta California, leaving Baja California with great relief and rejoicing.
1769	Abbot Chappe d'Auteroche head of Spanish scientific expedition to Cape to measure transit of Venus across the sun; dies in San José.
1780	First settlement established at Monterey, and Spanish interest shifts to the north.
1771–1846	Dominicans serve as missionaries on peninsula.
1772	Jesuit Johann Jakob Baegert, who served on the peninsula 1751–1768, publishes *Nachtrichten von der Amerikanischen Halbinsel Californien* in Mannheim.
1773	Galleons directed to put in at Monterey and to bypass the Cape.
1777	Separation of Baja and Alta California into two provinces.
1784–1800	Sealers and whalers visit coast of Lower California.
1789	Jesuit Francisco Xavier Clavijero, scholarly historian who did not serve on peninsula, compiles *The History of Lower California,* published posthumously in Italy by his brother as *Storia della California.*
1790	Miguel del Barco dies, having served on the peninsula 1738–1768; his *Adiciones y Correcciones a la Noticia de Miguel Venegas* published posthumously.
1791–92	First botanical trip to peninsula made by José Longinos Martínez.
1804	California becomes province of Mexico.
1811	La Paz resettled.
1813	Ferdinand VII cancels the Manila galleon trade.
1810–21	Mexican Wars of Independence.
1815	Last voyage of Manila galleon.
1817	Bad hurricane and flooding at San José del Cabo.
1821	Baja California becomes part of Territory of California; Mexico proclaims itself an empire, independent of Spain.
1822	San José del Cabo looted by armada of Lord Thomas Cochrane.
1830	Missions ordered secularized to become "pueblos"; La Paz becomes capital of Baja California Sur.
1833	Law passed to secularize all missions.
1835	President Andrew Jackson's offer to buy northern California refused.
1836	Battle of the Alamo.
1837	One of first collections of vertebrates when Herr F. Deppe collects birds and mammals on the peninsula.
1839	*H.M.S. Sulphur* exploring the Pacific Coast of peninsula; Richard Brinsley Hinds, surgeon, makes botanical collection, published in 1844 by George Bentham, English botanist, reporting on 78 new plant species.
1841–42	Russian botanist Voznesenskii collects on Gulf side of peninsula.
1843	Daniel Webster's offer, as Secretary of State, of $20 million for Baja California is turned down.
1845	James Polk's offer to buy Lower California for $40 million spurned.
1846	U.S. declares war on Mexico.
1847	Lt. José Antonio Mijares, a Spaniard, killed at San José del Cabo trying to storm an American position; at the Battle of Buena Vista General Winfield Scott captures Mexico City.
1848	Treaty of Guadalupe Hidalgo ends war; by it, the United States gains Texas, California, and New Mexico territory, cancels Mexican debt and pays $15 million.

1848–49	William Redmond Ryan, English sailor, publishes letters home as *Personal Adventures in Upper & Lower California.*
1853	"Colonel" William Walker claims "Republic of Lower California" for the United States.
1855	*Ley Juárez* abolishes special jurisdiction of military and ecclesiatic courts in civil cases, followed in 1856 by *Ley Lerdo* which authorized church lands to be sold, limited corporation holdings, redistributed Indian *ejidos*, etc.
1857	New constitution of Mexico adopted and Benito Juárez becomes President of Mexico.
1858	Lower California declares itself an independent territory of Mexico.
1859	Juárez, determined to destroy economic power of church, confiscates church property, suppresses monastic orders, etc.
1859–61	John Xantus at Cabo San Lucas as U.S. Tidal Observer, collecting for the Smithsonian Institution.
1866–67	J. Ross Browne explores peninsula for Lower California Company which had land grants from the Mexican government for more than two-thirds of the peninsula.
1879–80	Melitón Vargas y Gutiérrez to peninsula to adjudicate dispute between church and local government; finds ecclesiastic affairs in dire shape and recommends withdrawal of Baja California's Vicariate Apostolic status which is not restored until 1921.
1887–88	M. Abbot Frazor spends 9 months at Cape, collects 4,400 birds for William Brewster at Harvard, who publishes "Birds of the Cape Region of Lower California" in 1902.
1888	Lower California divided into Norte and Sur "districts."
1888–94	California Academy of Sciences begins a systematic program of exploration in Baja California and the adjacent islands, carried out by Walter Bryant, A.W. Anthony, Gustav Eisen collecting for CAS and T. S. Brandegee collecting on his own; collecting stops when Academy runs out of funds for expeditions.
1895	U.S. Biological Survey Expeditions touch on Baja California.
1903–10	U.S. fleet uses Magdalena Bay for coaling, drills, and target practice.
1905–06	First scientific expedition mounted by U.S. National Museum, under direction of Edward W. Nelson, Chief of Bureau of Biological Survey, U.S. Department of Agriculture, with E. A. Goldman. traveling the entire length of the peninsula; report not published until 1922.
1906	San Francisco earthquake destroys much of CAS collections of Baja California material.
1910	Mexican Revolution begins.
1911	C. H. Townsend, U.S. Bureau of Fisheries, on *U.S.S. Albatross,* collects plants, fish, mammals, invertebrates, reptiles, insects, and small number of algae.
1918	Revolution ends. Hurricane partially wrecks La Paz; two U.S. ships reported lost.
1920	U.S. suspends diplomatic relations after fall of Carranza government; Obregón becomes president of Mexico; emphasizes building schools, economic stability, recognizes labor unions (CROM).
1923	William M. Mann makes first extensive insect collection in the southern part of the peninsula.
1927	First road opened between San José del Cabo and San Lucas.
1929	Dr. Ira Wiggins begins botanical work on peninsula, culminating in *Flora of Baja California,* published in 1980.
1931	Lower California separated into Norte and Sur territories.
1933	1,250,000 hectares recovered from foreign grants and returned to Mexican ownership.

1934	First Allan Hancock Foundation Expedition, resulting in a series of papers on the area.
1936	William Beebe on the Templeton Crocker Expeditions, oversees the publication of a series of scientific papers in cooperation with the American Museum of Natural History.
1938	Michelbacher and Ross, collecting for CAS, take 50,000 insect species; John Steinbeck and Ed Ricketts make collecting trip that becomes *Sea of Cortez*, published in 1941.
1940	President Cárdenas distributes 45 million acres to the *ejidos;* by 1942 nearly half the land under cultivation is held in *ejidos* rather than private holdings.
1941	Disastrous hurricane in September destroys San Lucas with great loss of life.
1952	Northern territory of Baja California becomes Mexico's 29th state; Baja California Sur remains a territory because it lacks 80,000 minimum population for statehood.
1958	Lower California determined to be second only to Mexico City in having the largest number of automobiles per capita.
1961	Joseph Wood Krutch publishes *The Forgotten Peninsula*.
1975	Baja California Sur population reaches 83,433 and the territory becomes a state.

PLANTS OF THE CAPE REGION

Of the 2,958 plant species that Dr. Ira L. Wiggins lists in *Flora of Baja California*, almost 40 percent (around 880) of these grow at the Cape. At the Cape some 272 endemics make for a higher degree of endemism, 30.9 percent, than for the peninsula as a whole. Endemic species are marked with an *. Plants are listed alphabetically by scientific family name with the English equivalent at the end of this list. Common names, both English and Spanish, are given when possible, for which I am deeply indebted to Dr. Wiggins who searched his field notes, and Miss Annetta Carter, University Herbarium, University of California at Berkeley.

Blooming times are indicated by months:

JA	January	MY	May	SP	September
FB	February	JN	June	OC	October
MR	March	JL	July	NV	November
AP	April	AU	August	DC	December

In some instances, plants bloom only after rains, or may be expected any time of year, indicated by RAIN and YEAR.

In an effort to give the most likely habitats in the simplest fashion, it has seemed most flexible to cite a basic habitat (first column) with or without a modifying adjective following in the second and third columns:

A	Arroyo	W	Wet, all of which are fresh-	V	Valley/Ravine
B	Beach		water unless designated as	L	Lagoon/Estuary
H	Hillside/Cliffs	SW	Saltwater	P	Plains
M	Meadow/Fields	R	Roadside/Waste Places	AK	Alkaline
S	Sand	W	Woods	R	Rocky
D	Dry	D	Desert	SC	Scrub/Thicket
M	Moist/Damp	C	Canyons	G	Gravelly

The most common designation is H D/R—a dry and rocky hillside; A M indicates a seepy or damp habitat in an arroyo.

Because some Cape plants can be found only at certain altitudes, such as the flora growing high in the Sierras de la Laguna or Victoria, the following altitudinal designations may sometimes be used:

MT Mountains   FT Foothills   SL Sea level

Some plants have been introduced and escaped, and these are so indicated. For definitive information, see Dr. Wiggins' *Flora of Baja California*, and Paul C. Standley, *Trees and Shrubs of Mexico*, 5 parts (Washington, D.C.: U.S. Government Printing Office, 1920–1926).

Common and Scientific Names		Habitat	Blooming Times	Spanish Name
ACANTHUS FAMILY (Acanthaceae):				
Hummingbird flower	Beloperone californica	H	S/D	AU-MY	Chuparosa
*Hummingbird flower	B. purpusii	H	R/D	NO-AP	Chuparosa
Berginia	See Holographis				
Carlowrightia	Carlowrightia arizonica	H	R/D	MR-MY	
Carlowrightia	C. californica	H	D/G	ANY	Aretito
Carlowrightia	C. cordifolia	H	D/S	AU-NO	
Carlowrightia	C. pectinata	H	D/R	FB-NO	
*Dicliptera	Dicliptera formosa	H	D/R	SP-MY	
Dicliptera	D. resupinata	S	R/S	SP-MY	
Dyschoriste	Dyschoriste decumbens	C		OC-MY	Hierba de la vibora
Elytraria	Elytraria imbricata	H	D/R	SP-MY	Cordoncillo
Henrya	Henrya insularis	H/A	R/S	FB-MY	
Holographis[1]	Holographis virgata var. virgata	D		FB-MY	
*Holographis	H. v. var. glandulifera	H	R/D	NO-AP	
Jacobinia	Jacobinia spicigera	H/A	R/G	OC-JN	Mohuitli, Hierba azul
*Justicia	Justicia insolita var. insolita	A/H		OC-AP	
*Justicia	J. i. var. tastensis	H	D/R	DC-MY	
*Justicia	J. palmeri	H	D/R	AU-MR	
Ruellia	Ruellia leucantha	H	D/R	OC-MY	
Ruellia	R. peninsularis	H	D/R/G	OC-AP	Rama parda
Tetramerium	Tetramerium fruticosum	A	R/S	OC-MY	
Tetramerium	T. hispidum	C	M/W	SP-JN	
AGAVE FAMILY (Agavaceae):				
*Century Plant	Agave aurea	H	D/R	DC-MR	Mescal
*Century Plant	A. datylio var. datylio	MT		NV-JA	Mescal
Century Plant	A. promontorii	MT/FT		DC-MR	Mescal
Century Plant	A. sullivanii	CULTV		NV-FB	Mescal
*Nolina[2]	Nolina beldingii	MT/W	R	AP-MY	Palmita
*Yucca	Yucca valida	H	D/S	MR-AP	Datilillo
AIZOON FAMILY (Aizoaceae Family):				
Ice plant	Mesembryanthemum crystallinum	S/D	S	MR-OC	Flor de sol, Molina
Ice plant	M. nodiflorum	S/D	S	AP-NV	Flor de sol, Molina
Carpet-weed/ Indian chickweed	Mollugo verticillata	R/S	S/D	MY-NV	
Horse purslane	Trianthema portulacastrum	R/B	S/D	JN-NV	Verdolaga blanca

Common and Scientific Names		Habitat	Bloom-ing Times	Spanish Name
AMARANTH FAMILY (Amaranthaceae):				
Alternanthera	*Alternanthera repens*	R	S/G	AU-NV	
Pigweed	*Amaranthus fimbriatus*	D	S	AU-NV	
Pigweed	*A. palmeri*	R/D	S/G	AU-NV	Quelite
Pigweed	*A. spinosus*	R	S/G	JN-OC	Quelite espiroso
Pigweed	*A. watsonii*	S/D	S	AU-SP	
*Celosia	*Celosia floribunda*	S/G		MR-OC	Cresta de gallo, Bledo
Dicraurus	*Dicraurus alternifolius*	H	D/R	JL-SP	
Froelichia	*Froelichia interrupta*	H	D/R	MR-OC	
Gomphrena	*Gomphrena sonorae*	MT		AU-MR	
Iresine	*Iresine augustifolia*	A/C	R/G	JA-AP	
Iresine	*I. calea*	A/H	R/G	NV-FB	
AMARYLLIS FAMILY (Amaryllidaceae):				
*Behria	*Behria tenuiflora*	H	D/R	SP-MR	
BATIS FAMILY (Batidaceae):				
Saltwort	*Batis maritima*	B	SW/S	JY-OC	
BEGONIA FAMILY (Begoniaceae):				
*Begonia	*Begonia californica*	C	MT	SP-OC	
BIGNONIA FAMILY (Bignoniaceae):				
Bignonia	*Bignonia unguis-cati*	A/V	SC	RAINS	Bignonia
Desert Willow	*Chilopsis linearis*	A/C	S	AU-AP	Mimbre
Trumpet Bush	*Tecoma stans*	A/V	S/G	RAINS	Palo de arco
BIRTHWORT FAMILY (Aristolochiaceae):				
*Dutchman's pipe	*Aristolochia monticola*	V		JY-SP	Yerba del Indio
Dutchman's pipe	*A. porphyrophylla*	A/H	R/S	JY-SP	Yerba del Indio
BLACK MANGROVE FAMILY (Avicenniaceae):				
Black mangrove	*Avicennia germinans*	L		NV-MY	Mangle negro, Mangle salado
BLUEBELL FAMILY (Campanulaceae):				
*Heterotoma	*Heterotoma aurita*	C/FT	S/D	DC-MY	
Lobelia	*Lobelia laxiflora* var. *angustifolia*	MT	R	AP-OC	Jarritos, Aretitos
Triodanis	*Triodanis biflora*	SL	S/G	AP-MY	
BORAGE FAMILY (Boraginaceae):				
Bourreria	*Bourreria sonorae*	H	R/S/D	NV-JA	Juanita, Vanita, Chocolatillo
Coldenia	*Coldenia cuspidata*	A	R/S	AU-SP	
Cordia	*Cordia brevispicata*	C/A	S	OC-AP	Trompillo
*Cryptantha	*Cryptantha echinosepala*	SL/FT	S	FB-AP	
Cryptantha	*C. grayi* var. *cryptochaeta*	P	D/S	SP-JA	Espumila

Common and Scientific Names		Habitat		Blooming Times	Spanish Name
*Cryptantha	C. pondii	P	S	FB-AP	
Heliotrope, Chinese Pusley	Heliotropium curassavicum var. oculatum	B/V	S	YEAR	Heliotropo Cimorrón, Cola de mico, Robo de mica
Heliotrope, Chinese Pusley	H. procumbens	A	S/SW	AU-MY	
Tournefortia	Tournefortia hartwegiana	C/A	R/S	NV-AP	Ortiguilla
Tournefortia	T. volubilis	S	S	OC-MY	

BOX FAMILY (Buxaceae):

Goatnut	Simmondsia chinensis	H/A	D	FB-MY	Jojoba

BUCKTHORN FAMILY (Rhamnaceae):

Colubrina	Colubrina triflora	H	D/R	AP-SP	
Colubrina	C. viridis	H/A	D/S	SP-OC	Palo colorado
Condalia	Condalia globosa var. globosa	A/P	G/S	OC-NV	Sarampión
Condaliopsis	Condaliopsis lycioides var. canescens	D		AP-JN	
*Condaliopsis	C. rigida	P	S	AP-MY	
Goatnut	Simmondsia chinensis	H/A	D	MY	Jojoba
Gouania	Gouania rosei	SC		JY-SP	
Karwinskia	Karwinskia humboldtiana	A/H	R	MR-OC	Cacachila
Karwinskia	K. parvifolia var. pubescens	H	D	AP-JY	
Zizyphus	Zizyphus sonorensis	A/D/P		AU-SP	

BUCKWHEAT FAMILY (Polygonaceae):

Coralvine	Antigonon leptopus	H/A	D/S	AP-NV	San Miguel, San Miguelito
Buckwheat	Eriogonum fasciculatum var. polifolium	H	R/D	MR-OC	
Buckwheat	E. inflatum var. deflatum	FT/MT	D/R	FB-AP	
Knotweed	Polygonum hydropiperoides var. asperifolium	SL	M	MY-OC	Chilillo
Knotweed	P. punctatum	W		MY-OC	
Dock, Sorrel	Rumex crispus	R/H	M/W	YEAR	
Dock, Sorrel	R. inconspicuus	W		YEAR	

BUTTERCUP FAMILY (Ranunculaceae):

*Buttercup	Ranunculus harveyi var. australis	MT	M/W	JY-SP	Boton de oro
Clematis	Clematis drummondii var. californica	R	R/SC	MR-SP	Chilillo
*Meadowrue	Thalictrum peninsulare	MT/W	D/W	JL-SP	

CACTUS FAMILY (Cactaceae):

*Bartschella	Bartschella schumannii	H	D/D/S	MY-SP	
*Cochemia	Cochemia poselgeri	C/H	R/S	JY-AU	

Common and Scientific Names		Habitat	Bloom- ing Times	Spanish Name
*Strawberry Cactus Hedgehog	*Echinocereus brandegeei*	H/P	R/S	JY-OC	Casa de rata
Hedgehog	*E. sciurus*	H/P	S/G	AP-JY	
*Barrel cactus	*Ferocactus townsendianus* var. *townsendianus*	P	D/S	MY-AG	Viznaga
*Organ Pipe Cactus	*Lemaireocereus thurberi* var. *littoralis*	B	S/R	AP-JY	Pitahaya
Organ Pipe Cactus	*L. t.* var. *thurberi*	DH/S	AP-JY	AP-JY	Pitahaya dulce
Old Man Cactus	*Lophocereus schottii* var. *australis*	H/B	S	JN-SP	Garambullo
Old Man Cactus	*L. s.* var. *schottii*	H/P	R/S	AP-AU	Garambullo
Galloping Cactus	*Machaerocereus gummosus*	H	R/S/G	JY-AU	Pitahaya agria
*Pincushion	*Mammillaria albicans*	D	S	JY-AU	Junco
*Pincushion	*M. arida*	H/A	D/S	JN-JY	
*Pincushion	*M. baxteriana*	H/B	R/G/S	AP	Bisnaguita
*Pincushion	*M. capensis*	H	R/G	AP-MY	
Pincushion	*M. dioica*	H	D/G	AP/JY	Biznaga
*Pincushion	*M. evermanniana*	B	R/G	AP-MY	
*Pincushion	*M. gatesii*	S	G	MR-AP	
*Pincushion	*M. hutchinsoniana*	A/H	D/S/G	AP	
*Pincushion	*M. peninsularis*	H/P	G/S/R	AP-MY	
*Pincushion	*M. petrophila*	MT/V		AP-MY	
*Pincushion	*M. phitauiana*	H,FT	R	AP	
*Candelabra	*Myrtillocactus cochal*	H/C		YEAR	Cochal
Prickly pear	*Opuntia bravoana*	W/DC	R/S	MY-JY	Nopal, Tuna
*Prickly pear	*O. brevispina*	H	R	MR-JN	Nopal, Tuna
*Prickly pear	*O. burrageana*	H/V	D	SP-MY	
Cholla	*O. cholla*	D/H	R/S	AP-MY	Cholla
*Prickly pear	*O. ciribe*	D	R	AP-MY	Ciribe
*Prickly pear	*O. invicta*	B	S/G	AP-MY	
*Prickly pear	*O. tapona*	H/A	R/S	AP-MY	
*Prickly pear	*O. tesajo*	H/A	D/S	MY-JN	
Cardón	*Pachycereus pecten-arboriginum*	D/P	D/S	MR-AP	Cardón hecho, Cardón-barbón
Cardón	*P. pringlei*	DP	D/S	AP-JU	Cardón
*Cactus	*Peniocereus johnstonii*	B	S	FB-MR	
*Cactus	*Pereskiopsis porteri*	P/H	SC/S	SP-OC	
Wilcoxia	*Wilcoxia striata*	P	S/SC	JY	

CALTROP FAMILY (Zygophyllaceae):

Fagonia	*Fagonia californica*	P/D	S/R	SP-AP	
*Fagonia	*F. villosa*	C/H	G/S/R	FB-MY	
*Guaiacum	*Guaiacum unijugum*	H/S	S/R	AU-SP	Guayacán
Kallstroemia	*Kallstroemia californica*	A	S/RS	MY-OC	

Common and Scientific Names		Habitat		Bloom-ing Times	Spanish Name
*Kallstroemia	*K. peninsularis*	P	S/G	AU-MR	
Creosote bush	*Larrea tridentata*	H/P/A	S	FB-AP/ YEAR	Gobernadora
Tribulus	*Tribulus cistoides*	B/P	S	JY-OC	Abrojo de tier-ra caliente
Tribulus	*T. terrestris*	R	S/G	JY-OC	
CAPER FAMILY (Capparidaceae);					
Atamisquea	*Atamisquea emarginata*	A/P	S	MR-AP	Palo hediondo
Beeplant	*Cleome guianensis*	P/H/A	S	JY-DC	Barbona
Beeplant	*C. tenuis* subsp. *tenuis*	P	S	MY-AU	
Forchammeria	*Forchammeria watsonii*	D	R/S	MR-AP	Palo San Juan
Wislizenia	*Wislizenia refracta* var. *mammillata*	B	S	MY-OC	
CATTAIL FAMILY (Typhaceae):					
Cattail	*Typha domingensis*	M/A	W	MY-JY	Maza de Aqua
CLIMBING FERN FAMILY (Schizaeaceae):					
Climbing fern	*Anemia hirsuta*	MT	R		
COMBRETUM FAMILY (Combretaceae):					
Conocarpus	*Conocarpus erecta*	L/B	SW	SP-DC	Mangle prieta
Laguncularia	*Laguncularia racemosa*	B	S	JY-OC	Mangle chino, Mangle blanco
COTTON-TREE FAMILY (Bombaceae):					
Kapok	*Ceiba pentandra* (Introduced)	INTR		FB-MR	Ceiba, Ceibo, Pochote
DAISY/ASTER FAMILY (Asteraceae):					
*Alvordia	*Alvordia brandegeei*	H	D/G	SP MY	
*Alvordia	*A. fruticosa*	FT		MR-AP/NV-JA	
*Amauria	*Amauria brandegeana*		R/S	OC-AP	
Ragweed	*Ambrosia ambrosioides*	C	S	FB-MY	Hierba amar-gosa, Chicura
*Ragweed	*A. bryantii*	A/P	S/R/G	JN-AP	
*Ragweed	*A. carduacea*	H/C/A	D/R	YEAR	
Ragweed	*A. chenopodifolia*	H	D	FB-MY	
Aster	*Aster spinosus*	A	W	MY-DE	Buena mujer
Baccharis	*Baccharis glutinosa*	A/P	W	MR-DC	Huatamote*
Sweetbush	*Bebbia juncea* var. *atriplicifolia*	H/C	R	YEAR	Ápa
Sweetbush	*B. j. juncea*	A	R/S	YEAR	Ápa
*Beggar's ticks	*Bidens amphicarpa*	MT/M	W	JY-OC	
Beggar's ticks	*B. aurea*	M	D/W	JY-OC	
Beggar's ticks	*B. bigelovii* var. *pueblensis*	MT/FT	M/W	JY-OC	
Beggar's ticks	*B. lemmonii*	MT	M/W	JY-OC	
*Beggar's ticks	*B. leptocephala* var. *hammerlyae*	FT	DW	AU-OC	

Common and Scientific Names		Habitat		Bloom-ing Times	Spanish Name
Beggar's ticks	*B. leptocephala* var. *leptocephala*	W	D	AU-OC	
*Beggar's ticks	*B. nudata*	MT/M/W	D	JY-SP	
Beggar's ticks	*B. pilosa* var. *radiata*	M	D	AU-SP	Aceitilla, Te de milpa blanca
Beggar's ticks	*B. tenuisecta*	MT	M	JY-SP	
*Brickellia	*Brickellia brandegeei*	A/H/MT	S/R	SP-JA	
Brickellia	*B. coulteri*	C/H	D/R	SP-MY	Hierba de la Cruz
Brickellia	*B. glabrata*	H/C	R/D	OC-MR	
*Brickellia	*B. hastata*	P	R/S	FB-AP	Apan
*Brickellia	*B. peninsularis*	R/DH/G		OC-AP	
Thistle	*Circum mexicanum*	B/P	S	JA-AU	Abrojo, Cardo
Conyza	*Conyza bonariensis*	S		JN-AU	
Conyza	*C. canadensis*	SL	S	JN-SP	
*Coreocarpus	*Coreocarpus parthenioides* var. *heterocarpus*	P/H	D	DC-AP	
*Coulterella	*Coulterella capitata*	B	R	OC-MY	
*Dogweed	*Dyssodia anthemidifolia*	P	S/G	FB-AP	
*Dogweed	*D. littoralis*	B	S	FB-MY	
*Dogweed	*D. speciosa*	P/B	S/G	YEAR	
False daisy	*Eclipta alba*	F/A	W	MR-NV	
Brittlebush	*Encelia farinosa* var. *phenicodonta*	D/P	S	SP-MY	Incienso
*Brittlebush	*E. f.* var. *radians*	H/P	R	MR-JY	
*Brittlebush	*E. palmeri*	P/A	S	FB-JN	
*Eupatorium	*Eupatorium purpusii*	MT/C	R	FB-AP	
*Eupatorium	*E. peninsulare* var. *epipolium*	MT/H	R	NV-MR	
*Eupatorium	*E. p.* var. *peninsulare*	MT/H	R	NV-MR	
Eupatorium	*E. sagittatum*	C/H	R/D	YEAR	
*Faxonia	*Faxonia pusilla*	MT		SP	
Galinsoga	*Galinsoga ciliata*	MT/M/W		SP-NV	
Galinsoga	*G. parviflora*	MT/M	D	AU-NV	Estrellita, Mercurial
Galinsoga	*G. semicalva* var. *percalva*	MT/W		SP-NV	
Cudweed	*Gnaphalium oxyphyllum*	MT/W	D	MR-DC	Manzanilla del rio
Cudweed	*G. palustre*	V/M	M/W	MR-OC	Bardolobo
Cudweed	*G. pedunculosum*	P/A	S/W	JY-OC	
Cudweed	*G. purpureum*	MM/M	W	JY-AU	
*Gochnatia	*Gochnatia arborescens*	MT/C	R/G	MR-MY	
*Haplopappus	*Haplopappus arenarius*	B	S	MY-OC	
Haplopappus	*H. sonorensis*	P/A	S	MR-DC	Romerillo amargo
*Sunflower	*Helianthus similis*	MT/W		JY-OC	
*Heliopsis	*Heliopsis parviflora* var. *rubra*	C	R	OC-AP	Mirasol

Common and Scientific Names		Habitat		Blooming Times	Spanish Name
*Heterosperma	Heterosperma coreocarpoides	MT/A	R/G	SP-MR	
*Heterosperma	H. xantii	MT	R/S	MR-OC	
Hawkweed	Hieracium fendleri	MT/M	W	MR-MY	Lechuguilla
Hawkweed	H. wrightii	FT	S/G	AU-OC	Lechuguilla
*Hofmeisteria	Hofmeisteria fasciculata var. xantii	B	R	MR-AP	
Burrobush	Hymenoclea monogyra	S/G/R		SP-OC	Romerillo dulce
Hymenoxys	Hymenoxys odorata	A/C	D	JA-JY	
*Malacothrix	Malacothrix xantii	A/H	R/D	SP-MY	Clavelito del monte
*Melampodium	Melampodium sinuatum		DH	AU-NV	
*Nicolletia	Nicolletia trifida	SL	S	NV-MY	
Spanish Needle	Palafoxia linearis var. linearis	B	S	JA-MY	
*Parthenice	Parthenice mollis var. peninsularis		MT/R	FB-AP	Nendo de burro
*Parthenium	Parthenium confertum var. lyratum	R	D	AP-SP	
*Cinchweed	Pectis multiseta var. multiseta	SL	S/R/G	JA-AP	Limoncillo
Cinchweed	P. palmeri	C/H	M	FB-OC	
Cinchweed	P. urceolata	MT	W	JY-OC	
Rock daisy	Perityle californica	MT/C		DC-JN	Manzanilla
*Rock daisy	P. cuneata	B	S	YEAR	
*Rock daisy	P. crassifolia var. crassifolia	B	S	YEAR	
*Rock daisy	P. incompta	D/P	S	NV-JN	
Rock daisy	P. microglossa	H/A	W	YEAR	
Plucea	Plucea adnata	A	D/W	AU-OC	
Plucea	P. odorata	A/P	D/W	YEAR	
Porophyllum	Porophyllum gracile	H/A	D/S	MR-OC	Hierbo del venado
Porophyllum	P. pinifolium	H/A	R	JN-SP	
Porophyllum	P. porfyreum	B	R	OC-MR	
*Porophyllum	P. ochroleucum	A/C	G/R	RAINS	
*Rumfordia	Rumfordia connata	MT/A	W	JY-OC	
Sclerocarpus	Sclerocarpus divaricatus	FT/MT		AU-OC	
Stevia	Stevia rhombifolia	W	W/M	SP-FB	
Marigold	Tagetes filifolia			AU-OC	
*Marigold	T. lacera	MT/W		SP-NV	
Marigold	T. micrantha	MT/W		SP-NV	Anisillo
Marigold	T. subulata	MT/W		SP-FB	
*Trixis	Trixis angustifolia	A	R/S	MR-SP	Falsa arnica, Plumilla
Trixis	T. californica	H/A	R	FB-JN/ OC-NV	Santa Lucia
*Trixis	T. peninsularis	P/H	S/G	JA-MR	
*Crownbeard	Verbesina erosa	H		JY-SP	Capitaneja
*Crownbeard	V. pustulata	MT/C	R	AU-OC	

Common and Scientific Names		Habitat		Bloom-ing Times	Spanish Name
*San Diego sunflower	*Viguiera deltoidea* var. *deltoidea*	P/A/H		NV-AP	
*San Diego sunflower	*V. deltoidea* var. *tastensis*	H/A	R	MR-NV	
*San Diego sunflower	*V. tomentosa*	C/H	R	SP-MR	Tecote
Cockle bur[3]	*Xanthium strumarium*	R/A	S	FB-OC	Abrojo
DOGBANE FAMILY (Apocynaceae):					
*Macrosiphonia	*Macrosiphonia hesperia*	C/H	R/D	AU-NV	Jasmín de la Sierra
Oleander	*Nerium oleander* (Introduced, cultivated)			SUMM	Aldelta, Rosa laurel
Plumeria	*Plumeria acutifolia*	C/FT	D	MR-SP	Cacalosúchil
Stemadenia	*Stemadenia insignis*	ESC		JY-SP	
*Vallesia	*Vallesia laciniata*	C/A	S	DC-AP	Huitatave
Periwinkle	*Vinca rosea* (Escaped)	R/A		YEAR	Maraville de España
DUCKWEED FAMILY (Lemnaceae):					
Duckweed	*Lemna minima*	A	W		Lentejilla
Duckweed	*L. minor*	MT	W		Lentejilla de agua
ELM FAMILY (Ulmaceae):					
Hackberry	*Celtis pallida*	P/H	R	MR-AP	
Hackleberry	*C. reticulata*	A/C/H		MR-AP	Garabato blanco, Bainor, Vainor
EVENING-PRIMROSE FAMILY (Onagraceae):					
Fireweed	*Epilobium adenocaulon* var. *parishii*	A/M	W	JN-SP	
Gaura	*Gaura parviflora*	R/P	S	MY-AU	Linda tarde
*Lopezia	*Lopezia clavata*	A	S/R/W	OC-MY	
Ludwigia	*Ludwigia octovalvis*	A	W	YEAR	
Ludwigia	*L. peploides* subsp. *peploides*	A	W	AP-SP	Verdolaga acuatica, Verdolaga de agua
*Evening-primrose	*Oenothera drummondii* var. *thalassaphila*	B	S	MR-AP	
Evening-primrose	*O. laciniata* subsp. *pubescens*	FT/MT/A	W	JY-AU	
Evening-primrose	*O. tetraptera*	A/H	S/R	MR-AU	Linda tarde
FERN FAMILY (Polypodiaceae):					
Maidenhair fern	*Adiantum concinnum*	MT/C	R		Culatrillo de México

Common and Scientific Names		Habitat		Bloom-ing Times	Spanish Name
Maidenhair fern	*A. poirettei*	MT/W	D		
*Spleenwort	*Asplenium blepharodes*	C	D		
Lip fern	*Cheilanthes lindheimeri*	MT	D		Hierba de la peña
Lip-fern	*C. pyramidalis*	MT	D		
*Lip-fern	*C. peninsularis*	C	D/W		
Wood fern	*Dryopteris patula* var. *rossii*	MT/W	D		
Cloak fern	*Notholaena candida* var. *candida*	MT/W	D		
Cloak fern	*N. lemmonii* var. *lemmonii*	MT			
*Cloak fern	*N. peninsularis*	MT	R		
Cloak fern	*N. standleyi*	MT/C	R/W		
Cliff brake fern	*Pellaea ternifolia* var. *ternifolia*	MT	R		
Cliff brake fern	*P. t.* var. *wrightiana*	C/H	R		
Gold fern	*Pityrogramma triangularis* var. *viscosa*	V	SC/D		
Polypody	*Polypodium guttatum*	MT/C	W		
Polypody	*P. lanceolatum*	MT/W	D		Lengua de ciervo, Mananepile
Thelypteris	*Thelypteris puberula* var. *sonorensis*	MT	D		
Thelypteris	*T. rudis*	MT/C	W		
FIG FAMILY (Moraceae):					
*Fig	*Ficus brandegeei*	MT/C	R/D	DC-FB	Zalate, Higuera silvestre
Fig	*F. palmeri*	C/H	D	DC-AP	Anaba, Higo
FIGWORT FAMILY (Scrophulariaceae):					
Snapdragon	*Antirrhinum cyathiferum*	H	S/G	OC-MY	
Bacopa	*Bacopa monnieri*	M	D/W	YEAR	
Indian paint-brush	*Castilleja bryantii*	A/H	R	MR-AP	
*Clevelandia	*Clevelandia beldingii*	A	S	RAIN	
Conobea	*Conobea intermedia*	H/A	S	SP-NV	
Conobea	*C. polystachya*	H/C	R	FB-AP	
*Galvezia	*Galvezia juncea* var. *foliosa*	C	G/R	NV-MR	
*Galvezia	*G. j.* var. *juncea*	H/B	R/D	FB-OC	
*Galvezia	*G. j.* var. *pubescens*	B		MR-NV	
Toad-flax	*Linaria texana*	C	S/D?	MR-JN	
*Mecardonia	*Mecardonia exilis*	A/M	S/D	MR-AP	
Mecardonia	*M. vandellioides*	A	D/W	MR-SP	
Monkey-flower	*Mimulus dentilobus*	C	W	FB-NV	
Monkey-flower	*M. floribundus*	MT	W	FB-MY	
Monkey-flower	*M. glabratus*	MT/FW		DC-AP	
Monkey-flower	*M. guttatus*	A	W	FB-AU	
Monkey-flower	*M. nasutus*	C	W/S/G	AP-SP	

337

Common and Scientific Names		Habitat		Bloom-ing Times	Spanish Name
Scoparia	*Scoparia dulcis*	A	W/S	NV-AP	Escobilla amarga
Stemodia	*Stemodia durantifolia*	H/A	D/W	YEAR	
Stemodia	*S. pusilla*	A/C/M	D/W/S	NV-FB	
Speedwell	*Veronica peregrina* subsp. *xalapensis*		M	MR-AP	Veronica
FOUR-O'CLOCK FAMILY (Nyctaginaceae):					
Windmills	*Allionia incarnata*	S	S/R	AP-SP	Hierba de golpe
Boerhaavia	*Boerhaavia coccinea*	P	S	JN-SP	Sembecerambe
Boerhaavia	*B. erecta*	R	S/G	JY-AP	
*Boerhaavia	*B. gracillima*	FT		SP-MY	
Boerhaavia	*B. intermedia*	P/H	S/D	JY-SP	
Boerhaavia	*B. maculata*	H/A	S/G	AU-NV	
Boerhaavia	*B. spicata*	S	S	SP-OC	
Boerhaavia	*B. xantii*	H	S/G/R	SP-JN	
Bougainvillea	*Bougainvillea spectabilis* (Escaped)	C/A	D	AP-JY	Azalia de guia
*Commicarpus	*Commicarpus brandegeei*	C/H	R	OC-MR	Guananiquil
Commicarpus	*C. scandens*	H	R	SP-AP	
*Four-o'clock	*Mirabilis exserta*	MT/H		JY-OC?	Arrebolera
Four-o'clock	*M. triflora*	MT/C		OC-AP	
*Pisonia	*Pisonia flavescens*	C		MY-JN	Garabato
FRANKENIA FAMILY (Frankeniaceae):					
Alkalai heath	*Frankenia palmeri*	B	S/SW	NV-MY	Hierba reuma
GENTIAN FAMILY (Gentianaceae):					
*Centaury	*Centaurium capense*	MT/A	D/W	MR-MY	
Centaury	*C. exaltatum*	MT/M	D/W	AP-MY	
*Centaury	*C. nudicaule*	MT/M	D/W	MR-MY	Conchíta
Catchfly gentian	*Eustoma exaltatum*	M	S/A	JN-SP	
GERANIUM FAMILY (Geraniaceae):					
*Geranium	*Geranium flaccidum*	MT/W	D	SP-OC	Alquimila
GOODENIA FAMILY (Goodeniaceae):					
Scaevola	*Scaevola plumieri*			JA-MY	Bosborón, Caralillo
GOOSEBERRY FAMILY (Grossulariaceae):					
*Currant	*Ribes brandegeei*	MT/W	D	DC-AP	Ciruelillo
GOOSEFOOT FAMILY (Chenopodiaceae):					
Iodine bush	*Allenrolfea occidentalis*	S	A	JN-AP	Hierba del burro
Saltbush	*Atriplex barclayana* subs. *barclayana*	B	S/A	FB-JN	
Saltbush	*A. b.* subsp. *sonorae*	B	S/A	FB-JN	

Common and Scientific Names		Habitat		Bloom-ing Times	Spanish Name
Saltbush	A. canescens subsp. canescens	P	D	MR-SP	Cenizo
Saltbush	A. c. subsp. linearis	S	D/A	MY-JY	
*Saltbush	A. magdalenae	P/B	S	FB-MY	
Goosefoot	Chenopodium ambrosioides	R	D	JN-DC	Epazote
Goosefoot	C. murale (Introduced)	R	D	AP-JY/YEAR	

GOURD (SQUASH) FAMILY (Cucurbitaceae):

Brandegea	Brandegea bigelovii	A/C/H	D	MR-MY	
Melon	Citrullus vulgaris (Escaped)	S		AP-AG	Citron, Sandía
Cucumber	Cucumis dipsaceus (Escaped)	A	D	MR-MY	Pepino
*Gourd	Cucurbita cordata	A/P	S/R/G	MR-MY	Calabaza
Cyclanthera	Cyclanthera tamnoides	MT/W	D	JY-OC	
*Echinopepon	Echinopepon minimus	A	R/S	NV-AP	
*Echinopepon	E. peninsularis	A	R/S	DC-MY	
*Ibervillea	Ibervillea sonorae var. peninsularis		S/G/R	AU-NV	Melón coyote
Momordica	Momordica charantia	R	R	YEAR	Cundeamor
*Sicyos	Sicyos peninsularis	FT/H	D	JY-OC	
*Vaseyanthus	Vaseyanthus brandegei	A	S/R	NV-AP	
*Coyote Melon	V. insularis var. inermis	B	S/G	NV-AP	

GRAPE FAMILY (Vitaceae):

Cissus	Cissus trilobata	M	W	MY-AU	Molonqui
Grape	Vitis peninsularis				Narras

GRASS FAMILY (Poaceae):[4]

Aegopogon	Aegopogon cenchroides	MT/H	R	MR-SP	
Spike bentgrass	Agrostis exarata	P	D	JN-AU	
Water bentgrass	A. semiverticillata	MT	D	MY-JN	Castillitos de Agua
Anthephora	Anthephora hermaphrodita	R/M	D	JY-AP	
Three-awn	Aristida adscensionis	H	R	FB-JN	Zacate de agua tres barbas
Three-awn	A. glabrata	H	D/G	JN-MY	
Three-awn	A. schiediana	H	R/DH	SP-OC	
Spidergrass	A. ternipes	S	R/S	OC-AP	Tres aristas argueado
Giant reed	Arundo donax	A	W	MR-SP	Carrizo
Needle grama	Bouteloua aristidoides	A/H	D	JN-OC	Navajita aguja
Sideoats grama	B. curtipendula	H/C	R	AP-OC	Navajita banderilla
Hairy grama	B. hirsuta	H/P	R/D	AU-OC	Navajita velluda
Palmer sandbur	Cenchrus palmeri	B/S	S	MR-AP AU-OC	Huizapol
*Finger grass	Chloris brandegeei	A/R	M	MR-OC	Zacate colorado
Finger grass	Chloris crinita [Escaped]	H	R	JN-OC	
Finger grass	C. virgata	M	M	MR-SP	Zacate mota, Verdillo plumerito

Common and Scientific Names		Habitat	Blooming Times	Spanish Name
Job's tears	*Coix lacryma-jobi* [Cultivated, escaped]		JY-AU	Lagrimas de Job
Bermuda grass	*Cynodon dactylon*	R	AP-AU	Gallitos Pato de gallo
Durban Crow-foot grass	*Dactyloctenium aegypticum*	R D	RAIN	Pato de pollo
Jungle rice grass	*Echinochloa colona*	R/M W	JN-SP	Arroz de monte
Jungle rice grass	*E. crus-galli*	R	JY-OC	
Goose grass	*Eleusine indica*	R D	JY-OC	Zacate guácima
Lovegrass	*Eragrostis spicata*	P S	AU-OC	
Teosinte	*Euchaena mexicana* [Cultivated]		JN-AU	Acecé
Hackelochloa	*Hackelochloa granularis*	R	AU-OC	
Grass	*Heteropogon contortus*	H/R		Retorcido moreno
Glaucous barley	*Hordeum glaucum* [Introduced]	R	MR-MY	
Barley	*H. vulgare* [Escaped]	R	AP-JY	Cebada
Jouvea	*Jouvea pilosa*	P S	JN-SP	
Lasiacis	*Lasiacis ruscifolius*	W	JY-SP	
Sprangletop	*Leptochloa uninervia*	R M/W	JN-OC	
Microchloa	*Microchloa kunthii*	MT/H R	JY-OC	
Littleseed Muhly	*Muhlenbergia microsperma*	S S/R	MR-MY	Zacatón
Pappophorum	*Pappophorum vaginatum*	P/V	JY-SP	Barbón puntiagudo
Dallis-grass	*Paspalum dilatatum*	R	MY-NV	
Hairyseed paspalum	*P. publiflorum*	S/D/A	MR-OC	Camalote velludo
Pereilema	*Pereilema crinitum*	MT G/R	JY-SP	
Reed	*Phragmites australis*	A W	JY-NV	
Pinyon rice grass	*Piptochaetium fimbriatum*	MT/W R	JY-SP	Falso espartillo del pinar
Natal grass	*Rhynchelytrum repens*	B/S S	JY-OC	Zacate natal
Sugar cane	*Saccharum officinarum*	CULTV	AP-OC	Caña de Azúcar
Johnson grass	*Sorghum halepense*	R/M D/W	AP-AU	Zacata Johnson
Sorghum	*S. bicolor*	ESC	AP-AU	Sorgo, Milo maiz
Sand dropseed	*Sporobolus cryptandrus*	W/H R	MY-AU	Zacatón desgranador
Whorled drop-seed	*S. pyramidatus*	B/R S	AU-OC	Zacatón pyramidal
Seashore drop-seed	*S. virginicus*	B D/S	JN-OC	
Spike burgrass	*Tragus berteronianus*	P D	SP-OC	Abrojo espigada
HEATH FAMILY (Ericaceae):				
*Arbutus	*Arbutus peninsularis*	H/C/W	FB-MR	Madroño
HOLLY FAMILY (Aquifoliaceae Family):				
Holly	*Ilex tolucana*	MT/C M	MR-MY	

Common and Scientific Names		Habitat	Blooming Times	Spanish Name
KRAMERIA FAMILY (Krameriaceae):				
Krameria	*Krameria parvifolia* var. *parvifolia*	H/D	S/D	MR-SP	Mezquitillo
Krameria	*K. paucifolia*	H/A	R/S	FB-AU	
LINDEN FAMILY (Tiliaceae):				
Linden	*Triumfetta semitriloba*	H/A	D/M	AU-AP	Cadillo
LIZARD'S TAIL FAMILY (Saururaceae):				
Lizard's tail	*Anemopsis californica*	S	W	MR-AU	Yerba del Mansa
LOASA FAMILY (Loasaceae):				
Eucnide	*Eucnide cordata*	D	S	RAIN	Pega pega
Eucnide	*E. rupestris*	D	S	RAIN	
*Mentzelia	*Mentzelia adhaerens*	H/C/S	R/S	OC-JN	Pega pega
Mentzelia	*M. aspera*	S	S/G/R	JY OC	Pega pega
LOGANIA FAMILY (Loganiaceae):				
*Buddleia	*Buddleia crotonoides*	C/A	M	RAIN	
LOOSESTRIFE FAMILY (Lythraceae):				
Ammania	*Ammania coccinea*		M	MY-SP	
Heimia	*Heimia salicifolia*	C/A		YEAR	Granadillo
Lythrum	*Lythrum acinifolium*	MT/M	M	AP-MY	
*Lythrum	*L. bryantii*	A/P	M	DC MR	
MADDER FAMILY (Rubiaceae):				
Bouvardia	See *Hedyotis*				
Diodia	*Diodia teres* var. *angustata*	A	S/M	MR-JY	
Bedstraw	*Galium microphyllum*	A/H	R	MR-OC	
Bedstraw	*G. uncinulatum*	MT/W		YEAR	
*Hedyotis [5]	*Hedyotis alexanderae*	MT	R	DC-MR	Trompetilla
*Houstonia	*Houstonia asperuloides* var. *asperuloides*	A/S	S	SP-MY	
*Houstonia	*H. a.* var. *brandegeana*	B/P	S	SP-MY	
*Houstonia	*H. arenaria*	B	S	SP-AP	
*Houstonia	*H. australis*	C/A	S/G	OC AP	
*Houstonia	*H. mucronata*	B/A	S	AU-JN	
*Houstonia	*H. peninsularis*	MT/C	R	NV-AP	
*Houstonia	*H. prostrata*	A	G/S	AU-JN	
Mitracarpus	*Mitracarpus hirtus*	A	S	SP-MR	
*Mitracarpus	*M. linearis*	S	S/G	NV-AP	
Mitracarpus	*M. schizangius*	C/A	S	SP-MY	
Randia	*Randia armata*	H	D/R	JY-AU	Papache
Randia	*R. obcordata*	A/H	D/R	JY-AU	Papache
Richardia	*Richardia scabra*	R/S	S/M	SP-FB	Alcatraz
Staelia	*Staelia scabra*	SL	S/G	JA-NV	
MALLOW FAMILY (Malvaceae):				
*Abutilon	*Abutilon aurantiacum*	V/C	R	MR-MY	Polatazo
Abutilon	*A. californicum*	P/C		MR-SP	

Common and Scientific Names		Habitat		Bloom-ing Times	Spanish Name
Abutilon	*A. carterae*	MT/C	R	MR-MY	
Abutilon	*A. palmeri*	C/S		MR-MY	
Abutilon	*A. pringlei*	MT/S	S	MR-MY	
*Abutilon	*A. xantii*	H/A		SP-JN	
Anoda	*Anoda acerifolia*	M		MY-NV	
Anoda	*A. crenatiflora*	MT	R	AU-SP	
Anoda	*A. pentachista*	R/P		JN-OC	
Cotton	*Gossypium barbadense*	ESC		SP-MR	Algodón comun
Cotton	*G. herbaceum*	ESC		SP-MR	Algodón
Cotton	*G. harknessii*	A	S/R	OC-MY	Algodón
Cotton	*G. klotzschianum* var. *davidsonii*	C/H		SP-MY	
Herissantia	*Herissantia crispa*			YEAR	
Hibiscus	*Hibiscus biseptus*	A/P	S/G	AP-OC	
Hibiscus	*H. denudatus*	A/H	D	JA-OC	
*Hibiscus	*H. ribifolius*		S/G	DC-OC	
Horsfordia	*Horsfordia alata*	H/A/PS/R		MR-OC	
Horsfordia	*H. newberryi*	H/P	D	MR-OC	
Horsfordia	*H. rotundifolia*	A/H	R/S	AU-MR	
Malvastrum	*Malvastrum coromandeli-anum*	A/H/C	R	JY-NV	Escoba blanca
Sida	*Sida ciliaris*	S	S/G	AU-DC	
Sida	*S. glutinosa*	R	M	YEAR	
Sida	*S. rhombifolia*	H/R		RAIN	
Sida	*S. xantii*	A/H	S/R	YEAR	
*Mallow	*Sphaeralcea axillaris* var. *violacea*	S		JA-AP	
*Mallow	*S. coulteri* var. *californica*	S		JA-AP	

MALIPIGHIA FAMILY (Malpighiaceae):

Janusia	*Janusia californica*	A/H	S/G	JA-SP	
*Malpighia	*Malpighia diversifolia*	H/A/C	D	AU-OC	
Mascagnia	*Mascagnia macroptera*	H/P	R/S	RAIN	Gallineta
Thryallis	*Thryallis angustifolia*	A/H	R/G	SP-MR	

MANGROVE FAMILY (Rhizophoraceae):

Mangrove	*Rhizophora mangle*	L	W	MR-NV	Mangle Rojo, Mangle colorado

MILKWEED FAMILY (Asclepiadaceae):

Milkweed	*Asclepias albicans*	P/H/A	S/D	MR-JN	Yumete
Milkweed	*A. subulata*	B/P/H	S/D	YEAR	Yumete
Cryptostegia	*Cryptostegia grandiflora* [Introduced, escaped]	M/C	M	OC-MY	
*Cyanchum	*C. peninsulare*	B/P	S/D	NV-FB	
Matelea	*Matelea cordifolia*	A/P	S	AU-OC	Talayote
*Matelea	*M. fruticosa*	H/P	D	SP-NV	
Matelea	*M. pringlei*	H/A	R/S	AU-MR	

Common and Scientific Names		Habitat		Bloom-ing Times	Spanish Name
*Matelea	*M. umbellata*	MT/A		SP-NV	
Metastelma	*Metastelma californicum*	H/A	S/G/R	AU-MR	
Metastelma	*M. pringlei*		S/R/G	RAINS	
Sarcostemma	*Sarcostemma clausum*	C/A	M	YEAR	
Sarcostemma	*S. pannosum*	H/C		JY-NV	

MILKWORT FAMILY (Polygalaceae):

Milkwort	*Polygala apopetala*	H/C	R	FB-MY, JY-SP	Cordoncillo
Milkwort	*P. herlandieri*	P/H		SP-NV	
Milkwort	*P. glochidiata*	P		AU-NV	
*Milkwort	*P. magdalenae*	P	D	MR-MY	
*Milkwort	*P. xantii*	A	D	MR-MY	

MINT FAMILY (Labiatcae):

*Desert lavender	*Hyptis collina*	H/A	R	SP-FB	
*Desert lavender	*H. decipiens*	H/C		OC-MR	
*Desert lavender	*H. emoryi* var. *amplifolia*	C/A	R	SP-AP	Salvia
*Desert lavender	*H. laniflora*	C/A	S/R	SP-MY	Salvia real
Desert lavender	*H. tephrodes*	A/P	R/M	AU-MR	
Pitcher sage	*Lepechinia hastata*	MT/W	M	JN-SP	
Monardella	*Monardella lagunensis*	MT	W	MR-JY?	
Prunella	*Prunella vulgaris* subsp. *lanceolata* [Introduced]	R		MY-SP	
Sage	*Salvia misella*	A/C/H		AU-FB	
Sage	*S. riparia*	A/M/H	M	NV-MR	
Sage	*S. setosa*	M/H		AU-SP	
*Sage	*S. similis*	A/C/H	M	SP-AP	
Stachys	*Stachys bigelovii*	C	M	MR-SP	
Stachys	*S. coccinea*	M/W	M	JA-SP	
*Stachys	*S. tenerrima*	C/P	M	OC-JA	

MISTLETOE FAMILY (Loranthaceae):

*Misteltoe	*Phoradendron digeutianum* [Parasite on many shrubs]	MT		AP-JN	Toji
Phrygilanthus	*Phrygilanthus sonorae* [Parasite on *Bursera* and *Cyrtocarpa*]			OC-DC	

MOONSEED FAMILY (Menispermaceae):

Cissampelos	*Cissampelos pareira*	M/W		RAIN	Pareira brava, Butua

MORINGA FAMILY (Moringaceae):

Moringa	*Moringa oleifera* [Introduced, escaped]			JY-OC	

MORNING-GLORY FAMILY (Convolvulaceae):

Calonyction	*Calonyction aculeatum*	A/C/V		NV-FB	
Calonyction	*C. muricatum*	A/C/V		SP-JA	

Common and Scientific Names		Habitat		Blooming Times	Spanish Name
*Calonyction	*C. tastense*	C/H	R	SP-JA	
Morning-glory	*Convolvulus soldanella*	B	S	AP-AU	
Cressa	*Cressa truxillensis*	S	A	YEAR	
Dodder	*Cuscuta campestris* [Parasite]			MR-DC	Chochear
Dodder	*C. corymbosa* [Parasite]			AG-NV	
Dodder	*C. desmouliniana* [Parasite on *Euphorbia*]			SP-FB	
Dodder	*C. leptantha* [Parasite]			NV-MY	
Dodder	*C. macrocephala* [Parasite]			NV-MY	
Dodder	*C. salina* [Parasite on *Salacornia*]			AP-NV	
Dodder	*C. umbellata* var. *reflexa* Parasite			JN-DC	
Evolvulus	*Evolvulus alsinoides* var. *acapulcensis*	H/P	D	MR-DC	
Evolvulus	*E. sericeus* var. *discolor*	H/P	R	MR-SP	
Exogonium	*Exogonium bracteatum*	H/A	M	DC-MY	
Morning-glory	*Ipomoea hederacea*	A/P	S	MY-DC	
*Morning-glory	*I. jicama*	A/P	S/R	SP-DC	Jicama
Morning-glory	*I. leptotoma*	A/H/M		AG-DC	
Morning-glory	*I. nill*	A/P	S	SP-DC	
*Morning-glory	*I. peninsularis*	A/H		OC-FB	
Morning-glory	*I. perlonga*	A/H		SP-NV	
Morning-glory	*I. pes-caprae*	B	S	DC-AP	Pata de vaca
Morning-glory	*I. purpurea*	A	R/S	MY-NV	
Morning-glory	*I. scopulorum*	A/H	R	SP-DC	Aurora, Yedra movada, Jalapa limoncilla
Morning-glory	*I. stolonifera*	B	S	YEAR	
Morning-glory	*I. triloba*	R/M		SP-FB	
Jacquemontia	*Jacquemontia abutiloides* var. *abutiloides*	H/C/A	R	SP-JN	
*Jacquemontia	*J. a.* var. *eastwoodiana*	C/A/H	R	DC-MY	
Jacquemontia	*J. palmeri*	A/V	S/R	AU-NV	
*Merremia	*Merremia aurea*	H/C	D	YEAR	Yuca
Merremia	*M. quinquefolia*		S/R	SP-MR	
Quamoclit	*Quamoclit pinnata*	P/H/A	SP-JA		
Quamoclit	*Q. coccinea* var. *coccinea*	P/H/A		AU-DC	Cundeamor, Yedra colorado
Quamoclit	*Q. c.* var. *hederifolia*	P/H/A		AU-MR	Chiqueo de monjas

MUSTARD FAMILY (Brassicaceae):

Common and Scientific Names		Habitat		Blooming Times	Spanish Name
*Dryopetalon	*Dryopetalon crenatum*	MT/FT		AU-SP	
Dryopetalon	*D. palmeri*	C/H		FB-MR	
*Lyrocarpa	*Lyrocarpa xantii*	P/A	S/D	AU-OC	
Cress	*Rorippa nasturtium-aquaticum*	A	W	YEAR	Berros

Common and Scientific Names		Habitat		Blooming Times	Spanish Name
OAK FAMILY (Fagaceae):					
*Oak	*Quercus brandegei*	A/V		MR-AP	Encina negra
*Oak	*Q. devia*	MT		FB-MR	Encina negra
,Oak	*Q. reticulata*	MT/M/A		AP-MY	Encina demiel
Oak	*Q. tuberculata*	MT/A/C		MR-AP	Encina demiel
OCOTILLO FAMILY (Fouquieriaceae):					
*Ocotillo	*Fouquieria burragei*	H	D	FB-MR	Palo Adán
Ocotillo	*F. diguetti*	SL	S/G	JA-MY	Palo Adán
OLAX FAMILY (Olaceae):					
Schoepfia	*Schoepfia californica*	D	S	FB-AP	Higuajin
OLIVE FAMILY (Oleaceae):					
*Desert olive	*Forestiera macrocarpa*	C/H	D	FB-MR	
ORCHID FAMILY (Orchidaceae):					
*Arethusa	*Arethusa rosea*	MT	D	JY-OC	
Epipactis	*Epipactis gigantea*	MT/W/M	D	MY-AU	
Malaxis	*Malaxis soulei*	MT/	M	JY-NV	
Malaxis	*M. tenuis*	MT/H	R	JY-OC	
Malaxis	*M. unifolia*	MT	M	JY-OC	
Spiranthes	*Spiranthes cinnabarina*	MT/C	R/M	AU-FB	Cutzis
PALM FAMILY (Arecaceae):					
Coconut	*Cocos nucifera* [T] [Cultivated]	B		FB-MR	Cocotera, Coco de aqua
*Fan palm	*Erythea brandegeei*	A/C		FB-MR	La Palmia, Palma de Taco
Date Palm	*Phoenix canariensis* [T] [Introduced, cultivated]			FB MR	Datil
Date Palm	*P. dactylifera* [Introduced, cultivated]			FB-MR	Datil
*Fan palm	*Washingtonia robusta*	A/C	M/W		Palma
PARSLEY FAMILY (Apiaceae Family):					
Celery	*Apium leptophyllum*	M	M/W	AP-SP	
*Arracacia	*Arracacia brandegeei*	MT	W	AU-JA	Acocote
Eryngium	*Eryngium nasturtiifolium*	P	D	NV-MY	Perejilillo
Hydrocotyle	*Hydrocotyle umbellata*	MT/FT	M/W	MY-DC	Ombligo de Venus
PASSION-FLOWER FAMILY (Passifloraceae):					
Passion-flower	*Passiflora arida* var. *arida*	A/H	R	FB-OC	
*Passion-flower	*P. a.* var. *cerralbensis*	H/A		MR-SP	
*Passion-flower	*P. a.* var. *pentachista*	H/A	R	MR-SP	
*Passion-flower	*P. palmeri*	A/H	R	MR-OC	Granaditos, Bolsita de víbora
PEA/LEGUME FAMILY (Fabaceae):					
*Acacia	*Acacia brandegeana*	A/P	S/D	FB-MR	Vinorama

Common and Scientific Names		Habitat		Blooming Times	Spanish Name
Acacia	*A. cymbispina*	H/P	S/R	JY-NV	
*Acacia	*A. goldmanii*	MT/C	R	MR-MY	Frijollilo
Acacia	*A. farnesiana*	A/P/H	D	AP-NV	Vinorama, Huisache
*Acacia	*A. peninsularis*	P/A	S	MR-AP	Palo Chino
*Aeschynomene	*Aeschynomene nivea*	H/A	R	NV-AP	Bara prieta
*Aeschynomene	*A. vigil*	H/A/P	R/G	DC-FB	
Albizzia	*Albizzia lebbeck* [Introduced]			JY-SP	
Albizzia	*A. occidentalis*	A/V/H		JN-JY	Palo escopeta
*Locoweed	*Astragalus francisquitensis*	MT/W		FB-MY	Cascebelito
Locoweed	*A. nuttallianus* var. cedrosensis	C/H/D	R	JA-MY/ SP-OC	
*Bauhinia	*Bauhinia peninsularis*	B/P	S	AU-SP	
Bauhinia	*B. purpurea* [Introduced]			MR-AP	
Benthamantha	*Benthamantha brandegeei*	DH/R		JY-SP	
*Brongniartia	*Brongniartia peninsularis*	H/A	R/D	SP-NV	
*Brongniartia	*B. trifoliata*	MT/A	R		
*Caesalpinia	*Caesalpinia arenosa*	B/S	S	JA-MR	Barba de gallo
*Caesalpinia	*C. californica*	H/A	D/R	FB-MR/RAINS	
*Caesalpinia	*C. pannosa*	A/H	D	DC-FB	
*Caesalpinia	*C. placida*	H/A	D/R	FB-MR	
*Caesalpinia	*C. pulcherrima* [Escaped]			JY-OC	Flor del camarén, Tabachino
*Fairy duster	*Calliandra brandegeei*	MT/C		AU-OC	Tabachín
*Fairy duster	*C. californica*	H/A	S/G	FB-MY	Tabardillo
*Fairy duster	*C. peninsularis*	H/A	R	NV-MR	
Cassia	*Cassia biflora*	P/H/A	S	OC-AP	
*Cassia	*C. confinis*	D		JA-MR/ OC	Ojasén, Hojasén
Cassia	*C. covesii*	P/A	S	AP-OC	Ojasén
Cassia	*C. emarginata*	H/A	S	YEAR	Palo Zorillo
*Cassia	*C. goldmanii*	MT/C	M	JN-JY	
Cassia	*C. occidentalis*			JY-DC	Bricho, Ecapatli
Cassia	*C. villosa*	A	G/S	AU-MY	
Cercidium	*Cercidium microphyllum*	A/H/P	S/G/R	MR-MY	Dipua
*Cercidium	*C. floridum* subsp. peninsulare	H/V/A	G/S	MR-JN	Palo Verde
Cercidium	*C. praecox*	P/D	S	MR-MY	Palo Brea
Coursetia	*Coursetia glandulosa*	H/A	G/R	MR-AP	Samo Prieto
Crotalaria	*Crotalaria angulata*	R	S/G	JY-OC	
Crotalaria	*C. incana*	R/A	S	JY-OC	
Crotalaria	*C. pumila*	P/R	S/G	AU-OC	Tronadora
Crotalaria	*C. sagittalis*		S/G	SP-AP	
*Dalea	*Dalea chrysorhiza*	S		OC-MY	
*Dalea	*D. divaricata* subsp. *anthonyi*	B	S	NV-MY	

346

Common and Scientific Names		Habitat		Blooming Times	Spanish Name
*Dalea	D. d. subsp. divaricata	P		NV-MR	
Dalea	D. emoryi	D		MR-MY/AU-SP	
*Dalea	D. maritima	B	S	NV-MR	
Dalea	D. parryi	D	D	MR-JN	
Dalea	D. peninsularis	S		NV-AP	
*Dalea	D. tinctoria var. arenaria	H/A	R/S	NV-AP	
*Dalea	D. t. var. tinctoria	H/A	R/S	NV-AP	
*Dalea	D. vetula	S		NV-MR	
Dalea	D. mollis subsp. mollis	S		DC-MY	
Desmanthus	Desmanthus covillei	A/P	G/S	AU-OC	Frutilillo
*Desmanthus	D. fruticosus	H	D	AU-NV	Frutilillo, Dái, Frijolillo
*Desmanthus	D. oligospermus	A/P	G/S	AU-SP	
Desmodium	Desmodium neomexicana	MT/C		AU-SP	
Desmodium	D. procumbens var. exiguum	MT/FT/C/A		AU-SP	
*Desmodium	D. prostratum	MT	M/W	SP-NV	
Desmodium	D. scorpiurus	S		SP-JA	
Desmodium	D. tortuosum	M/H		AU-OC	
Enterolobium	Enterolobium cyclocarpum [Introduced, escaped]	R/C		MR-AP	Parote, Piche
Coral tree	Erythrina flabelliformis	C/H	R	MR-MY/SP	Colorin, Corcho, Coralina
Haematoxylon	Haematoxylon brasiletto	H/A	D/G	RAINS	Brasil, Palo de tinta
*Indigo plant	Indigofera fruticosa	H/C	R	AU-SP	
*Indigo plant	I. nelsonii	H/A	R	AU-SP	
Indigo plant	I. suffruticosa	R		MR-NV	Añil montes
*Leucaena	Leucaena brandegeei	FT		JY-OC	Guaje
Leucaena	L. microcarpa	H/A	R	SP-OC	
Lupine	Lupinus sparsiflorus var. barbatulus	D/A	S/R	JN-AP	
*Lupine	L. s. var. insignitus	D/A	S/R	JY-AU	
*Palo blanco	Lysiloma candida	H/A/V	R/D	MR-MY	Palo blanco
Lysiloma	L. divaricata	H/V		JY-SP	Mauto
Sweet clover	Melilotus indica [Introduced]	R		MR-AU	
Mimosa	Mimosa brandegeei	H	D	JY-OC	
*Mimosa	M. margaritae	S		AP-MY	
Mimosa	M. purpurascens	DH/R		MR-MY/SP-OC	Garabatillo
Mimosa	M. xanti	P	S	MR-MY/SP-OC	Celosa
Neptunia	Neptunia plena	M	M/W	SP-OC	
*Nissolia	Nissolia setosa	MT/C		JY-SP	
Ironwood	Olneya tesota	D		MY-JN	Tesota, Una de Gato
Parkinsonia	Parkinsonia aculeata	A/H	R	AP-MY	Junco, Palo verde, Retama

Common and Scientific Names		Habitat		Blooming Times	Spanish Name
Petalostemon	*Petalostemon evanescens*	P/A	S/D	FB-MR/AU-OC	
Beans	*Phaseolus atropurpureus* var. *atropurpureus*			MR-OC	
Beans	*P. a.* var. *sericeus*			RAIN	
Beans	*P. filiformis*	H/A	S/R	RAIN	
Beans	*P. speciosus*		SC	RAIN	
*Pithecellobium	*Pithecellobium confine*	A/H	G	FB-AP	Palo fierro, Ejotón
Pithecellobium	*P. dulce* [Cultivated]			NV-JN	Guamúchil
Pithecellobium	*P. mexicanum*	A/V	S/D	MR-AP	Chino, Palo chino
Pithecellobium	*P. undulatum*				Ébano
Mesquite	*Prosopis articulata*	H/A	S/G	JA-JN	Mesquite
*Mesquite	*P. palmeri*	A/C	D	SP-MR	Palo hierro, Palo fierro
Psoralea	*Psoralea rhombifolia*	A/H	R	JY-DC	Contra hierba
Rhynchosia	*Rhynchosia minima*	MT/M		RAIN	Negritos
Rhynchosia	*R. praecatoria*	MT/H	R	AP-SP	
Sesbania	*Sesbania exaltata*	R	W	AU-OC	
Sphinctospermum	*Sphinctospermum constrictum*	H/P	S	JY-SP	
Stylosanthes	*Stylosanthes viscosa*	S		FB-SP	
Tamarindus	*Tamarindus indicus*	CULT		RAINS	Tamarindo, Hoaxinus
*Tephrosia	*Tephrosia cana*	MT/C	S/R	MR-AP AU-OC	Barbasco
Tephrosia	*T. palmeri*	H	D/R	JA-MY/AU-OC	
Tephrosia	*T. tenella*	A	S	AP-NV	Añil
Clover	*Trifolium microcephalum*	MT/M/V		AP-AU	
Vetch	*Vicia exigua* var. *hassei*	FT		MR-JN	
Zornia	*Zornia reticulata*	S		AU-OC	

PEPPERWORT FAMILY (Marsiliaceae):

Pepperwort	*Marsilia fournieri*	Ponds			

PERSIMMON FAMILY (Ebenaceae):

*Persimmon	*Diospyros californica* var. *californica*	A	S	JY-AU	Zapote, Chapote
*Persimmon	*D. c.* var. *tonsa*			JY-AU	
*Maba	*Maba intricata*	C	R	JY-AU	Zapotillo

PHLOX FAMILY (Polemoniaceae):

*Gilia	*Gilia palmeri* var. *palmeri*	H/P	R/S	DC-AP	
Linanthus	*Linanthus nuttallii* subsp. *nuttallii*	MT	G	JN-SP	
Loeselia	*Loeselia ciliata*	A/H	D	OC-MY	Hierba de la Virgen

PINE FAMILY (Pinaceae):

Piñon	*Pinus cembroides*	MT/H	D	MR-AP	Piñon

Common and Scientific Names		Habitat		Bloom-ing Times	Spanish Name
PINEAPPLE FAMILY (Bromeliaceae):					
Hechtia	*Hechtia montana*	H	R/D	FB-MR	Datillo
*Ballmoss	*Tillandsia ferrisiana*	MT		OC-NV	
Ballmoss	*T. recurvata*			OC-NV	Heno Pequeño, Gallitos, Agare palo
PINK FAMILY (Caryophyllaceae):					
Achyronychia	*Achyronychia cooperi*	C/P	S	MR AP	
Sandwort	*Arenaria lanuginosa* subsp. *saxosa*	MT/M	M	JN-SP	
*Drymaria	*Drymaria arenarioides* subsp. *peninsularis*	S	S	JY-SP	
*Drymaria	*D. debilis*	A	S/G	NV-MY/AU	
*Drymaria	*D. glandulosa*	H/A	S/G	RAIN	Encaje
*Drymaria	*D. gracilis* subsp. *carinata*	H/C	R/S/G	JY-NV	
*Drymaria	*D. holosteoides* var. *crassifolia*	S	S/G	RAIN	
Drymaria	*D. leptophylla*		S/G	JN-OC/RAIN	
*Drymaria	*D. viscosa*		S	RAIN	
Paronychia	*Paronychia mexicana* subsp. *monandra*	B/P	S	JY-NV	
*Catchfly	*Silene laciniata* subsp. *brandegeei*	MT/M		JY-OC	
Starwort	*Stellaria nemorum*	MT		JN-SP	
PLANTAIN FAMILY (Plantaginaceae):					
Plantain	*Plantago hirtella* var. *galleottiana*	M	W	ANY	
Plantain	*P. linearis* var. *mexicana*	MT/M	W	MR-OC	Lantén
PLUMBAGO FAMILY (Plumbaginaceae):					
Plumbago	*Plumbago scandens*		R	MY-SP	Hierba alacrán, Plumbago blanco
POKEBERRY FAMILY (Phytolaccaceae):					
Petiveria	*Petiveria alliacea*			YEAR	Hierba de las gallinitas, Zorillo
Phaulothamnus	*Phaulothamnus spinescens*	P/H		JY-AU	
Pokeweed	*Phytolacca octandra*	R/M	M	ANY	Conguarán, Japonera, Verbachin
Rivina	*Rivina humilis*	C/A	M/W	ANY	Coral
Stegnosperma	*Stegnosperma halimifolium*	B/H		OC-MY	Hierba del cuervo
PONDWEED FAMILY (Potamogetonaceae):					
Pondweed	*Potamogeton foliosus*	A	W	JY-OC	

Common and Scientific Names		Habitat		Bloom-ing Times	Spanish Name
Pondweed	*P. illinoensis*		W	JN-AU	
Ditch-grass	*Ruppia maritima*	L	W	MR-OC	
POPPY FAMILY (Papaveraceae):					
Prickly poppy	*Argemone gracilenta*	D/P	S/G	DC-JN	Chicalote, Cardo
Prickly poppy	*A. ochroleuca*	A/H/P	S/G	DC-MY	
California poppy	*Eschscholzia mexicana*	P	S/G	FB-MY	Amapola amailla
POTATO FAMILY (Solanaceae):					
Pepper	*Capsicum annuum*	CULT		FB-SP	Chile, Cahúas
Jimsonweed	*Datura inoxia*	H/P/A/C	S	MR-OC	Toloache, Belladona
Lycium	*Lycium berlandieri* var. *peninsulare*	H/V	D	MR-SP	Garambullo
Lycium	*L. brevipes*	A/P	G/S	FB-AP	
Lycium	*L. carolinianum*	V/P	S	SP-MR	Frutilla
Lycium	*L. fremontii* var. *congestum*	A/H	R	AU-SP	
Lycium	*L. f.* var. *fremontii*	A/H	R	FB-MY/AU-SP	
*Lycium	*L. megacarpum*	P/A	R/G/S	FB-MY	
Tomato	*Lycospersicon esculentum* [Cultivated, escaped]			FB-AU	Jitomate
Tree Tobacco	*Nicotiana glauca*	A/P	R/S	YEAR	Levántate Don Juan, Tabaco amarillo
Tree Tobacco	*N. trigonophylla*	A	S/G	YEAR	Tobdeo cimarrón
Ground cherry	*Physalis angulata*	P	S/M	AP-JN	Tomate, Tomatillo
Ground cherry	*P. crassifolia* var. *crassifolia*	A/D	S/G	FB-JN/AU-DC	
*Ground cherry	*P. glabra*	B/S	S	AU-JN	
Ground cherry	*P. nicandroides*	R		FB-AP/AU-NV	
Ground cherry	*P. leptophylla*		S/G/R	JY-OC	
Ground cherry	*P. maxima*	R/A	M/W	JY-OC	
Ground cherry	*P. philadelphica*	P	S	JY-OC	
Ground cherry	*P. pubescens*	R	S	SP-OC	Tomate
Nightshade	*Solaunum hindsianum*	H/A/C	S	AU-AP	Mariola
Nightshade	*S. nodiflorum*		S	YEAR	
PRIMROSE FAMILY (Primulaceae):					
Pimpernel	*Anagallis arvensis*	R/A	M	FB-SP	Anagálide, Hierba del pararo, Saponaria
Centunculus	*Centunculus minimus*	MT	M/W	MR-MY	
Water pimpernel	*Samolus ebracteatus*	MT/V	M/W	DC-MY	
Water pimpernel	*S. vagans*	FT/M	M	AP-AU	

Common and Scientific Names		Habitat		Bloom-ing Times	Spanish Name
PURSLANE FAMILY (Portulaceae):					
Portulaca	*Portulaca halimoides*		S	JN-SP	
Portulaca	*P. lanceolata*	P?	M	JY-SP	
Portulaca	*P. mundula*	A	S/G	MR-MY/JY-SP	
Portulaca	*P. oleracea*	R/H		FB-SP	Verdolaga
Portulaca	*P. parvula*		G	JN-SP	
Portulaca	*P. pilosa*	S/D	S	MR-NV	
Portulaca	*P. suffrutescens*		G	MR-AP	
Talinum	*Talinum paniculatum*	C	R/M	JA-MY	
QUILLWORT FAMILY (Isoetaceae):					
Quillwort	*Isoetes howellii* var. *minima*	MT	W		
Quillwort	*I. h.* var. *howellii*	MT	W		
RAFFLESIA FAMILY (Rafflesiaceae):					
Pilostyles[6]	*Pilostyles thurberi* Parasite on *Dalea*	D		JA-JN	
RIVERWEED FAMILY (Podostemonaceae):					
Oserya	*Oserya coulteriana*	A/V	W	AP MY	
Podostemon	*Podostemon ceratophyllum*	A/V	W	FB-MY	
ROCKROSE FAMILY (Cistaceae):					
Rockrose	*Helianthemum glomeratum*	MT/W		JY-SP	Juanita
Lechea	*Lechea tripetala*	MT/W/C R		JY-NV	
ROSE FAMILY (Rosaceae):					
Alchemilla	*Alchemilla aphanoides* var. *subalpestris*	MT/M	D/M	JY-SP	
Strawberry	*Fragaria mexicana*	MT/W	D/M	MR-AU	Fresa
Christmas berry, California holly	*Heteromeles arbutifolia*	H/V		AP-JY	Toyon, Tollon
Holly-leaved cherry	*Prunus ilicifolia*	H/C/W		AP-MY	Islay
Prunus	*P. serotina* subsp. *virens*	MT		MR-AP	Capulín
Raspberry	*Rubus scolocaulon*	MT/C/V M		MR-SP	
RUE FAMILY (Rutaceae):					
*Esenbeckia	*Esenbeckia flava*	H/C	D/R	AU-SP	Palo amarillo
Zanthoxylum	*Zanthoxylum arborescens*	C/A/V	D/R	SP-OC	
Zanthoxylum	*Z. sonorense*	H	R	FB-MR	
RUSH FAMILY (Juncaceae):					
Rush	*Juncus mexicanus*		M/W	MY-AU	Junco
SALVINIA FAMILY (Salviniaceae):					
Mosquito fern	*Azolla filiculoides*	Pools/streams S			Chilacaxtli
SAPOTE FAMILY (Sapotaceae):					
Bumelia	*Bumelia occidentalis*	A	S	FB-MR	Bebelama
*Bumelia	*B. peninsularis*	C/A		DC-FB	

Common and Scientific Names		Habitat		Bloom-ing Times	Spanish Name
SEDGE FAMILY (Cyperaceae):					
*Sedge	*Carex lagunensis*	MT/M	W		
*Sedge	*C. longissima*	MT/C	R		
Cyperus	*Cyperus aristatus* var. *inflexus*	A/FT	W	JN-NV	Tule
Cyperus	*C. ferax*	D		JY-OC	Tule
Cyperus	*C. hermaphroditus*	MT	M	JY-SP	Tule
Cyperus	*C. ligularis*	A	M/W	AP-SP	Tule
Cyperus	*C. niger* ver. *capitatus*	MT/M	M/W	JY-NV	Tule
Cyperus	*C. perennis*	M/A	M/W	JA-SP	Tule
Cyperus	*C. subambiguus* var. *pallidicolor*		W	JY-SP	Tule
Cyperus	*C. surinamensis*		W	JY-NV	Tule
Cyperus	*C. tenuis*	A	W	JY-NV	Tule
Spikerush	*Eleocharis montevidensis*	MT/C	M/W	MY-SP	
Fuirena	*Fuirena simplex*	A	S/W	AP-OC	
Hemicarpha	*Hemicarpha micrantha*		W	JY-NV	
Scirpus	*Scirpus americanus*	B/A	S/M	MY-AU	Tule
Scirpus	*S. cernuus* var. *californicus*	S/B	M	AP-SP	Tule
Scirpus	*S. olneyi*		W	JU-AG	Tule
SILK-TASSEL FAMILY (Garryaceae):					
*Silk-tassel	*Garrya salicifolia*	MT/W	D	AU-DC	
SOAPBERRY FAMILY (Sapindaceae Family):					
Tronador	*Cardiospermum corindum*	P	A	YEAR	Tronador
*Tronador	*C. spinosum*	H/C	R	RAIN	
*Tronador	*C. tortuosum*	P/D	D/S	RAIN	
Paullinia	*Paullinia sonorensis*	C/H	R	AU-NV	
Sapindus	*Sapindus saponaria*	V	M/W	MY-AU	Matamuchacho
*Serjania	*Serjania californica*	A/H		DC-FB	
SPIKE-MOSS FAMILY (Selaginellaceae):					
Spike-moss	*Selaginella bigelovii*	H	D/R		
Spike-moss	*S. pallescens*	H	D/G		
Spike-moss	*S. lepidophylla*	C	R/G		Siempreviva
SPIDERWORT FAMILY (Commelinaceae):					
Aploleia	*Aploleia monandra*	MT/FT?		AU-NV	
Commelina	*Commelina erecta* var. *angustifolia*	A	D/W	AU-OC	Rosilla
Commelina	*C. e.* var. *crispa*	A	D/W	AU-OC	
Commelina	*C. dianthifolia*	C/A	D/W	JL-OC	
Commelina	*C. diffusa*	C/H/A	M/W	IRREG	
*Gibasis	*Gibasis heterophylla*	MT	M/W	JL-NV	
*Gibasis	*G. linearis*	MT/M/C	M	JL-OC	
*Tinantia	*Tinantia modesta*		M	JL-NV	Hierba del pollo, Felvira
Tradescantia	*Tradescantia peninsularis*		M	JL-NV	Hierba del pollo
Tripogandra	*Tripogandra angustifolia*		M	JL-OC	

Common and Scientific Names		Habitat	Bloom-ing Times	Spanish Name
SPURGE FAMILY (Euphorbiaceae):				
Acalypha	*Acalypha aliena*	M	M	AU-OC	Hierba del cancer
Acalypha	*A. californica*	H/A	D	FB-NV	Hierba del cancer
*Acalypha	*A. comonduana*	H/C	M	MR-OC	Hierba del cancer
Adelia	*Adelia virgata*	H/A	R	AU-OC	Pimentilla
*Andrachne	*Andrachne ciliato-glandulosa*		R/M	OC-AP	
Bernardia	*Bernardia mexicana*	P/H/A	D/R	RAIN	
*Bernardia	*B. lagunensis*	H	R	RAIN	
Tread softly	*Cnidoscolus maculatus*[7]				Caribe
Tread softly	*Cnidoscolus palmeri*	R/S	D/S	MY-JN	Mala Mujer, Ortigilla
*Croton	*Croton caboensis*	H	R/G	AU-OC	
*Croton	*C. boregensis*	FT		unkwn	
Croton	*C. californicus* var. *californicus*	P/H	S/G	FB-OC	
Croton	*C. c.* var. *tenuis*	P/H	S/G	FB-OC	
Croton	*C. ciliato-glanduliferum*	H/C	R/D	MR-NV	Trucha, Xonaxe
*Croton	*C. magdalenae*	C	R	JA-JN	José gris, Durasnillo
Ditaxis	*Ditaxis serrata*	D/A	D/S	FB-NV	
*Spurge	*Euphorbia apicata*	MT/M	S/G/M	JY-AU	Golondrina
*Spurge	*E. brandegeei*	A/H/P	S	AU-MR	Golondrina
*Spurge	*E. californica* var. *californica*	A/H/P	S/G	NV-MR	Liga
*Spurge	*E. c.* var. *hindstana*	H	R/G	RAINS	Liga
Spurge	*E. capitellata*	P/H	R/S	MR-OC	Liga?
*Spurge	*E. dentonsa*	H/A	S	SP-FB	Liga
Bettle spurge	*E. eriantha*	H/A	G/S	FB-NV	Liga
Spurge	*E. heterophylla* var. *graminifolia*	H/A	M	AU-OC	Liga
Spurge	*E. h.* var. *heterophylla*	H/A	M	AU-OC	Liga
*Spurge	*E. h.* var. *eriocarpa*	H/C	R	SP-DC	Liga
Spurge	*E. hyssopifolia*	A	S/G	RAINS	Liga
Spurge	*E. incerta*	B	S	JN-NV	Liga
Spurge	*E. leucophylla*	B	S/D	AU-MY	Liga
*Spurge	*E. magdalenae*	H/A	G/S	FB-OC	Liga
Spurge	*E. pediculifera* var. *pediculifera*	H/A	D	FB-SP	Liga
Spurge	*E. p.* var. *linearifolia*	H	R	MR-OC	Liga
*Spurge	*E. peninsularis*	B	S	OC-MY	Liga
Spurge	*E. polycarpa* var. *intermixta*	H	R/G	RAINS	Liga
*Spurge	*E. p.* var. *mejamia*	A/B	S/D	RAINS	Liga
Spurge	*E. tomentulosa*	H/A	R/S	FB-OC	Liga

Common and Scientific Names		Habitat		Blooming Times	Spanish Name
*Spurge	*Euphorbia xantii*	H/A	D/R	DC-AP	Liga, Jumetón
Jatropha	*Jatropha cinerea*	P/H	R/S	AP/	
				AU-OC	Lomboy, Lombol
*Jatropha	*J. giffordiana*	B	S	AU-SP	
*Jatropha	*J. moranii*		R/S/G	JL-AU	
Jatropha	*J. purpurea*	H	R/G	JL-AU	
*Jatropha	*J. vernicosa*	MT/H	R	JL-AU	Sangre agrado, Sangre de drago
Manihot	*Manihot chlorosticta*		D	JN-OC	Yuca
Wax plant [8]	*Pedilanthus macrocarpus*	P/H/A	D	FB-MY/ AU-OC	Candelilla
Phyllanthus	*Phyllanthus acuminatus*	C/H	M	OC-AP	Ciruelillo
Phyllanthus	*P. galeottianus*	A/H	R	AU-AP	
Castor bean	*Ricinus communis*	A	S	YEAR	Ricino
Sapium	*Sapium biloculare*	A/H	R	MR-NV	Herba de la flecha
Sebastiana	*Sebastiana pavoniana*	C		AU-NV	Palo de la flecha
*Tetracoccus	*Tetracoccus capensis*	H	S	JY-OC	
STAFF-TREE FAMILY (Celastraceae):					
Schaefferia	*Schaefferia cuneifolia*	H	R	AP-JY	Capul
Schaefferia	*S. shrevei*	H/C	R/D	MY-JY	Piel de león
Maytenus [9]	*Tricerma phyllanthoides*	B/L	SW/M	AP-NV	Mangle dulce
STERCULIA FAMILY (Sterculiceae):					
Ayenia	*Ayenia compacta*	H/A	R	SP-AP	
Ayenia	*A. glabra*	H/C/P	R	SP-AP	
*Ayenia	*A. peninsularis*	C/P		JY-NV	
Ayenia	*A. pusilla*		R/G	FB-NV	
Hermannia	*Hermannia palmeria*	H/A	R	JA-AP	
Waltheria	*Waltheria americana*	H/A	R/S		Malva
STONECROP FAMILY (Crassulaceae):					
*Siempreviva	*Dudleya albiflora*	H	R	AP-JN	Siempreviva
STORAX FAMILY (Styraceae):					
Storax	*Styrax argenteus*	MT/C	M	AU-SP	Chilacuate
SUMAC FAMILY (Anacardiaceae):					
*Plum-tree	*Cyrtocarpa edulis*	A	S	MY	Ciruelo
*Lemonade Berry	*Rhus integrifolia* var. *cedrosensis*	H/C		FB-AP	
Sumac, Poison ivy	*R. radicans* var. *divaricata*	A	S	MR-SP	Hiedra
Sumac, Poison ivy	*R. tepetate*	H	R/D	JY-SP	

Common and Scientific Names		Habitat		Blooming Times	Spanish Name
TAMARISK FAMILY (Tamariaceae):					
Tamarisk	*Tamarix* sp.	AR	S	MR-AU	Pino salado
TORCHWOOD FAMILY (Burseraceae):					
Bursera	*Bursera cerasifolia*	H		DC-MR	Copal
Bursera	*B. epinnata*	H	R/S	SP-DC	Copal
*Bursera	*B. filicifolia*	H		AG-SP	
Bursera	*B. hindsiana*	H/A	R/S	SP-OC	Copal
Bursera	*B. microphylla*	H	R/S	JL-AU	Torote, Torote colorado
Bursera	*B. odorata*	H	R	JL-AU	Torote blanco
TURNERA FAMILY (Turneraceae):					
Turnera	*Turnera diffusa*	H/A	S/G	JA-JY	Damiana
Turnera	*T. pumila*		S/G	SP-OC	
UNICORN PLANT FAMILY (Martyniaceae):					
Devil's Claw	*Proboscidea altheaefolia*	S/A	S	MY-AU	Espuela del diablo, Cuernos del diablo
VALERIAN FAMILY (Valerianaceae):					
Valerian	*Valeriana sorbifolia*	MT/M	M	AU-OC	
VERVAIN FAMILY (Verbenaceae):					
*Aloysia	*Aloysia barbata*	A/H		FB-MY	
Citharexylum	*Citharexylum flabelliformis*	H	R/S	SP-MR	
Duranta	*Duranta repens*	A	S	AP-SP	Espina blanca, Garbancillo
Lantana	*Lantana scorta*	MT/A/H		MY-DC	
Lantana	*L. velutina*	MT/A/P	S	MR-DC	Confiturilla
*Lippia	*Lippia formosa*	A/P	R/S/G	DC-AP	Orégano
Priva	*Priva lappulacea*	H/P	M/S	JY-OC	
Verbena	*Verbena carolina*	FT/MT/P/H		JY-OC	Verbena
*Verbena	*V. macrodonta*		G	?	
Verbena	*V. scabra*	M	M/W	MR SP	
VIOLET FAMILY (Violaceae):					
Hybanthus	*Hybanthus attenuatus*	MT/FT	M	JY-AU	
Hybanthus	*H. fruticulosus*	MT	M	JA-MY	
Hybanthus	*H. mexicanus*	MT		JY-AU	
Hybanthus	*H. verticillatus*	H/A	G	DC-MR	
WATERLEAF FAMILY (Hydrophyllaceae):					
Mountain Balm	*Eriodictyon trichocalyx*	H/C		MY-AU	Yerba Santa
Nama	*Nama coulteri*	MT/M	S	NV-MY	Hierba de la punzada
Nama	*N. stenocarpum*	A/C/V	M/S	MR-MY	
*Phacelia	*Phacelia scariosa*	C/H	R	NV-AP	

Common and Scientific Names		Habitat	Bloom-ing Times	Spanish Name
WILLOW FAMILY (Saliaceae):				
*Cottonwood	*Populus brandegeei* var. *brandegeei*	A	M/W	FB-MR	Güeribo
*Cottonwood	*P. b.* var. *glabra*	MT	M/W	FB-MR	Güeribo
Willow	*Salix bonplandiana* var. *bonplandiana*		W	FB-MR	Sauce, Sauz
Willow	*S. taxifolia*	A	D/W	FB-MR	Sauce, Sauz
WOODSORREL FAMILY (Oxalidaceae):				
Oxalis	*Oxalis albicans*	MT/W		MR-SP	
Oxalis	*O. corniculata* (Introduced)	R		MR-NV	Acedera
Oxalis	*O. nudiflora*	A/M	M/S	JY-OC	

1. *Holographis* now replaces *Berginia*, according to Annetta Carter.
2. Wiggins does not list any *Nolinas* for the Cape; N. *beldingii* is, according to Jeanette Coyle, Norman C. Roberts, *A Field Guide to the Common and Interesting Plants of Baja California* (La Jolla: Natural History Publishing Company, 1975), "abundant" on the higher peaks of the Cape Region. I found it more prevalent at La Laguna than on the eastern side of the mountains, but would not call it plentiful.
3. Wiggins (1980) does not list *Xanthium* for the Cape; Brandegee noted it in 1892 and it is to be found in dry arroyo bottoms and waste places.
4. Scientific and vernacular names of the grasses follow Frank W. Gould and Reid Moran, "The Grasses of Baja California, Mexico," *San Diego Society of Natural History, Memoir No. 12* (1981).
5. *Hedyotis* replaces *Bouvardia*, according to Carter.
6. Wiggins says *Pilostyles thurberi* "possibly" ranges into the Cape Region.
7. *Cnidoscolus maculatus* is *C. angustidens* in Wiggins.
8. Wiggins lists *Pedilanthus macrocarpus* "almost to Cape Region," while Coyle and Roberts find it to the "tip of the peninsula."
9. *Tricerma* replaces *Maytenus*, according to Carter.

LATIN TO ENGLISH NAMES

Acanthaceae
  Acanthus
Agavaceae
  Agave
Aizoaceae
  Aizoon
Amaranthaceae
  Amaranth
Amaryllidaceae
  Amaryllis
Anacardiaceae
  Sumac
Apiaceae
  Parsley
Apocynaceae
  Dogbane
Aquifoliaceae
  Holly
Arecaceae
  Palm
Aristolochiaceae
  Birthwort
Asclepiadaceae
  Milkweed
Asteraceae
  Daisy/Aster
Avicenniaceae
  Black Mangrove
Batidaceae
  Batis
Begoniaceae
  Begonia
Bignoniaceae
  Bignonia
Bombacaceae
  Cotton-tree
Boraginaceae
  Borage
Brassicaceae
  Mustard
Bromeliaceae
  Pineapple
Buxaceae
  Box
Cactaceae
  Cactus
Campanulaceae
  Bluebell

Capparidaceae
  Caper
Caryophyllaceae
  Pink
Celastraceae
  Staff-tree
Chenopodiaceae
  Goosefoot
Cistaceae
  Rockrose
Combretaceae
  Combretum
Commelinaceae
  Spiderwort
Convolvulaceae
  Morning-glory
Crassulaceae
  Stonecrop
Curcurbitaceae
  Gourd/Squash
Cyperaceae
  Sedge
Ebenaceae
  Persimmon
Ericaceae
  Heath
Euphorbiaceae
  Spurge
Fabaceae
  Pea/Legume
Fagaceae
  Oak
Fouquieriaceae
  Ocotillo
Frankeniaceae
  Frankenia
Garryaceae
  Silk-tassel
Gentianaceae
  Gentian
Geraniaceae
  Geranium
Goodeniaceae
  Goodenia
Grossulariaceae
  Gooseberry
Hydrophyllaceae
  Waterleaf

Isoetaceae
  Quillwort
Krameriaceae
  Krameria
Juncaceae
  Rush
Labiateae
  Mint
Lemnaceae
  Duckweed
Loasaceae
  Loasa
Loganiaceae
  Logania
Loranthaceae
  Mistletoe
Lythraceae
  Loosestrife
Malvaceae
  Mallow
Malpighiaceae
  Malpighia
Marsiliaceae
  Pepperwort
Martyniaceae
  Unicorn Plant
Menispermaceae
  Moonseed
Moraceae
  Fig
Moringaceae
  Moringa
Nyctaginaceae
  Four-o'clock
Olaceae
  Olax
Oleaceae
  Olive
Onagraceae
  Evening-primrose
Orchidaceae
  Orchid
Oxalidaceae
  Woodsorrel
Passifloraceae
  Passion flower
Papaveraceae
  Poppy

Pinaceae
 Pine
Phytolaccaceae
 Pokeberry
Plantaginaceae
 Plantain
Plumbaginaceae
 Plumbago
Poaceae
 Grass
Podostemonaceae
 Riverweed
Polemoniaceae
 Phlox
Polygalaceae
 Milkwort
Polygonaceae
 Buckwheat
Polypodiaceae
 Fern
Portulacaceae
 Purslane
Potamogetonaceae
 Pondweed
Primulaceae
 Primrose
Rafflesiaceae
 Rafflesia

Ranunculaceae
 Buttercup
Rhamnaceae
 Buckthorn
Rhizophoraceae
 Mangrove
Rosaceae
 Rose
Rubiaceae
 Madder
Rutaceae
 Rue
Saliaceae
 Willow
Salviniaceae
 Salvinia
Sapindaceae
 Soapberry
Sapotaceae
 Sapote
Saururaceae
 Lizard's Tail
Schizaeaceae
 Climbing Fern
Scrophulariaceae
 Figwort
Selaginellaceae
 Spike-moss

Solanaceae
 Potato
Sterculiaceae
 Sterculia
Styraceae
 Storax
Tamariaceae
 Tamarisk
Tiliaceae
 Linden
Turneraceae
 Turnera
Typhaceae
 Cattail
Ulmaceae
 Elm
Valerianaceae
 Valerian
Verbenaceae
 Vervain
Violaceae
 Violet
Vitaceae
 Grape
Zygophyllaceae
 Caltrop

BIRDS OF THE
CAPE REGION

At most, there are around 250 birds that might be seen at the Cape Region and surrounding waters; almost half are sea coast or open sea birds. A small and distinctive group is associated with the high mountains of the Cape, and those common in low scrub and dry open country are often the same or similar species to be found in our southwest.

The list has been checked by Sanford R. Wilbur, Chief of the Division of Endangered Species, U.S. Fish and Wildlife Service, who has a book in preparation on the birds of Baja California. Dr. Richard Beidelmann of The Colorado College has offered comments. Nomenclature has been checked against the American Ornithologists' Union Committee on Classification and Nomenclature, *Check-list of North American Birds,* 5th ed., Baltimore: American Ornithologists' Union, 1957, and "Thirty-fourth Supplement to the American Ornithologists' Union Check-List of North American Birds," Supplement to the *AUK* 99(3) (1982).

For convenience, birds are listed alphabetically by common name, with Spanish names included where known; those birds that are rare or accidental, or have only been sighted a very few times, have their common name set in italics. When a species is present at the Cape is indicated by

W Winter   S Summer   R Resident, year-round   A Accidental   M Migrant

An * signifies that the species is rare. Baja California is not on one of the main waterfowl/shorebird flyways, but many birds follow the Pacific Coast between their wintering and summering grounds.

Following the name, habitats are indicated by the following abbreviations, with the caveat that in order to make this table useful and not overly complex, designations are broad:

OC   Open Country, includes the open semi-desert scrub, a general catch-all for the kind of country that prevails at the Cape.

TH   Thickets, may be cactus, shrubs, or low trees, or any combination thereof, low and thick-growing and often impenetrable.

D   Desert, is predominantly dry and open country with less than 50 percent plant cover.

M   Marsh, or lagoon (S or F may be appended for salt or fresh water)

FW   Freshwater, includes running arroyos or *tinajas,* marshes or lagoons.

OO   Open Ocean, away from the immediate sea coast.

SC   Sea Coast, beaches and inlets, the wide band of interface between land and sea.

TF   Towns and/or Farms, around man's habitations, ranches, etc.

MT   Mountains

OP   Oak-Pinon woodlands; these are invariably in the mountains and the only "woodlands" existing at the Cape.

Wilbur notes that northern birds wintering in the south are usually not as selective about habitat as when on breeding grounds. For more precise delineation of habitat, see John K. Terres, *The Audubon Society Encyclopedia of North American Birds* (New York: Knopf, 1980); Roger Tory Peterson and Edward L. Chalif, *A Field Guide to Mexican Birds* (Boston: Houghton Mifflin, 1973); Emmet R. Blake, *Birds of Mexico: A Guide for Field Identification* (Chicago: University of Chicago Press, 1953); and Ernest P. Edwards, *A Field Guide to the Birds of Mexico* (Sweet Briar, VA: Ernest P. Edwards, 1972). (However, Edwards uses "BC" for the entire peninsula with no differentiation between *Norte* and *Sur;* since this is considerable, the designation is often misleading.)

Season	Common and Scientific Names		Habitat	Spanish Name
A*	Albatross, Black-footed	*Diomedea nigripes*	OO	Albatross Pies Negros
A*	Albatross, Laysan	*D. immutabilis*	OO	Albatros
R*	Auklet, Cassin's	*Ptychoramphus aleuticus*	OO	Alcuela Norteamericana
W	Avocet, American	*Recurvirostra americana*	FW	Piquicurvo
M*	Bittern, Least	*Ixobrychus exilis*	M	Garcilla
M/W	Bittern, American	*Botaurus lentiginosus*	FW	Torcomon
W	*Blackbird, Brewer's*	*Euphagus cyanocephalus*	OC,F	Tordo de Ojos Amarillos
W	Blackbird, Red-winged	*Agelaius phoeniceus*	FW	Tordo Charretero
A	*Bluebird, Western* [1]	*Siala mexicana*	MT	Ventura Azul
R*	Booby, Blue-footed	*Sula nebouxii*	SC/OO	Bubia Pies Azules
R	Booby, Brown	*S. leucogaster*	SC/OO	Bubia Vientre Blanco
A	Booby, Masked	*S. dactylatra*	SC/OO	Bubia Carlazel
W*	Brant, Black	*Branta bernicla*	SC	Ganso de Collar
W	Bunting, Lark	*Calamospiza melanocorys*	OC	Gorrion Canero
M/W	Bunting, Lazuli	*Passerina amoena*	OC	Gorrion Cabeziazul
R	Bunting, Varied	*P. versicolor*	OC/MT	Gorrion Morado
R	Bushtit	*Psaltriparus minimus*	PO/MT	Sastrecito Sencillo
W*	*Canvasback*	*Aythya valisineria*	OO/FW	Pato Coacostle
R	Caracara, Crested	*Polyborus plancus*	OC	Quebrantahuesos, Queleli
R	Cardinal, Northern	*Cardinalis cardinalis*	OC/TH	Cardenal Comun
W	Coot, American	*Fulica americana*	M/F&S	Gallareta Gris
R	Cormorant, Brandt's	*Phalacrocorax penicillatus*	SC	Sargento Guanero
R	Cormorant, Double-crested	*P. auritus*	SC	Cuervo Marino
W	Cowbird, Brown-headed	*Molothrus ater*	OC/TH	Tordo Negro
S*	Cuckoo, Yellow-billed	*Coccyzus americanus*	TH	Platero Piquiamarillo
W*	Curlew, Long-billed	*Numenius americanus*	SC/OC	Picolargo
A	Dickcissel [2]	*Spiza americana*	OC	Gorrion Cuadrillero
R	Dove, Common Ground-	*Columbina passerina*	F/M	Mucuy
R	Dove, Mourning	*Zenaida macroura*	W/F	Huilota Comun
R	Dove, Rock	*Columba livia*	TF	Pichon de las Rocas
R	Dove, White-winged	*Zenaida asiatica*	W/F	Tortola
M/W	Dowitcher, Short-billed	*Limnodromus griseus*	FW/SC	Agachona Gris

Season	Common and Scientific Names		Habitat	Spanish Name
M/W	Dowitcher, Long-billed	*L. scolopaceus*	FW	Agachona Piquilarga
W*	Duck, Ring-necked	*Aythya collaris*	F/SW	Pato Chaparro
W	Duck, Ruddy	*Oxyura jamaicensis*	F/SW	Pato Tepalcate
M/W	Dunlin	*Calidris alpina*	SC	Tinguis Lomo Rojo
R*	*Eagle, Golden*	*Aguila chrysaetos*	OC/MT	Aquila Real
R	Egret, Cattle	*Bulbulcus ibis*	TF/FW	Garza de Ganado
W*	Egret, Great	*Casmerodius albus*	FW	Garzon Blanco
R	Egret, Reddish	*Egretta rufescens*	SC	Garza Melenuda
R	Egret, Snowy	*E. thula*	SC/FW	Garcita Nivea
R	Falcon, Peregrine	*Falco peregrinus*	OC	Halcon Peregrino
R*	Falcon, Prairie	*F. mexicanus*	OC	Halcon Cafe
R	Finch, House	*Carpodacus mexicanus*	TF/TH	Gorrion Comun
R	Flicker, Northern Gilded	*Colaptes auratus mearnsi*	OC	Carpintero Aliamarillo
R	Flycatcher, Ash-throated	*Myiarchus cinerascens*	W/C	Copeton Cenizo
M*	Flycatcher, Dusky	*Empidonax oberholseri*	TH	Mosquerito Oscuro
W	Flycatcher, Gray	*E. wrightii*	OC	Mosquerito Gris
A	Flycatcher, Scissor-tailed	*Tyrannus forficatus*	OC	Papamoscas Tijereta
R	Flycatcher, Vermilion	*Pyrocephalus rubinus*	OC	Cardenalito
R	Flycatcher, Western	*Empidonax difficilis*	MT/OP	Mosquerito Barranqueño
A	Flycatcher, Brown-crested	*Myiarchus tyrannulus*	FT/TH	Copeton Portuguesito
M	Flycatcher, Willow (Trail's)	*Empidonax traillii*	TH	Mosquerito Palido
R	Frigatebird, Magnificent	*Fregata magnificens*	SC	Fregata Magnifica
W	Gadwall	*Anas strepera*	M/F	Pato Pinto
R	Gnatcatcher, black-tailed	*Polioptila melanura*	OC	Perlita Colinegra
R	Gnatcatcher, Blue-gray	*P. caerulea*	W	Perliata Comun
M/W	Godwit, Marbled	*Limosa fedoa*	SC	Agachona Real
W*	*Goldeneye, Common*	*Bucephala clangula*	SC/FW	Pato Chillon Ojos Dorados
M/W	Goldfinch, Lawrence's	*Carduelis lawrencei*	OC	Dominquito de Lawrence
R	Goldfinch, Lesser	*C. psaltria*	PO	Dominiquito Dorado
M/W	Grebe, Eared	*Podiceps nigricollis*	SC	Zambullidor Orejudo
W/A	Grebe, Horned	*P. auritus*	SC	Zambullidor Cornudo
R	Grebe, Least[3]	*Tachybaptus dominicus*	FW	Zambullidor Chico
R/W	Grebe, Pied-billed	*Podilymbus podiceps*	FW/SC	Zambullidor Pico Pinto
W	*Grebe, Western*[4]	*Aechmophorus occidentalis*	F/SM	Achichilique
M/W	Grosbeak, Black-headed	*Pheucticus melanocephalus*	OP	Tigrillo

Season	Common and Scientific Names		Habitat	Spanish Name
W	Grosbeak, Blue	*Guiraca caerulea*	FT/MT	Piquigordo Azul
M/W	Gull, Bonaparte's	*Larus philadelphia*	SC	Apipizca Blanca
W	Gull, California	*L. californicus*	SC/OO	Gaviota Californiana
M*	Gull, Franklin's	*L. pipixcan*	SC	Apipizca de Franklin
W	Gull, Glaucous-winged	*L. glaucescens*	SC	Gaviota de Alas Glaucas
R	Gull, Heermann's	*L. heermanni*	SC	Apipizca de Heermann
W	Gull, Herring	*L. argentatus*	SC	Gaviota Plateada
W	Gull, Laughing	*L. atricilla*	SC	Gaviota Risuena
W	Gull, Ring-billed	*L. delawarensis*	SC	Apipizca Pinta
M*	Gull, Sabine's	*Xema sabini*	OO	Gaviota de Sabine
R	Gull, Western	*Larus occidentalis*	SC	Gaviota Occidental
W	Harrier, Northern	*Circus cyaneus*	M	Gavilan Ratonero
M*	Hawk, Broad-winged	*Buteo platypterus*	OC	Gavilan Aludo
M/W	Hawk, Cooper's	*Accipiter cooperii*	W	Esmerejon de Cooper
W*	Hawk, Ferruginous	*Buteo regalis*	OC	Aguililla Patas Asperas
R	Hawk, Harris'	*Parabuteo unicinctus*	OC	Aguililla Cinchada
	Hawk, Pigeon, see Merlin			
	Hawk, Sparrow, see Kestrel			
R	Hawk, Red-tailed	*Buteo jamaicensis*	OC/MT	Aguililla Ratonera
R*	Hawk, Sharp-shinned	*Accipiter striatus*	W	Esmerejon Coludo
M*	Hawk, Swainson's	*B. swainsoni*	OC	Gavilan Chapulinero
R*	*Hawk, Zone-tailed*	*Buteo albonotatus*	OC/TH	Aguililla Cola Cinchada
R	Heron Black-crowned Night	*Nycticorax nycticorax*	FW/TH	Pedrete Gris
R	Heron, Great Blue	*Ardea herodias*	FW/SC	Garzon Cenizo
R	Heron, Green-backed	*Butorides striatus*	FW	Garcita Verde
W	Heron, Little Blue	*Egretta caerulea*	FW/SC	Garcita Azul
R	Heron, Tricolored	*Hydranassa tricolor*	FW/SC	Garza Flaca
R	Heron, Yellow-crowned Night-	*Nyctanassa violaceus*	FW	Pedrete Enmascarado
R	Hummingbird, Black-fronted[5]	*Hylocharis xantusii*	MT/D	Chuparossa de Xantus
M*	Hummingbird, Broad-billed	*Cyanthus latirostris*		Chupaflor Piquiancho
R	Hummingbird, Costa's	*Calypte costae*	OC/TH	Chupaflor Garganta
M	Hummingbird, Rufous	*Selasphorus rufus*	OP/TF	Chupaflor Dorado
R	Ibis, White	*Eudocimus albus*	SC/FW	Ibis Blanco
M*	Ibis, White-faced	*Plegadis chihi*	M/FW	Atotola
R	Jay, Scrub	*Aphelocoma coerulescens*	OC/TH	Queixque de Ceja Blanca
R	Junco, Yellow-eyed[6]	*Junco phaeonotus*	MT/OP	Ojilumber Mexicano
W*	Junco, Dark-eyed	*J. hyemalis oreganus*	OC/TH	Carbonero Oregonense
R	Kestrel, American	*Falco sparverius*	OC	Cernicalo Chitero

Season	Common and Scientific Names		Habitat	Spanish Name
R	Killdeer	*Charadrius vociferous*	FWM/F/OC	Tildio
W	Kingbird, Cassin's	*Tyrannus vociferans*	OC	Madrugador Chilero
A	Kingbird, Eastern	*T. tyrannus*	OC	Madrugador Viajero
A	Kingbird, Tropical	*T. melancholicus*	OC	Madrugador Abejero
M/W	Kingfisher, Belted	*Ceryle alcyon*	FW/SC	Pescador Norteno
W	Kinglet, Ruby-crowned	*Regulus calendula*	OC/TH	Reyezuelo de Rojo
W*	Kittiwake, Black-legged	*Rissa tridactyla*	OO	Rissa
M*	Knot, Red	*Calidris canutus*	SC	Chichicuilote Canuto
R	Lark, Horned	*Eremophila alpestris*	OC	Alondra
W	Loon, Arctic	*Gavia arctica*	SC	Somorgujo Artico
W	*Loon, Common[7]*	*G. immer*	FW/SC	Somorgujo Comun
W*	*Loon, Red-throated*	*G. stella*	SC	Somorgujo Gargantua
W*	Mallard	*Anas platyrhynchos*	FW	Pato de Collar
S*	Martin, Purple	*Progne subis*	OC	Martin Azul
W	Meadowlark, Western	*Sturnella neglecta*	OC	Triguero de Occidente
W*	Merganser, Hooded	*Lophodytes cucullatus*	SC/FW	Mergo de Caperuza
A	Merganser, Red-Breasted	*Mergus serrator*	SC	Mergo Copcton
M/W	Merlin	*Falco columbarius*	OC	Halconcillo
R	Mockingbird, Northern	*Mimus polyglottos*	OC	Cenzontle Norteño
R	Moorhen, Common	*Gallinula chloropus*	FW	Polla de Agua
R	Murrelet, Craveri's	*Synthliboramphus craveri*	SC/OO	Pato Nocturno
R	Nighthawk, Lesser	*Chordeiles acutipennis*	OC	Tapacamino Halcon
R	Nuthatch, White breasted	*Sitta carolinensis*	MT	Saltapalo blanco
R	Oriole, Hooded	*Icterus cucullatus*	OC/TH	Calandria Zapotera
R	Oriole, Scott's	*I. parisorum*	OC/OW	Calandria Tunera
R	Osprey	*Pandion haliaetus*	SC/FW	Gavilan Pescador
R	Owl, Common Barn	*Tyto alba*	FT/OC	Lechuza Mono
R	Owl, Burrowing	*Athene cunicularia*	OC	Lechucilla Llanera
R	Owl, Elf	*Micrathene whitneyi*	W,D	Tecolote Enano
R	Owl, Great Horned	*Bubo virginianus*	W	Tecolote Cornudo
R	Owl, Northern Pygmy-	*Glaucidium gnoma*	TH	Picametate
R	Owl, Western Screech	*Otus asio*	OC/TH	Tecolotito Chillon
W*	Owl, Short-eared	*Asio flammeus*	F/M	Tecolote Orejas Cortas
R	Oystercatcher, American	*Haematopus palliatus*	SC	Ostrero
R	Pelican, Brown	*Pelecanus occidentalis*	SC	Alcatraz Moreno
M	Petrel, Cook's	*Pterodroma cookii*	OO	
S	Pewee, Western Wood	*Contopus sordidulus*	OC/TH	Tengofrio Comun
R	Phainopepla	*Phainopepla nitens*	OC	Capulinero Negro
M	Phalarope, Red-necked	*Phalaropus lobatus*	OO/M	Chorlillo Norteño
M	Phalarope, Red	*P. fulicaria*	OO	Chorlillo Rojo

Season	Common and Scientific Names		Habitat	Spanish Name
M	Phalarope, Wilson's	*P. tricolor*	FW	Chorlillo Nadador
R	Phoebe, Black	*Sayornis nigricans*	FW/W	Papamoscas Negro
M/W	Phoebe, Say's	*S. saya*	OC	Papamoscas Boyero
R	Pigeon, Band-tailed	*Columba fasciata*	OP	Paloma Ocotera
W	Pintail, Northern	*Anas acuta*	FW/SW	Pato Golondrino
A	Pipit, Red-throated[8]	*Anthus cervinus*	FW	
W	Pipit, Water	*A. spinoletta*	OC/FW	Alondra Acuatica
M	Plover, Black-bellied	*Pluvialis squatarola*	SC	Ave Fria
M*	Plover, Lesser Golden	*P. dominica*	SC	Pluvial Dorado
W*	Plover, Mountain	*Charadrius montanus*	OC	Chichicuilote Montanes
W	Plover, Semipalmated	*C. semipalmatus*	SC/FW	Pluvial Frailecillo
R	Plover, Snowy	*C. alexandrinus*	SC	Chichicuilote Nevado
R	Plover, Wilson's	*C. wilsonia*	SC	Chichicuilote Picquigrueso
R	Poor-will, Common	*Phalaenoptilus nuttallii*	OC	Pachacua Comun
R	Pyrrhuloxia	*Cardinalis sinuata*	OC/TH	Cardenal Torito
R	Quail, California	*Callipepia californicus*	OC	Cordorniz Californiana niana
R	Rail, Clapper	*Rallus longirostris*	M/S/F	Rascon Picudo
M/W	Rail, Virginia	*R. limicola*	M/FW	Rascon de Agua
R	Raven	*Corvus corax*	OC/TH	Cuervo Grande
W*	Redhead	*Aythya americana*	FW/SW	Pato Cabeza Roja
M/W*	Redstart, American	*Setophaga ruticilla*	M/TH	Calandrita
R	Roadrunner, Greater	*Geococcyx californianus*	OC/TH	Correcamino Californiano
R	Robin, American[9]	*Turdus migratorius*	FT	Primavera Real
M/W	Sanderling	*Calidris alba*	SC	Chichicuilote Blanco
M*	Sandpiper, Baird's	*C. bairdii*	FW	Chichicuilote de Baird
M/W	Sandpiper, Least	*C. minutilla*	FW/SM	Chichicuilote Minimo
M*	Sandpiper, Pectoral	*C. melanotos*	FW	Chichicuilote Manchado
M	Sandpiper, Solitary	*Tringa solitaria*	M/FW	Chichicuilote Solitario
M/W	Sandpiper, Spotted	*Actitis macularia*	M/SC/FW	Alzacolita
M/W	Sandpiper, Western	*Calidris mauri*	SC	Chichicuilote Occidental
M/W*	Sapsucker, Yellow-bellied	*Sphyrapicus varius*	OC/PO	Chupasavia
W	Scaup, Lesser	*Anas affinis*	FW/SW	Pato Bola
W	Scoter, Surf	*Melanitta perspicillata*	OO	Negreta de Marejada
M/S	Shearwater, Pink-footed	*Puffinus creatopus*	OO	Fardela
M/S	Shearwater, Sooty	*P. griseus*	OO	Fardela Gris
M/A	Shearwater, Townsend's	*P. auricularis*	OO	Fardela
M*	Shearwater, Wedge-tailed	*P. pacificus*	OO	Fardela Pacifica

Season	Common and Scientific Names		Habitat	Spanish Name
W	Shoveler	*Anas clypeata*	FW	Pato Cucharon
R	Shrike, Loggerhead	*Lanius ludovicianus*	OC/TH	Verdugo
M*	Skua, South Polar	*Catharacta maccormicki*	OO	
M	Snipe, Common	*Gallinago gallinago*	M/F&S	Agachona Comun
M	Sora	*Porzana carolina*	M/F&S	Gallineta de Cienaga
M/W	Sparrow, Black-chinned	*Spizella atrogularis*	TH	Chimbito Carbonero
R	Sparrow, Black throated	*Amphispiza bilineata*	OC	Chiero Barbanegra
M/W	Sparrow, Brewer's	*Spizella breweri*	OC/D	Chimbito de Brewer
W	Sparrow, Clay-colored	*S. pallida*	OC	Chimbito Palido
W*	Sparrow, Golden-crowned	*Zonotrichia atricapilla*	OC/FT	Zacatero Corona Dorada
M/W*	Sparrow, Grasshopper	*Ammodramus savannarum*	OC	Gorrion Chapulin
R	Sparrow, House	*Passer domesticus*	FT	Gorrion Ingles
W	Sparrow, Lark	*Chondestes grammacus*	OC	Chindiquito
M/W	Sparrow, Lincoln's	*Melospiza lincolnii*	MT/TH	Zorzal de Lincoln
R	Sparrow, Rufous-crowned	*Aimophila ruficeps*	OC	Zacatonero Corona Rojiza
M/W	Sparrow, Savannah	*Passerculus sandwichensis*	M	Gorrion Zanjero
M	Sparrow, Song	*Melospiza melodia*	FT/M	Zanjero Cantor
W	Sparrow, Vesper	*Pooecetes gramineus*	OC	Gorrion Torito
W	Sparrow, White-crowned	*Zonotrichia leucophrys*	FT/TH	Zacatero Mixto
A	Spoonbill, Roseate	*Ajaia ajaja*	M/F&S	Espatulata
A	Stork, Wood	*Mycteria americana*	FW/TH	Ciguenon
M*	Storm-petrel, Ashy	*Oceanodroma homochroa*	OO	Petrel Ceniciento
M*	Storm-petrel, Black	*O. melania*	OO	Petrel Negro
M	Storm-petrel, Leach's	*O. leucorhoa*	OO	Petrel Rabadilla Blanca
W*	Storm-petrel, Least	*O. microsoma*	OO	Petrel Minimo
M/S	Storm-petrel, Wedge-rumped	*Oceanodroma tethys*	OO	Petrel de la Tempestad
M	Swallow, Bank	*Riparia riparia*	OC/SC	Golondrina Riberena
M	Swallow, Barn	*Hirundo rustica*	FT	Golondrina Tijerilla
M	Swallow, Cliff	*H. pyrrhonota*	FT/CL	Golondrina Risquera
M/W	Swallow, Tree	*Trachycineta bicolor*	OC/FW	Golondrina Invernal
M	Swallow, Northern Rough-winged	*Stelgidopteryx serripennis*	MT/OC	Golondrina Aliaserrada
R	Swallow, Violet-green	*Tachycineta thalassina*	FW/W	Golondrina Verde
A	Swan, Tundra	*Cygnus columbianus*	SC/M	Cisne Chiflador
R	Swift, White-throated	*Aeronautes saxatalis*	OC/MT	Vencejo Montanes
M/W	Tanager, Western	*Piranga ludoviciana*	OP/OC	Piranga Cabeziroja
M*	Tattler, Wandering	*Heteroscelus incanus*	SC	Agachadiza Vagabunda
W	Teal, Green-winged	*Anas crecca*	M/F&S	Cerceta Comun
W	Teal, Blue-winged	*A. discors*	FW	Cerceta Aliazul
R	Teal, Cinnamon	*A. cyanoptera*	FW	Cerceta Café
M	Tern, Black	*Chlidonias niger*	OO	Charran Negro

Season	Common and Scientific Names		Habitat	Spanish Name
R*	Tern, Caspian	*Sterna caspia*	SC'	Charran Caspica
M*	Tern, Common	*S. hirundo*	SC/OO	Charran Comun
R	Tern, Elegant	*S. elegans*	SC/OO	Charran Elegante
M/W*	Tern, Forster's	*S. forsteri*	SC	Charran de Forster
R	Tern, Royal	*S. maxima*	SC	Charran Real
M*	Tern, Sooty	*S. fuscata*	SC/OO	Charran Oscuro
M/W	*Thrasher, Bendire's*	*Toxostoma bendirei*	OC	
R	Thrasher, Gray	*T. cinereum*	OC	Cuitlacoche Ceniciento
W	Thrasher, Sage	*Oreoscoptes montanus*	OC/D	Mirlo de las Chias
M/W	Thrush, Hermit	*Catharus guttatus*	TH	Mirlillo de la Selva
M	Thrush, Swainson's	*C. ustulatus*	TH	Mirlillo de Swainson
R	Titmouse, Plain	*Parus inornatus*	OP	Copetoncito Sencillo
R	Towhee, Brown	*Pipilo fuscus*	OC/TH	Llama
M/W	Towhee, Green-tailed	*P. chlorurus*	OP/TH	Toqui Cola Verde
R	Towhee, Rufous-sided	*Pipilo erythrophthalmus*	OP/TH	Chouis
R	Tropicbird, Red-billed	*Phaethon aethereus*	OO	Rabijunco Piquirojo
M/W	Turnstone, Ruddy	*Arenaria interpres*	SC	Chorlete Comun
R	Verdin	*Auriparus flaviceps*	OC/D	Valoncito
W	Vireo, Bell's	*Vireo bellii*	TH	Vireo Aceitunado
W	Vireo, Gray	*V. vicinior*	TH/MT	Vireo Gris
R	Vireo, Hutton's	*V. huttoni*	OP	Vireo Pardillo
R	Vireo, Solitary	*V. solitarius*	MT/OP	Vireo Solitario
S	Vireo, Warbling	*V. gilvus*	MT/OP	Vireo Gorjeador
R	Vulture, Turkey	*Cathartes aura*	OC	Aura Comun
W*	Warbler, Black-and-white	*Mniotilta varia*	OP	Mezcilla
W	Warbler, Black-throated gray	*Dendroica nigrescens*	OP	Verdin Gargantinegro
M/W	Warbler, Hermit	*D. occidentalis*	OP	Verdin Coronado
M*	Warbler, Lucy's	*Vermivora luciae*	OC	Gusanero
M/W	Warbler, MacGillivray's	*Oporonis tolmiei*	FT	Verdin de Tolmie
W	Warbler, Yellow-rumped	*Dendroica coronata*	OP	
M/W	Warbler, Orange-crowned	*Vermivora celata*	MT	Gusanero Cabezigris
M/W	Warbler, Townsend's	*Dendroica townsendi*	OP	Verdin Negriamarillo
M/W*	Warbler, Wilson's	*Wilsonia pusilla*	OP/TH	Pelucilla
R	Warbler, Yellow	*Dendroica petechia*	FT	Verdin Amarillo
M/W	Waterthrush, Northern	*Seiurus noveboracensis*	FW/SC	Verdin Charquero
M	Whimbrel	*Numenius phaeopus*	SC	Chorlo Real
W	Wigeon, American	*Anas americana*	FW	Pato Chalcuan
M/W	Willet	*Catoptrophorus semipalmatus*	SC	Zarapico
R	Woodpecker, Acorn	*Melanerpes formicivorus*	MT/OP	Carpintero Encinero
R	Woodpecker, Gila	*M. uropygialis*	OC	Carpintero del Gila
R	Woodpecker, Ladder-backed	*P. scalaris*	OC/D	Carpintero Listado

Season	Common and Scientific Names		Habitat	Spanish Name
W*	Wren, Bewick's	*Thryomanes bewickii*	OC/TF	Saltapared Tepetatero
R	Wren, Cactus	*Campylorhynchus brun-neicapillus*	D/OC	Matraca Grande
R	Wren, Canyon	*Catherpes mexicanus*	MT	Saltapared Risquero
M/W	Wren, House	*Troglodytes aedon*	TH	Saltapared Cucar achero
M/W	Wren, Marsh	*Cistothorus palustris*	M/F	Saltapared Pantanero
R	Wren, Rock	*Salpinctes obsoletus*	OC	Saltaladera
M/W	Yellowlegs, Greater	*Tringa melanoleuca*	FW/M	Tinguis Grande
M/W	Yellowlegs, Lesser	*Tringa flavipes*	FW/M	Tinguis Chico
R	Yellowthroat, Belding's	*Geothlypis beldingi*	M/S&F	Verdin de Antifaz
W	Yellowthroat, Common	*G. trichas*	M/F&S	Tapaojito Comun

1. According to Wilbur, there is only one record of a Western Bluebird in Baja California.
2. Wilbur cites only two records of a Dickcissel.
3. There are no recent records for the Least Grebe.
4. So far the Western Grebe has not been recorded south of Bahia Magdalena.
5. Black-fronted Hummingbird supersedes Xantus' Hummingbird as the recognized common name.
6. Baird's Junco is now considered part of this complex.
7. Wilbur has no records south of La Paz for the Common Loon.
8. The one sighting of a Red-throated Pipit occurred in 1883!
9. The San Lucas robin is considered a subspecies of the American Robin.

MAMMALS OF THE CAPE REGION

Insectivores—Order Insectivora

Ornate Shrew, *Sorex ornatus lagunae*
Desert Shrew, *Notiosorex crawfordi crawfordi*

Bats—Order Chiroptera

Peter's Bat, *Balantiopteryx plicata pallida*
Ghost-faced Bat, *Mormoops megalophylla megalophylla*
California Leaf-nosed Bat, *Macrotus californicus californicus*
*Long-tongued Bat, *Choeronycteris mexicana*
*Little Long-nosed Bat, *Leptonycteris yerbabuenae*
Mexican Funnel-eared Bat, *Natalus stramineus mexicanus*
California Myotis, *Myotis californicus californicus*
Yuma Myotis, *Myotis yumanensis yumanensis*
Peninsular Myotis, *Myotis peninsularis*
Long-legged Myotis, *Myotis volans volans*
*Long-eared Myotis, *Myotis evotis evotis*
Fish-eating Bat, *Myotis vivesi*
Western Pipistrelle, *Pipistrellus hesperus hesperus*
Big Brown Bat, *Eptesicus fuscus peninsulae*
Southern Yellow Bat, *Lasiurus ega xanthinus*
Red Bat, *Lasiurus borealis teliotis*
Hoary Bat, *Lasiurus cinereus cinereus*
Pallid Bat, *Antrozous pallidus minor*
Brazilian Free-tailed Bat, *Tadarida brasiliensis mexicana*
Pocketed Free-tailed Bat, *Tadarida femorosacca*
Big Free-tailed Bat, *Tadarida macrotis*

Rabbits—Order Lagomorpha

Brush Rabbit, *Sylvilagus bachmani peninsularis*
Desert Cottontail, *Sylvilagus audubonii confinis*
Black-tailed Jack Rabbit, *Lepus californicus xanti*

368

Rodents—Order Rodentia

White-tailed Antelope Squirrel, *Ammospermophilus leucurus extimus*
Botta's Pocket Gopher, *Thomomys bottae anitae* (lower elevations)
  and *T. b. alticolus* (higher elevations)
Bailey's Pocket Mouse, *Perognathus baileyi extimus*
Little Desert Pocket Mouse, *Perognathus arenarius arenarius*
  (Pacific side of Cape) and *P. a. sublucidus* (La Paz region)
Dalquest's Pocket Mouse, *Perognathus dalquesti*
Spiny Pocket Mouse, *Perognathus spinatus peninsulae*
Merriam's Kangaroo Rat, *Dipodomys merriami melanurus*
Marsh Rice Rat, *Oryzomys palustris peninsulae*
Cactus Mouse, *Peromyscus eremicus eremicus*
Eva's Desert Mouse, *Peromyscus eva eva*
Deer Mouse, *Peromyscus maniculatus coolidgei*
Piñon Mouse, *Peromyscus truei lagunae*
Desert Wood Rat, *Neotoma lepida arenacea* (coastal plains and lower hills) and *N. l. notia*
  (mountains)
†Black Rat, *Rattus rattus*
†Norway Rat, *Rattus norvegicus*
†House Mouse, *Mus musculus*

Whales, dolphins and porpoises—Order Cetacea

Minke Whale, *Balaenoptera acutorostrata*
Fin Whale, *Balaenoptera physalus*
Blue Whale, *Balaenoptera musculus*
Sei Whale, *Balaenoptera borealis*
Bryde's Whale, *Balaenoptera edeni*
Humpback Whale, *Megaptera novaeangliae*
*Black Right Whale, *Eubalaena glacialis*
Gray Whale, *Eschrichtius robustus*
*Japanese Beaked Whale, *Mesoplodon ginkgodens*
Goose-beaked Whale, *Ziphius cavirostris*
Sperm Whale, *Physeter macrocephalus*
Pygmy Sperm Whale, *Kogia breviceps*
Dwarf Sperm Whale, *Kogia simus*
*Rough-toothed Dolphin, *Steno bredanensis*
False Killer Whale, *Pseudorca crassidens*
Short-finned Pilot Whale, *Globicephala macrorhynchus*
Killer Whale, *Orcinus orca*
Pacific White-sided Dolphin, *Lagenorhynchus obliquidens*
*Fraser's Dolphin, *Lagenodelphis hosei*
Bottle-nosed Dolphin, *Tursiops truncatus*
Risso's Dolphin, *Grampus griseus*
Spotted Dolphin, *Stenella attenuata*
Spinner Dolphin, *Stenella longirostris*
Striped Dolphin, *Stenella coeruleoalba*
Common Dolphin, *Delphinus delphis*

Carnivores—Order Carnivora

Coyote, *Canis latrans peninsulae*
Kit Fox, *Canis velox devia*
Gray Fox, *Canis cinereoargenteus peninsularis*
California Sea Lion, *Zalophus californianus californianus*
Ringtail, *Bassariscus astutus palmarius*
Raccoon, *Procyon lotor grinnelli*
Badger, *Taxidea taxus berlandieri*
Western Spotted Skunk, *Spilogale gracilis lucasana*
Mountain Lion, *Felis concolor improcera*
Bobcat, *Felis rufus peninsularis*

Artiodactyls—Order Artiodactyla

Mule Deer, *Odocoileus hemionus peninsulae*

---

*Indicates mammals of probable, but unverified occurrence in the Cape Region.
†Indicates mammals introduced into the Cape Region.

REPTILES AND AMPHIBIANS OF THE CAPE REGION

The reptile and amphibian fauna is not as extensive as might be expected at the Cape for it is an isolated area for migration of terrestrial vertebrates, and the climatic changes and shifts have decimated successive populations. It is in general a relatively recent fauna.

These lists have been compiled from Robert C. Stebbins, *A Field Guide to Western Reptiles and Amphibians* (Boston: Houghton Mifflin Company, 1966); Joseph T. Collins, James E. Huhcey, James L. Knight and Hobart M. Smith of the Society for the Study of Amphibians and Reptiles Committee on Common and Scientific Names, "Standard Common and Current Scientific Names for North American Amphibians and Reptiles," *Herpetological Circular No. 7*, Miscellaneous Publications, 1978; and verified, extended and updated by Dr. John W. Wright, Curator of Herpetology, Los Angeles Museum of Natural History.

Frogs

Couch's Spadefoot, *Scaphiopus couchi*
Red-spotted Toad, *Bufo punctatus*
Pacific Treefrog, *Hyla regilla*
Bullfrog (Introduced), *Rana catesbeiana*

Lizards

Axolote, *Bipes biporus*
Cape Leaf-toed Gecko, *Phyllodactylus unctus*
Leaf-toed Gecko, *Phyllodactylus xanti*
Banded Gecko, *Coleonyx variegatus*
Desert Night Lizard, *Xantusia vigilis*
Chuckwalla, *Sauromalus obesus*
Desert Iguana, *Dipsosaurus dorsalis*
Spiny-tail Iguana, *Ctenosaura hemilopha*
Zebra-tailed Lizard, *Callisaurus draconoides*
Desert Spiny Lizard, *Sceloporus magister*
Granite Spiny Lizard, *Sceloporus orcutti*
Black-tailed Brush Lizard, *Urosaurus nigricaudus*
Side-blotched Lizard, *Uta stansburiana*

Baja Rock Lizard, *Petrosaurus thalassinus*
Coast Horned Lizard, *Phrynosoma coronatum*
Cape Skink, *Eumeces lagunensis*
Western Whiptail, *Cnemidophorus tigris*
Orange-throated Whiptail, *Cnemidophorus hyperythrus*
Cape Alligator Lizard, *Gerrhonotus paucicarinatus*

Snakes

Western Blind Snake, *Leptotyphlops humilis*
Rosy Boa, *Lichanura trivirgata*
Baja California Rat Snake, *Elaphe rosaliae*
Spotted Leaf-nosed Snake, *Phyllorhynchus decurtatus*
Coachwhip, *Masticophis flagellum*
Western Patch-nosed Snake, *Salvadora hexalepis*
Bullsnake, *Pituophis melanoleucus*
Common Kingsnake, *Lampropeltis getulus*
Western Water Snake, *Natrix valida*
Western Ground Snake, *Sonora semiannulata*
Banded Sand Snake, *Chilomeniscus cinctus*
Baja Sand Snake, *Chilomeniscus stramineus*
Western Black-headed Snake, *Tantilla planiceps*
Sorda Night Snake, *Eridiphas slevini*
Night Snake, *Hypsiglena torquata*
California Lyre Snake, *Trimorphodon biscutatus*
Western Diamondback Rattlesnake, *Crotalus atrox*
Speckled Rattlesnake, *Crotalus mitchelli*
Baja California Rattlesnake, *Crotalus enyo*
Yellow-bellied Sea Snake, *Pelamis platurus*

Turtles

Pond Slider, *Chrysemys scripta*
Leatherback Sea Turtle, *Dermochelys coriacea*
Green Sea Turtle, *Chelonia mydas*
Hawksbill Sea Turtle, *Eretmochelys imbricata*
Western Ridley Sea Turtle, *Lepidochelys olivacea*
Loggerhead Sea Turtle, *Caretta caretta*

---

* Endemic to Cape.

SELECTED BIBLIOGRAPHY

Most accounts pertain to Baja California as a whole, with sections devoted to the Cape in varying depth and detail. The best of these are:

Durham, J. Wyatt, and Edwin C. Allison, eds. "Symposium: The Biogeography of Baja California and Adjacent Seas." *Systematic Zoology* 9(2) 1960. The three parts—Part I. Geologic History (pp. 47–92); Part II. Marine Biotas (pp. 93–147); and Part III. Terrestrial and Fresh Water Biotas (pp. 148–232)—consist of a series of scholarly papers on these aspects of the peninsula, with specific bibliographies. Although there have been changes in twenty years, this group of papers remains the best overall reference for the natural history of the peninsula.

Krutch, Joseph Wood. *The Forgotten Peninsula*. New York: William Morrow & Company, 1961. A handsomely written, thoughtful book.

————, with Eliot Porter, edited by Kenneth Brower, *Baja California and the Geography of Hope*. San Francisco: Sierra Club, 1967. Large format, stunning photographs, quintessential Sierra Club.

Steinbeck, John, and Edward F. Ricketts. *Sea of Cortez*. New York: Viking Press, 1941. The original has been reprinted by Paul P. Appel, Mount Vernon, NY, 1982. It has also been issued in paperback as *The Log of the Sea of Cortez* (New York: Penguin Books, 1982) without the scientific appendices but with Steinbeck's masterful profile of Ricketts.

Johnson, William Weber, and the Editors of Time-Life, *Baja California*. New York: Time, Inc., 1972. Well-written and presented.

Bates, Ken and Caroline, with the *Sunset* Editorial Staff. *Baja California*. Menlo Park, CA: Lane Books, 1971. Pleasant travel guide, well illustrated.

Lewis, Leland R., and Peter E. Ebeling, *Sea Guide Volume II: BAJA Covering the Waters of Baja California from San Diego to Cabo San Lucas, to San Felipe, Including All the Offshore and Oceanic Islands*. Newport Beach, CA: SEA Publications, 1971. This offers much historical information and observation of landforms, as well as appendices useful to both landlubber and sailor.

Wheelock, Walt, and Howard E. Gulick, *Baja California Guidebook*. Glendale, CA: A. H. Clark Co. 1975. Well done, with maps and much historical information.

Three important bibliographies are:

Barrett, Ellen C. *Baja California, 1535–1956*. 2 vols. Los Angeles: Bennett and Marshall, 1957. A bibliography of "historical, geographical, and scientific literature relating to the peninsula," provides a thorough list of references in one handy place, and has been updated by

Silvera, Katharine M. *Baja California Bibliography, 1965-1966.* La Jolla, CA: Baja Californianos of the Friends of the University of California San Diego Library, 1968.

Schwartzlose, Richard A., and John R. Hendrickson. *Bibliography of the Gulf of California: Marine Sciences* (through 1981). Scripps Institution of Oceanography, forthcoming.

More specific references for the Cape Region follow, arranged according to category: Geology, History, Botany, Invertebrates and Vertebrates. Not included are the many field guides to the Rocky Mountain and California West that are of some use, even as far south as the Cape, nor general textbooks; it is assumed that both are widely available. They are cited in the footnotes as appropriate.

GEOLOGY

Allison, Edwin C. "Geology of Areas Bordering the Gulf of California." In "Marine Geology of the Gulf of California—A Symposium." Edited by Tj. U. van Andel and G. G. Shor, Jr. *American Association of Petroleum Geologists Memoir* 3 (1964):3-29.

Anderson, C. A., *et al.* "The 1940 E. W. Scripps cruise to the Gulf of California. Part I. Geology of Islands and Neighboring Land Areas." *Geological Society of America, Memoir* 43 (1950):1-47).

Anderson, F. M., and G. D. Hanna. "Cretaceous Geology of Lower California." *California Academy of Sciences* (4th series), 23(1935):1-34.

Darton, N. H. "Geological Reconnaissance in Baja California." *Journal of Geology* 29(1921):720-48.

Durham, J. Wyatt. "E. W. Scripps Cruise to the Gulf of California. Part II: Megascopic Paleontology and Marine Stratigraphy." *Geological Society of America, Memoir* 43 (1950):1-216.

Durham, J. Wyatt, and Edwin C. Allison. "The Geologic History of Baja California and Its Marine Fauna." In "Symposium: The Biogeography of Baja California and Adjacent Seas. Part I. Geologic History." *Systematic Zoology* 9(2) (1960): 47-91.

Eardley, Armand J. *Structural Geology of North America (Baja California and Sonora Systems).* New York: Harper & Row, 1962.

Gabb, William M. "Geological Survey Reports." In *Resources of the Pacific Slope.* Edited by J. Ross Browne, pp. 82-122. New York: D. Appleton & Company, 1869.

———. "Part 2: Geology. Notes on the Geology of Lower California." *California Geological Survey* (1882):137-148.

Gastil, Gordon, Richard P. Phillips, and Rafael Rodríguez-Torres. "Section 3: Tectonics. The Reconstruction of Mesozoic California." *International Geological Congress, Proceedings* (1972):211-29.

———, Richard P. Phillips, and Edwin C. Allison. "Reconnaissance Geology of the State of Baja California." *Geological Society of America Memoir* 140 (1975).

Hamilton, W. "Origin of the Gulf of California." *Geological Society of America Bulletin* 72 (1961):1307-18.

———. "Recognition on Space Photographs of Structural Elements of Baja California." *U.S.G.S. Professional Paper 718.* Washington, DC: U.S. Government Printing Office, 1971: 1-26.

Hammond, Edwin M. "A Geomorphic Study of the Cape Region of Baja California." *University of California Publications in Geography* 10(2) (1954):45-115.

Heim, Arnold. "Notes on the Tertiary of Southern Lower California (Mexico)." *The Geological Magazine* 59(12) (1922):529-47.

Hertlein, Leo George, "Pectens from the Tertiary of Lower California." *Proceedings of the California Academy of Sciences* (4th series), 14(1) (1925):1-35.

———. "Additional Pliocene and Pleistocene Fossils from Lower California." *Journal of Paleontology* 5 (1931):365-367.

————. "Pliocene Fossils from Rancho El Refugio, Baja California, and Cerralvo Island, Mexico." *Proceedings of the California Academy of Sciences* (4th series), 30(14) (1966):265–284.

Macdonald, Ken C., and Bruch P. Luyendyk. "The Crest of the East Pacific Rise." *Scientific American* 244(5) (1981):100–116.

Miller, Wade E. "The Late Pliocene Las Tunas Local Flora from Southernmost Baja California, Mexico." *Journal of Paleontology* 54 (4) (1980):762–805.

Normak, W. R., and J. P. Curray. "Geology and Structure of the Tip of Baja California, Mexico." *Geological Society of America Bulletin* 79(1968):1589–1600.

Phillips, Richard P. "The Geology." In *A Field Guide to the Common and Interesting Plants of Baja California,* by Jeanette Coyle and Norman C. Roberts, pp. 4–6. La Jolla, CA: Natural History Publishing Company, 1975.

Roden, G. I. "Oceanographic and Meteorological Aspects of the Gulf of California." *Pacific Science* 12 (1958):21–45.

————, and G. W. Groves. "Recent Oceanographic Investigations in the Gulf of California." *Journal of Marine Research* 18 (1959):10–35.

Shepard, F. B. "1940 *E. W. Scripps* Cruise to the Gulf of California. Part III: Submarine Topography of the Gulf of California." *Geological Society of America, Memoir* 43 (1950):1–32.

HISTORY

Alzola, Tomás de. "Declaration made by Tomás de Alzola, Master of the ship named SANTA ANA which the English robbed off Cabo San Lucas in California, relative to the events taking place at that time and afterward until his arrival at the Port of Acapulco with the same ship, a part of which was burned and destroyed by the enemy." In *The Capture of the Santa Ana.* Transcribed, translated and annotated by W. Michael Mathes, pp. 45–54. Los Angeles: Dawson's Book Shop, 1969.

Andrews, Kenneth R. *Elizabethan Privateering: English Privateering During the Spanish War, 1585–1603.* Cambridge, Eng.: The University Press, 1964.

Andrews, Thomas F., ed. *English Privateers at Cabo San Lucas. The Descriptive Accounts of Puerto Seguro by Edward Cooke (1712) and Woodes Rogers (1712).* Los Angeles: Dawson's Book Shop, 1979.

Ascención, Father Antonio. "Father Antonio de la Ascención's Account of the Voyage of Sebastián Vizcaíno." Edited by Henry R. Wagner. *California Historical Society Quarterly* 7(4) (1928):295–394 and 8(1) (1929):26–70.

Aschmann, Homer, ed. and trans. *The Natural and Human History of Baja California from Manuscripts by Jesuit Missionaries.* Los Angeles: Dawson's Book Shop, 1966.

Atondo y Antillón, Admiral Don Isidro de. *First from the Gulf to the Pacific. The Diary of the Kino-Atondo Peninsular Expedition.* Introduction and translation by W. Michael Mathes. Los Angeles: Dawson's Book Shop, 1969.

Baegert, Johann Jakob. "An Account of the Aboriginal Inhabitants of the California Peninsula." Translated by Charles Rau. *Annual Report of the Smithsonian Institution for 1863–64.* Washington, DC: U.S. Government Printing Office, 1865: 352–69.

————. *Observations in (Lower) California.* Translation with introduction and notes by M. M. Brandenburg and Carl L. Baumann. Berkeley: University of California Press, 1952.

————. *The Letters of Jakob Baegert, 1749–1761.* Translated by Elsbeth Schultz-Bischof, introduction and edited by Doyce B. Nunis, Jr. Los Angeles: Dawson's Book Shop, 1982.

Bancroft, Hubert H. *History of Mexico.* San Francisco: A. L. Bancroft & Co., 1883–1888.

————. *History of California.* San Francisco: The History Company, 1890.

Barco, Miguel del. *The Natural History of Baja California.* Introduction by Miguel Léon-Portilla, translated by Froylan Tiscareno. Los Angeles: Dawson's Book Shop, 1980.

_____. *Ethnology and Linguistics of Baja California*, introduction and notes by Miguel Léon-Portilla. Los Angeles: Dawson's Book Shop, 1981.

Beaglehole, J. C. *The Exploration of the Pacific*. London: A. & C. Black, 1934.

Betagh, William. In *English Privateers at Cabo San Lucas*. Edited by Thomas F. Andrews, pp. 105–12. Los Angeles: Dawson's Book Shop, 1979.

Browne, J. Ross. "Explorations in Lower California." *Harper's New Monthly Magazine* 37 (1868):578–91 and 740–52; and 38 (1868):9–23.

_____. *Resources of the Pacific Slope. A Statistical and Descriptive Summary of the Mines and Minerals, Climate, Topography, Agriculture, Commerce, Manufactures, and Miscellaneous Productions of the States and Territories West of the Rocky Mountains*. New York: D. Appleton & Co., 1869.

Bryant, Walter F. "The Cape Region of Baja California. *Zoe* 2 (1891):185–201.

Cabrillo, Juan Rodríguez. "Voyage of Cabrillo in 1542." Translated by Bartolomé Ferrer. *U.S. Geographical Survey West of the 100th Meridian* 7:299–314. Washington, DC: U.S. Government Printing Office, 1879.

Cardona, Nicolás de. *Geographic and Hydrographic Descriptions of the Discovery of the Kingdom of California (1632)*. Los Angeles: Dawson's Book Shop, 1974.

Carter, Annetta M. "I. G. Voznesenskii, Early Naturalist in Baja California, Mexico." *Taxon* 28(1,2,3) (1979):27–33.

Cavallero Carranco, Juan de. In *The Pearl Hunters in the Gulf of California, 1668*. Edited by W. Michael Mathes. Los Angeles: Dawson's Book Shop, 1966.

Cavendish, Thomas. "A Letter of M. Thomas Candish to the Right Honourable the Lord Hunsdon, Lord Chamberlaine, one of her Majesties most honourable Privy Councell, Touching the Successe of His Voyage about the World." In *Hakluyt's Voyages: Tales of Adventure and Exploration,* edited by Delbert A. Young. Toronto: Clarke, Irwin and Co., 1973.

Chappe d'Auteroche, Jean-Baptiste. *A Voyage to California*. Introduction by Kenneth Holmes. Richmond, Eng.: Richmond Publishing Co., Ltd., 1973.

_____. *The 1769 Transit of Venus. The Baja California Observations of Jean-Baptiste Chappe d'Auteroche, Vicente de Doz, and Joaquín Velázquez Cárdeñas de León*. Edited by Doyce B. Nunis. Los Angeles: Natural History Museum of Los Angeles County, 1982.

Clavijero, Francisco Javier. *The History of Lower California*. Translated and edited by Sara E. Lake and A. A. Gray. Stanford, CA: Stanford University Press, 1937.

Clinch, Bryan James. *California and Its Missions*. San Francisco: Whitaker & Ray Co., 1904.

Cochran, Robert T. "Cold-eyed Soldier of Fortune Who Became a 'President.'" *Smithsonian* 12(3) (1981):117–26.

Cooke, Captain Edward. *A Voyage to the South Sea and Round the World, Performed in the Years 1708, 1709, 1710, and 1711*. London: B. Lintot and R. Gosling, 1712.

_____. "A Voyage to the South Sea and Round the World in the Years 1708 to 1711." In *English Privateers at Cabo San Lucas*. Edited by Thomas F. Andrews, pp. 33–58. Los Angeles: Dawson's Book Shop, 1979.

Ducrue, Father Norberto. In *The Natural and Human History of Baja California*. Edited by Homer Aschmann. Los Angeles: Dawson's Book Shop, 1966.

Dunne, Peter M. *Black Robes in Lower California*. Berkeley and Los Angeles: University of California Press, 1952.

Dupetit-Thouars, L. M. Aubert A. *Voyage of the Venus*. Los Angeles: Dawson's Book Shop, 1956.

Eisen, Gustav. "Explorations in the Cape Region of Baja California in 1894, with References to Former Expeditions of the California Academy of Sciences." *Proceedings of the California Academy of Sciences* (2nd series), 5 (1895):733–55.

_____. "Explorations in the Cape Region of Baja California Made Under the Auspices of the California Academy of Sciences." *American Geographical Society of New York Bulletin* 29(3) (1897):271–80 and 32(5) (1907):397–429.

Elliott, Benjamin Franklin. *Lower California—1917*. [Pamphlet, no date, no publisher.]

Engstrand, Iris W. *Royal Officer in Baja California, 1768-1770, Joaquín Velázquez de León*. Los Angeles: Dawson's Book Shop, 1976.

Farquhar, Francis P. "A Footnote on the Name California." *California Historical Society Quarterly* 9(2) (1927):167-68.

Gerhard, Peter. *Pirates on the West Coast of New Spain 1575-1742*. Glendale, CA: Arthur H. Clark Co., 1960.

Hager, Anna M., ed. *The Filibusters of 1890*. Los Angeles: Dawson's Book Shop, 1968.

Hale, Edward Everett. *The Queen of California. The Origin of the Name of California with a Translation from the Sergas de Esplandian*. San Francisco: Colt Press, 1945.

Hatsutaro. *Kaigai Ibun*. Compiled by Maekawa Bunzo and Sakai Junzo. Translated by Richard Zumwinkle and Tadanobu Kawai. Los Angeles: Dawson's Book Shop, 1970.

Janes, John. "The Last Voyage of Thomas Cavendish as Told by Master John James." In *Hakluyt's Voyages: Tales of Adventure and Exploration*, edited by Delbert A. Young. Toronto: Clarke, Irwin and Co., 1973.

Janes, John F. "Lower California A New Empire." In *The Filibusters of 1890*. Edited by Anna M. Hager. Los Angeles: Dawson's Book Shop, 1968.

Kino, Eusebio Francisco. *First from the Gulf to the Pacific, the Diary of the Kino-Atondo Expedition, December 14, 1684—January 13, 1685*. Translated and edited by W. Michael Mathes. Los Angeles: Dawson's Book Shop, 1969.

Konnyu, Leslie. *John Xantus Hungarian Geographer in America (1851-64)*. Köln· American Hungarian Publishers, 1965.

León-Portilla, Miguel. *Voyages of Francisco de Ortega*. Los Angeles: Dawson's Book Shop, 1973.

———. ———. "Indian Place Names of Baja California Sur. A Report Attributed to Esteban Rodríguez Lorenzo." *Southwest Museum Leaflets* 38, 1977.

Link, Wenceslaus. *Reports and Letters 1762-1778*. Translated, edited and annotated by Ernest J. Burrus. Los Angeles: Dawson's Book Shop, 1967.

Lindsay, George E. "The Mission Period of Baja California." *Pacific Discovery* 18(4) (1965):2-8.

———. ———. "Some Natural Values of Baja California." *Pacific Discovery* 23(2) (1970):1-10.

Longinos Martínez, José de. *Journals*. Edited by Lesley Byrd Simpson. San Francisco: J. Howell—Books, 1961.

Madden, Henry Miller. *Xantus: Hungarian Naturalist in the Pioneer West*. Linz, Austria: Ober österreichischer Landesverlag, 1949

Martínez, Pablo. *A History of Lower California*. Translated by Ethel Duffy Turner. Mexico 14, D.F.: Editorial Baja California, 1960.

Massey, William C. "Tribes and Languages of Baja California." *Southwestern Journal of Anthropology* 5(3) (1949):272-307.

Mathes, W. Michael. *The Pearl Hunters in the Gulf of California, 1668*. Los Angeles: Dawson's Book Shop, 1966.

———. ———. *Vizcaíno and Spanish Expansion in the Pacific Ocean, 1580-1630*. San Francisco: California Historical Society, 1968.

———. ———, ed. and trans. *The Capture of the Santa Ana, Cabo San Lucas, November, 1587*. Los Angeles: Dawson's Book Shop, 1969.

———. ———, trans. *The Conquistador in California: 1535. The Voyage of Fernando Cortés to Baja California in Chronicles and Documents*. Los Angeles: Dawson's Book Shop, 1973.

———. ———, trans. and ed. *Spanish Approaches to the Island of California, 1682-1632*. San Francisco: The Book Club of California, 1975.

———. *A Brief History of the Land of Calafia: the Californias*, 1535 to 1995. La Paz: 1977.

———. *Las Misiones de Baja California. The Mission(s) of Baja California: 1649-1849*. La Paz: Governo del Estado de Baja California Sur & Ayuntamiento de la Paz, 1977.

_____, and J. Andrés Cata Sandoval. *Importancia de Cabo San Lucas.* La Paz, Baja California Sur: Fonapas,1980.

Meigs, Peveril. *The Dominican Mission Frontier of Lower California.* Berkeley: University of California Press, 1935.

Mendaña, Alvaro de. "The Voyage of Alvaro de Mendaña." Edited by Henry R. Wagner. *California Historical Society Quarterly* 7(3) (1928):228–76.

Murray, Spencer, ed. *Explorations in Lower California.* Studio City, CA: Vaquero Books, 1966.

Nelson, E. W. "A Land of Drought and Desert—Lower California. Two Thousand Miles on Horseback Through the Most Extraordinary Cacti Forests in the World." *National Geographic Magazine* 22(1911):443–74.

_____. "Lower California and Its Natural Resources." *National Academy of Sciences, Memoir* 16 (1921):1–194.

Nordoff, Charles C. *Peninsular California.* New York: Harper & Row, 1888.

Nordoff, Walter [Antonio de Fierro Blanco]. *The Journey of the Flame.* Boston: Houghton Mifflin Company, 1955.

Pretty, Francis. "The Admirable and Prosperous Voyage of the Worshipfull Master Thomas Candish of Trimley in the Countie of Suffolke Esquire, into the South sea, and from thence round about the circumference of the whole earth, begun in the yeere of our Lorde 1586, and finished 1588. Written by Master Francis Pretty lately of Ey in Suffolke, a Gentleman employed in the same action." In *Capture of the Santa Ana.* Edited by W. Michael Mathes, pp. 23–31. Los Angeles: Dawson's Book Shop, 1969.

Reid, J. M. "The Ensenada." *National Magazine* 4(6) (1854):502–5.

Rodríguez Cemeño, Sebastián. "The Voyage to California of Sebastián Rodríguez Cemeño." Edited by Henry R. Wagner. *California Historical Society Quarterly* 3 (1924):289–331.

Rogers, Woodes. *A Cruising Voyage Round the World.* Introduction and notes by G. E. Manwaring. New York: Longmans, Green & Co. 1928.

_____. *The Voyage of Woodes Rogers, Round the World, with the Discovery of Alexander Selkirk, the Origin of Robinson Crusoe.* London, 1806.

_____. "A Cruising Voyage Round the World Between August 1708 and October 1711." In *English Privateers at Cabo San Lucas.* Edited by Thomas F. Andrews, pp. 59–70. Los Angeles: Dawson's Book Shop, 1979.

Ryan, William Redmond. *Personal Adventures in Upper and Lower California 1848–1849.* New York: Arno Press, 1973.

Sales, Luis de. *Observations on California 1772–1790.* Edited by Charles N. Rudkin. Los Angeles: Dawson's Book Shop, 1956.

Salvatierra, Juan María de. *Selected Letters About Lower California.* Translated and biography by Ernest J. Burrus. Los Angeles: Dawson's Bookshop, 1971.

Sanchez, Facio Manuel. "The Truth About Lower California—Forfeiture of Contract Between Mexican Government and Mexican 'Colonization' Company." [No publisher, no date.]

Scammon, C. M. "Report of Captain C. M. Scammon, of the U.S. Revenue Service, on the West Coast of Lower California." In *Resources of the Pacific Slope.* Edited by J. Ross Browne, pp. 123–31. New York: D. Appleton and Co., 1879.

Schurz, William L. "The Manila Galleon and California." *Southwestern Historical Quarterly* 31 (1917):107–26.

_____. *The Manila Galleon.* New York: E. P. Dutton & Co., 1939.

Shelvocke, George. "A Voyage Round the World by Way of the South Sea in the Years 1719 to 1722." In *English Privateers at Cabo San Lucas.* Edited by Thomas F. Andrews, pp. 71–104. Los Angeles: Dawson's Book Shop, 1979.

Simpson, Lesley Byrd. "The Story of José Longinos Martínez, California's First Naturalist." *Hispanic American Historical Review* 20(4) (1940): 643–49.

————, ed. and trans. *The Journal of José Longinos Martínez.* San Francisco: John Howell—Books, 1961.

Taylor, Alexander S. "Historical Summary of Lower California from Its Discovery in 1532 to 1867." In *Resources of the Pacific Slope.* Edited by J. Ross Browne, pp. 5–77. New York: D. Appleton & Co., 1869.

Tirsch, Ignacio. *The Drawings of Ignacio Tirsch.* Narrative by Doyce B. Nunis, Jr., translation by Elsbeth Schulz-Bischof. Los Angeles: Dawson's Book Shop, 1972.

Townsend, C. H. "Voyage of the *Albatross* to the Gulf of California in 1911." *American Museum of Natural History Bulletin* 35 (1916): 399–476.

Turner, Ethel Duffy. *Revolution in Baja California.* Detroit: Blain Ethridge, 1981.

Unamuno, Pedro de. "The Voyage of Pedro de Unamuno to California in 1587." Edited by Henry R. Wagner. *California Historical Society Quarterly* 2 (1923): 140–60.

Venegas, Miguel. *A Natural and Civil History of California.* 2 vols. Ann Arbor, MI: University Microfilms, Inc., 1966.

Wagner, Henry R., ed. "The Voyage of Pedro de Unamuno to California in 1587." *California Historical Society Quarterly* 2 (1923):140–60.

————, ed.. "The Voyage to California of Sebastián Rodríguez Cemeño in 1695." *California Historical Society Quarterly* 3 (1924):3–24.

————, ed. "Spanish Voyages to the Northwest Coast in the Sixteenth Century." *California Historical Society Quarterly* 6(4) (1927):289–331.

————, ed. "The Voyage of Alvaro de Mendaña." *California Historical Society Quarterly* 7(3) (1928):228–76.

————, ed. "The Occupation of the Philippines and the Discovery of the Return Route." *California Historical Society Quarterly* 7(2) (1928):132–93.

————, ed. "Spanish Voyages to the Northwest Coast. The Voyage of Juan Rodríguez Cabrillo." *California Historical Society Quarterly* 7(1) (1928):20–77.

————. "Pearl Fishing Enterprises in the Gulf of California. *Hispanic American Historical Review* 10(2) (1930):188–220.

————. *The Cartography of the Northwest Coast of America to the Year 1800.* Berkeley: University of California Press, 1937.

Weber, Francis J. *The Missions & Missionaries of Baja California.* Dawson's Book Shop, 1968.

————, trans. and annot. *The Peninsular California Missions, 1808–1880.* Los Angeles: Dawson's Book Shop, 1979.

Woodward, Arthur, ed. *The Republic of Lower California, 1853–1854.* Los Angeles: Dawson's Book Shop, 1966.

Xantus, John. *Letters from North America.* Translated and edited by Theodore Schoenman and Helen B. Schoenman. Detroit: Wayne State University Press, 1975.

————. Letters. Archives of the Smithsonian Institution.

Young, Delbert A., ed. *Hakluyt's Voyages: Tales of Adventure and Exploration.* Toronto: Clarke, Irwin and Co., 1973.

BOTANY

Axelrod, Daniel I. "The Stratigraphic Significance of a Southern Element in Later Tertiary Floras of Western America. *Washington Academy of Sciences Journal* 28 (1938):313–22.

————. "Climate and Evolution in Western North America During the Middle Pliocene Time." *Evolution* 2 (1948):127–44.

————. *Studies in Late Tertiary Paleobotany.* Washington, DC: Carnegie Institution Publication 590, 1950.

Bentham, George. *The Botany of H.M.S. Sulphur Under Command of Capt. Sir Edward Belcher, During the Years 1836–42.* London: Smith, Elder & Co., 1844.

Brandegee, Katharine. "Notes on Cactaceae." *Zoe* 5(10) (1904):189–93.

Brandegee, Townshend S. "A New Species of Esenbeckia." *Zoe* 1 (1890):378.

_____. "Studies in Coreopsidea and Tagetineae, Especially of Lower California, with Descriptions of Some New Species." *Zoe* 1 (1890):308–14.

_____. "A New Nolina." *Zoe* 1 (1890):305–6.

_____. "A New Cottonwood from Baja California." *Zoe* 1 (1890):274–75.

_____. "Notes Concerning the Collection of Plants Made by Xantus at Cape St. Lucas and Vicinity." *Zoe* 1 (1890):269–72.

_____. "The Hedgerows of Todos Santos." *Zoe* 1 (1890):179–81.

_____. "A New Perityle." *Zoe* 1 (1890):54.

_____. "Field Notes on the Plants of Baja California." *Zoe"* 2 (1891): 145–52.

_____. "Drymaria in Baja California." Zoe 2 (1891):68–70.

_____. "Cactaceae of the Cape Region of Baja California." *Zoe* 2 (1891):18–22.

_____. "A New Rumfordia from Lower California." *Zoe* 2 (1891):241–42.

_____. "The Distribution of the Flora of the Cape Region of Baja California." *Zoe* 3(1892):223–31.

_____. "Southern Extension of California Flora." *Zoe* 4(3) (1893):199–210.

_____. "Additions to the Flora of the Cape Region of Baja California. II." *Zoe* 4 (1894):398–408.

_____. "New Species of Plants, Mainly from Baja California." *Zoe* 5(6,7,8) (1900):104–9.

_____. "A New Tapiria from Baja California." *Zoe* 5 (1900):78–79.

_____. "New Species of Mexican Plants." *Zoe* 5(11) (1906):244–62.

Cabrera, Dr. Jésus O. *Plantas Curativas de Mexico propiedades medicinales de las mas conocidas plantas de México, su aplicación correcta y eficaz.* [No publisher, no date.]

Carter, Annetta. "The Genus *Alvordia* (Compositae) of A [sic] Baja California, Mexico." *Proceedings of the California Academy of Sciences* (4th series), 30(8) (1964):157–74.

Coyle, Jeanette, and Norman C. Roberts. *A Field Guide to the Common and Interesting Plants of Baja California.* La Jolla, CA: Natural History Publishing Company, 1975.

Cupp, Easter E. "Marine Plankton Diatoms of the West Coast of North America." *Bulletin Scripps Institution of Oceanography* 5 (1943):1–238.

_____, and Allen, W. E. "Allan Hancock Pacific Expeditions; Plankton Diatoms of the Gulf of California Obtained by Allan Hancock Pacific Expedition of 1937." *Hancock Pacific Expeditions* 3(5) (1938):61–99.

Dawson, E. Yale. "Field Observations on the Algae of the Gulf of California." *Hancock Pacific Expeditions* 3(1941):115–19.

_____. "The Marine Algae of the Gulf of California." *Hancock Pacific Expeditions* 3(1944):189–464.

_____. "A Note on the Vegetation of a New Coastal Upwelling Area of Baja California. *Journal of Marine Research* 9 (1950):65–68.

_____. Marine Algae from the 1958 Cruise of the *Stella Polaris* in the Gulf of California." *Los Angeles County Museum, Contributions in Science* 27 (1959):1–39.

_____. "A Review of the Ecology, Distribution, and Affinities of the Benthic Flora." In "Symposium: The Biogeography of Baja California and Adjacent Seas. Part II: Marine Biotas." Edited by J. Wyatt Durham and Edwin C. Allison. *Systematic Zoology* 9(2) (1960):93–100.

Eaton, D. C. "A New Fern from Lower California." *Zoe* 1 (1890):197.

Gentry, Howard S. "The Agaves of Baja California." *California Academy of Sciences, Occasional Papers* 130 (1978):1–119.

Gilmartin, Amy Jean, and Mary L. Neighbours. "Flora of the Cape Region, Baja California Sur." *National Geographic Society Research Reports, 1969 Projects.* Washington, DC, 1978:219–25.

Selected Bibliography

Goldman, E. A. "Plant Records of an Expedition to Lower California." *Contributions, U.S. National Museum* 16 (1916):309–71.

Gould, Frank W., and Reid Moran. "The Grasses of Baja California, Mexico." *San Diego Society of Natural History, Memoir No. 12.* (Nov. 10, 1981). San Diego, CA, 1981:1–140.

Gray, Asa. "Enumeration of a Collection of Dried Plants Made by L. J. Xantus, at Cape San Lucas, etc., in Lower California, Between August, 1859, and February, 1860, and Communicated to the Smithsonian Institution." *Proceedings of the American Academy of Arts and Sciences* 5 (1861):153–73.

Hooker, J. W., and G. A. Walker Arnott. *The Botany of Captain Beechey's Voyage; Comprising an Account of the Plants Collected by Messrs. Lay and Colie, and other officers of the expedition, during the voyage to the Pacific and Bering's Strait, performed in his majesty's ship Blossom, under the command of Captain F. W. Beechey, R.N., F.R., & A.S., in the Years 1825, '26, '27, and '28.* London: Henry G. Bohn, 1841.

Johnson, Ivan Murray. "Expedition of the California Academy of Sciences to the Gulf of California in 1921. The Botany (The Vascular Plants)." *Proceedings of the California Academy of Sciences* (4th series), 12(30) (1921):951–1218.

———. "The Botany (the Vascular Plants) in: Expedition of the California Academy of Sciences to the Gulf of California in 1921." *Proceedings of the California Academy of Sciences* (4th series), 12 (1924):951–1218.

Lamson-Scribner, F. "Lower California Grasses. An Enumeration of the Grasses Collected by Mr. T. S. Brandegee in Lower California in 1893." *Zoe* 2 (1894):385–93.

Lindsay, George E. "Desert Plants of Baja California." *Pacific Discovery* 18(4): (1917):15–20.

Longinos Martínez, José. *The Journals of José Longinos Martínez.* Edited and translated by Lesley Byrd Simpson. San Francisco: John Howell—Books, 1961.

Millspaugh, C. F. "Euphorbiaceae Collected by T. S. Brandegee Principally in the Vicinity of Todos Santos, Baja California, January and February, 1890." *Zoe* 1 (1890):346–48.

Moran, Reid. "Brandegee's Tarweed, and the True Story of Its Rediscovery." *Environment Southwest* 440 (1972):3–6.

———. "Palms in Baja California." *Environment Southwest* 478 (1977):10–14.

Nash, T. H., III, G. T. Nebeker, T. J. Moser, and T. Reeves. "Lichen Vegetational Gradients in Relation to the Pacific Coast of Baja California: The Maritime Influence." *Madroño* 26(4) (1979):149–63.

Raven, Peter, and Daniel Axelford. "Origin and Relationships of the California Flora." *University of California Publications in Botany* 72 (1978):1–134.

Setchell, William Albert, and Nathaniel Lyon Gardner. "XXIX Expedition of the California Academy of Sciences to the Gulf of California in 1921. The Marine Algae." *Proceedings of the California Academy of Sciences* (4th series), 12(29) (1924):695–949.

Shreve, Forrest. "The Vegetation of the Cape Region of Baja California." *Madroño* 4 (1937):105–13.

Stanley, Paul C. *Trees and Shrubs of Mexico.* 5 parts. Washington: U.S. Government Printing Office, 1926.

Wiggins, Ira L. "New Plants from Baja California." *Contributions, Dudley Herbarium* 1 (1933):161–87.

———. "Investigations in the Natural History of Baja California." *Proceedings of the California Academy of Sciences* (4th series), 30(1) (1960): 1–45.

———. "The Origin and Relationships of the Land Flora." In "Symposium: The Biogeography of Baja California. Part III. Terrestrial and Fresh-water Biotas." Edited by J. Wyatt Durham and Edwin C. Allison. *Systematic Zoology* 9(2) (1960):148–65.

———. "New Species of Plants from Baja California, Mexico." *Proceedings of the California Academy of Sciences* (4th series), 36 (1965):317–46.

————. "Notes on Three Ferns from Baja California, Mexico." *American Fern Journal* 63 (1974):152–57.

————. *Flora of Baja California.* Stanford, CA: Stanford University Press, 1980.

INVERTEBRATES

Aitken, Thomas H. G. "Contributions Toward a Knowledge of the Insect Fauna of Lower California. No. 6. Diptera: Culcidae." *Proceedings of the California Academy of Sciences* (4th series), 24(6) (1942):161–70.

Arnaud, Paul H. "The Sefton Foundation *Orca* Expedition to the Gulf of California, March–April, 1953. General Account." *Occasional Papers of the California Academy of Sciences.* September 18, 1970.

Baker, Fred, G. D. Hanna, and A. M. Strong. "Some Rissoid Mollusca from the Gulf of California." *Proceedings of the California Academy of Sciences* (4th series), 19(4) (1930):23–40.

————. "Some Mollusca of the Family Epitoniidae from the Gulf of California." *Proceedings of the California Academy of Sciences* (4th series), 19(5) (1930):41–56.

————. "Some Pyramidellidae from the Gulf of California." *Proceedings of the California Academy of Sciences* (4th series), 17(7) (1928):205–46.

Banks, Nathan. "Arachnida from Baja California and Other Parts of Mexico." *Proceedings of the California Academy of Sciences* (3rd series), 1(7) (1898):205–309.

————. "Contributions Toward a Knowledge of the Insect Fauna of Lower California. No. 4. Neuroptera: Myrmeleonidae." *Proceedings of the California Academy of Sciences* (4th series), 24(4) (1942):133–52.

Barr, William F. "Contributions Toward a Knowledge of the Insect Fauna of Lower California. No. 12. Coleoptera: Cleridae." *Proceedings of the California Academy of Sciences* (4th series), 24(12) (1942):485–519.

Blaisdell, Frank E. "Contributions Toward a Knowledge of the Insect Fauna of Lower California. No. 7. Coleoptera: Tenebrionidae." *Proceedings of the California Academy of Sciences* (4th series), 24(7) (1942):171–288.

Bohart, Richard M. "Contributions Toward a Knowledge of the Insect Fauna of Lower California. No. 9. Hymenoptera: Eumeninae." *Proceedings of the California Academy of Sciences* (4th series), 24(9) (1942):313–36.

Boone, Lee. "Scientific Results of the First Oceanographic Expedition of the 'Pawnee' 1926. Mollusks from the Gulf of California and the Perlas Islands. The Brigham Oceanographic Collection." *Peabody Museum of Natural History* 2(5) (1928):1–17.

Brusca, Richard C. *A Handbook of the Common Intertidal Invertebrates of the Gulf of California.* 2nd rev. ed. Tucson: University of Arizona Press, 1981.

————, and D. A. Thomson. "The Pulmo Reefs of Baja California—True Coral Reef Formation in the Gulf of California." *Cincias Marinas* 1(3) (1977):37–53.

Calvert, Philip P. "The Odonate Collections of the California Academy of Sciences from Baja California and Tepic, Mexico, of 1889–1894." *Proceedings of the California Academy of Sciences* (4th series), 23(41) (1947):603–9.

Carpenter, Philip P. "Notice of Shells Collected by Mr. J. Xantus, at Cape St. Lucas." *Philadelphia Academy Proceedings* (1859):331–32.

————. "Diagnoses of New Forms of Mollusks Collected at Cape St. Lucas by Mr. J. Xantus," *Annals and Magazine of Natural History* (series 13), (1864):311–15, 474–79; and (series 14), (1864):45–49.

————. "Supplementary Report on the Present State of Our Knowledge with Regard to the Mollusca of the West Coast of North America." *Report of the British Association for the Advancement of Science for 1863.* Washington, DC: Smithsonian Miscellaneous Collections 252 (1872), pp. 517–686.

Chace, Fenner A., Jr. "The Templeton Crocker Expedition. VII. Caridean Decapod Crustacea from the Gulf of California and the West Coast of Lower California." *Zoologica* 22 (1937):109–38.

Chamberlin, R. V. "Expedition of the California Academy of Sciences to the Gulf of California in 1921. The Spider Fauna of the Shores and Islands of the Gulf of California." *Proceedings of the California Academy of Sciences* 12 (1924):561–694.

Church, Clifford C. "Shallow Water Foraminifera from Cape San Lucas, Lower California." *Proceedings of the California Academy of Sciences* (4th series), 30(17) (1968):357–80.

Cooper, J. G. "On Land and Freshwater Shells of Lower California." *Proceedings of the California Academy of Sciences* (2nd series), 3 (1890–1892).

Crane, Jocelyn. "The Templeton Crocker Expedition. III: Brachygnathous Crabs from the Gulf of California and the West Coast of Lower California." *Zoologica* 22 (1937):47–78.

————. "The Templeton Crocker Expedition. VI: Oxystomatous and Dromiaceous Crabs from the Gulf of California and the West Coast of Lower California." *Zoologica* 22 (1937):97–108.

Czaier, M. A. "The Origin, Distribution, and Classification of the Tiger Beetles of Lower California (Coleoptera: Cicindelidae)." *American Museum Novitiates* 1382 (1948):1–28.

Dall, W. H. "Land Shells of the Genus *Bulimulus* in Lower California, with descriptions of several new species." *U.S. National Museum Proceedings* 16 (1893): 639–47.

Deichmann, Elisabeth. "The Templeton Crocker Expedition. IX: Holothurians from the Gulf of California, the West Coast of Lower California and Clarion Island." *Zoologica* 22 (1937): 161–76.

————. "Holothurians from the Western Coasts of Lower California and Central America, and from the Galápagos Islands." *Zoologica* 23 (1938): 361–87.

Farmer, Wesley. *Tidepool Animals from the Gulf of California.* San Diego, CA: Wesword Co., 1968.

Ferris, Clifford D., and Martin F. Brown. *Butterflies of the Rocky Mountain States.* Norman: University of Oklahoma Press, 1980.

Garth, J. S. "Distribution and Affinities of the Brachyuran Crustaceae." In "Symposium: The Biogeography of Baja California. Part II. Marine Biotas." Edited by J. Wyatt Durham and Edwin C. Allison, pp. 205–223. *Systematic Zoology* 9 (2) (1960).

Glassell, S. A. "The Templeton Crocker Expedition. I. Six New Brachyuran Crabs from the Gulf of California." *Zoologica* 21 (1936): 213–18.

————. "The Templeton Crocker Expedition. IV. Porcellanid Crabs from the Gulf of California." *Zoologica* 22 (1937):79–89.

————. "The Templeton Crocker Expedition. XI. Hermit Crabs from the Gulf of California and the West Coast of Lower California." *Zoologica* 22 (1937):241–63.

Grossbeck, John A. "Lists of Insects Collected by the *Albatross* Expedition in Lower California in 1911, with Description of a New Species of Wasp." *American Museum of Natural History Bulletin* 31 (1912):323–26.

Hanna, G [sic] Dallas, and A. L. Brigger. "Fossil Diatoms from Southern Baja California." *Proceedings of the California Academy of Sciences* (4th series), 30(15) (1966):285–308.

————, and Allyn G. Smith. "The Diguet-Mabille Land and Freshwater Mollusks of Baja California. *Proceedings of the California Academy of Sciences* (4th series), 30(18) (1968):381–99.

Howe, William H. *Butterflies of North America.* Garden City, NY: Doubleday & Co., 1975.

LeConte, J. L. "Notes on the Coleopterous Fauna of Lower California." *Philadelphia Academy Proceedings* (1861):335–38.

Leech, Hugh B. "Contributions Toward a Knowledge of the Insect Fauna of Lower California. No. 11. Coleoptera: Haliplidae, Dytiscidae, Gyrinidae, Hydrophilidae, Limnebiidae." *Proceedings of the California Academy of Sciences* (4th series), 24(11) (1942):375–484.

Linsley, E. Gorton. "Contributions Toward a Knowledge of the Insect Fauna of Lower California. No. 2. Coleoptera: Cerambycidae." *Proceedings of the California Academy of Sciences* (4th series), 24(2) (1942):21–96.

————. "The Origin and Distribution of the Cerambycidae of North America with Special Reference to the Fauna of the Pacific Slope." *Proceedings of the Sixth Pacific Scientific Congress* 4 (1960):269–82.

Macneill, C. Don. "A Preliminary Report on the Hesperidae of Baja California (Lepidoptera)." *Proceedings of the California Academy of Sciences* (4th series), 30(5) (1962):91–116.

Michelbacher, A. E. "Contributions Toward a Knowledge of the Insect Fauna of Lower California. No. 5 Symphyla." *Proceedings of the California Academy of Sciences* (4th series), 24(5) (1942):153–60.

————, and E. S. Ross. "Contributions Toward a Knowledge of the Insect Fauna of Lower California. No. 1 Introductory Account." *Proceedings of the California Academy of Sciences* (4th series), 24(1) (1942):1–20.

Rindge, Frederick H. "Contributions Toward a Knowledge of the Insect Fauna of Lower California. No. 8 Lepidoptera: Rhopalocera." *Proceedings of the California Academy of Sciences* (4th series), 24(8) (1942):289–312.

Ross, Herbert H. "The Trichoptera of Lower California." *Proceedings of the California Academy of Sciences* (4th series), 27(3) (1951):65–76.

Saylor, Lawrence W. "Contributions Toward a Knowledge of the Insect Fauna of Lower California. No. 10. Coleoptera: Scarabaeidae." *Proceedings of the California Academy of Sciences* (4th series), 24(10) (1942):337–74.

Soule, John D. "The Distribution and Affinities of the Littoral Marine Bryozoa (Ectoprocta)." In "Symposium: The Biogeography of Baja California. Part II: Marine Biotas." Edited by J. Wyatt Durham and Edwin C. Allison. *Systematic Zoology* 9(2) (1960):100–104.

————. "Results of the Puritan-American Museum of Natural History Expedition to Western Mexico, 6: Anascan Cheilostomata (Bryozoa) of the Gulf of California." *American Museum Novitiates* 1969 (1969):1–54.

Stahnke, Herbert L. "Some Diplocentrid Scorpions from Baja California del Sur, Mexico." *Proceedings of the California Academy of Sciences* (4th series), 35(14) (1968):273–320.

Stimpson, William. "Notes on North American *Crustacea* in the Museum of the Smithsonian Institution. No. II." *Lyceum Annals* 7(1862):176–246; and "No. III." 10(1874):92–136.

Treadwell, Aaron L. "The Templeton Crocker Expedition. VIII: Polychaetous Annelids from the West Coast of Lower California, the Gulf of California and Clarion Island." *Zoologica* 22 (1937):139–59.

Truxal, Fred S. "The Entomofauna with Special Reference to Its Origins and Affinities." In "Symposium: The Biogeography of Baja California. Part III: Terrestrial and Fresh-Water Biotas." Edited by J. Wyatt Durham and Edwin C. Allison. *Systematic Zoology* 9(3) (1960):165–70.

Uhler, P. R. "Observations upon the Heteropterous *Hemiptera* of Lower California, with Descriptions of New Species." *California Academy of Sciences Proceedings* (2nd series), 4 (1893–1894):223–95.

Usinger, Robert L., ed. *Aquatic Insects of California.* Los Angeles: University of California Press, 1956.

Van Dyke, Edwin C. "Contributions Toward a Knowledge of the Insect Fauna of Lower California. No. 3. Coleoptera: Buprestidae." *Proceedings of the California Academy of Sciences* (4th series), 24(3) (1942):97–132.

Williams, S. C. "Scorpion Fauna of Baja California, Mexico: Eleven New Species of Vejovis (Scorpinida Vejovidae)." *Proceedings of the California Academy of Sciences* 37 (1970):275–331.

Wirth, Willis N. "The Shore Flies of the Genus *Canaceoides* Cresson (Diptera: Canaceidae)." *Proceedings of the California Academy of Sciences* (4th series) 36(19) (1969):551–70.

Ziesenhenne, Fred C. "The Templeton Crocker Expedition. X: Echinoderms from the West Coast of Lower California, the Gulf of California and Clarion Island." *Zoologica* 22 (1937):109–239.

VERTEBRATES

Anthony, A. W. "General Ornithological Notes. 1. Nesting Habits of the California Brown Pelican *(Pelicanus californicus)*." *Proceedings of the California Academy of Sciences* (2nd series), 2 (1889):83–85
————. "Notes on the Cactus Wren." *Zoe* 1 (1891): 133–34.

Asplund, K. K. "Ecology of Lizards in the Relictual Cape Flora, Baja California." *American Midland Naturalist* 77 (1967):462–75.

Bailey, Vernon. *Mammals of the Southwestern United States.* 1931 reprint. New York: Dover Publications, 1971.

Baird, Spencer F. "Notes on a Collection of Birds Made by Mr. John Xantus, at Cape St. Lucas, Lower California, and Now in the Museum of the Smithsonian Institution." *Proceedings of the Academy of Natural Sciences of Philadelphia* (1859): 199–306.
————, Thomas F. Brewer, and Robert Ridgway. *A History of North American Birds.* 3 vols. Boston: Little, Brown and Company, 1874.

Banks, Richard C. "Birds and Mammals of La Laguna, Baja California." *Transactions of the San Diego Society of Natural History* 14(17) (1967):205–32.

Belding, Lyman. "Second Catalogue of a Collection of Birds Made Near the Southern Extremity of Lower California." *Proceedings of the U.S. National Museum* 6(1883):344–52.
————. "The Deer of Southern Lower California." *West American Scientist* 6(1889):26–27.

Blake, E. R. *Birds of Mexico: A Guide for Field Identification.* Chicago: Chicago University Press, 1953.

Bohlke, James E., and John C. Briggs. "The Rare Cirrhitid Fish Genus *Oxycirrhites* in American Waters." *California Fish and Game* 39(3) (1953):375–80.

Brewster, William. "Descriptions of Supposed New Birds from Lower California, Sonora, and Chihuahua, Mexico, and the Bahamas." *Auk* 5 (1888):82–95.
————. "Birds of the Cape Region of Lower California." *Bulletin of the Museum of Comparative Zoology, Harvard College* 41(1) (1902).

Bryant, Walter F. "A Catalogue of the Birds of Lower California, Mexico." *Proceedings of the California Academy of Sciences.* (2nd series), 2 (1889):236–320.
————."El Zorillo." *Zoe* 1 (1890):272–74.
————."Descriptions of the Nests and Eggs of Some Lower Californian Birds, with a Description of the Young Plumage of Geothlypis beldingi." *Proceedings of the California Academy of Sciences.* (2nd series), 1 (1890):20.
————. "The Cape Region of Baja California." *Zoe* 2(1891):185–201.

Davis, John. "The Sierra Madrean Element of the Avifauna of the Cape District, Baja California." *Condor* 61 (1959):75–84.

Denburgh, J. van. "The Reptiles and Amphibians of the Islands of the Pacific Coast of North America from the Farallons to Cape San Lucas and Revilla Gigedos." *Proceedings of the California Academy of Sciences* (3rd series), 4(1) (1905):1–40.
————. "Description of a New Lizard *(Dipsosaurus dorsalis lucasensis)* from Lower California." *Proceedings of the California Academy of Sciences.* (4th series), 10 (1920):33–34.
————."Description of a New Species of Rattlesnake *(Crotalus lucasensis)* from Lower California." *Proceedings of the California Academy of Sciences* (4th series), 10(2) (1920):29–30.
————, and Joseph R. Slevin. "A List of the Amphibians and Reptiles of the Peninsula of Lower California, with Notes on the Species in the Collection of the Academy." *Proceedings of the California Academy of Sciences* (4th series), 11(4) (1921):49–72.

Edwards, Ernest P. *A Field Guide to the Birds of Mexico.* Sweet Briar, VA: E. P. Edwards, 1972.

Follett, W. I. "The Fresh-water Fishes—Their Origins and Affinities." In "Symposium: The Biogeography of Baja California and Adjacent Seas. Part III. Terrestrial and Fresh-water Biotas." Edited by J. Wyatt Durham and Edwin C. Allison. *Systematic Zoology* 9(2) (1960):212–32.

Gilbert, C. H. "Scientific Results of Explorations by the U.S. Fish Commission Steamer *Albatross.* No. XII. A Preliminary Report on the Fishes Collected by the Steamer *Albatross* on the Pacific Coast of North America During the Year 1889, with Descriptions of Twelve New Genera and Ninety-two New Species." *Proceedings of the United States National Museum* 13 (1980):49–126.

Grinnell, Joseph. "A Distributional Summation of the Ornithology of Lower California." *University of California Publications in Zoology* 32 (1928):1–300.

Hoffmeister, D. F. "A Taxonomic and Evolutionary Study of the Piñon Mouse, *Peromyscus truei.*" *Illinois Biological Monograph* 21(4) (1951):1–104.

Hubbs, Carl L. "Changes in the Fish Fauna of Western North America Correlated with Changes in Ocean Temperature." *Journal of Marine Research* 7 (1948):459–82.

———. "The Marine Vertebrates of the Outer Coast." In "Symposium: The Biogeography of Baja California. Part II. Marine Biotas." Edited by J. Wyatt Durham and Edwin C. Allison. *Systematic Zoology* 9(2) (1960):134–47.

Huey, L. M. "The Pocket Gophers of Baja California, Mexico, with Descriptions of Nine New Forms." *Transactions of San Diego Society of Natural History* 10(1945):245–68.

———. "The Kangaroo Rats (Dipodomys) of Baja California, Mexico." *Transactions of the San Diego Society of Natural History* 11 (1951):105–56.

———. "The Mammals of Baja California, Mexico." *Transactions of the San Diego Society of Natural History* 13 (1964):85–168.

Jameson, D. L., J. P. Mackey, and R. C. Richmond. "The Systematics of the Pacific Tree Frog, *Hyla regilla.*" *Proceedings of the California Academy of Sciences* (4th series), 33 (1966):551–620.

Johnson, Martin W. "The Larval Development of the California Spiny Lobster, *Panulirus interruptus* (Randall), with Notes on *Panulirus gracilis* (Streets)." *Proceedings of the California Academy of Sciences* 29(1) (1956):1–19.

Jones, J. K., Jr., J. D. Smith, and T. Alvarez. "Notes on Bats from the Cape Region of Baja California." *Transactions of the San Diego Society of Natural History* 14(1965):53–56.

Jordan, D. S., and C. H. Gilbert. "Catalogue of the Fishes Collected by Mr. John Xantus at Cape San Lucas, Which Are Now in the United States National Museum, with Descriptions of Eight New Species." *U.S. National Museum Proceedings* 5(1882):353–71.

Klauber, Laurence M. "The Gopher Snakes of Baja California, with Descriptions of New Subspecies of *Pituophis catenifer.*" *Transactions of the San Diego Society of Natural History* 11(1) (1946):1–40.

Lamb, Chester C. "Some Birds New to the Cape San Lucas Region." *Condor* 27 (1925):117–18.

———. "Observations on the Xantus hummingbird." *Condor* 27 (1925):89–92.

———. "The Viosca Pigeon." *Condor* 28 (1926):262–63.

Lawrence, George N. "Descriptions of Three New Species of Humming Birds of the Genera Heliomaster, Amazilia, and Mellisuga." *American Lyceum of Natural History* 7 (1860):109–45.

Leviton, A. E., and B. H. Banta. "Midwinter Reconnaissance of the Herpetofauna of the Cape Region of Baja California, Mexico." *Proceedings of the California Academy of Sciences* 30 (1964):127–56.

Linsdale, Jean M. "Amphibians and Reptiles from Lower California." *University of California Publications in Zoology* 38 (1932):345–86.

Miller, A. H. "Speciation in the Avian Genus *Junco.*" *University of California Publications in Zoology* 44 (1941):173–434.

_____ _____, and L. Miller. "Geographic Variation of the Screech Owls of the Deserts of Western North America. *Condor* 53 (1951):161-77.

Orr, Robert T. "An Analysis of the Recent Land Mammals." In "Symposium: The Biogeography of Baja California. Part III. Terrestrial and Fresh-water Biotas." Edited by J. Wyatt Durham and Edwin C. Allison. *Systematic Zoology* 9(2) (1960):171-79.

Osburn, R. C., and J. T. Nichols. "Shore Fishes Collected by the 'Albatross' Expedition in Lower California with Descriptions of New Species." *American Museum of Natural History Bulletin* 35 (1916):139-81.

Peterson, Roger Tory, and Edward L. Chalif. *A Field Guide to Mexican Birds.* Boston: Houghton Mifflin Company, 1973.

Ridgway, Robert. "The Humming Birds. Annual Report of the Board of Regents of the Smithsonian Institution for the Year Ending June 30, 1890." *Report of the United States National Museum,* pp. 253-383. Washington, DC: U.S. Government Printing Office, 1891

Roth, E. L. "A New Species of Pocket Mouse (*Perognathus: Heteromyidae*) from the Cape Region of Baja California Sur, Mexico." *Journal of Mammology* 57(3) (1976):562. 50.

Rutter, Cloudsley. "Notes on Fishes from the Gulf of California, with the Description of a New Genus and Species." *Proceedings of the California Academy of Sciences* (3rd series), 3(8) (1904):251-54.

Sanborn, Sherburn R., and Richard B. Loomis. "Keys to the Amphibians and Reptiles of Baja California, Mexico, and the Adjacent Islands." Mimeographed. Long Beach: California State University, 1976.

Savage, Jay M. "Evolution of a Peninsular Herpetofauna." In "Symposium. Biogeography of Baja California. Part III. Terrestrial and Fresh-water Biotas." Edited by J. Wyatt Durham and Edwin C. Allison. *Systematic Zoology* 9(1) (1960):184-219.

Schmidt, Karl P. "The Amphibians and Reptiles of Lower California and the Neighboring Islands." *American Museum of Natural History Bulletin* 46 (1921):606-707.

Sibley, C. G. "The Warbling District of the Cape District of Lower California." *Condor* 42 (1940):255. 9).

Stager, Kenneth E. "The Composition and Origin of the Avifauna." In "Symposium: The Biogeography of Baja California. Part III. Terrestrial and Fresh-water Biotas." Edited by J. Wyatt Durham and Edwin C. Allison. *Systematic Zoology* 9 (1960):179 83.

Smak, Karl H. "Reptile Hunting in Baja California. *Pacific Discovery* 285 (15):16-26.

Tanner, W. W. "The Night Snakes of Baja California." *Transactions of the San Diego Society of Natural History* 16(15) (1966):189 90.

Thayer, John E. "Some Rare Birds and Sets of Eggs from the Cape Region of Lower California." *Condor* 11 (1909):10-11

Thompson, Donald A., Lloyd T. Findley and Alex N. Kerstitch *Reef Fishes of the Sea of Cortez.* New York: John Wiley & Sons, 1979.

Townsend, C. H. "Birds Collected in Lower California." *Bulletin of the American Museum of Natural History* 48(1923):1-51.

Verrill, A. E. "Contributions to Zoology from the Museum of Yale College. No. VI: Descriptions of Shells from the Gulf of California." *American Journal of Scientific Arts* 49 (1870):235-76

Walker, Boyd W. "The Distribution and Affinities of the Marine Fish Fauna of the Gulf of California." In Symposium: The Biogeography of Baja California. Part II. Marine Biotas." Edited by J. Wyatt Durham and Edwin C. Allison. *Systematic Zoology* 9(2) (1960):123-33.

Wright, N. Pelham. *A Guide to Mexican Mammals and Reptiles.* Mexico City: Minutiae Mexicana, 1970.

Xantus, John. "Description of Three New Species of Starfishes from Cape St. Lucas." *Philadelphia Academy of Sciences Proceedings* 1860:568.

INDEX

Page numbers in *italic* indicate illustrations.